THE AMERICAN ALPINE JOURNAL

2018

[Front Cover] Alex Honnold in the Monster Offwidth section of Freerider during his free solo ascent of El Capitan (see p.12). *Tom Evans | Elcapreport.com* [This page] The final section of the summit ridge during the second ascent of Kang Nachugo in Nepal (see p.326). *Genki Narumi*

2018   VOLUME 60 ISSUE 92

CONTENTS

RECON

98 JEBEL MISHT BY GEOFF HORNBY
Forty years of adventurous climbing on Oman's massive limestone mountain.

[Photo] Heading back to camp in the Double Peak area of the Chigmit Mountains in Alaska (see p.147).
Joe Stock

CLIMBS & EXPEDITIONS

The American Alpine Journal, 710 Tenth St. Suite 100, Golden, Colorado 80401
Telephone: (303) 384-0110 E-mail: aaj@americanalpineclub.org
www.publications.americanalpineclub.org

ISSN: 0065-6925
ISBN: 978-0-9998556-0-7
ISBN: (hardcover edition): 978-0-9998556-2-1

FIND MORE AT THE *AAJ* WEBSITE. Our online stories frequently contain additional text, photographs, videos, maps, and topos. Look for these symbols at the end of a story indicating additional resources at *publications.americanalpineclub.org.*

 FULL-LENGTH REPORT

 ADDITIONAL PHOTOS

 MAPS OR TOPOS

 VIDEO OR MULTIMEDIA

[Photo] The incredible rock of the Tafoni Pillar on Mt. Turcotte in the Pirrit Hills of Antarctica (see p.238). *GMHM*

FRIENDS OF THE AAJ

Gordon A. Benner
Robert M. Branch
Yvon & Malinda
 Chouinard
Carla L. Firey

Eric D. Green
Bryan Heifner
Richard E. Hoffman M.D.
Dougald MacDonald
William A. Oliver

[Photo] He Chuan and Liu Yang making the first ascent of the incredible Christmas Tree ice climb in China (see p.351). *Lie Feng*

2017 GREAT RANGES FELLOWSHIP

[EIGER]

Anonymous
Yvon and Malinda Chouinard
Kevin Duncan
Timothy Forbes
Clark Gerhardt Jr.

Peter Horan
Craig McKibben
Mark and Teresa Richey
Carey Roberts
Naoe Sakashita

Steve and Paula Mae Schwartz
Cody J Smith
Jerry Stritzke
Steven Swenson and Ann Dalton
Roger and Sha Sha Walker

[ALPAMAYO]

Warren Adelman
Audrey Borisov
Edmund and Betsy Cabot
   Foundation
Philip Duff
Rocky Henderson

Nick Horbaczewski
Mark Kroese
Phil Lakin Jr.
George Lowe III
Garry Menzel
Peter and Kathleen Metcalf

Miriam Nelson and Kinloch Earle
John Sirois
William and Barbara Straka
Lawrence True and Linda Brown

[ROBSON]

Anonymous
Mark Aiston
Jon Anderson
William Atkinson
Sumit Bhardwaj
Tanya Bradby and Martin Slovacek
John Catto
Dan Cohen
Matt and Charlotte Culberson III
Elizabeth and Joseph Davidson
Kit DesLauriers
The Duckworth Family
James M Edwards and Michele
   Mass

Dan Emmett
Chas Fisher
Charlotte Fox
Bruce Franks
Eiichi Fukushima
Suzanne Hartman
Seth Hawkins
Richard E. Hoffman M.D.
Thomas Hornbein M.D.
Thomas Janson
David Landman
Randy Luskey
Michael Morgan Family Foundation
Paul Morrow

Dan Nordstrom
Michael Pantelich
Brian Peters
John Reppy
Melissa Arnot Reid
David Riggs
Vik Sahney
Richard Salisbury
John B. Soebbing
Theodore Streibert
Joshua Swidler
Niels Tietze
Winston Warme
Christopher Warner

[TEEWINOT]

Anonymous
Jonah Adelman
Conrad Anker
George Basch
Douglas Beall
Robert Bechaud
Vaclav Benes
Gordon A. Benner M.D.
John Bird
Brent Bishop
Nate Bondi
Donald Brier
Pete Brownell
Deanne Buck
Thomas Burch
Mitch Campbell
Robert "RJ" Campbell
Brian Cannard
Kevin Capps
Jimmy Chin
Brianna Chrisman
Jeffrey Cohen
Kevin Cooney
John Costello
Christopher Croft
Paul Brunner and Coleen
   Curry
Lee Davis
Larina Davis
Scott Davis
Tom Degenhardt
Gretchen Dennison

Ed Diffendal
John Donlou M.D.
Richard Draves
Ken Ehrhart
Charles Eilers
Stuart Ellison
Terrence English
Chuck and Lisa
   Fleischman
James Frank
Jim Frush
Ken and Rebecca Gart
Marilyn Geninatti
Michael Gibbons
Bill and Sandra Givens
Dunham Gooding
Wayne and Cynthia Griffin
Roger Hartl
Diane Heasley
Scot Hillman
Mark Hingston
Marley and Jennifer
   Hodgson
John Hutchinson
Alex Intermill
Richard Johnston
Steven Kasoff
Diane Kearns
William Kilpatrick M.D.
Joel G. Kinney
Ron and Yael Kohavi
Michael Lederer

Richard LeDuc
Paul Lego
Chris Lynch
Ryan Maitland
Brent Manning
Geoff Martin
Edwards Matthews
Patrick Mauro
Dan McCoy
Danny McCracken
Chris McCullough
Brad McQueen
Roger Mellem
Mark Miller
Scott Milliman
Halsted "Hacksaw" Morris
Robert Morse
Andrew Muller
Mie Nakane
Sean O'brien
Matt Ochs
Bob Palais
Jed Paulson
Mark Powers
Andrew Puhl
John Rehmer
Louis Reichardt
Wolf Riehle
Michael Riley
David Robertson
Joel Robinson
Arthur Rock

John Rudolph
David Ryon M.D.
Jeb Sanford
Charles Sassara III
Janet Schlindwein
Mark Schumacher M.D.
   and Ulrika Schumacher
Stephen Scofield
George Shaw
Lauren Sigman
George N. Smith
Katherine Song
Robert and Jennifer
   Stephenson
Pamela and Bob Street
Sam Streibert
Duncan Stuart
Pavan Surapaneni
Jack and Pat Tackle
Steve and Krista Taylor
Mark Twight
Dieter Von Hennig
Jeff Wagener
Brian Weihs
Mark Wilford
Douglas Wilson
Tracie Winbigler
Todd Winzenried
Jason Wolfe
Donald Woods
Brian Young
Rob Ziegler

THE AMERICAN ALPINE JOURNAL

EXECUTIVE EDITOR
Dougald MacDonald

SENIOR EDITOR
Lindsay Griffin

ASSOCIATE EDITORS
Andy Anderson, Chris Kalman, Erik Rieger

CONTRIBUTING EDITORS
Whitney Clark, Geoff Hornby, David Stevenson (Book Reviews), Drew Thayer

ART DIRECTOR
David Boersma

ILLUSTRATIONS AND MAPS
Dallin Carey, Marty Schnure, Drew Thayer

PROOFREADERS
Christine Blackmon, Dillon Blanksma, Rolando Garibotti, Damien Gildea, Anna Kramer, Will McFarland, Bruce Normand, Mason Osgood, Eric Rueth, Katie Sauter, Azissa Singh

TRANSLATORS
Zbyšek Česenek, Fanny Deplace, Chris Kalman, Emily Laskin, Guillaume Lavigueur, Tamotsu Nakamura, Oh Young-hoon, Heikki Ruuska

INDEXERS
Ralph Ferrara, Eve Tallman

REGIONAL CONTACTS
Steve Gruhn, Mark Westman, *Alaska*; Ian Welsted, *Canada*; Sevi Bohorquez, Sergio Ramirez Carrascal, *Peru*; Luis Pardo, *Colombia*; Damien Gildea, *Antarctica*; Rolando Garibotti, Marcelo Scanu, *Argentina-Chile*; Alex von Ungern, *Bolivia*; Geoff Hornby, *Middle East*; Harish Kapadia, Nandini Purandare, *India*; Rodolphe Popier, Richard Salisbury, *Nepal*; Tamotsu Nakamura, Hiroshi Hagiwara, *Japan*; Peter Jensen-Choi, Oh Young-hoon, *Korea*; Elena Dmitrenko, Anna Piunova, *Russia, Tajikistan, and Kyrgyzstan*; Xia Zhongming, *China*

ADVISORY BOARD
Whitney Clark, Alison Criscitiello, Kelly Cordes, Damien Gildea, Colin Haley, Mark Jenkins, Chris Weidner, Graham Zimmerman

WITH HEARTFELT THANKS TO...
Christine Blackmon, Elizabeth Cromwell, Tom Evans, Alex Honnold, Marc Piché, Nick Wilder, members of the American Alpine Club, and our hundreds of authors, photographers, and supporters

THE AMERICAN ALPINE CLUB

AAC Board member Graham Zimmerman pulls through on Crack-A-No-Go, Smith Rock, OR. *AAC member Jim Aikman.*

The Journal depends on the Club.

And the Club depends on you.

The AAJ is only possible because of thousands of hours invested by the AAC and its volunteers. Please consider supporting the publication of this information by volunteering your time or making a donation to the American Alpine Club.

americanalpineclub.org

[Photo] Angela Eiter on Planta de Shiva (9b/5.15b) in Spain. Eiter made the third known ascent of the climb—the first 9b climbed by a woman—in October 2017. *Javipec | ASP | Red Bull Content Pool*

MILESTONES

BIG-WALL FREE SOLOS and mountaineering first ascents don't happen in a vacuum—they are part of (and are influenced by) the broader evolution of climbing performance. To provide context for the long climbs we have documented in this edition, we record here some of the most notable achievements in 2017 on the world's shorter cliffs. –The Editors

FEBRUARY

MARGO HAYES (USA), 19 at the time, redpointed La Rambla at Siurana, Spain, the first solid 9a+ (5.15a) free climbed by a female climber. She followed up this performance by making the first female ascent of Biographie (also 9a+) at Ceüse, France, in September.

AUGUST

GORDON MCARTHUR, A 37-year-old Canadian, redpointed Storm Giant, a dry-tooling route that climbs out a gigantic cave near Fernie, British Columbia, and took two and a half years to complete. The 80-meter pitch has more than 50 bolts and some manufactured holds, and is the first dry-tooling route to be given the grade of D16.

SEPTEMBER

ADAM ONDRA (CZECH), 24, completed Silence, a 45-meter free climb in Norway for which he proposed the world's first 9c (5.15d). The first half of the climb is 8b (5.13d), followed by three distinct boulder problems: 8C (V15), 8B, and 7C+. The route climbs the roof of a granite cave near Flatanger, Norway, where, in 2012, Ondra freed Change, the first 9b+ (5.15c) in the world.

SEPTEMBER

ANAK VERHOEVEN, 21, from Belgium became the first female climber to do the first ascent of a climb graded 9a+/5.15a (and the second woman ever to free a route of this difficulty): Sweet Neuf at Pierrot Beach in France. This new linkup extended Sang Neuf (9a/5.14d), a route that Verhoeven had climbed for its first free ascent one day earlier, with the 5.14 upper section of Home Sweet Home.

OCTOBER

ANGELA EITER, 31, from Austria, redpointed La Planta de Shiva (9b/5.15b) at Villanueva del Rosario, Spain, the first route of this grade free climbed by a woman. The route was first freed in 2011 by Adam Ondra and is believed to have been repeated only once before.

FREERIDER

FREE SOLO ON EL CAPITAN

ALEX HONNOLD

On June 3, I free soloed Freerider on El Capitan, the culmination of an eight-year dream. The year and a half I took to actually realize the climb has, at this point, been well documented. The story of that journey is told in an upcoming documentary film, tentatively titled *Free Solo*. I also added 30,000 words to a revised edition of my book, *Alone on the Wall*, which will come out this year. In this space, I simply aim to cover the nuts and bolts—the exact variations and methods I used, just in case anyone wants to repeat a very minor new route.

What I mean by "new route" is that I didn't exactly free solo the original Salathé Wall and Freerider link-up. (*Freerider, first climbed by Alex Huber in 1995, is a series of variations to the 1961 Salathé Wall route, creating a 5.12d/13a climb that is significantly easier than the original Salathé as a free climb*.) I followed most of the traditional route but also pioneered a few variations here and there to avoid insecure moves and sections that I didn't like.

It may not sound like a big deal, but for me there was a significant mental shift when I realized that I didn't need to stay on the original line. When you're not constrained by the need to place protection, it turns out you can go anywhere you want on the wall. In this way, soloing is actually kind of liberating. My goal was simply to climb El Cap without a rope; I didn't care about any specific route or grade.

I HAD PREVIOUSLY free soloed the West Face (5.11c) and the East Buttress (5.10b) of El Capitan, but neither of them is considered a *real* El Cap route. These two routes bookend the nearly 115 *real* routes that climb the iconic, sheer face. Of these, some 16 routes have been free climbed (a total that increases every year or two), and most of them are much too hard and insecure to imagine ever free soloing.

Over the many years that I dreamed of free soloing El Cap, the only two routes I seriously considered were Freerider (5.12d or maybe 5.13a if you climb the Boulder Problem) and Golden Gate (5.13a and quite sustained). Golden Gate was really just a worst-case backup for the Freerider. If I ended up deciding that the crux of Freerider, pitch 23, simply felt too insecure to solo, then I could plan to branch onto Golden Gate a few pitches lower and follow that to the summit instead.

I also briefly considered climbing the first 10 pitches of the Muir Wall as a possible alternative to the Freeblast (*the first 10 pitches of the Salathé Wall, rated 5.11*), because the Muir is mostly crack climbing and therefore more secure than the tenuous friction slabs on the Freeblast. But the Muirblast also includes a 5.13b undercling traverse, which seemed less than ideal for free soloing.

These are the tradeoffs of free soloing. Is it worth climbing something harder to feel more secure? At what point is the added physical difficulty not worth it? There are no set answers—I just considered every option and followed my gut.

Alex Honnold completing the downclimb before traversing left to Hollow Flake. The 5.12a variation is one key to free climbing the Salathé and Freerider. Preparing for his solo, Honnold sought an alternative to the downclimb but eventually committed to simply rehearsing the moves. A friend revealed a hidden hold that made this section feel secure. *Tom Evans | Elcapreport.com*

IN THE FALL of 2016 I worked the Freerider extensively in preparation for the potential solo, but I ran into a few problems. There was limited shade on the wall in the fall—it was quite cold in the morning before the sun rose, but as soon as the sun crested the opposite rim of the Valley it beat directly onto the wall, creating a solar oven. It went from too cold to too hot almost instantly, which made it challenging to climb the 3,000-foot route in decent conditions. But the bigger problem was that I seriously sprained my ankle in a careless slip on the Freeblast slabs. It didn't break, thankfully, and would eventually recover fully, but I struggled to hike or put on a climbing shoe for the full time I was in the Valley that season.

Nevertheless, by the middle of November I'd done enough rehearsal on the Freerider that I felt vaguely close to being able to solo the route. The weather was closing down for the season, and I figured I should give it one good try before winter.

I started in the dark since I needed to get to the crux before the sun hit it. It felt cold and my shoe felt too tight—my injured foot was still swollen. I felt nervous and climbed poorly. I climbed up to the crux of the Freeblast slab (pitch five) before I finally succumbed to my uneasiness and grabbed a bolt. Then I French-freed my way up the rest of the slab, disappointed that I wasn't sending but happy to be done. From Heart Ledge, I rappelled to the ground with a borrowed sling and carabiner. I'd failed to free solo Freerider. But I had climbed the Freeblast without a rope, which was at least a first step. I considered the whole experience to be good progress.

Approximate line of the Salathé Wall–Freerider linkup, showing key landmarks: (1) Solo variation to pitch six of the Freeblast. (2) Variation off Heart Ledges. (3) Downclimb and traverse to Hollow Flake. (4) Monster Offwidth. (5) Boulder Problem Pitch. (6) Round Table Traverse. *Chris Falkenstein / Yosemiteprints.org*

WHEN I CAME back to the Valley for the spring season, I spent the first week exploring some new free climbing potential on the right side of El Cap with Sonnie Trotter. At the time, it felt like a distraction from my real mission, but everything was still super wet from the winter, so I didn't mind the delay. It took me a little longer to understand that the days that we spent swinging around and looking for holds fundamentally shifted my perception of what might be possible for my solo.

After Sonnie left, I returned to preparations on the Salathé and Freerider with much broader vision. Suddenly the route was less defined. If I didn't like a few moves on a certain pitch, I would consider traversing in above them or even try to avoid the entire pitch. Don't like a particular sequence? Find a way to skip it! That became my new motto.

Honnold on top of El Capitan, preparing to fix ropes to work on the climb. *Sanni McCandless*

There had always eight sections that I considered scary to solo, listed here from most to least serious: the 5.13a Boulder Problem on pitch 23, the two Freeblast slab pitches, the Enduro Corner (5.12d), the 5.12a traverse to the Round Table, the 5.11c slab leaving Heart Ledges, the 5.12a downclimb to reach the Hollow Flake, and the 5.11d traverse to the Monster Offwidth.

The Boulder Problem, the Enduro Corner, and the Round Table traverse were each immutable—there was no way to avoid any of them. Each was a key weakness linking distinct parts of the wall.

The Freeblast slab pitches, by contrast, are an arbitrary line meandering through an enormous sea of granite. These pitches were defined only by where Royal Robbins, Chuck Pratt, and Tom Frost had chosen to go on the first ascent of the Salathé. While their ascent was visionary, they mostly weren't free climbing—in fact, sticky rubber shoes hadn't yet been invented. No one had ever really looked around for the easiest possible passage.

Before investigating alternatives to the slabs, however, I found my first successful variation on the pitch leaving Heart Ledges. This is a fun pitch of mostly 5.10 crack climbing that has one extremely slippery 5.11c slab move in the middle. I jugged up the fixed lines to the Heart and rope soloed the pitch above with the intention of rehearsing that thin slab move until I could make it feel secure. But once I began swinging around on rappel, I realized that I could probably just loop around the thin slab problem and rejoin the cracks above. To my delight, I discovered the variation was 5.10c knob climbing—it was completely unprotectable and probably impossible to lead in the normal sense, but much easier and more secure than the original route. I couldn't wait to apply my new strategy to the rest of the pitches on my list.

I spent a few mornings rappelling down the Freeblast, swinging from side to side and looking for straighter or easier possibilities. I even considered harder but more secure possibilities—again, the tradeoffs of soloing. Rob Miller had placed bolts near pitch five on the Freeblast as part of a new route between the Nose and Salathé that would later become the Platinum Wall (39 pitches, 5.13+, *see page 114*). For a brief time I thought that I preferred the Platinum Wall slab because, unlike the Freeblast, it had handholds (albeit marginal), but ultimately I decided to stick with the original line—the insecure 5.11b on the Freeblast that I'd done dozens of times over the years beat out the slightly more secure 5.12a on the Platinum Wall. The Freeblast slab also held a much smaller chance of breaking a foothold than the newer route to the right.

Eventually I realized that I could bypass most of the second Freeblast slab (pitch six, 5.11a) by simply climbing 25 feet to the right and following a big, blocky buttress-like feature. To exit this feature, I had to pioneer a challenging traverse back left onto the normal pitch. But this variation cut off the majority of a slab that I'd always found terribly insecure. Instead of 20 moves on glassy, tenuous smears, I would have a 10-move traverse with only one really insecure move. The full pitch remained 5.11a, since I would still do the same crux at the top, but at least I could get there more securely.

My NEXT "VARIATION" was one that had already been established: the traverse left to Bermuda Dunes before the Ear on pitch 18 of the Salathé. This is an alternative way to access the very bottom of the Monster Offwidth on Freerider, where it's still a pleasant hand crack. (It's also much easier for short people who can't make the span to the Monster up above.) While I can't take credit for the discovery, I did clean it up; after rappelling to the ground with a backpack full of rocks, I could tick this one off the list as well.

The final section of the wall that I investigated was the traverse to the Hollow Flake, a pitch that normally requires at least 100 feet of polished downclimbing. I considered climbing higher up into the Heart formation and skipping this traverse pitch entirely, but it seemed too difficult to get back over to the Salathé. I also considered traversing left a few hundred feet lower, but that slab looked futuristically difficult. I spent two different sessions examining the options around the Hollow Flake. Ultimately, I just practiced the normal sequence as much as I could. There was no better option, so I set myself to the task of making the normal way feel as secure as possible.

During this time, I discussed the Hollow Flake traverse with my friend James Lucas, expressing my concern for the thin tips liebacking on the downclimb.

"Why don't you use the big block out to the left?" he asked.

"What block? I think you're thinking of the wrong pitch," I responded. I'd spent two full sessions on that section of the wall. There wasn't some secret jug hidden off to the side.

"No, there's a block off to the left. I've always done it that way. You'll see," James replied.

Sure enough, the next time I was on the pitch, I found the little wedged block off to the left, hidden by a tiny overlap in the wall, right where I needed it. With James' new beta, the pitch suddenly felt secure.

Preparing for the rest of the route simply meant rehearsing the Boulder Problem and the upper corners, memorizing the difficult moves that I knew I couldn't avoid. The beauty of the crux boulder problem and the Enduro Corner was that they involved relatively "normal" climbing. Unlike the Freeblast slabs and similar pitches, which required smearing my feet against seemingly random patches of smooth rock, the difficult upper pitches had actual holds. That meant that as I got stronger and knew the pitches better they actually felt easier, whereas the Freeblast slabs never really felt easy or hard, just slippery and insecure.

My WHOLE SPRING season in Yosemite was focused around the list of pitches that I needed to work on. By the end of May, I'd scratched everything off my list. If I was ever going to solo the route, now was the time. But then it rained a day, which required rappelling the wall again to make sure nothing had gotten too wet or started seeping. And that took a whole day of effort, which necessitated yet another day to rest. Well, if I was ever going to solo this route, *now* was really the time.

On June 3 I woke up early, drove to the east end of El Cap meadow, and strolled up to the base of the wall with nothing but my shoes and chalk bag. I started climbing at first light, knowing that I had about five hours of shade until the crux went into the sun. It was slightly warmer and more humid than I would have liked, but it didn't really matter anymore—I was committed. I was an Olympic gymnast starting up a 3,000-foot floor routine, executing a long-rehearsed sequence on autopilot. All I had to do was lace up and perform.

The climbing went even more smoothly than I could have hoped. My only scary moment was on the second Freeblast slab, when I had to do the awkward step down from my new variation into the crux of the normal route. I knew it would be a scary move and it was, but I also knew exactly how to do it. So I ignored the scariness and did what I was supposed to do.

Safely on the summit, a little under four hours after starting. "Honestly, I feel like I could go do another lap right now," Honnold told National Geographic later that day. *Jimmy Chin | Natonal Geographic*

As I climbed higher, I felt more and more confident. My feet felt welded to the wall and my body felt light and strong. There was no fatigue. If anything, I felt stronger as I got higher.

At the Boulder Problem I dropped even deeper into autopilot mode—I climbed it exactly as I always had in rehearsal but without the rope this time. It felt perfect. And when I reached the finishing jug, after the ten most important moves of climbing in my life, I knew the route was in the bag. I still had the Enduro Corner and traverse to the Round Table above me—three guidebook pitches of 5.12 in a row, with no great rests—but they weren't nearly as intimidating as the crux. I felt strong and knew they wouldn't be a problem.

I forced myself to stay calm and not rush, but as soon as I made it around to the Round Table I checked my phone and saw that I was on track to break four hours for the ascent. With all the hard climbing now below me, I stopped holding back and charged for the finish.

The last four pitches got easier and easier, and I summited at a near jog, racing up the final slab. Years of dreaming and several seasons of effort had all come together in 3 hours and 56 minutes of climbing. I'd done the first free ascent of a very minor new route on El Cap. I'd set some kind of speed record. But most importantly, I'd finally climbed El Cap without a rope.

SUMMARY: Free solo of Freerider (33 guidebook pitches, with variations, 5.12d/13a) by Alex Honnold—the first free solo of one of the main faces of El Capitan in Yosemite Valley. Honnold climbed the route in 3 hours 56 minutes on June 3, 2017.

ABOUT THE AUTHOR: *Alex Honnold, 33, is an aspiring sport climber.*

STARTING OVER

THREE YEARS FOR A NEW ROUTE ON NUPTSE'S VAST AND DIFFICULT SOUTH FACE

FRÉDÉRIC DEGOULET

Trying, failing, and starting over: It's the basis of any experience, the thing that pushes us forward. What would we do if everything were easy?

Nuptse was a beautiful challenge—an extremely difficult climb in every imaginable way. The technical level of the face seemed very high, given the few lines on it and the number of failed attempts, and the project we were considering appeared even steeper. To the technical difficulty we had to add sheer length—about 2,200 vertical meters on a previously untried line—as well as the altitude. Our high point would be well over 7,700 meters. And so we were facing a truly enormous challenge. Some might even say the challenge of a lifetime.

In 2015, Benjamin Guigonnet and Hélias Millerioux made their first attempt on the south face. I chose not to go. At the time I felt the project was too ambitious for my skill level, my past experiences being too scarce. On previous expeditions I had never climbed above 6,850 meters, a difference of nearly 1,000 meters with Nuptse. I'm someone who likes to take challenges step by step, and the gap was simply too big.

I told Ben and Hélias I would have to pass, but I'd definitely be there the following year. I let them go knowing they'd gain a lot of experience, and it was clear to me they might need more than one try to reach the summit. Only Hélias had climbed at similar altitude, and only once, on easy terrain. So what I thought was, "Go ahead, get your ass kicked, and then I'll come." In the end they weren't even able to attempt the line. The heat during the fall of 2015 led to huge rockfall that made the whole south face of Nuptse impracticable.

In 2016, Le Gang des Moustaches ("The Mustache Gang") was reunited, as Robin Revest and I decided to join Ben and Hélias in Nepal. That had been our nickname since 2014, when we climbed a new route on the west face of Siulá Chico in Peru (*AAJ 2015*). With the full team back together and great conditions on the face, we got up to 7,400 meters on Nuptse—perhaps one day below the top—but were forced down due to equipment and strategic mistakes, combined with a lack of experience.

Coming back down to base camp, our morale was at an all-time low, and we wondered what had gone wrong. Everyone on the team was deeply frustrated about having to turn back so close to the summit. It was clear to all of us that we wouldn't leave it at that.

When people ask me how it was on Nuptse in 2017, all I think is, "We finally did it." It's

Benjamin Guigonnet heads into the difficulties on day four of the new route on Nuptse's south face: seven pitches up to WI5+ M5+ at nearly 7,000 meters. *Degoulet | Guigonnet | Millerioux*

Le Gang des Moustaches after the climb. Their route is the first to ascend the south face of Nuptse's northwest summit: (A) Nuptse Nup II (7,742m). The trio bivouacked five times during the ascent and once on the way down, plus a six-hour stop at Camp 2 to wait for nightfall before descending to advanced base camp. One year earlier, the same trio, plus Robin Revest, reached 7,400 meters (near Camp 5) o n the same line. (B) Nuptse Main (7,861m), first climbed in 1961. *Degoulet | Guigonnet | Millerioux*

quite strange that these are the only words that come to mind, considering how much this adventure brought me. It's not every day that we make our dreams come true. Finishing the climb was like a huge weight being lifted off our shoulders, like an assignment we'd taken too long to do. To me, going back to Nuptse was an obligation, because it had been within our grasp, because the mistakes we had made the year before were easily avoidable. We knew we could do it.

In retrospect, I believe the only thing we lacked was experience under our belts. We were impatient, arrogant even, when instead Nuptse should have commanded more respect. Our mistake was to see it as just another mountain. This one was different in its magnitude, its altitude, its physical and mental commitment, and the risks involved. We had to review our whole game plan.

As soon as we got back to France, Ben sealed our fate when he announced that he would try the line again in the fall of 2017. Robin wanted to wait a year, but I definitely wanted to go back. The difference was that I didn't feel the excitement that usually comes with new expeditions. I knew where we were going, and I also knew pretty much everything that would happen, including the the discomfort, the stress, the commitment, and the opinion of our family and friends who knew the risks we were taking yet again. However, the thought of making the first ascent, getting up that face and standing on the summit, eclipsed everything else. That one thought allowed me, perhaps subconsciously, to disregard every argument against going back. In the end no one could have reasoned with me or stopped me because that one thought, that selfish desire, was simply too strong. In my opinion, it is this ability to disregard harsh reality and only focus on possibilities that allows us to undertake this type of challenge.

Now that our project is over, I realize how this process is essential to me but also extremely dangerous. I recognize that undertaking a number of projects with this level of commitment considerably decreases your life expectancy. Yes, there is an element of chance, but we do make our own luck, or at least part of it.

It will be a while before I reconsider projects of this size (even if we all tend to forget the bad parts and only keep the great memories). Many people ask us, "So what's next?" as if they expect us to always aim higher, to always try harder. In reality, I don't have to do anything. What I do is only decided by me and my selfishness. Of course, I will always look for new challenges, because that's what motivates me. But I'll try as much as possible to pick less risky ones

Anyway, we climbed Nuptse....

THE CLIMB

AFTER ACCLIMATIZING BY climbing Cholatse, we moved up to advanced base camp at 5,400 meters on October 13. Our plan for the first day was to climb an obvious crux ice pitch and leave a rope fixed for the next day. As it turned out, we didn't use the rope, but it seemed essential to have this option, because we knew the following day would be very long.

After three hours of approach from ABC, we started the face with five pitches up moderate snow (65°) to reach the WI6 pitch, right above our first bivy site. One of us dug out a campsite at 5,950 meters, at the base of a steep rock wall, while the other two climbed this crux pitch.

We started the second day at midnight. The whole team climbed the pitch that had been fixed the previous day, without using the fixed rope. Than we simul-climbed up and left across a huge 45° ice field to reach more difficult terrain. Four tough pitches followed (WI4+ to WI5+), followed by three easier pitches to reach a snowfield shaped like a flying bird, where we began to work on our next bivy site at 6,580 meters.

It took two and a half hours to dig a good site for the tent—we dug deep into the snow slope to create a high wall behind the tent and hopefully protect it from rockfall. The previous year, at this same site, a rock had ripped through the tent wall and landed close to Ben. Despite our efforts, the tent was still threatened, so we had to sit up all night with our backs against the snow.

The wind blew hard throughout the night, ending only at 8 a.m., and we did not start climbing until 10 a.m.

Hélias Millerioux leading WI5 ice below the second bivouac. Millerioux would be badly injured by rockfall during the team's descent from the summit. *Degoulet | Guigonnet | Millerioux*

Benjamin Guigonnet leads a very steep ice and mixed pitch on the ramp-like *goulotte* that brought the team to the upper couloir. *Expedition Photo*

That day, October 16, was short but tough: six pitches at WI5, gaining only 220 meters. There was less snow at the site we'd used for Camp 3 the previous year, and we had to traverse off-route to the right to find a better site, leaving a 60-meter rope fixed horizontally across the snowfield. We chopped a ledge into a snowy spur protected from rockfall at 6,800 meters.

Day four on the route was again packed with difficult climbing: seven pitches up to WI5+ M5+ along a ramp-like *goulotte*. At 3:30 p.m. we began the daily routine of digging a ledge in steep snow, a reasonably protected site at 7,013 meters.

Now we were in the grand couloir angling directly toward the northwest summit. After 120 meters of solo climbing up a snow slope, we climbed seven pitches at 55° to 60°. The crux came at the end of this day: two pitches in a very steep snow flute, with loose, insecure climbing. We arrived at our bivy site at 7,443 meters after climbing eight and a half hours. And our sleep was not easy that night: Camp 5 was perched precariously on a snow mushroom—safe from rockfall, but we were not 100 percent convinced of its stability.

Summit day, October 19, began with three steep mixed pitches (WI4 M4) up la Virgule ("The Comma") to reach a 55° snow slope, which we simul-climbed for 200 meters to reach the ridgeline. A final 100-meter traverse along the ridge gained the top of Nuptse Nup II (7,742 meters) at 3 p.m. in perfect weather. [*This peak was first climbed in 1977 by the northwest ridge.*] Downclimbing and rappelling, we were back at Camp 5 on the snow mushroom by 6 p.m.

The descent began smoothly the next day, rappelling from pickets and Abalakov anchors, but at 7,100 meters, as Hélias was standing at a belay anchor, he was hit on the back of his shoulder by a big block of ice or rock. (Back in France, he learned that he had broken three ribs and parts of two vertebrae.) We had hoped to reach the safer bivy that we'd used on the third night of our ascent, but Hélias could only use one of his arms and was unable to climb back across the traverse to this site, so we had to continue down toward Camp 2. As the day warmed, a lot of rock began falling and we had to cross a dangerous couloir very quickly, helping Hélias as much as we could. At noon, after a total of about 15 rappels, we finally reached the site of Camp 2.

Without bothering to set up the tent, we sat in our sleeping bags on the ice ledge we had dug five days earlier, waiting for the face to go into shadow and the temperature to drop. We called a doctor in France on a sat phone and treated Hélias with painkillers and anti-inflammatory medicine.

Finally, at 6 p.m., we started down again. There was no moonlight, making it difficult to find the right way. But after 16 more rappels and three hours of walking down the glacier and moraine, we safely reached advanced base camp at 3 a.m. on October 21, having descended about 2,000 meters in less than 20 hours, the last 1,700 meters with an injured partner. When

we finally returned to the lodge at Chukhung, we were like zombies. Our friends who run the lodge welcomed us with a full bottle of Nepali liquor—an excellent recovery drink. The next day, with Hélias urgently needing medical attention, the full team was evacuated by helicopter.

SUMMARY: Alpine-style new route on the south face of Nuptse, reaching the northwest summit (Nuptse Nup II, 7,742 meters), by Frédéric Degoulet, Benjamin Guigonnet, and Hélias Millerioux (all from France), October 14–21, 2017. They summited on October 19 and descended the same route.

ABOUT THE AUTHOR: *Frédéric Degoulet, 35, lives below the Massif des Écrins, near Briançon, France, and works as a mountain guide. This was his tenth foreign expedition.*

Translated from the French by Guillaume Lavigueur.

[Top] A magnificent view over Camp 5, perched on a mushroomed snow ridge on Nuptse's south face, looking down beyond advanced base camp and the Nuptse Glacier toward the village of Chukkung, Ama Dablam, Kangtega, and other peaks high in the Khumbu. [Bottom] On the summit (left to right): Hélias Millerioux, Benjamin Guigonnet, and Frédéric Degoulet, with the southwest face of Mt. Everest behind. *Degoulet | Guigonnet | Millerioux*

CULMINATION

THE COMPLETE SOUTHWEST RIDGE OF K7 WEST

KATSUTAKA YOKOYAMA

In the summer of 2014, Ryo Masumoto, Takaaki Nagato, and I aspired to reach the summit of unclimbed Badal Peak (ca 6,100m) and then traverse to K7 West (6,615m). Badal is located on the north side of the Charakusa Glacier in the eastern Karakoram. Although we had some success, making the first ascent of Badal Peak by a 58-pitch new route, over four days of climbing, we could not complete the traverse. After seven more pitches along the ridge toward K7 West, poor weather, lack of food, unstable conditions, and an injury to Masumoto's knee forced us to retreat.

Badal Peak was named after the first route climbed up one of the huge rock walls along the west and southwest sides of the mountain. Four climbers completed the west face over 15 days in 2007, but they did not continue to the summit. Since then, at least five parties have attempted or climbed various routes on these walls and pinnacles, but none got higher than the 2007 team until our climb.

In the summer of 2017 we were back on the Charakusa Glacier. This time, Masumoto and Yusuke Sato had their eye on a big-wall free climb (*see page 283*). Nagato and I had two possible objectives in mind. One was the southwest ridge of K7's main peak (6,934m), one of the last major projects remaining in this area. But since much of this ridge had already been traced by various parties, there was less of the unknown, and so it no longer had as much appeal. On the other hand, the traverse from Badal Peak to K7 West felt more alluring, especially if we started the lower wall with the untouched buttress just to the left of the line we had previously climbed.

Upon arriving at base camp in July, we began acclimatization in the surrounding mountains. However, because of bad weather, we were unable to go higher than 5,800 meters.

On August 2, Nagato and I gathered all of our ropes and headed for the foot of Badal's southwest face at about 4,300 meters. Ordinarily, we might have tried the climb to K7 West in one push, but this lower section would be one of the keys to the climb and would take some time to negotiate. We'd be unlikely to enjoy much free climbing en route to K7 West. Therefore we decided to spend a day fixing ropes, with thoughts to take pleasure in free climbing for at least one day. Both the leader and follower free climbed all day, on solid 5.11 terrain. After nine pitches we deposited some gear on a small terrace and descended, fixing all the ropes. [*This new start ascends a prominent pillar in between the 2014 Japanese route (on the right) and a 900-meter pillar climbed by Marko Prezelj and Maxime Turgeon in 2007.*]

We rested for two days and then left base camp at 3 a.m. on August 5. As the light grew in the east, we started up our fixed ropes. At our high point, we threw down a haul bag with six ropes that were now unnecessary (safely recovered on the day after our descent). Above this point, we had already decided that Nagato would lead all the remaining pitches on the rock wall, and then I would take the lead higher up. Nagato had the ability to easily cope with the rock climbing, and I was more experienced for the alpine terrain of the traverse, plus I

Beyond Badal Peak the traverse is a complex mix of
rock towers and ice walls. "The challenge is created
more by route-finding than by technical difficulty."

[Above] K7 group showing (A) Badal Peak, (B) K7 West, (C) K7 Central, (D) K7 Main, and (E) Link Sar massif. Route 2 shows Japanese climb to Badal Peak in 2014. Route 1 shows 2017 route to Badal Peak and continuation to K7 West (much of the upper traverse is hidden). Other routes and attempts not shown. *Jon Griffith* [Below] K7 from Beatrice to the northwest. The Badal Wall is the large rock face in right center, culminating in Badal Peak. The Japanese traversed the pinnacled skyline left to K7 West. They descended the sunlit northwest face in center. *Masumoto | Sato*

was accustomed to climbing with heavy loads. Unless we sought maximum efficiency, the difficulty of this mountain could not be overcome.

Up to 5.10, Nagato led with light loads and I carried a 15kg pack. The angle of the wall generally did not allow simul-climbing. On harder pitches, Nagato led with no pack and hauled our heavier pack, using a thin rope we had brought; I then followed him with a light load, sometimes climbing with a Micro Traxion for self-belay, sometimes jugging.

At the end of our second day—the third day including fixing—we

Nagato leading on the lower wall. The pair climbed and fixed nine pitches, with much 5.11, three days before starting their push for the summit. *Katsutaka Yokoyama*

joined our earlier route at approximately 5,600 meters, after 27 pitches of climbing. The route-finding on the buttress was complicated, and the wall was so steep in places that we relied on aid climbing many times. This was more time-consuming than we had expected, and it wasn't until the afternoon of the third day that we finished the lower rock wall. The top was guarded by a 60-meter rock face with just a single crack splitting it, which we aided up. Above this we carried on, simul-climbing for another 1,000 meters of ice and snow mixed with rocks, losing elevation to four rappels off gendarmes that blocked the way. We stood on top of Badal Peak right at sunset. It was our second time on this summit, and we knew we still had a long way to go.

The ridge beyond Badal Peak toward K7 West is a complex mix of rock towers and snow and ice walls, with the challenge created more by complicated route-finding than by technical difficulty. Speedy and wise use of tactics such as rappelling and simul-climbing was essential. The big question mark on the upper route was a steep rock buttress in the last part of the ridge. As we neared the buttress on the fourth day of the climb, we suddenly changed plans and decided to detour around on the north side of the ridge, which would mean climbing beneath a 30-meter-high serac. The serac had looked awful from a distance, but as we got closer it seemed relatively stable. We could not say there was no danger, but to go the other way would have caused another risk. Our first priority was how speedily we passed through this crucial point. If we had gone for the other route, we would have failed to reach the summit.

To reach the ice below the serac, we first made a full 60-meter rappel off the ridge. Then, for two hours, we climbed across a 60–65° ice wall. This was roughly the same path followed in 2011 by the Slovenians Nejc Marcic and Luka Strazar, who reached this point after climbing the northwest face, while making the third ascent of K7 West. Near the top, we found a crevasse through the serac wall that gave access to the summit plateau. Nagato joined me and we decided we'd bivouac there. As there was still plenty of light, we started climbing toward the summit, about 200 meters above us. But the snow was so soft in the afternoon sun that we were forced to make a snowplow to the waist. In ten minutes we gave up. We got into our sleeping bags, planning to start again before dawn the next day.

We woke at 1 a.m. with snow falling on our tent. The snowfall got stronger and blasts of powder snow incessantly hit the tent. We spent a sleepless night, wondering, "Will it be possible to reach the summit tomorrow?"

At 4 a.m. we looked outside: Luck was with us—the snow had stopped. Though we were worried about bad conditions, there was less new snow than expected and the snow was firmer on the slope above the tent. We filled a small pack with water and simple food and started up. For two hours we climbed the broad snow ridge until finally Nagato belayed me up a 30-meter pitch to where the slope eased off. In thick clouds, we couldn't even see our own feet. We crouched and felt the snow around us, and finally determined we were right on the summit.

We took a few pictures, buried a snow picket, and rappelled off the summit five minutes after getting there. When we got back to the bivouac site, we could see glimpses of blue sky. We packed the tent and started down the northwest face, more or less following the Slovenian line. The free-hanging rappel off the first serac from a single snow picket was dreadful. However, once we were onto the northwest face, we found good anchors on rock spikes and V-threads. Another storm moved in during the descent, and soon we were soaked. Finally on the glacier, we set up the tent and recovered the feeling of life and comfort. Before noon the next day we were safely back in base camp. The six long days were over.

NEITHER NAGATO NOR I indulged in happy and pleasant moods throughout our time on the mountain. We were preoccupied from early morning until night. The only time I felt I could relax was while having some instant soup in the tent each evening. Nonetheless, I cannot remember experiencing more fulfilling and satisfactory climbing in my 30 years of mountaineering life. Which was the most interesting or most difficult among my climbs in the past? I can't simply compare or rank them. The only answer to this question is that the K7 West traverse was the outcome of a lifetime of achievements in mountaineering so far.

My experiences on the frozen giants of Alaska, the Himalaya, and South America fostered not only an improvement of mixed climbing technique but also stepping up skills and mental strength, making it possible not to give up climbing even in the most miserable conditions. The enchainment of two hard routes on Denali over a week of climbing in 2008 and the first ascent of Mt. Logan's southeast face in 2010 are good examples.

Next we focused on the Fitz Roy massif in Patagonia, where real rock climbing feats were essential—both improved rock technique and sustained power for speedy and long-time climbing were required. During five seasons in Patagonia I made some first ascents and free climbs. But it was always my aim and serious desire to put the abilities gained in Patagonia to practical use in the high Himalaya. I believed that the experiences in Patagonia would only be fully rewarded when they were actually practiced in all-round mountaineering.

To be frank, our technique and power of ten years ago would not have been sufficient for this expedition. The lower rock wall on Badal Peak was so huge and difficult to climb that the experiences in Patagonia were undoubtedly very useful. However, even greater skills and technique than those we'd mastered in Yosemite and Patagonia would not have ensured our success on the traverse to K7 West. Here, the route required tougher strength, complex route-finding, speedy and right action to minimize danger, and the mental pressure inevitable in alpine-style climbing. Unless we had these abilities, acquired in the greater ranges of Alaska and the Himalaya, we could not have succeeded on the full K7 West traverse.

During this expedition the sun came and went. Often the sky was covered with clouds, and we were often tossed about by rain and snow. Sometimes the bright sun of the Karakoram appeared, not only to softly warm us but also to scorch us as if we were in hell. Good weather

[Above] **Moving toward the difficult exit through the serac wall on day four of the climb.** *Takaaki Nagato* [Right] **Nagato (left) and Yokoyama on the summit. "The K7 West traverse was the outcome of a lifetime of achievements in mountaineering."** *Katsutaka Yokoyama*

blessed us during most of the final climb, but on the morning of the summit day we were filled with uneasiness due to snowfall. Recollecting that we had been at the mercy of sun, we chose the name Sun Patch Spur for our route.

This name has an additional meaning too. Coincidentally, all four of us on this expedition were born in the same year, 1979, and thus we were all 38 years old during our time in the Karakoram. The number 38 is pronounced *sanju-hachi* or *san-pachi* in Japanese, the latter being not just a casual but also endearing way to say it. Since Sun Patch sounds very similar to *san-pachi* in Japanese, the name felt like a way to bless these 38-year-old climbers, who were all very happy to achieve their ideal ascents in the greater Himalaya.

SUMMARY: First complete ascent of the southwest ridge of K7 West (6,615m) by the Sun Patch Spur (ED+ 5.11c R A2 M5 90°), by Takaaki Nagato and Katsutaka Yokoyama, August 5–10, 2017. The two Japanese first climbed a partial new route up the southwest face of Badal Peak (ca 6,100m), then traversed the upper southwest ridge of K7 West to the summit. With six rappels en route, the climb gained well over 2,300 meters; the total climbing distance was approximately six kilometers. They descended the northwest face.

ABOUT THE AUTHOR: *Katsutaka "Jumbo" Yokoyama was born in 1979 and began mountaineering at age eight. He lives in Yamanashi Prefecture, Japan, with his wife, Chihiro, and two sons, Yoh and Kan. Tamotsu Nakamura assisted with translation for this article.*

[Photo] Kenro Nakajima nearing Camp 1 on the northeast face of Shispare. *Kazuya Hiraide*

SHISPARE

THE LONG QUEST FOR AN ELUSIVE SUMMIT

KAZUYA HIRAIDE AND KENRO NAKAJIMA

Starting the second day of the climb, with more than 2,000 meters of the northeast face still looming overhead. Camp 2 would be found amid the rocks in upper left. *Kazuya Hiraide*

THE QUEST, *BY KAZUYA HIRAIDE*

SHISPARE WAS ALWAYS there, living in the back of my head. A mountain worth spending my life upon.

In 2002, I went to Pakistan alone with a map of the Karakoram on which I had marked routes ascended by previous parties. The objective was to find out what treasures—mountains without ascents, unclimbed routes—I could find in the blank spots on the map. In one of those places, I met with Shispare. I remember it as if it were yesterday: falling in love with this pyramid-shaped, 7,611-meter mountain, with its grand, unclimbed northeast face. However, I also realized I did not have the experience to attempt Shispare anytime soon.

Gradually building up my skills and waiting for a chance, I finally made an attempt five years later, in 2007, with Yuka Komatsu. The intent was to draw a new line up the middle of the northeast face. Unfortunately, we retreated at 6,000 meters due to unstable snow conditions. I thought afterward, "There's no mountain I couldn't climb if only I would throw everything at it." My young and immature self couldn't accept defeat as defeat.

My climbing from then on had good moments and bad moments. On the plus side, I won many prizes in the alpine community. On the negative, one of our expeditions ended in the death of people who came to rescue us. [*During a rescue attempt on Ama Dablam in 2010, a helicopter crashed and killed the two crew members on board.*] During those years, I didn't give a second go at any mountain I bailed from. But somehow Shispare was different. I wanted to return to the beginning. I had a hunch that this mountain could teach me what I was lacking, both as an alpinist and as a person.

Thus I returned, in 2012, with Takuya Mitoro. This time we attempted the southwest face. It is also a grand unclimbed face, and it too called to me. We were thrown back by bad weather at 5,350 meters. But by then, I had learned to accept defeat a little: "Even if I throw my everything at them, some mountains I may not be able to climb."

I couldn't give up the thought of climbing Shispare, though, so I came back the next year

with Kei Taniguchi. She was the ultimate partner—I had climbed the southeast face of Kamet in India with her five years earlier (an ascent that won a Piolet d'Or), and I had high hopes of finally standing on Shispare's summit. We attempted the southwest face again, having seen its promise the year before. However, a serac high on the route terrified us, so we retreated at 5,700m. I was despairing and pretty sure I would not return to Shispare. "Perhaps," I thought, "it's alright to have one mountain I can't climb in my life."

The northeast face of Shispare (7,611 meters) and the line of Shukriya ("Thanks"). Hiraide and Nakajima bivied four times on the face, including two nights at the highest camp shown, plus two more nights during the descent. The mountain had only been climbed twice before, both times by the eastern ridge (left), which is the route the 2017 climbers descended. *Kazuya Hiraide*

In 2015, my longtime partner Kei died in a mountaineering accident in Japan. The sudden tragedy made me question my motivation for mountaineering. At the end of much pondering, I decided to continue climbing, with her climbing alongside in spirit. The following year, I partnered up with Kenro Nakajima and we succeeded on the first ascent of the north face of Loinbo Kangri (7,095m) in Tibet in a clean, fast, direct line. But my heart was still restless. I decided that I needed to settle with Shispare. If I could only climb the mountain that started it all, I could forge a new path for myself. Luckily, my new partner understood my relationship with Shispare, and I knew I could rely on him. The stage was set for the final showdown.

We started preparing for the expedition in January, but back-to-back photography assignments at Everest and Denali saw the summer arriving in a rush. Still, the knowledge that I'd be warmly welcomed in Hunza, which by now had become a second home, allowed me to relax. This year's harvest of Tibetan apricots was plentiful, and meeting old friends brought smiles to our faces. Thus we found ourselves arriving at base camp in high spirits.

A Pakistani expedition aiming for Pasu Peak was also at the base camp. They didn't like the conditions of the glacier and left for home more than a month ahead of schedule. In the suddenly quiet camp, we could finally get down to business. The weather was predominantly bad, as usual, and we ended up spending long stretches in camp. Maintaining motivation was tough.

Once we began climbing, we were constantly threatened by avalanches and covered by spindrift. But one thing was different this time. In the past, during moments of danger and duress, I had sought excuses to quit and, having found one, chose to retreat. This time, every time such a decision was required, even if there was only a one percent chance of success, we would go on. I feel that this was because my old partner Kei had passed away without fulfilling all of her goals, while I was still alive, and, since I had the motivation, the opportunity, and the capability to go on, giving up too easily would be unfair. Making countless decisions of this kind is what led to our success.

I wonder if I will ever find another mountain as fulfilling as Shispare.

Day three: Kenro Nakajima traverses steep ice toward the route's crux at about 6,500 meters: a 60° wall of thin ice and mixed that gave access to the upper ice slopes. *Kazuya Hiraide*

THE CLIMB, *BY KENRO NAKAJIMA*

ON JULY 26, after two days of light trekking, we climb steeply to Patundas, on top of a ridge, and Shispare stands in front of us, with a carpet of wildflowers at our feet. We descend a gentle slope to base camp on the bank of the Pasu Glacier.

Two days later we head to Shispare's east ridge, the first and only prior route up the mountain, to acclimatize and to check out conditions and our descent route. (*This long ridgeline, first climbed in 1974, descends generally eastward from the summit, but mostly to the northeast in the section that has been climbed.*) The glacier is a complete maze of crevasses. The northern spur used to access the main ridge is difficult to reach; we finally end up ascending snow slopes on the west side of the spur. The next day, we follow the spur to 5,600m, not far below the east ridge. Having checked the descent route to our satisfaction, we return to base camp.

After resting for two days, we leave camp on August 1 to attempt Pasu Peak (7,478m), eight kilometers to the northwest of Shispare. Unfortunately, bad weather shuts us down and we can't summit, but after camping for two nights at 6,400 meters and climbing up to 6,750 meters, we do at least manage to acclimatize.

We intend to climb Shispare in the next weather window, but as the forecast is hideous for multiple days to come, we decide to return to Hunza for a three-day rest before further attempts. Back at base camp, the weather still isn't agreeable, and we pass time in the tent with cloudy skies and snowfall outside.

Nine days after our acclimatization on Pasu Peak, we decide to stretch our legs and give it a go. Perhaps the bad weather won't affect the lower route too much. We leave base camp under overcast skies, and it starts to snow in the afternoon—we can't find our way forward in the whiteout. We camp at 5,000 meters to see if conditions will improve, but with 40 to 50 centimeters of fresh snow, getting on the wall would be a fool's errand. Humbled, we return to base camp again on August 14.

We decide to stay in camp until the snow on the wall stabilizes and it's safer to climb. The waiting is making us anxious and wearing us down. Even when the forecast calls for clear skies, the summit stays shrouded in clouds.

On the morning of August 17, the sky clears for a few hours and we see Shispare's face gleaming in the sun. On the next day, the weather isn't all that convincing, but we still decide to go for it. The maze of the glacier is familiar by now, and finally we start to climb the northeast face.

We had worried about the seracs hanging over our approach gully, and our worries prove to be well founded. First, a small serac fall causes us to be covered in a bit of snow, but this isn't too much of a problem. Soon, however, we hear a thunderous bang and see a cloud of snow above us—clearly something we can't ignore. In a rush, we scurry out of the fall line, but one of my feet gets stuck in a crevasse, the rope goes tight, and neither of us gets into proper cover. When the avalanche reaches us, we endure a deluge of snow and crushing wind for a full minute. It's difficult to breathe, but luckily neither of us is buried or injured. Paradoxically, enduring such a big serac fall without a scratch boosts our spirits—we pretend there won't be a new one anytime soon. Thus we pass through the gully successfully. Since we had started a bit later than intended, we set up camp earlier than planned by flattening part of a snow ridge at 5,450 meters.

Next morning we cross over a ridge and reach a 60–70° degree ice wall. It has a thin cover of snow, but it's possible to use ice screws for runners. To maintain speed, we simul-climb with one piece of protection between us. My calves start screaming, but that's the price to pay for speed. After finishing up the S-shaped wall of ice and snow, we encounter a rock wall. Traversing to the left for four pitches, we arrive at a gully. The weather turns for the worse and continuous spindrift slides down the wall. We had intended to bivy at the base of the rock, but there are no suitable spots. It's a choice of either climbing in bad weather or returning to our previous bivy site. We steady our resolve and start climbing.

The ice is shallow, but with some difficulty we manage to find screw placements. Occasionally a big snow slide tries to rip us off the wall, but we manage to hold on and clear the rock face in two pitches. Still no sign of a bivy spot. We climb a steep snow wall for three more pitches, up and right, off our intended route, and get onto a snow ridge that should be safe from avalanches. It's narrow, but we manage to cut a ledge at about 6,500 meters, just big enough for both of us to lie down. We've climbed over 1,000 meters that day.

On August 20 we wait until the sun hits the wall in hopes of the snow consolidating a little, then do two rappels to get back onto our intended route. After traversing steep snow and ice for a further three pitches, we reach the second rock band. The rock isn't too steep, only 60°, but it's a slab without a covering of solid snow or ice. I leave my pack with Hiraide and head up.

For the first half of the pitch, I can get ice screws halfway in, but they feel really suspect. Then the ice and snow disappear and there's no protection whatsoever on the smooth slab. My legs and arms feel like they're approaching the limit, so there's no time to waste. I commit to climbing without pro. Suddenly both feet come off, but an axe catches on something solid higher up. For the first time ever at an altitude like this, I let out a victory yell. I manage to get in another half screw and feel a bit better. Then one of my tools slips at the next move and I fall. I imagine all the runners zippering out below me, but by some miracle they hold. Shaken but determined, I finish the pitch to the top of the rock band.

Above, we simulclimb ice for three pitches. Then it starts snowing again and we are attacked by spindrift, so we start belaying. We cut a campsite on the ridge at the top of the ice wall at about 6,860 meters.

During the night, the snowfall continues and our tent is assaulted by spindrift. In the morning, the tent is more than half buried. The visibility is bad. We stay in the tent for the whole day. It's above our acclimatization altitude, and I'm feeling it. I've lost my appetite.

The next day, August 22, we wake early, hoping to reach the summit. However, it keeps snowing so we stay in the tent for a while. Around 6 a.m. the visibility improves and we pack up and leave. In all the new snow, we are faced with arduous post-holing. We try to keep motivation high. Forcing a way through the deep snow is reminiscent of winter mountaineering back in Japan. However, at this altitude the body refuses to perform, and it feels like it's taking forever. After a pitch of steep snow, a three-pitch traverse to the right brings us to a snow ridge that we follow for another four pitches, finally reaching the east ridge at about 7,200 meters.

It's already past 11 a.m. We manage to get a signal on the satellite phone and make a call to Japan for a weather update. It seems we should be standing under clear skies, which is a bit hard to believe with the blizzard raging around us. The weather for the next day is supposed to be similar. It's hard to know what to think. The visibility isn't terrible, though, despite the snowfall, so we cache everything we can and hurry toward the summit, about 400 meters above us, with one rope, a minimal set of pro, and a bit of food.

The wind is strong, but we see glimpses of Rakaposhi to the south between the clouds. Then we are completely engulfed by clouds, and we take care to note the way back as we proceed, crossing over countless false summits. At 2 p.m. we suddenly find ourselves on the real summit. There's no view, and we're worried about the way down. Hiraide's frozen beard makes him look like Santa Claus. We make a quick phone call, and he scrapes a hole in the snow and places a photo of Kei Taniguchi inside it, and then we start down right away.

Our path has already mostly disappeared, so we use a compass to navigate and somehow reach our cache just before dark. We would have liked to descend further, but there is no visibility, so we cut a ledge and bivy. During the night, snow showers assault our tent again.

We wake up to a blizzard. Rather than being happy about having summited, we are worried about getting down alive. We had chosen the east ridge for our descent due to fewer dangers from avalanches and seracs, but in no way is it an easy route. The plateau is broad and it is necessary to climb over three minor peaks along the way. Finding the way down in zero visibility would be impossible. We wait in the tent, praying for the weather to improve.

At around 6:30 a.m. the visibility is ever so slightly better, though the wind is as strong as ever. We catch a glimpse of the route toward the northern spur and head that way, but our scouting had only covered the lower part of the descent, and this area is unknown to us. We end up having to traverse around some big seracs, rappelling off the tops of others. But gradually the visibility improves and the wind quiets. When we finally reach the high point of our scouting climb, we stop for a final night on the mountain. For the first time in six days, we sleep at a safe, flat spot without snow sliding onto us.

[Top] Hiraide prepares to leave a photo of Kei Taniguchi on the summit of Shispare. The two were favorite partners and had attempted Shispare in 2013. She died in a climbing accident in Japan in 2015. *Kenro Nakajima* [Bottom] Kazuya Hiraide (left) and Kenro Nakajima. *Expedition Photo*

Arriving at base camp the next day is much, much more emotional than reaching the summit had been. We are off the mountain—alive.

SUMMARY: First alpine-style ascent of Shispare (7,611m) in the Batura Muztagh of Pakistan via the first ascent of the northeast face (2,700m, WI5 M6), by Kazuya Hiraide and Kenro Nakajima from Japan, August 18–24, 2017. The climbers descended the east ridge and north spur. They called their route Shukriya ("Thanks" in Urdu). Shispare had been climbed only twice before, by a Polish-German expedition in 1974 and a Japanese team in 1994. Both previous ascents followed the east ridge and climbed expedition-style, using fixed ropes.

ABOUT THE AUTHORS: *Kazuya Hiraide, 38, lives in Yokohama, Japan. He is a professional mountaineer and mountain cameraman. Kenro Nakajima, 33, is self-employed and lives in Kawasaki, Japan.*

Translated from Japanese by Heikki Ruuska.

SATISFACTION!

FIVE EPIC EXPEDITIONS AND FINALLY SUCCESS ON GASHERBRUM I'S SOUTHWEST FACE

MAREK HOLEČEK

"As you get closer to the summit, the exponential curve of adversities gets ever steeper. Everything costs more energy the farther you get from the point of safe return. Despite this we are still able to fight and chase our goal. The human body is just a perfect machine, provided one´s head will not quit."

If only I had known how much time, sacrifice, sorrow, and disappointment it would cost me to finish a new route on Gasherbrum I, never would I have started down this road. But I am not a Sibyl, an oracle, and actually it is better this way, because if I saw the negatives ahead of me it might paralyze my forward progress, which is certainly undesirable. What if, instead, we just see the future in bright colors and then tackle impediments when they occur? In this way we can enjoy every new day, because we never know which might be our last.

In 2007 I saw the Beautiful Mountain for the first time—that is the rough translation of Gasherbrum from the Baltí dialect. At that time I was not focused on Gasherbrum I but on the west face of her sister mountain, Gasherbrum III. But G-I became my lover at first sight. Since then I've done five expeditions to Gasherbrum I with the goal of making the first ascent of the southwest face. [*In 1983, Jerzy Kukuczka and Voytek Kurtyka (Poland) climbed the southwest face to the final rock band, then moved right and followed the south ridge to the summit. In 2008, Viktor Afanasiev and Valery Babanov (Russia) climbed the left side of the southwest face to a col at 7,200 meters, then followed the southwest ridge to the summit. The complete southwest face remained unclimbed.*] All in all, my time on this mountain has totaled eight months, with each expedition so epic as to cover at least a chapter of the whole book.

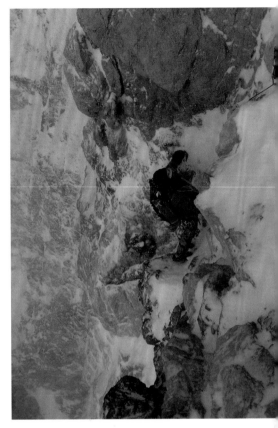

[Above] **Ondra Mandula at the first crux of the route, at 7,400 meters, in 2016. On this attempt, he and Marek Holeček were trapped for seven nights at 7,750 meters before retreating.** [Left page] **Zdeněk Hák (left) and Holeček on the summit. "We looked like fish fillets in a freezer."** *Marek Holeček*

Let me skip right into the last sequence of the drama. It was the summer of 2017, and Zdeněk "Hook" Hák was my latest climbing partner for the steep face. After four consecutive days of climbing and bivouacs, now at 7,800 meters, every move we made represented sheer toil. The massive rock barrier at the top of the face rose in front of our eyes. Our observations through binoculars had suggested there were ice gullies promising easier progression toward the summit. We had hoped for something other than rock climbing at this altitude. However, the reality surpassed even the most horrific dreams. The snow that promised easier climbing was like cotton candy over rotten rock—a frightful combination, but retreating 2,500 meters would be next to impossible. We knew there was no option but up. Occasional snow flurries filled the air. Luckily, the usual strong wind was not blowing. Considering the altitude and the setting, the weather actually was not that bad.

The next pitch took me really a long time, at least in my view. I even had to take off my gloves and hide them inside my down jacket to proceed, climbing with bare hands. I could not feel my fingers, but I did not care about that. At this altitude you have to make a sequence of a few quick and precise moves, then catch your breath before continuing. You cannot get into oxygen debt or you might lose control over your body or even lose consciousness. This would result in a fatal fall—perhaps for both of us, as the protection between us was very poor.

The day's summary was not really encouraging: a mere 80 meters gained during 12 hours of climbing. I managed to drive in a relatively good piton and shouted to Zdeněk to follow me. It was about time to find the bivy spot, but there was no good place for the tent. There was no choice but to dig into a tiny ice slab on a rocky balcony with a 70° slope. After endless chopping of ice, we managed to pitch our tent and take shelter in this tiny, airy house. With no need for words, we started to make dinner. This was our third day high above 7,000 meters, which takes its toll. Inside the tent at last, I started to recall other desperate moments on this face. My first attempt, with Zdeněk Hrubý in 2009, was like a Hollywood horror movie in my memory.

Zdeněk and I had solved the first crux of the face, the rock barrier at nearly 7,400 meters, blocking the way from the broad couloir on the left to the central snowfields. His health problems began at the next bivouac. It was impossible to know at that time he was about to experience the bursting of a gastric ulcer and massive internal bleeding. I still cannot comprehend the miracle we were about to fulfill. Zdeněk had to rappel a 200-meter rock band while vomiting and suffering terrible pains. In the ice couloir he was forced to rappel full pitches, place ice screws, and wait until I downclimbed to his stance. This continued for nearly 1,700 meters. We had to bivouac in a serac cave before we reached the glacier at the foot of the face. After a dreadful march across the rugged glacier, he was finally evacuated from base camp by helicopter two days later.

I was left at camp without a partner, still with some time before leaving the area. So I took advantage of the situation and climbed the classical route (the Japanese Couloir) on the completely abandoned mountain. This was my first time to look around the lonely Karakoram from Gasherbrum I's 8,068-meter summit.

Four years later, Zdeněk and I began our expedition season by completing my longtime project on the northwest face of Talung, near Kangchenjunga. It was a great climb that made it onto the red carpet at the Piolets d´Or in Chamonix. If only these happy times could have remained, but they did did not. A month after Talung we were at the foot of Gashebrum again.

Suddenly the noise from boiling water and flaring flames disturbed my recollections. Once again I missed the right moment to switch off the stove, and hot water bubbled up from below the lid and onto my sleeping bag. Damn it…but this happens. The sleeping bag was damp anyway—the vapors inside had frozen to the bone in my backpack, and now I warmed it up with my body. We call this a "Priessnitz pack." [*In the early 19th century, Vincenz Priessnitz popularized a treatment for various maladies that involved wrapping patients in wet bandages and then bathing them in cold water.*] It simultaneously shows the glory and misery of a climber´s life.

I put a teabag in the pot and added a spoonful of sugar from our thinning supplies. Our dehydrated stomachs received the first drops of badly needed liquid. The instantaneous relief was replaced by suffocating coughs. Sounds even worse than those of a tuberculosis ward—in this case the highest in the world, without a doubt. A new dose of snow for our fast-boiling pot took me back into my reveries, observing the melting snow crystals on Hook's hand after he'd dug into the white powder outside of the tent. We resembled two unhappy rooks on an airy perch in deep, deep frost.

It is unbelievable what a human body can withstand in adverse conditions. We already had lost many kilos, first from our fat reserves—not very big at the time, really—followed

by our muscles. Literally we ate ourselves alive. At high altitude the opponents are predefined and expected—the cold, the lack of oxygen, the daily multiple marathons of cruel toil, the lack of sleep (if any), the stressful concentration on thousands of steps, the threats from avalanches or falling rocks or weather. Also there remains the question of whether the chosen route may even be climbable—or at least climbable by us. Strangely enough, as you get closer to the summit, the exponential curve of adversities gets ever steeper. Everything costs more energy the farther and farther you get from the point of safe return. Despite this we are still able to fight and chase our goal. The human body is just a perfect machine, provided one´s head will not quit.

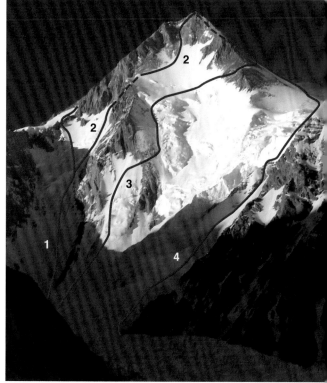

It was like a bolt from the blue. Just a slight outcry and then silence again. I looked below and saw Zdeněk´s body gathering speed over the ice slopes. One hit on the rock, another in an ice gully, and then it was just a lifeless body falling lower and lower. It seems strange, but very pragmatic ideas went through my brain immediately: Zdeněk is dead—what will happen to me? It was 2013; we had reached 7,000 meters. Now I was hanging from an ice screw next to another screw on which a half-opened carabiner still rocked and swayed. The biner was

[Top] The alluring headwall on Gasherbrum I: It took three days to climb this final 250 meters. [Bottom] The southwest face, about 2,600 meters high. (1) Babanov-Afanasiev (2008, to summit). (2) Satisfaction (Hák-Holeček, 2017). (3) Kurtyka-Kukuczka (1983). (4) Spanish (1983). *Marek Holeček*

supposed to be clipped to Zdeněk's rappel rope. But there was neither a rope nor my friend. What exactly happened was not the issue—all that counted was what would happen next. We did not take a second rope, and all the gear was gone with my partner, who was already more than a kilometer below me. I had no choice but to try downclimb if another obituary note was not to be issued today. There was no time to wait, as the sun would turn to the face soon, releasing more falling rocks. I began to climb down toward Zdeněk.

For Hook and me, the fifth morning on the face was pretty much in line with the previous ones. Climbing close to our limits, combined with suffocating with every move from lack of oxygen. According to the forecast, we needed to make it over the summit this day at any cost. A spell of high wind with more snow was supposed to arrive from India to the south. We would be slightly sheltered from the wind beyond the crest, on the northwest slopes of the mountain.

Time passed so fast, yet we climbed as if in slow motion. Dusk approached and Hook shouted at me through the roaring wind that there was no way upward. This woke me from my lethargy. How could there be no way? For God´s sake, we had to get up this, otherwise we were dead alive! I reached his stance and continued up the loose rock above. I had managed to climb some ten meters when suddenly I felt that nothing was holding my hands and feet. The next moment my apprehension had come true and I started falling. Then the rope tightened and a big rock that I had grabbed rolled over my thigh. A camming device in the crack had saved our expedition. My leg was OK—just the Gore-tex pants torn and our rope disclosing its inner threads. Otherwise, nothing serious.

All this prompted me to continue with the resolute moves of a machine, the whole pitch nearly unprotected. After fixing the belay station, I shouted at Hook to follow as the sun set, giving the wild scenery a purple tint. An endless carpet of lower summits stretched around us. At this moment I realized we were above the rock barrier, and also that a bivy at 8,000 meters was inevitable, with tough weather coming the next day. We would not make it over the summit today.

Two years after Zdeněk's death, I was back with Tom Petreček, climbing in freezing cold by headlamp to minimize the danger of the nearly two-kilometer couloir above us. Climbing at night gave a false feeling of safety, as the threat above was not visible and the frost made the rock more solid. Despite that, it was imperative to be fast and decisive. As soon as the sun returned to the face, about 10 in the morning, it became a shooting gallery of falling stones.

Toward the end of the next day, 200 meters of hard mixed climbing led us to the col that joins the plateau and the final rocky headwall. The weather forecast seemed to be positive, and we fell asleep with this happy thought. However, in the morning we woke to a blizzard that endured for six long days. We were trapped. There was no chance to continue up, and the way down was blocked by avalanches. After all those days and nights in a tiny bivouac tent, we abseiled down and reached base camp 11 days after our departure.

How could I know that my fourth attempt, together with Ondra Mandula, the following year, would resemble the real Dante´s inferno? This time we reached 7,750 meters, only to be trapped at this altitude for seven nights! We finally reached base camp after 14 days, having stretched food and gas supplies that were barely sufficient for nine. It was not a surprise when I removed my boots and found severely frostbitten toes. The ensuing three-day journey back to civilization did not help my condition, resulting in the amputation of parts of a few toes.

Day six on the face, July 30, at just below 8,000 meters, started out very windy. While we were packing the tent, the temperature dropped far below -20°C, and Hook and I had not even reached the open summit crest. Anyway, we had no choice but to start climbing.

The terrain was not really difficult, and we climbed unroped. The wind beat us with great brutality. For a time, Hook and I lost sight of each other. After about half an hour of navigating between rock spires, we met again at the summit of Gasherbrum I. This was my second and surely the last time to be here. Freezing smiles in front of the camera. We looked like fish fillets

Day five on the southwest face, about 7,900 meters. The climbers hoped to reach the summit this day but climbed only 150 meters on this difficult terrain, forcing another night on the face. *Marek Holeček*

in a freezer. Only a few words to exchange, mainly concerning how we would descend through the worsening weather as fast as our condition and the snowpacked terrain would allow. Pure intuition helped us find the way down through the white inferno to Camp 3 above the Japanese Couloir. Hook disappeared from sight for a moment, but shouts and whistles helped us find each other.

The next day was as beautiful as one could imagine, but rappelling and downclimbing the avalanche-prone Japanese Couloir cost us some more nerves. No wonder that not a single expedition was successful on the route that year. Nonetheless, we had to get down the couloir to reconfirm our existence yet again. Hook belayed as I tried my luck in white powder up to my waist. A horrific 600 meters, where any move might set off an uncontrolled ride. These lines confirm that we successfully reached the Gasherbrum La and, after one more bivouac, returned to base camp the next morning, eight days after leaving.

Five expeditions and five epic chapters on the southwest face of Gasherbrum I. A route that even Jerzy Kukuczka, Wojciech Kurtyka, Valery Babanov, and Viktor Afanasiev did not complete. Compared with those legends, we were just luckier, I reckon.

SUMMARY: Alpine-style first ascent of the complete southwest face of Gasherbrum I (a.k.a. Hidden Peak, 8,068m), by Zdeněk Hák and Marek Holeček, July 25 to August 1, 2017. The two summited at approximately 1 p.m. on July 30 and descended by the Japanese Couloir on the upper northwest face. The ca 2,600m route, named Satisfaction!, was graded ED+ WI5+ M7.

ABOUT THE AUTHOR: *Czech climber Marek Holeček was born in 1974 and wrote about the first ascent of Talung's northwest face in AAJ 2014. He has dedicated this ascent to the memory of Zdeněk Hrubý. This article was translated from Czech by Zbyšek Česenek.*

Tenuous downclimbing while following a traverse between the second and third towers on the south ridge. *Clint Helander*

STONE GOOD, SNOW BAD

MT. HUNTINGTON'S TWO-MILE SOUTH RIDGE

CLINT HELANDER

A fierce gust of wind blew across the summit ridge of Mt. Huntington. The snow hissing across the tent's thin fabric sounded like the moan of a haunting wraith. The chill penetrated beyond my physical core, intensifying the dark emotions that had lurked in my mind throughout the past week. Our breath frosted the tent's inner walls, and icy feathers knocked loose by the gusts stung our faces. Jess Roskelley curled in the fetal position next to me, and I felt him shivering under his wet sleeping bag. "Well," he said with a raspy cough, "at least we aren't still on that ridge." Darkness fell.

Snow filled our tent whenever we opened the door, so instead we choked on carbon monoxide and suffered raging headaches. The pungent aroma of week-old socks blended with an acrid stench of ammonia from muscle tissue being consumed. Dinner that night consisted of four bullion cubes and some warm water: 22 calories per man. *How much snow would this storm dump? Could we survive if we were trapped up here for a week?*

For five days, we had struggled over paper-thin cornices and blade-like gendarmes during the first ascent of Mt. Huntington's complete south ridge. We clawed our way to the 12,240-foot (3,731-meter) summit through a rising storm, then conceded to the stinging, windblown snow and set up the tent. We tried to convince ourselves that we were just recovering and waiting for a break in the weather, but as I prepared for my second night near the top, I began to come to terms with the idea that we could perish on the summit after climbing the biggest route of our lives.

MT. HUNTINGTON IS a mountain devoid of subtleties. Its features are sharp and appear exaggerated—its monstrous seracs and house-size cornices seem more in place atop the higher flanks of Denali or Foraker than on the narrow ridges of this "lesser" peak of the Alaska Range. Huntington is a technical climber's mountain—one with no easy path to the summit. The walls surrounding the Tokositna Glacier form one of the most precipitous corners of the range. A storm may encase Huntington in three feet of snow while the Ruth Gorge, just five miles away as the raven flies, barely receives a trace.

"The most beautiful mountain in Alaska," as it has often been called, has captivated technical climbers since its first ascent in 1964 by a French team led by Lionel Terray. Those who have written the history of Huntington's arching ridges and icy faces include the names that inspired me most as a passionate young Alaskan alpinist: David Roberts, John Waterman, Glenn Randall, Jack Roberts, Jay Smith, and Jack Tackle. Though I had few qualifications to justify such dreams, I longed to add my own story on such a magnificent mountain. I thought I had been born a few years too late; it seemed that every distinct feature had been ascended long ago—until I discovered that Huntington's longest and most prominent ridge had never been completed.

I first noticed the south ridge in 2013 during a summertime flight-seeing tour with my family. From the air, the two-mile-long ridge resembled a jagged saw blade. Kurt Hicks and I had climbed the Phantom Wall, on Huntington's southwest face, several months before, but in our rush to beat an incoming storm I hadn't noticed the seemingly infinite chaos of cornices and serrated gendarmes to our right.

Back home in Anchorage, I tore through my collection of Alaska climbing literature. "[The] south ridge looked incredibly difficult; it was not so much a ridge as five separate, serrated peaks, each increasingly higher," David Roberts wrote in his 1967 classic *The Mountain of My Fear*. "To traverse them all would involve gaining perhaps three times as much altitude as the east ridge would require, and the necessity of cutting oneself off from the base camp might be unavoidable."

During the 1970s, when Alaska was still in its "ridge phase," several teams poked around the lower south ridge without much success. In the 1973 *AAJ*, Jeb Schenck wrote, "An attempt in early July to climb the entire south ridge was an utter failure. Rotten sugar snow without any base prevailed, due to the lack of the normal spring thaw. Avalanching was considerable." Before making the first ascent of Huntington's southeast spur in 1978 with three other climbers, Angus Thuermer Jr. ran into a group of 13 mountaineers from Sapporo, Japan, on the glacier. They had retreated from the south ridge after a month of sieging up to the second of the ridge's peaks. "Over ceremonial coffee we tried to communicate," Thuermer noted in the 1979 *AAJ*. "Queries had to be rephrased before we drew their response: 'Stone good, snow bad.'"

In May 1979, David Jay, Jay Kerr, Jeff Thomas, and Scott Woolums bypassed the first four towers along the ridge by climbing a couloir from the east to reach the upper south ridge, between Huntington and its 10,700-foot southern subpeak (now called Idiot Peak), then continued up the ridge to the top. In the *AAJ*, Thomas wrote, "[T]o climb the entire ridge was enticing, but it would be terribly difficult."

Will Mayo and Chris Thomas made the first ascent of Idiot Peak in 2005, approaching from the west. In 2009, Jay Smith and Jack Tackle established several impressive routes on the east face of the south ridge, including one to just below the summit of Idiot Peak, but none of the lines continued up the ridgeline toward Huntington.

After several reconnaissance flights and countless hours studying photos, it was apparent the complete south ridge would demand total commitment. The approach would involve traversing avalanche slopes, scurrying under numerous seracs, and navigating complex crevasse fields. The first tower (Point 9,460') appeared to be overhanging on its north side—it might be impossible to reclimb, if necessary, after rappelling into the col beyond it. If a storm arrived halfway up the ridge, there might be no way to move safely in any direction. Even so, each spring from 2014 to 2016, I convinced myself and potential partners that the ridge would be possible to climb. But a suitable weather window never arrived.

In March 2017, my would-be partner injured his shoulder. With the prime season only a few weeks away, I scavenged for a high-caliber replacement. Jess Roskelley and I had climbed Fitz Roy at the same time, but we had never shared a rope. I was impressed with his calm and confident approach to technical climbing, and we enjoyed the same grade-school humor. When I called him and he agreed to attempt Huntington without even seeing a photograph of the ridge, I was sure he was just the right type of crazy. Two weeks later, an ideal high-pressure system rotated north toward Alaska from the Pacific Ocean. Jess was on a plane to Anchorage the very next day.

I'VE ALWAYS HELD that every Alaska Range adventure should begin and end at the bar of Talkeetna's Fairview Inn. It felt strange, then, to fly from Anchorage in my friend Conor's little

To access the south ridge of Mt. Huntington from the glacier landing strip, the climbers descended alongside the icefall of the east fork of the Tokositna Glacier to reach Death Valley, where they bivouacked. After traversing around the toe of the ridge, they climbed to the first tower (A), then traversed on or alongside the ridge crest over the second tower (B), third tower (C), and Idiot Peak (D) to the top of Huntington (E). They spent four nights along the ridge and two nights near Huntington's summit before they could descend the West Face Couloir and return to the landing strip. *Clint Helander*

plane and bypass Talkeetna, thereby avoiding the hangover that seemed to mark the start of every expedition. On April 18, as we flew past Huntington toward the landing strip on the upper East Fork of the Tokositna, I flashed a thumbs-up to Jess: Conditions looked great for our route, with far less snow than I had seen in years past.

Less than two hours after setting up our base camp, Jess and I began the painstaking and dangerous approach to Death Valley, the narrow cwm of the lower East Fork. Directly below Huntington's southwest face, we bypassed a Khumbu-like icefall by dropping 2,000 feet down a steep and slender couloir.

At the bottom of the valley, we felt like the proverbial fish in a barrel. Towering walls encased with massive seracs surrounded us on nearly every side. Large chunks of sharp blue ice littered the basin. Debris piles from fresh avalanches crisscrossed in every direction. Above us, the Phantom Wall turned a sinister red in the late evening.

Darkness fell as we navigated through a minefield of crevasses—Jess' diligent arrest kept me from falling too deep into one hole. Rather than risk another fall while trying to navigate in the dark, we heeded to prudence and established camp among the trenches. We convinced ourselves that we were out of reach of the seracs adorning the south ridge, but dawn couldn't arrive soon enough.

At first light we escaped Death Valley and wrapped around the tip of the south ridge. At 5,700 feet, we began to climb up a left-slanting ramp. Already, it felt like an entire expedition lay behind us, and we had only just finished the approach. I pushed against my instincts as we

Death Valley in the lower East Fork of the Tokositna Glacier, below the menacing seracs on Huntington's south ridge. Darkness forced an unwelcome bivouac amid this minefield of crevasses. *Clint Helander*

climbed up old avalanche runnels. It hadn't snowed for several weeks and the face felt safe. But what if it snowed even an inch? We wouldn't dare come back this way. But the 3,750-foot climb up the funneled south face of Point 9,460' went smoothly, and late in the evening we found a ledge and settled into a comfortable bivy. In our tent, nestled in our 20°F sleeping bags, we studied photos of the route ahead, knowing we would be totally committed if we chose to continue along the ridge.

In the morning we peered into a vertigo-inducing gunsight notch between the north side of the first tower and a rotten gendarme. Scuds of cirrus boiled into an ominous gray tempest. Just as I had feared, the north face was overhanging and composed of shattered black crud. Rocks bombarded the notch as I balanced onto a narrow ledge. Clouds enveloped us and Jess squinted into blowing sleet that froze onto his face.

"Do you feel good with this?" I asked him.

"Is this only a localized storm?" he asked.

Across the Tokositna, Mt. Hunter faded behind a wall of white as more snow began to fall. Powerful sloughs washed down the ridge.

"Yes," I said. "I hope." Jess rappelled without saying another word.

After what seemed like an eternity, I screamed to Jess but the only sound was the wind rushing against my hood and the rumbles of small sloughs below me. I feared he had been hit by a falling rock as his ropes raked across the fractured wall, and I had begun to panic when I heard a faint "off rappel." Mounds of stacked blocks shifted as I carefully pushed away from the wall. When I swung back, falling rocks shrieked downward. I watched in horror as they peppered around Jess, who held his pack overhead as a makeshift shield.

Jess was clipped to one cam in an icy crack. We smashed two pitons behind a frozen block as waves of snow washed over us. I stared westward beyond the whirling shrouds of snow. Mt. Hunter was illuminated in brief moments of sunshine. We suppressed our doubts and put our faith in the forecast. As we watched the ropes fall toward us, we knew we were committed to the summit, at least four days away.

After another rappel, I led two traversing pitches across jutting snow flutings and some steep mixed sections along the left side of the ridge. If Jess was alarmed, he didn't show it, but it was terrifying to witness the power of the sloughs caused by even a light snowfall. Jess calmly dispatched a difficult traverse along the fracture line between solid granite and decaying schist. His feet sunk through vertical, aerated snow while he torqued his picks across the thin rock seam.

Stone good, snow bad.

We barely noticed that the weather had improved as we bypassed overhanging snow mushrooms and chopped up through cornices. "I don't know how you would ever downclimb that," said Jess as he arrived at one stance.

After hours of the most technical snow climbing either of us had ever done, we reached a broadening ridge at the base of the second tower (Point 9,800'). We were wet to the core, and as light faded our clothes gelled into ice. I searched for any place good enough to chop out a ledge, but every site that looked promising from below proved too small or sloping when I reached it.

Twilight cast a purple hue upon the snow as I waded upward toward a giant boulder. When I arrived, I was startled to see two ancient pitons encased in ice. It took some time to chop them out, but after testing them with my hammer, I clipped them and belayed Jess up. Throughout the last two days, I had searched for any sign of the 1978 Japanese expedition, but had seen nothing. Now I hacked away at the ice beside me as Jess climbed, exposing aluminum aid ladders, pickets, and strings of fixed line. "Have I got a surprise for you!" I yelled to him. As we widened the expansive ledge, we found 35 pitons and a gallon of gas. Old rope showed that the Japanese had most likely accessed the second tower from a gully to the east. We were now sure they had not come the way we had just climbed, and surmised that we had been the first people to stand atop the first tower.

IN THE MORNING we added 15 Japanese pitons to our rack, wondering if we should take more. On the summit of the second tower, we saw the last signs of the Japanese climbers. Beyond, we lost more elevation than we gained. Tedious route-finding across complex gullies and buttresses on the west side of the ridge, beneath looming cornices and blank rock, often meant that we would finish a pitch significantly lower than where we had started, leaving the second climber exposed to dangerous falls. Tension traverses, difficult mixed climbing while simul-climbing, and the feeling of cornices settling under body weight became the standard. After a while, 100 feet between hand-placed pickets hardly merited a thought. Throughout this, Jess' morose humor never waned, and I laughed at his jokes almost as much as he did. "Don't tell my wife about this," he'd say as he pulled out a picket by hand. Our new partnership had quickly developed into what felt like an ancient friendship. Thousands of feet below, I noticed, our meandering tracks through Death Valley had been covered in two spots by large slides.

Gear cache below the second tower on the south ridge from a Japanese attempt in 1978. The pitons were a welcome addition to the 2017 climbers' depleted rack. *Clint Helander*

[Above left] Roskelley nearing the end of a long simul-climbing block toward the top of the third tower. In the background is the Tokositna Icefall, which the pair bypassed during their approach via a couloir on looker's right. Mt. Hunter (left) and the Kahiltna Queen rise in the distance. *Clint Helander* [Top right] Roskelley starts a rock step high on the third tower. *Clint Helander* [Bottom right] Helander studies the clouds from an open bivouac on the fifth morning on the route. *Jess Roskelley*

As night fell, we reached the base of the third tower. Our tent in the col hung halfway over a cornice. That night, the aurora borealis danced across the sky in vibrant flashes of greens and purples.

Moving up the steep side of the 10,100-foot third tower the next day, Jess led two incredible pitches of immaculate granite, jamming bare hands into sun-warmed cracks while his crampons skittered upon flawless stone. After leaving anchors for at least a dozen rappels, our rack felt dangerously light. We took inventory on the summit of the third tower: Of the ten titanium pitons we had brought, plus the 15 we had raided from the Japanese cache, only six pitons remained, plus a few nuts, cams, and ice screws. We made two rappels off the narrow peak to reach the col, and then started up the craggy, unclimbed south face of Idiot Peak. Far below, we could see our tent in base camp, as insignificant as a single fleck of feldspar upon a sprawling granite wall.

Jess led through a steep mixed face and fixed the rope. As I prusiked up, the taut rope slipped over a large boulder and I tumbled violently backward. I clawed at the slope. Had the rope been cut? Did the anchor blow? The rope came tight and I crashed into a rock, too full of adrenaline to feel any pain. After gathering my breath, I tugged on the rope and continued ascending. The bivy site that night was too small to erect the tent, so we slept on the edge of a great precipice with slings tied around our bodies. I struggled to close my eyes as another spectacular display of the aurora borealis illuminated the sky.

Scuds of gray cirrus wafted high across the sky in the early morning. Our marathon was about to become a sprint against an incoming storm. Jess placed psychological protection in deep snow near the summit of Idiot Peak while Mt. Hunter disappeared into broiling clouds. We should have been numb to it by now, but as Jess crept 50 feet across overhanging cornices without finding any protection, the worst-case scenarios of anchor-ripping falls kept playing through my head.

We used the last of our 120 feet of rappel cord while descending Idiot Peak and then began leaving slings. Dark mist curled around us and wind lashed our faces, cutting short a much-needed break. Two more rappels to the east ate up another cam and the last of our nuts. Snow whipped off the summit of Huntington. "My picks are so dull, I'd might as well be swinging with those foam pool-noodle things," Jess yelled as I joined him at a stance. I led a long block up the southeast face, kicking through deep snow on unclimbed terrain in a couloir crowned by a suspicious serac. Every step required double the effort from days before.

At 11,600 feet, I brought Jess up and willed him to take us to the top. Rime encased our faces and clothing. Idiot Peak disappeared in the blanket of rising darkness. Jess climbed into a growing lenticular and I lost sight of him. My fingers and toes were numb, and my thoughts became slow and murky. I reached Jess just below the summit and navigated by snowy braille, feeling for the hardest snow and knowing that the cornices were perilously close. A slight tinge of gray several meters away delineated the sky from snow.

On top we quickly agreed that attempting to descend would be foolish. A mistake felt inevitable in the storming dusk. We set up the tent just below the summit and crashed to sleep without melting any snow to rehydrate. We had little food to cook anyway. The weather the next day was just as bad, and our mental capacity had improved little, if at all. We tried to descend, but as I searched for the route, all I saw was a featureless gray murk. Descending blindly with our pathetic rack would be foolish. After swinging around for an hour, I ascended the ropes and we re-pitched our tent on the summit ridge for a second night.

The weather cleared just enough on our eighth morning on the mountain so I could spot the trajectory toward the west face couloir—our planned descent route. We still felt utterly wasted. As I led the 15 rappels, light snow fell and sloughs, some impressively powerful, hit us as we descended. I left screws when V-threads became too much work in the storm. Jess had a near miss when a carabiner came unclipped from the anchor as he leaned back to weight the rope. We were barely keeping it together.

We staggered into base camp past two teams who had given us up for dead. Nearly two feet of snow fell soon afterward, and we shuddered to imagine that storm arriving while we were still on the ridge. On our fourth night stuck in base camp, a 5.2 magnitude earthquake shook the glacier and caused multiple seracs to calve in the distance. Confined in the tent, I felt helpless and honestly wondered if, after all we had experienced, we might die in base camp. When Paul Roderick of Talkeetna Air Taxi flew us out two days later, the south ridge of Huntington was almost unrecognizable. Gigantic cornices had formed where we had crossed only days before. Hundreds of avalanches had scoured every aspect. Any trace of our passage had been erased.

SUMMARY: First ascent of the complete south ridge of Mt. Huntington (The Gauntlet Ridge, 2,500m, VI M6 A0 95°) by Clint Helander and Jess Roskelley, April 18–25, 2017. The two bivouacked once during the approach, four times on the south ridge, and twice on the summit before descending the West Face Couloir.

ABOUT THE AUTHOR: *Clint Helander moved to Anchorage from Seattle in 2003. He has ventured into the Alaska Range every year since 2007 and doesn't plan on missing a season for the next few decades. Other articles about this climb are in Alpinist 59 and Rock and Ice 244.*

THE TRIFECTA

ALL FREE, NO FALLS, IN A DAY
ON THE THREE HOWSER TOWERS

WILL STANHOPE

The idea of linking the three Howser Towers in a single day dawned on me back in 2010. It was my second season in a row climbing above the East Creek Basin; the year before, Jason Kruk, Matt Segal, and I had done the first free ascent of the west face of Central Howser. Now, as Andrew Rennie and I raced up the 1,000-meter All Along the Watchtower on the North Tower, I thought about some of my climbing heroes. Peter Croft, Dave Schultz, Sean Leary, Tommy Caldwell, Dean Potter, and Leo Houlding had enchained multiple walls free in a day in Yosemite. Why not bring the same concept to the alpine arena of the Bugs?

In January of 2016, I sent Leo an email out of the blue with an image of the towers—three rocket-ship needles, side by side—and spilled my guts about the idea. Given his busy schedule and young family, I didn't really think he'd be able to swing the trip. To my surprise and elation, he responded that he was in. The next summer we teamed up for a couple of weeks in the Bugs and climbed the Beckey-Chouinard, the classic route up South Howser's west side, along with All Along the Watchtower and a first free ascent on the Minaret. Individually, they went down

Will Stanhope leads the 5.12+ slab crux of the Central Howser Tower. *Adrian Samara*

easily enough. But the trifecta seemed intimidating and unlikely.

This past August, Leo and I arrived in the Bugaboos with Wilson Cutbirth, Waldo Ether-
ington, and Adrian Samarra, who were hoping to get some virtual-reality footage of the
Beckey-Chouinard and to make a short film about our planned linkup. I was psyched to have
them there, but also felt nervous. I had convinced these guys to come all the way to the Bugaboos to make a film about a linkup I wasn't even sure I could achieve.

We fixed ropes top to bottom on the Central Tower to facilitate training laps on Chocolate
Fudge Brownie, the hardest of the three climbs, and to enable a fast descent. Not the best style,
I'll be the first to admit, but at the time it felt like a necessary step. After two weeks we were still
unsure whether it would be safe to climb the North Howser after climbing Central, because of
all the simul-climbing that would be required. And the Beckey on the south tower after that?
We vowed to play it as safe as possible and "stay on the right side of the wild line," as Leo put it.

On the evening of August 28, we stood at the Howser bivy boulder and each took a nip of

The southwest faces of the Howser Spire massif. (1) Central Tower, Chocolate Fudge Brownie. Leo Houlding and Will Stanhope rappelled fixed lines to approach their next route. (2) Howser Spire (a.k.a. North Tower), Spicy Red Beans and Rice and All Along the Watchtower linkup. After descending the far side and hiking back to base camp (BC), the climbers set out for their third route of the day. (3) South Tower, Beckey-Chouinard Route. *Marc Piché*

Captain Morgan's Spiced Rum, toasting a gorgeous sunset over the wild, uninhabited valley to the west. Leo and I woke at 3:30 a.m., marched up to the base of the Central Howser, and started climbing at dawn. After about five hours of grueling cracks, corners, and the delicate 5.12+ slab crux of Chocolate Fudge Brownie, we had reached the summit.

Buoyed by our fast time, we zipped down our fixed lines to the base and guzzled some Red Bull. We were nervous about rappelling into the basin below North Howser and the mad dash we'd have to make across a bowling-alley snowfield on our way to the climb, especially at high noon, the most dangerous part of the day. But we were both feeling more or less OK, so we decided to go for it.

The next few hours, climbing up the first half of the North Howser, were the most demoralizing part of the day for me. Low-angle, tedious climbing, carrying a huge rack, water, and crampons, all in the blazing afternoon sun—I was worried that this might have been a really bad (read: stupidly dangerous) idea. Luckily, Leo seemed to have hit his stride and playfully teased me out of my negative thoughts. This pattern repeated itself throughout the day: both of us riding the undulating waves of psyche, and one picking up the slack when the other was feeling down.

The sun started to set just as we started up the centerpiece 200-meter open-book corner of All Along the Watchtower, and I instantly felt better. We both fired the powerful and footsy 5.12c crux pitch. (We each led or followed every pitch free on all three towers.) With the redpoint crux of the day behind us, Leo took the lead and guided us through the technical maze of ridge climbing to the summit of North Howser Tower.

After a technical descent and berg-schrund hop, we tried to motivate for the final push as we hiked across the Upper Vowell Glacier, through Pigeon-Howser Col, and down a steep, loose gully into the East Creek Basin. Even though the final tower would be nowhere near as hard as the first two, the Beckey-Chouinard is still a 15-pitch, 600-meter route. Back at camp, the boys had prepared some food for us and were openly jazzed about our progress. Fueled by their psyche, and after some more caffeinated and electrolyte beverages, Captain Leo announced, "We leave in 15 minutes, yeah?"

Around 3 in the morning, we started up the Beckey in a simul-climbing blur of endless granite hand cracks, Leo in the lead. Two-thirds of the way up the route, Leo groggily handed over the sharp end,

Stanhope (left) and Houlding celebrating at dawn on the summit of South Howser Tower. *Leo Houlding*

and I gunned it to just below the summit ridge as the sky turned from pitch black to a muted gray. On top, with minutes to spare before the 24-hour mark, we gazed over at the central and north towers. It was hard to believe we'd just stood on each of them. The sky had turned smoky orange from the wildfires blazing across British Columbia. My fatigue was strangely gone—I felt infused with boundless energy by the rising sun. We shuffled down the standard rappels and arrived back at camp to hugs from the boys.

For a few weeks after our trip to the Bugaboos, one of my big toes remained numb and I felt distant and dazed toward the world around me. Eventually, pure gratitude for the experience seeped in. The word "inspiration" is perhaps overused these days, but I'd like to extend a warm tip of the hat to our fallen friends Sean "Stanley" Leary and Dean Potter, who in no small way helped spawn this idea. And thanks of course to Leo, who had believed in the vision and was rock-solid on the climb. On paper, it had all added up, but I don't think I've ever felt such trepidation before. In the end it was a perfect project: within reach, but barely.

SUMMARY: All-free linkup of the west faces of the Howser Towers in the Bugaboos, British Columbia, Canada, by Leo Houlding (U.K.) and Will Stanhope (Canada), August 29–30, 2017. The two climbed Chocolate Fudge Brownie (5.12+, 11 guidebook pitches) on Central Howser; Spicy Red Beans and Rice and All Along the Watchtower (5.12c, 34 pitches) on Howser Spire; and the Beckey-Chouinard Route (5.10, 15 pitches) on South Howser. They used fixed ropes for the descent from Central Howser and the rappel approach to Howser Spire, and made the standard descent from Howser Spire; all fixed ropes were later removed. From the base of Central Howser to the summit of South Howser, their total time was 23 hours 36 minutes.

ABOUT THE AUTHOR: *Will Stanhope wrote about his first free ascent of the Tom Egan Memorial Route on Snowpatch Spire in the Bugaboos in AAJ 2016. He lives in Squamish, British Columbia. An interview with Stanhope about this climb was featured in episode one of the Cutting Edge Podcast.*

Alik Berg in full sun on the traverse toward the headwall on Chacraraju's east face. Completing this section before the mountain dangerously heated up was key to success. *Quentin Lindfield Roberts*

NOBODY KNOWS ANYTHING

TWO NEW ROUTES IN THE CORDILLERA BLANCA OF PERU

ALIK BERG

The idea of going to Peru wasn't sparked by some coveted unclimbed line. It was simply out of convenience and practicality. As the winter season in the Canadian Rockies wound down, I was getting antsy to go on a trip. Peru seemed ideal: big mountains in a country I had never visited, a chance to see how my body did at altitude, with simple logistics and low costs to boot. My schedule would allow me a month to "train" (i.e., go climbing), and I could go right in the middle of Peru's dry season. Finding a willing partner with the same open schedule proved more challenging, but eventually I convinced my friend Quentin Lindfield Roberts to take three weeks off. I booked a ticket for six weeks, with no clear plan for the second half of my trip.

Upon arriving in Huaraz, Quentin and I quickly found our favorite breakfast hang at Café Andino. Over an endless stream of espresso, we bounced ideas off each other for what to do with his brief time in the country. Eventually we agreed to acclimatize in the Santa Cruz Valley and then consider trying something new.

We departed a day later with packs light on climbing gear and heavy with good food, wondering why we'd decided not to cough up the $20 to get our loads hauled

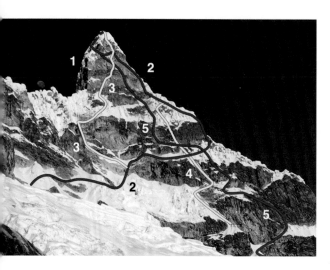

East face of Chacraraju Este (6,001m). (1) Upper southeast ridge (Kondo-Yoshino, 1976). (2) French Route (1962, first ascent of peak). (3) The Devil's Reach Around (Berg–Lindfield Roberts, 2017), believed to be first free ascent of the face. (4) Slovenian Direct Start (Kozjek-Krezel, 1993, to ridge). (5) The Shriek of the Black Stone (Juhasz-Markovic, 1999). Baró-Corominas direct finish not shown. *Quentin Lindfield Roberts*

in on burros. After a rest day in Alpamayo base camp and a riveting game of bocce ball among the boulders at the moraine camp, at 5,000 meters, we slogged up to the Alpamayo-Quitaraju col, where we decided we still had enough daylight and energy to head up Alpamayo that afternoon. Ditching the camping gear, we relished in the light packs as we slowly simuled the pleasant 300-meter ice face. Next morning we climbed the north face of Quitaraju, grateful for our friends César and Vincent's hard work in digging the impressive snow bollards we used on the descent. Returning to the valley, we were dismayed to find that some gear and food we'd stashed had been stolen. On the bright side, our packs were somewhat lighter for the hike out.

Back in Huaraz, we spend a luxurious morning at Café Andino scarfing breakfast burritos, drinking coffee, and hashing out a plan for the rest of Quentin's trip. After banging around several options, we decided to attempt an unclimbed line on the east face of Chacraraju Este (6,001m). The south face of spectacular, twin-summited Chacraraju rises above Laguna 69, one of the hottest tourist attractions in the area, and has been climbed by numerous routes, but the other aspects are rarely climbed. Chacraraju's eastern peak was first climbed in 1962 by a French party that traversed left to right across the lower east face, moved up the south ridge, then diagonaled back left across the upper east face to summit via the southeast ridge. A direct line up the east face had been attempted several times over the years, culminating in Slovenians Jure Juhasz and Andrej Markovic finally pushing a route through the headwall over six days in 1999. In photos of the face, we had noticed an appealing corner system breaching the left side of the roughly 250-meter headwall, and a potentially moderate passage snaking up the left edge of the lower wall. It was a bit of a gamble, as we hadn't yet seen the face in person—picking a route from a 20-year-old photo has its risks in a range with such rapid glacial recession.

We left town with six days remaining before Quentin's scheduled return to Canada. We had decided to approach from the Llanganuco Valley, which would intersect our planned descent route on the south face, allowing us to stash some gear for our return. On the second day we gained a 5,000-meter col below the southeast ridge of Chacraraju and began a surprisingly complex traverse to the base of the east face, with some tricky route-finding and technical scrambling.

We took a rest day to study the face and acclimatize, which unfortunately was quite exhausting due to the total lack of shade. Both of us were not feeling 100 percent, and we would have to move swiftly through the lower half of the face to avoid falling rock and ice in the morning sun. Quentin, being the eternal optimist, convinced me that it was worth a shot.

If we went home empty-handed, we would feel a lot better for having given it an honest effort.

We went to bed early and set the alarm for the ungodly hour of 9:30 p.m. We both barely slept, and when we headed out an hour later, I was battling waves of nausea. Quentin led for the first six hours, and I sluggishly followed, the gentle tug of the rope the only thing spurring me onward. He took us through the first rock band, a pitch of splitter granite crack climbing, and, forced to focus on the tricky and fun mixed climbing, I started to feel a bit better.

At the belay below the next rock band, I offered to take over the lead as we continued to simul-climb. Diverging from the original French route, which we'd basically followed to this point, I deked way left until I could gain the deteriorating remnants of an ice fluting, which brought me to a point level with and about 80 meters left of the easy snow slopes we needed to reach. From below, this crucial section had looked blocky and featured but not dead easy. Gingerly balancing over stacked blocks and loose flakes, I felt right at home—just like the Rockies! Luckily, most of the rubble was frozen together, and we finished the traverse just as the mountain began to heat up.

Reaching the base of the headwall in midmorning heat, we hacked out a ledge and siestaed for a few hours. Once things cooled off in the afternoon, I led the first pitch of the headwall, a full rope of beautiful mixed climbing—not too hard but intricate and engaging, and with perfect gear in bomber granite. I left the rope fixed and headed down for an early bivy.

Lying in the tent that evening the air was perfectly still, and as the sun set I left the door wide open and enjoyed the beautiful moment. Perched on our tiny oasis, surrounded by stark granite walls and otherworldly snow mushrooms, I watched as tiny ice crystals tumbled down the headwall and the stars came out one by one. In that moment of stillness and tranquility, the raw power and beauty of the mountains held me transfixed. The climbing had been good, but really this was what it was all about.

Early the next morning, Quentin self-belayed the pitch I'd enjoyed the day before while I jugged the fixed line with the heavy bag. The next pitch held the last big question mark: The crack system I'd followed the day before dead-ended in large overhangs above, and we needed to connect to a small hanging snowfield to the right, near the exit gully. Quentin traversed around the corner and found a steep crack choked with loose blocks. He tried another option farther right that also dead-ended but put him within spitting distance of the first crack. With no pro but positive edges, he holstered his tools and carefully tiptoed his way back to splitter hands, solid pro, and before long a good belay at the end of the hard climbing.

A couple more pitches of loose but easy simul-climbing brought us into the exit gully we had spied from below. Unfortunately, in the late-morning heat, the gully was running with water, and the first step of ice fell down when Quentin gave it the gentlest of taps. I started up easy-looking rock to the right and soon found myself balancing past more precarious stacked blocks. A few tense minutes later, I gained another ledge and decided I'd had enough.

Lindfield Roberts high on Chacraraju's east face on day two. *Alik Berg*

The next pitch was obvious: another short but steep step of ice, with water pouring behind the pillar. With the summit so close, we briefly tried to convince ourselves the pillar was solid enough to climb. Luckily, common sense prevailed as we realized the sun would be off the face in an hour or so. Time for another siesta!

Once the face was in shadow, the pillar refroze in a matter of minutes—an impressive thing to watch. I won a hard-fought rock-paper-scissors round and took off up a beautiful pitch of water ice that brought us to a wild ice cave below the final snow mushroom. In the final rays of another perfect day, I plowed a path up the steep sugar guarding the summit. After two full days of climbing, we found ourselves on the flattest ground since leaving the glacier. We dug into the facets and called it a night.

With Quentin's bus out of Huaraz leaving in a little over 24 hours, we woke a couple of hours before dawn. In temps below -20°C, we packed up and left the summit without ever actually seeing anything outside the spheres of our headlamps—I assume the view was very nice. The south face afforded us a straightforward descent via 10,000 V-threads, and before we knew it we were jockeying for position on the crowded Laguna 69 trail. We made it to Huaraz that evening, and the next morning I said good-bye to Quentin and embarked on the second half of my trip.

Aritza Monasterio, a longtime local climber, originally from the Basque Country of Spain, owns the Albergue Andinista, where we'd been staying in Huaraz. He had some free time at the end of July, and we agreed to do some climbing after he finished guiding a group up Pisco. Elated to have found a solid partner, I needed something to do until Aritza was free. I decided on the beautiful Parón Valley and spent four days alone there.

My first objective was the once-classic Renshaw-Wilkinson route of Pirámide de Garcilaso. Spooked by serac danger on the standard route, I attempted a safer line to the left, but poor climbing conditions sent me down from about halfway up. I later learned that, only a couple of days after my attempt, three climbers were tragically killed by serac fall on this face, and that there had been several similar incidents in past years. It seems that some of the old classics in the Blanca are no longer what they once were. I salvaged my Parón outing by hopping across the valley and climbing the south arête of Artesonraju, a pleasant slog up another very picturesque peak.

Back in town, Aritza called me into the guestroom that holds his climbing wall. He pointed to an old photo of an intimidating face pinned to the wall.

"What do you think of this? Do you want to climb this?" he asked.

"What is it?"

"North face of Hualcán. It's hidden from the road and not visible from any of the popular treks, so nobody knows about it. The face is 1,000 meters and has never been climbed. Probably never attempted."

That was enough to get my attention. Turns out Aritza had first laid eyes on this face 12 years earlier while attempting the south face of Nevado Ulta (which he later climbed in 2008), and he had returned a couple times to attempt 6,125-meter Hualcán but never had good enough conditions. It was settled.

Our planned descent would bring us down the opposite side of the mountain, so we left town prepared to carry everything over the top. With double boots on our feet and day packs overloaded with food for six days, we boarded the 6 a.m. bus toward Chacas, on the other side of the range, and settled into a bumpy three-hour ride over a nearly 5,000-meter pass and through the Punta Olimpica tunnel. Not long after descending onto the eastern slope of the Cordillera Blanca, we were dropped off at the head of the Cancaracá Grande Valley.

Starting up the pastoral valley, I confidently strode ahead through open meadows and soon found myself mired in a small bog. I looked back and found I was alone. A quick scan of the valley found Artiza waving at me from the dry cattle track along the edge of the meadow. Variations of this continued for the next two days, as Aritza's mastery of mountain navigation became clear and my lack thereof even clearer. The glacier we traversed on the second day had caused Aritza some grief on a previous attempt, and he was pleased that we were able to find a relatively painless though time-consuming route to the base of the north face. By midafternoon we had established a safe campsite on the glacier near the wall's east end.

Unfortunately, the face was enshrouded in clouds and we still hadn't had an opportunity to study it in detail. The bottom was clearly much drier than it had been in the 2006 photo that Aritza had shown me. Feeling the pressure of my impending departure, I worried that we wouldn't even get a chance to try the face. Aritza was *tranquilo* about it all and pointed out that we still had plenty of time—we just needed to be patient and let the mountains dictate the schedule.

The next day the clouds broke enough to give us a few brief views of the entire face. The mile-wide, kilometer-high wall reminded me of the glacier-capped north face of Mt. Kitchener, back home in the Rockies—only this face lacked the convenient couloir breaching the upper headwall. Additionally, Hualcán's central ice slopes were guarded by smooth rock slabs along the base of the face. Below the biggest (and most rockfall-prone) gullies, melt-

The north face of Hualcán (6,125m) and the line of the first ascent. Berg and Monasterio bivouacked once on the face and once on top. The 1,000-meter face is hidden from roads or popular trails and may never have been attempted before 2017. Monasterio had pinned a photo of the face to his home climbing wall in Huaraz as inspiration. *Aritza Monasterio (top) and Alik Berg*

Aritza Monasterio follows the key pitch on the second morning on the north face of Hualcán. *Alik Berg*

water would freeze overnight, offering fleeting delicate passages through these slabs, but neither of us much liked the idea of entering these bowling alleys. Aritza eventually spotted a slender, partially hidden snow ramp that breached the lower slabs on the right side. It appeared to provide rapid access to the central ice slopes—just what we needed! The upper headwall was another story, but it looked featured enough to be worth a shot.

We started early under clear skies. The last bit of glacier travel below the face proved more complex than expected, and we lost precious predawn hours, but by 5:30 we were simul-climbing up the ramp. At dawn, a tricky bit of mixed climbing gained a thin ribbon of ice streaming down from the central face. Pitch after pitch of calf-burning 60° ice in unrelenting heat followed, but the face remained quiet. Near the top of the ice, Aritza led an impressive near-vertical pitch, and soon we were at the base of the headwall. Chopping out a bivy ledge took several hours, and we finally collapsed into the tent after an exhausting day of climbing in the sun.

Our tiny ledge provided just the right amount of respite from the exposure and stress of being on a big face, and soon we were brewing hot soup, recharging, and talking politics and life. It was great to learn more about Aritza's path and philosophy in life, from an upbringing in

Basque Country to becoming a young guide in Huaraz and starting a family and business in Peru. Before leaving Huaraz we'd barely known each other, but over the last few days we'd become good friends, balancing our time between pushing hard on the mountain and relaxing at the bivies.

At daybreak we returned to the unfortunate reality of the looming headwall. Intimidating as it was, it did have a very obvious break, so there was no question about where to start. Two rope lengths of challenging but not outrageously difficult rock and mixed climbing got us to a distinct crux: a short, gently overhanging wall guarding an exit ramp that was so close we could have lobbed a snowball onto it. A squeeze chimney onto a small curtain of ice seemed like the way to go. I wormed my way as high as possible, plugged some gear, and stretched for good sticks in the curtain. As soon as I committed to the curtain, I realized the feet were terrible and I was weak as a kitten at this altitude. Luckily, it was only a couple of moves, and soon I was back on my frontpoints, gasping for air. One more pitch of mixed climbing brought us to easy ice slopes and the summit plateau, just as the sun was setting. We dropped the packs and after 30 minutes of post-holing reached the rarely trodden main summit of Hualcán.

After a cold night on the plateau, we began the long descent down the south glacier, with Huaraz visible in the distance. Over the next 10 hours we dropped over 3,000 meters and experienced a 40°C temperature change. At dusk, our taxi dropped us off at Aritza's house and we could finally remove our boots after a memorable traverse of the width of the Cordillera Blanca.

"We should call the route Nadie Sabe Nada," Aritza said. *Nobody knows anything*—a nod to the fact that the north face of Hualcán had been veiled in obscurity, despite over 100 years of climbing in the Cordillera Blanca, and that many people consider these mountains to be "climbed out." For such a well-trodden range, the Cordillera Blanca still has plenty of secrets.

SUMMARY: New route and first free ascent (The Devil's Reach Around, 900m, 5.10 M6 90°) on the east face of Chacraraju Este in Peru's Cordillera Blanca, by Alik Berg and Quentin Lindfield Roberts, July 14–16, 2017. First ascent of the north face of Hualcán in the Cordillera Blanca: Nadie Sabe Nada (1,000m, 5.9 M6 85°), by Alik Berg and Aritza Monasterio, July 28–30, 2017.

ABOUT THE AUTHOR: *Alik Berg, 30, is a self-described "obsessive climber" living in Canmore, Alberta. In his free time, he works as a high-angle industrial access technician to fund future climbing trips.*

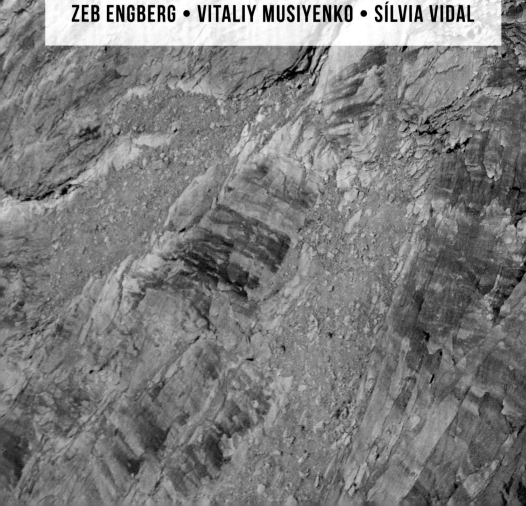

XANADU

At the heart of the Arrigetch Peaks in Alaska is a hulking granite peak that may have been climbed only once before, in 1974, via the moderate southwest ridge. Despite whispers in climbing circles for years, Xanadu's golden, near-vertical west face had never been climbed. Then, in the summer of 2017, three new routes went up this impressive wall, climbed in three dramatically different styles. Even on a solitary peak, there's still room for all kinds of adventure in the far north.

ZEB ENGBERG • VITALIY MUSIYENKO • SÍLVIA VIDAL

GOLDEN PETALS
THE FIRST ASCENT OF XANADU'S WEST FACE

BY ZEB ENGBERG

I sag deep into my harness and absently stare upward into a mesmerizing plane of granite. From my precarious hanging position, I am doing my best to keep the moist arctic wind from blasting my skin. Despite wearing every layer that I packed for this month-long trip into Alaska's Arrigetch Peaks, the cold air still chills me to the core. With only two days left in the trip, our team is feeling pressure to free the wall we've just climbed. Billy is below me, screaming as I reel in slack. There is no blood in his icy fingers as he tries to manhandle the granite knobs. He screams as he chalks up before reaching for the crux holds; he even screams as he gasps for air. As he arrives at the belay, we eke out smiles and wordlessly share the love for the brutal situation we have thrown ourselves into.

[Previous pages] **Billy Braasch connects the golden plates of the Corn Flakes Pitch (5.11) on Golden Petals (V 5.13+ or 5.12 AO), the first route up Xanadu's west face.** [This page] **Gabe Boning contemplates the seeping, flared feature on pitch three that the team nicknamed the Buttcrack.** *Zeb Engberg*

DAVID BAIN, Gabe Boning, Billy Braasch, and I began dreaming of this trip soon after our close friend Chris Vale died in a rappelling accident on El Cap's East Ledges in September 2016. The five of us had connected through our involvement in the Dartmouth Mountaineering Club, and now we wanted to do something to commemorate Chris' enthusiasm and sense of adventure. It seemed appropriate to attempt a first ascent in his honor, and we were drawn to the wildness and remoteness of the Arrigetch Peaks.

Xanadu is the centerpiece of the Arrigetch, a small subrange of the Brooks Range above the Arctic Circle. At 7,160', the summit is not the highest in the region, but the peak's ever-present mass, steep, aesthetic geometry, and its position at the headwaters of Arrigetch Creek give it a feeling of utmost prominence within this cluster of granite towers. Its eastern aspect is shadowed, stark, and glaciated. But under a cloudless summer sky, the western wall is illuminated in glowing, golden light from noon until midnight.

Knowledge of Xanadu's west face has been passed by word of mouth through various climbing circles. The late Mugs Stump dreamed of climbing it, and the wall lured Tommy Caldwell, Hayden Kennedy, and Corey Rich into making a trip in 2011 (*AAJ 2012*); they ended up climbing a neighboring cliff. We learned of Xanadu's west face from Jon Krakauer, who, together with Bill Bullard, made the only known ascent of Xanadu, via its southwest ridge (*AAJ 1975*). I was apprehensive to reach out to such a well-known figure, but Jon responded enthusiastically almost immediately. Between email exchanges and phone calls, he provided valuable information, insight, and encouragement. He vividly described his vision of a line up the west face—beautiful and bold face climbing through vertical and occasionally overhanging granite flakes. His hypothetical route closely matched what we eventually climbed.

After three days of hiking heavy loads, David, Gabe, Billy, and I caught our first glimpse of the gold-plated west face of Xanadu. Until that moment, all of the granite we'd seen along Arrigetch Creek seemed cold and dreary. Though we were weary and had contemplated stopping for the night, the sight of Xanadu rejuvenated us like a jolt of caffeine. Without words, we unanimously decided to push on to our base camp for the next few weeks, located in a lush alpine meadow below this massive piece of rock.

Gazing through binoculars, we looked for vertical weaknesses. The 1,500-foot wall was

ONE MORE STEP
A 17-DAY SOLO NEW ROUTE

BY SÍLVIA VIDAL

LAST SUMMER I spent 53 days in the Arrigetch—36 days of hauling loads and 17 days on the west face of Xanadu, where, from July 5 to 21, I completed a new route called Un Pas Més (530m, 6a A4/A4+). During this time, although I was not always completely alone in the area, I had no external assistance, no GPS, and no radio, phone, or communication device to obtain weather forecasts.

The amazing pilots at Brooks Range Aviation agreed to pick me up on a specific day two months after dropping me off—an exercise in trust. From the airstrip, I spent 16 days getting my 150 kilograms of food and big-wall gear in position, repeating the approach 11 times. After the climbing I spent 20 days carrying everything down, doing the descent nine times. I estimate that I hiked around 540 kilometers total, not counting the multiple times I became lost due to not having a GPS.

In June, the little path that climbs up the valley is barely visible, and it's easy to get lost. In August, the trail is easy to follow and accessible, due to the number of people headed in and out of the valley throughout the summer. To be alone in such a place is not easy. I did encounter bears and everything ended well, but I was really scared until I was able to transform my fear and enjoy the whole trip.

Instead of making base camp in the main valley beneath Xanadu's west face (which would have required additional load carrying), I climbed up to a pass on the north side of Xanadu to access a ledge that I'd seen in photos. This ledge system led to the base of the vertical face. Before the trip, I could see the ledge in photos, but I did not know if the access to the pass was feasible nor if the ledge would reach all the way across the base of the wall. However, this approach allowed me to avoid the lower slabs below the main face—alone and with haul bags, it would have been a nightmare.

Most of my route's 11 pitches featured technical aid climbing (up to A4/A4+), which is the style that allows me to open a route alone and have the kind of experience and climbing style I am looking for. The hardest pitches had short but precarious crux sections—steep faces that featured multiple hook moves in a row. I placed three lead bolts (no hangers) and 12 anchor bolts on the route, and rappelled my line of ascent (not all the belays have bolts).

Self-portrait during the solo new route on Xanadu's west face. Vidal spent 53 days almost entirely alone in the Alaskan wilderness. Silvia Vidal

Vidal repeated the approach to Xanadu 11 times to get her 150 kg of gear into position for the climb. After the climb, it took her 20 days to get everything back out. *Silvia Vidal*

The rock was generally good granite, but was sometimes sandy, and therefore small copperheads didn't hold. There were some loose blocks, and more face climbing than crack systems. There are expanding and inverted flakes that made the solo ascent more complicated, as the ropes below me often got stuck and I had to rap down to remove them, sometimes multiple times in a single pitch.

While in the valley, I met four American climbers who put up a new route to the right of mine; they were the first to summit the west face of Xanadu. In August, when I was carrying my gear down, three other American climbers came to put up another route to the left of mine. Both camped down in the valleys, and I stayed on the wall. Different base camps, logistics, styles, and dates allowed all of us to have our space and solitude.

After this kind of experience, being alone in a wild place for weeks, with no communcation and many uncertainties— only your doubts, fears, joy and happiness—the route is never the most difficult part. The challenge lies in the rest.

ABOUT THE AUTHOR: *Catalan climber Sílvia Vidal has done solo big-wall first ascents around the world.*

mostly devoid of cracks—instead, it was a mosaic of flakes. Although such features tend to encourage free climbing, we had read enough trip reports of loose, rope-chopping flakes in the Arrigetch to feel concerned. After much deliberation, we set our sights on a flake system on the right side of the face, below a looming overhang near the top of the ridge first climbed by Krakauer and Bullard.

As we contemplated our strategy, we contrasted our plan with that of Sílvia Vidal, who we encountered on our hike in. We were shocked to see another person, and even more surprised to learn that her goal was the same as ours. She was taking a rest day because her eyes were swollen shut from 11 days of non-stop exertion, ferrying loads to the base of Xanadu. Sílvia had budgeted nearly two months for her incredible solo mission, hauling an immense kit, including a portaledge, and committing to the face without returning to a cushy base camp like ours. Every couple of days we would shout "Hi Sílvia!" across the sea of granite. She would chime back with a friendly "Hello!" Most days, though, we tried to honor her solitary journey by not bothering her with our shenanigans. Sílvia topped out her masterpiece as we were flying out of the Arrigetch.

Between our base camp at 4,200 feet and the foot of the wall at 5,800 feet sat a loose and shifting talus field and a Half Dome–style death slab. Studying the approach through binoculars, we noticed a mysterious peach-colored object strung out along the slabs.

"Is it a piece of parachute? Maybe some trash from an air drop?"

"No way! It's a giant bag of Cheetos!"

"It's too big to be Cheetos! Could it be a tent that blew in there?"

"No, I think it's just a *really* big bag of Cheetos."

"God, I hope so."

We soon discovered a 65-meter static rope, abandoned by some party. Though it clearly had been absorbing UV light, vast amounts of water runoff, and rockfall for several years, we resourcefully put this bonus rope to use on our route. (Later, we carried out the rope and gave it to our bush pilots, who used it to tie their planes to shore.) As we started to work on our line, we split into teams of two and alternated days on the wall. Although our ultimate goal was to open a free climb, we knew that our initial climbing strategy might involve yo-yoing, French-freeing, and occasional direct aid to make progress. We had carried in enough rope to fix three-quarters of the wall, and we put it to use.

Atop the death slab we approached the intimidating vertical wall, anxiously pressing our palms against it, hoping for a sign. We soon discovered a thin, overhanging seam that would allow upward progress. Using blades and beak-style pitons, I nailed my way up what we christened Sílvia's Seam, an homage to our new friend. Above, the angle of the wall eased, but the protection also evaporated. A scary moment of 5.10 R face climbing allowed me to gain the main flake system, and our first pitch was established. This pitch was indicative of what was to come—the climbing was slow and intricate, and on many days we only succeeded in advancing our route several hundred feet.

The next day, David set off from my high point, leading several pitches of thin cracks and enticing laybacks. The rock was solid enough to pull on, but the protection was often questionable. We frequently placed small beaks, and our anchors morphed into nests of slings and cams. Gabe pushed the rope higher, aiding through a seeping and overhanging flared crack. From there, Billy took the lead, moving through a beautiful collage of layered and disconnected orange flakes. At the end of our third day of climbing we reached July 4th Ledge. The terrain we had covered was steep and exhilarating, and though we did not hesitate to aid through difficult sections, it seemed as though nearly all of it could go free.

Above Boomerang Ledge, a broken system that marked the halfway point up the wall, the vertical system we had been climbing dwindled into a labyrinth of isolated features. Billy and I meandered higher, negotiating the astonishing Portal Flake and the evocative Frosted Flakes— the beautiful expanses of metamorphic granite foretold by Krakauer, varnished and mostly solid, but with flakes that often felt hollow under our fist-tapping probes. Jugging after one lead, Billy prepared to make a 40-foot horizontal lower-out from a single brass nut. "It looks bomber," he said—right before freefalling in a tangle of gear, rope, and aiders.

"I'm OK!" he optimistically screamed as he swung below me at high speed.

Reaching 7-Hour Ledge, an awkward hanging stance with which Gabe and David would

become intimately familiar later in the trip, we had nearly fixed all of our 1,000 feet of rope (including the bootied orange rope). The angle of the wall steepened again, and the flakes above appeared fractal and menacing. We had visions of falling onto their jagged edges and slicing our rope.

David took over on the sharp end, slowly aiding up the run-out Pepper Flake pitch, a puzzling lead that required creative protection, including many beaks

The west face of Xanadu. (1) Arctic Knight (5.11+). (2) Un Pas Més (6a A4/A4+). (3) Golden Petals (5.13+ or 5.12/A0). (4) Southwest ridge (5.7, Bullard-Krakauer, 1974). *Zeb Engberg*

[Above left] The Arrigetch Peaks are known for remote granite towers, but also for foul weather—David Bain (left) and Zeb Engberg wait it out. *Gabe Boning* [Below left] View down Arrigetch Creek from the Escape Col approach to Xanadu's west face. *Zeb Engberg* [Above right] Zeb Engberg nailing up Silvia's Seam, named in honor of Catalan soloist Silvia Vidal, who put up a neighboring route on Xanadu's west face around the same time. This pitch eventually went free at 5.13+. *Billy Braasch*

and micro-nuts. "I want to come down, but I'll try to get in just one more piece of gear," David shouted for the sixth time. After several hours of this he finally lowered from his high point, and he and Gabe rappelled back to camp.

Up until then we'd been lucky to have about 15 days of good weather, with six days on the wall, but now the weather deteriorated into rain and fog. We were starting to run low on food, and for two days we ate half rations and moped in our soggy tents.

On the second day of this, around 8 p.m., Billy pointed out that no rain had fallen that afternoon. "Hey," he asked me with a grin, "want to head up there and finish that Pepper Flake? We can just climb through the night."

He was bluffing, but I was game to try.

"Seriously?" he asked. "Alright, let's do it!"

We jugged the fixed ropes through blowing fog, arriving at 7-Hour Ledge around midnight. After finishing David's last lead, I hammered in a bolt for a belay. Billy took over, leading a bold pitch of 5.12 face climbing. The S Pitch, named for the wandering, run-out slab, involved thin smears and committing high steps above dubious protection. As morning dawned, another pitch of run-out face climbing (easier at 5.10+) brought us to a seeping ramp. This, we were pleased to see, led over to a notch on the upper southwest ridge, avoiding the final overhanging mushroom. In the notch, we found an ancient nut and blue webbing, likely from the 1974 ascent. We felt comfort in seeing this minuscule sign of civilization.

Billy and I continued up the easy, lichen-covered summit ridge to the apex of Xanadu. We embraced and stood in awe of the huge vertical relief in all directions. Then we heard David and Gabe bellowing below. They had jugged up behind us and spent seven hours on the ledge at the end of our fixed ropes—hence the name—waiting for us to rappel so they could begin their own summit pilgrimage. We slowly descended and passed the torch to our friends, who topped out that afternoon in pea-soup fog. It was July 12, and we felt extremely privileged to make the probable second ascent of Xanadu and the first ascent of its west face. But we still had about a week remaining before we were to be picked up at Circle Lake, and we knew that we could climb our route in better style.

First, we set about cleaning up our anchors, some of which consisted of half a dozen equalized cams strung out over 10-foot swaths of rock. Although we had made a point of avoiding placing bolts mid-pitch, we decided to leave robust belay and rappel anchors. To some, this decision may go against wilderness principles, and we did agonize over this decision to add bolts. But, knowing that we'd need to leave fixed gear of some form in order to rappel, we decided to make them high-quality anchors that would last for decades. We placed a total of 17 bolts at the rappel stations on our route.

We then focused our energies on free climbing, rehearsing the moves that were accessible from our fixed ropes. The climbing was classic, often involving delicate laybacking with thin smears for the feet and handholds serendipitously appearing when the macro-features faded. Of the 14 pitches of technical climbing, many fell within the 5.9 to 5.11 range.

As the time to hike out neared, Gabe and David started up the route late one night, swinging leads and freeing every pitch from the second through the 11th. Then, over two consecutive windy and cold days, Billy and I freed the route from the second pitch all the way to Xanadu's summit, leading and following each pitch without falls. Finally, on the last climbing day of our trip, I successfully led the crux first pitch, Sílvia's Seam. Essentially a V10 boulder problem, this pitch required thin edging, unlikely foot pastes, and other granite wizardry. The west face of Xanadu could have been blank or perilously loose, but instead it permitted a demanding free route as good as anything we had ever climbed. We called our line Golden Petals (1,500', V 5.13+ or 5.12 A0).

On that last day, while Billy and I toiled on Sílvia's Seam, David and Gabe repeated the Bullard-Krakauer route to the top of Xanadu. They returned with huge grins, describing endless Type-1 fun and displaying a vintage hex they had bootied from the ascent 43 years earlier.

Throughout this trip, we were constantly reminded of the unique ways in which Chris Vale had entered each of our lives. He gladly would have taken the sharp end on any of the run-out pitches that left us shaking in our rock shoes. Chris would never say no to an adventure, and I'm certain he would have been proud of our success. ◙

ABOUT THE AUTHOR: *After earning a Ph.D. in mathematics, Zeb Engberg moved from New England to Utah, where he teaches math and climbs as often as possible. This trip was supported by the Dartmouth Outing Club's Chris Vale Adventure Fund and the Copp-Dash Inspire Award.*

Adam Ferro en route to the Albatross, prominent in right center. The team climbed the Direct Southeast Face (left side). Xanadu, hidden in the clouds, was accessed by a pass in upper right. *Vitaliy Musiyenko*

IN A PUSH
BOLD NEW ROUTES ON THE ALBATROSS AND XANADU

BY VITALIY MUSIYENKO

THE NEWS THAT I'd been hired to work in the emergency department of a large trauma center was bittersweet. My friends Brian Prince, Adam Ferro, and I had been planning to travel to the Arrigetch Peaks to attempt the unclimbed west face of Xanadu. Grant funding would cover most of our travel expenses. Now I might have to let my friends go on the trip of a lifetime without me. Fortunately, sending my supervisor the press release about our Mugs Stump Award and stacking up shifts worked magically—I was granted 19 days off.

Having less than three weeks for the expedition did not allow much time for screwing around. After arriving in Anchorage, we drove over 600 miles and about 15 hours north to the town of Coldfoot in one long push. Unfortunately, it was raining and we had to wait a few days before we could fly out. With the only hotel in town being prohibitively expensive, we crashed in an abandoned building.

When the weather allowed us to fly into Circle Lake on August 4, we learned that the biggest sandbag of the trip was the approach. Brian had thought it was about five miles—he obviously hadn't looked at the map very closely. It took us about two hours just to find a place to cross a small fork of the Alatna River—usually benign but now raging from the recent storms. We had to set up a Tyrolean to get our packs across. The trail up Arrigetch Creek that we eventually found was a muddy groove with water pouring down it. After walking for a few hours, Xanadu still looked very far away.

On the second day of our approach, we spotted a peak named the Albatross. Although not something we had planned to climb, it was a striking granite fin with what looked to be an

After days of rain, a Tyrolean was necessary to ferry packs over a normally placid creek and access the Arrigetch Valley. *Brian Prince*

exhilarating summit block. Soon after passing beneath it, we were caught in a raging thunderstorm and had to camp short of Escape Pass (our route to Xanadu). On the morning of August 6, the beautiful southeast face of the Albatross was illuminated by the sun. We quickly changed plans and set off to find a direct line up the face.

We climbed all sorts of terrain, from solid rock with fun, pumpy moves to dangerous overhangs with stacked flakes waiting for someone to carelessly give them a good pull. All three of us had a good amount of experience with route-finding on varied alpine terrain, and we tried to stretch our 70m ropes to the limit on every pitch, and consequently we made a relatively quick ascent. The Direct Southeast Face was approximately 1,700 feet, with difficulties to 5.10+—taller than the west face of Xanadu (which appears bigger on the map due to several hundred feet of slabs below the face). On top we found a summit register with only the signatures of the men who did the first documented ascent of the formation: Arthur Bacon and George Ripley, who climbed the peak in August 1969. *[Editor's note: The exact line of the first ascent is unknown but was described in the summit register "south face to S.W. ridge via shit gully." The second ascent was made by Lorna Corson and Norm Larson in 1993, via a parallel crack system on the south face (5.9, AAJ 1995). In 2016, Katie Mills and Nick Pappas climbed the Albatross' north buttress via the Eye of Sauron (1,200', 5.10c), but did not continue all the way along the ridge to the true summit (AAJ 2017).]*

We were physically beat from a tough three-day stretch of hiking and climbing, but the following morning the weather was fairly clear. So, only a few hours after we returned from the Albatross, we decided to load up on coffee and get after the main objective: the west face of Xanadu.

We got over Escape Pass, as well as a second unnamed pass, to reach the base of the wall in good time. *[The group approached the west face from looker's left via a ledge system that avoids the lower slabs.]* Zeb Engberg had sent us an overlay of the route he and his partners had finished less than a week prior to our departure, and had pointed out the line Sílvia Vidal was working on. With so little time available, we knew we'd have to climb in a push. When we got to the base and saw a beautiful corner system and steep cracks leading up the wall, we all thought it was the most natural and striking option for a possible free route.

But by then the wind had picked up and the clouds thickened. We started up the wall anyway, climbing a 70-meter, five-star corner and three and a half more pitches before the first drops of rain and a healthy dose of arctic wind forced a retreat from about halfway up.

After that, we were tent-bound by intermittent storms. After two days of tent festering, we only had half a day's worth of snacks and one dinner left. Though it wasn't raining, clouds surrounded the mountains. We had two choices: Hike out and retrieve more food from our cache at the airstrip or hike back up and over two passes, attempt our route, and then go out to the airstrip to get food after the climb. We chose the latter.

Brian Prince finding a path through numerous overlaps on the west face of Xanadu during the first ascent of the Arctic Knight (5.11+ R). *Vitaliy Musiyenko*

Midway up the wall, above our previous high point, the difficulties picked up. We were able to get past several serious runouts without placing bolts, and several cruxes up to 5.11+ went free—the most memorable being a big roof that required campusing on finger locks. Doing all that with frozen fingers—and climbing in a whiteout—provided more drama than most would want on a remote alpine route, but after about seven pitches of climbing, most of which were a full 70 meters, we were standing on top of the wall. About 400 feet of simul-climbing along the ridge took us to the true summit, where we dubbed our route the Arctic Knight (1,600', IV 5.11+ R).

Although happy with the result, the thick clouds and freezing winds didn't allow us to see much or stay long. We rappelled our line of ascent with two 70m ropes.

It was a shame the weather didn't cooperate, as the wall had great rock and amazing climbing that would have been much more fun without the screaming barfies.

Because we had to get down from the wall, pack up camp, move five miles down the valley, hike all the way out to the landing site, pick up seven days worth of food, and hike back up to our new camp, the true crux of this day was endurance and willpower. We found our food cache at dusk, and shortly afterward it started to rain heavily. By the time we returned to camp the next morning, 29 hours after initially setting out for Xanadu, we were exhausted, drenched, and ready to ask any nearby grizzly bears to end this sufferfest for us.

Unfortunately, after all that effort, it rained for several days in a row and climbing was out of the question, though a few short weather windows were big enough to pick blueberries. We ended up flying out of the Arrigetch four days early to meet up with Brian's stepdad for a few days of salmon fishing. Despite only getting two marginal climbing days, the trip featured great partners, challenging days in the mountains, blueberries, fishing, learning to operate a plane, and not getting eaten by a bear—the full-on Alaska experience! ▤ ▣ ▢

ABOUT THE AUTHOR: *Vitaliy Musiyenko lives in California. His feature article about new routes in the High Sierra appeared in AAJ 2017.*

RUNGOFARKA

THE FIRST ASCENT OF A DIFFICULT
6,500-METER PEAK IN INDIA

ALAN ROUSSEAU

Even as a child, knowing very little about the world, I remember conjuring images of India. These mental snapshots were total Indiana Jones fantasies: chaotic scenes filled with noisy, swirling crowds of people. Decades later, as the time for my first expedition to India approached, I wondered what chaos we might actually find, especially since we were hoping to climb in Kashmir, an area with a recent history of war and terrorism. My anxiety oscillated between the unknowns of traveling to such a place and the unknown climbing we would face. In the end, we found the travel easy to navigate. The rest, well, we will get into that.

Jammu and Kashmir (J&K) has a past as dramatic as its mountains. The zone has been subject to intense conflict since the British withdrew from Asia in 1947 and Pakistan separated from India. Showing up only as a dotted line on maps, the India-Pakistan border in this area has been disputed ever since and is referred to as the "Line of Control." The largely peaceful population of Kashmir has been victimized by this conflict for generations.

Having fought three wars and endured frequent terrorist attacks in Kashmir, the Indian government long restricted tourist access to the area's valleys and mountains. With the election of Asif Ali Zardari as Pakistan's leader in 2008, however, the conflict seemed to calm. In 2010, India opened more than 100 peaks to expeditions in Kashmir. To attract tourism and climbers, the Indian Mountaineering Foundation (IMF) streamlined the permit process and instated affordable peak fees.

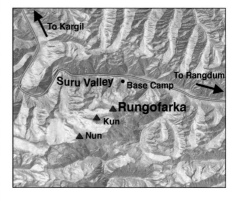

My climbing partner, Tino Villanueva, and I hoped to attempt one of these newly opened peaks. We scanned the IMF list and typed the names and coordinates into Google and the AAJ database. I was looking for peaks that were aesthetic, had big technical features, and had no record of exploration. We found several photos taken near Gulmatongo, in the Suru Valley, showing a striking, steep peak in the Zanskar Range, which is smack in the middle of J&K, west of the city of Leh. But the photos were all from the same vantage and quickly went blurry as we enlarged them and looked for possible lines. Although each aspect of the mountain obviously dropped well over 1,000 meters, on Google Earth the peak appeared as barely a blip on a ridgeline. We were able to find low-resolution maps on iPhone apps, but these had a datum shift on the mountain, making elevation lines difficult to follow.

The information about this area was so incomplete, in fact, that as I write this I'm still not sure of the name of the peak we ended up climbing. Captions from the few photos called it Rungofarka. The IMF lists the peak at this latitude and longitude as Techafarka (6,495m). We asked locals of the Suru Valley, who shepherd in the area, what they called it. One person said Kun (a well-known 7,000-meter peak nearby), while others told us they had no name for our mountain.

Despite the lack of information, Tino and I decided the north aspect of Whatever-farka was worthy of an expedition. Fortunately, the Mugs Stump Award and Copp-Dash Inspire

[Left] Alan Rousseau heading into the crux (the spotty ice smears to his right) on day four of the first ascent of Rungofarka. Finishing this challenging lead "was more of a highlight than standing on the summit a few hours later." *Tino Villanueva* [Above] Though access to the region has been difficult in the past because of security concerns, the base camp for Rungofarka itself is just one day's walk from the Kargil–Padum road. *Base map by Dallin Carey*

[Top] **Rungofarka (6,495m) from the north.**
(1) Approximate line of the first ascent by the
north ridge. (2) Attempt on direct north face.
(3) Descent by the west face. *Alan Rousseau*
[Bottom] **The north ridge (sunlit prow in right**
center) from the northeast. *Seth Timpano*

Award committees agreed, making our expedition possible. After Tino and I wrapped up our summer guiding seasons in Chamonix, we took off for India on September 6.

ALTHOUGH VIOLENCE IN the area has decreased over the last decade, the wounds are still fresh in Kashmir. Our journey to the Suru Valley began by driving along the Indus River, which flows into Pakistan and is a major water source. The Indus Waters Treaty, signed in 1960, ensures the river will not be dammed or diverted. India has threatened to break this treaty, and Pakistan has responded that it will not hesitate to retaliate with nuclear action.

Later that day we drove by a pass that Pakistani militants had flooded over in 1999, igniting the Kargil War. The next day, as we drove into the Suru Valley, frequent military checkpoints required us to show our visas and other documentation. That night we reached an outpost where we would start our short trek to base camp. This checkpoint was established in the mid-2000s in response to a terrorist attack on a busload of German tourists and the killing of several monks from the nearby Rangdum monastery. Loud trucks occasionally bounced down the rough road as I struggled to sleep in my tent, and each time I was relieved to hear them continue past.

With the help of local horsemen, we established an idyllic grassy base camp at 3,900 meters, just one day from the road. We spent the following days acclimatizing, exploring nearby boulders, scouting our approach, and establishing a cache at 4,900 meters. The north face of Whatever-farka rose directly to our south, about five kilometers away. Hidden behind it was Pinnacle Peak (now usually called Lingsarmo), a nearly 7,000-meter peak where American Fanny Bullock Workman set an early altitude record for women in 1906. Though we did not sleep above base camp, we hiked and bouldered to nearly 5,500 meters. Twelve days after arriving at BC, when we got word of an approaching high-pressure system via our InReach device, we decided it was time to get face-to-face with our objective.

On September 24 we spent the night in the bergschrund below the north face at 5,300 meters. The next morning the climb was on us as soon as we stepped out of the tent door. The aerated, overhanging wall of the 'schrund required extensive chopping and excavating just to find the marginal protection that allowed us to aid through it. Above, deep snow lay on the access ramp where we'd hoped to find névé, and the effort required to wallow up the 50° slopes at this altitude was as mentally crushing as it was physical. The true angle of the face above soon revealed itself—it was much steeper than it had let on.

Darkness engulfed us after climbing about 40 percent of the north face, including a seven-pitch runnel with difficulties to AI5+ M5. The high pressure was not as high as predicted—we climbed through light snowfall all day. Finally, with destroyed calves and no bivy ledge in sight, too many factors seemed against us and we pulled the plug. We rappelled through the night to get back to our 'schrund bivy.

DURING THE WALK down to base camp we started to craft a new plan. We had carried a small bivy tent for the mountain, but it seemed as though we would have needed hammocks to succeed on our north face line. The north ridge, to the left, however, appeared to have better options for bivy sites. In the few photos we'd seen before the trip, the north ridge had seemed less appealing than the main face—we thought it might even be a walk-up, linking snow slopes on the hidden east side. Now that we'd seen it in person, we realized the ridge was more like a prow—the central facet in the diamond-shaped north wall. It looked like it had plenty of difficult climbing. By the time we stepped off the glacier on our way back to camp, Tino and I had set our sights on the north ridge for our next attempt on Whatever-farka.

After a few days of needed rest, a huge high-pressure window opened. It was perfect timing because our porters were scheduled to arrive back at base camp just six days later. We only would get one more attempt—and we might not have time for that.

On September 30, Tino and I packed up and headed to an ABC at 4,900 meters for the night. Walking across the glacier the following morning, I was feeling nauseous and experiencing general malaise. *Why am I trying this again?* If Tino had expressed similar feelings, I'm sure I would have suggested bailing. Thankfully, he was fine and my lethargy faded as we crossed the 'schrund. The meditative mantra of swing-kick-kick-swing took over as we climbed nine rope lengths of AI3 to a prominent col below the north ridge. We quickly stomped out a platform and had a restful first night on the route (5,700 meters).

While our bodies rested, our minds raced. The next morning we would have to negotiate 200 to 300 meters of near-vertical mixed terrain.

"It's dry up there—the rock better be solid."

"Real steep, too, and it looks like some shale bands."

"Maybe there is a more moderate terrain on the east side?"

It was hard to find something positive to say about the terrain ahead, other than, "Well, we came here to climb something hard."

Heading up on October 2 with open minds, we found the climbing to be slow, thought-provoking, at times loose, and mostly in the M5 or M6 range. The pitches often traversed, and the anchors were marginal to the point that jugging never seemed like a great option. We both free climbed all but one short tension traverse on this section.

One pitch remains vividly seared into my mind: a long, ever-steepening, styrofoam-like strip of névé that narrowed to around a foot wide and a couple of inches thick. The nearly vertical névé line ended at a 15-foot-tall overhanging block that was somehow pasted to the

Looking down the difficult wide crack at nearly 6,200 meters, the 19th pitch on the third day on the climb. *Alan Rousseau*

mountain. From the top of this block, we traversed left, frontpoints nestled into coarse-grained igneous horizontals, then balanced up to gain a four-inch-wide ledge with little more for an anchor than highly fractured shale blocks frozen in place.

After 10 pitches, we were above the first big question marks of our route, searching for a bivy ledge. But the terrain above only steepened, so we decided to rappel back to some lower-angle terrain. Poking our heads behind an ice pillar, we discovered a cave that was 15 feet long and wide enough for the tent, with a flat floor. Surrounded by otherwise unrelenting terrain, at just under 6,000 meters, it was paradise.

IN THE MORNING, as we loaded our packs, Tino verbalized a harsh reality about our progress: "You know, we've only climbed 19 pitches in two days. We've got a long way to go. And the porters are going to be here three days from now."

"Yeah, I know. And that upper headwall looks complicated, for sure."

"If we only get up another ten pitches again today, we're going to have to bail."

"For sure, but let's give it everything we have today and see what happens."

Fortunately, the day started with some easier terrain. The pitches fell away, along with some of the mental weight.

Halfway through the day, the ridge steepened into more M6 cruxes. An ice runnel to nowhere and a featureless steep slab both required tension traverses off knifeblades to access more climbable terrain.

All afternoon, as we neared our planned high bivy at 6,200 meters, we could see above us an obvious dead-vertical wide crack. It stared us down for hours. When we got there, we realized with dismay there was no way around this six-inch crack. It was our 19th pitch of the day. I'd put in some serious time on wide cracks at Indian Creek and elsewhere, so I took the lead, but I had to laugh at the contrast with those sun-soaked sandstone walls, climbing in tape gloves and sticky-soled shoes—here I was chicken-winging with a puffy jacket and heel-toe camming in crampons. Fortunately the techniques transferred to this inhospitable locale, and though Tino later pulled out the protection pitons with his fingers, another piece of the puzzle soon had fallen into place.

Our bivy was perched on top of a rock feature that was a dead ringer for the Prow on the Moonflower Buttress of Mt. Hunter. We were relieved to reach this spot, but it was less than ideal. After two hours of chopping into a 50° snow arête in the dark, with winds gusting 40 to 50 mph, we had created a ledge about three-quarters the width of our tent. Despite our best attempts to be delicate with the platform, it quickly deteriorated to half a tent width. We spent that night bracing the tent from the wind and sharing the uphill side of our ever-shrinking ledge. I slept a few hours, which was a couple more than Tino did. I guess my bony backside didn't make for a great pillow!

In the morning we were gifted with clear, calm skies. The chimney line directly above us was choked with loose blocks, and it seemed our only option was to rappel about 45 meters off the prow to the right and try to reach the ice runnel we believed to be there. Even from the lower anchor, after the rappel, we couldn't quite see into the heart of this runnel and verify if it

Tino Villanueva heading toward the summit, finally on good névé. In back is a partial view of LIngsarmo (a.k.a. Pinnacle Peak, 6,955m). *Alan Rousseau*

held ice or cracks. All we knew was that if we could make it through the next 15 or 20 meters of unknown, only one pitch of WI3 would remain before the summit ice slopes. If it didn't go, we weren't sure we could go back the way we'd came, but after 40-plus pitches it seemed like a good gamble. Both of us were breathing hard as we pulled the ropes.

"Man, I hope this goes," I said as Tino put me on belay.

Tino replied in his usual steady tone: "Dude, with how you have been climbing, one way or another it's going to happen."

The trust and confidence of an old friend filled me with calm, as if, after nearly a dozen serious trips together, Tino knew exactly what I needed to hear. I purposefully unclipped from the belay and moved toward the hidden runnel.

Thin, emaciated ice and committing M6 moves linked one icy seam to the next. The pitch turned out to one of the most challenging—and elegant—of the route. Clove-hitching into the anchor was more of a highlight for me than standing on the summit a few hours later.

After a short stay on top, we began our descent by the lower-angle west face. We'd hoped this might be a walk, but instead it involved around 20 rappels, threatened at times by seracs, coupled with breaking trail through shin-crushing snow crust. We trudged on into the night, descending 2,700 vertical meters in around nine hours, and arrived in base camp just 12 hours before our porters.

It was a privilege to climb in such a spectacular range, and visiting these areas and hiring locals can only help the situation in Kashmir. The people of the Suru Valley that we encountered were friendly and hard-working. For their sake, I hope these peaks remain open to climbers and tourism continues to be encouraged. There's no shortage of unclimbed objectives!

SUMMARY: First ascent of Rungofarka (a.k.a. Techafarka, 6,495m or 21,309', GPS 6,485m), by the north ridge, by Alan Rousseau and Tino Villanueva, October 1–4, 2017. Their route, the T&A Show, was 1,200m, ca 50 pitches, and rated VI M6 WI4+ A0. The pair descended glacial slopes to the west. This climb was featured in episode two of the AAJ's Cutting Edge Podcast.

ABOUT THE AUTHOR: *Alan Rousseau is an IFMGA/UIAGM mountain guide living in Salt Lake City, Utah, and working primarily in Utah, Alaska, and Chamonix, France. He loves developing new routes, whether it's short bolted lines near home or virgin peaks in the greater ranges.*

Travis Foster takes in the view from the top of the Red Alert Wall in the Daniels River Valley after the first ascent. The wall in back, Super Unknown, was climbed just a few weeks later. *Drew Leiterman*

THE BIG WALL BELT

THREE HUGE NEW WALLS—AND A WHOLE LOT OF POTENTIAL—IN THE COAST MOUNTAINS OF BRITISH COLUMBIA

INTRODUCTION: **CHRIS KALMAN**

REPORTS: **TRAVIS FOSTER • EVAN GUILBAULT • AUSTIN SIADAK**

In the spring of 2017, I was looking for something big, remote, and wild to climb in the upcoming summer, but I didn't have the time or money for a place like the Ruth, Baffin, or Karakoram. I knew that a 50-pitch rock route had been climbed on Mt. Bute in the Coast Mountains, not too far from Vancouver, and I figured there just had to be good granite between there and Squamish. So I hopped on Google Earth and started playing with the controls—zooming, panning, spinning, adjusting the angle. Suddenly my jaw hit the keyboard. What the hell was *that*? The somewhat distorted imagery seemed to show a sheer buttress of white rock jutting 1,400 meters into the sky. The shade from that apparent rocket ship of stone, and some nearby peaks, cast an entire valley into toothy darkness. Not knowing any other name for the place, I called it the Dark Valley.

A few months later, my friends Miranda Oakley and Austin Siadak and I crested the snowcone summit of that massive buttress in the last golden light of a long summer day. What had started as a deep dive into Google Earth's vortex of pipe dreams and half-baked ideas had somehow manifested into the biggest first ascent—actually, so far, the biggest ascent—of my life.

But if I was surprised at our success, I was downright flabbergasted to discover, not long after our return from the Dark Valley, that two *other* first ascents of roughly the same length had just been done, not far to the south. Upon further research, I came to learn that the valley we'd visited was merely the tip of a very large, very exciting iceberg. I have taken to calling it the Big Wall Belt of Canada.

The Big Wall Belt runs along the western flank of the vast, sprawling, and seldom-traveled Coast Mountains, extending generally northwest from Squamish for several hundred miles, all the way to the Alaska border. To come up with a reasonable estimate of the amount of exposed and climbable rock here would require data modeling tools far beyond my comprehension and a helicopter with an unlimited fuel budget. But spend a few minutes on Google

Earth exploring the map area shown at right. You see those seemingly endless granite walls lining deeply bifurcated valleys and alpine gorges? Most of them are unclimbed. Now multiply what you see there by the entire Pacific Coast of Canada.

The most developed portion of the Big Wall Belt is undoubtedly the Eldred Valley, northeast of the town of Powell River. Climbing there dates back to 1988, when Rob Richards and his brother Casey put up Psychopath (600m, V 5.10+) on Psyche Slab. In 1993, Richards brought Yosemite big-wall tactics to the valley when he and Colin Dionne climbed West Main Wall in capsule style over seven days, establishing Mainline (VI 5.11 A4). Six years later, Matt Maddaloni and John Millar spent three weeks in the valley establishing Funk Soul Brother (12 pitches, VI 5.10 A4+) on Carag Dur. Later that season, Aaron Black and Dionne teamed up to climb Amon Rûdh—Black would go on to make at least four trips to the Eldred, eventually partnering with Sean Easton to climb Call of the Granite (23 pitches, V 5.12 C1) on West Main Wall in 2005.

In the years since, the Eldred has matured as a climbing destination, though it remains rarely visited. It can even be found on Mountain Project, and was described in greater detail in the *Climbers Guide to Powell River* (Chris Armstrong, 2002). Still, the Eldred is anything but climbed out. In 2014, the 500m West Main Buttress finally saw its first route with Brent Goodman and Matt Hodgson's Against the Current (500m, V 5.11+ C1). Rob Richards himself was still at it in 2017, nearly 30 years after he authored the Eldred's first route, climbing Mormegil (500m, 5.10 C1) on Amon Rûdh with Evan Guilbault and Matt Hodgson. According to Guilbault, 30-plus pitches were added to Amon Rûdh in 2017. More importantly, logging projects threatening old-growth forests surrounding Amon Rûdh were postponed in early spring of 2018 for two years due to public pressure.

Less than 20 miles northwest of the Eldred as the crow flies is a much less-visited region called the Daniels River Valley. In the 1985 *Canadian Alpine Journal*, the prolific Coast Mountains explorer John Clarke described the Daniels as "the most beautiful arctic alpine wilderness, studded with lakes, small glaciers, and heather ridges." He noted that the upper valley hosted enormous cliffs, one of which he estimated at 3,500 feet high. "This is probably the least traveled area within a hundred miles of Vancouver," he said, "a marvelous stretch of wilderness, still left to the goats, wolverines, and ravens." Clarke extolled the Daniels in the *CAJ* again in 1990, even sharing a picture of a huge and attractive wall. But nobody took the bait until 1998, when

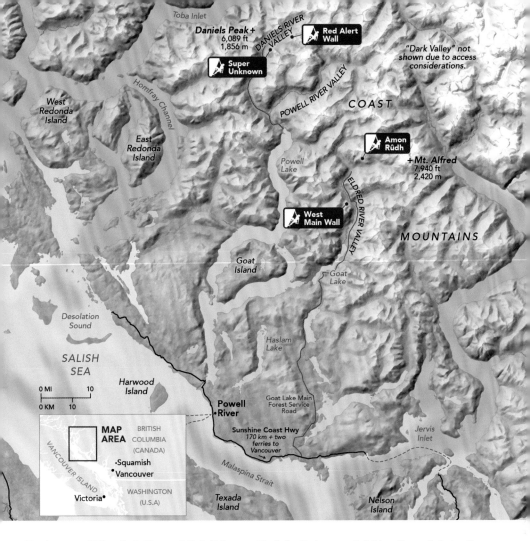

The map contains the following labels:

Toba Inlet

Daniels Peak +
6,089 ft
1,856 m

DANIELS RIVER VALLEY

Red Alert Wall

"Dark Valley" not shown due to access considerations.

Super Unknown

POWELL RIVER VALLEY

COAST

Homfray Channel

West Redonda Island

East Redonda Island

Amon Rûdh

+ Mt. Alfred
7,940 ft
2,420 m

Powell Lake

ELDRED RIVER VALLEY

MOUNTAINS

West Main Wall

Goat Island

Goat Lake

Desolation Sound

Haslam Lake

SALISH SEA

Harwood Island

0 MI   10
0 KM   10

Goat Lake Main Forest Service Road

Powell River

Sunshine Coast Hwy
170 km + two ferries to Vancouver

Jervis Inlet

MAP AREA

BRITISH COLUMBIA
(CANADA)

· Squamish
· Vancouver

WASHINGTON
(U.S.A)

Victoria ·

VANCOUVER ISLAND

Malaspina Strait

Texada Island

Nelson Island

[Previous page] **Miranda Oakley and Chris Kalman settle in for their second night on the wall during the first ascent of Northwest Passage.** *Austin Siadak* [Above] **The Eldred and Daniels valleys are accessed from the isolated town of Powell River, BC. To the north, the "Big Wall Belt" extends for hundreds of miles. Map sources: NASA, Government of Canada.** *Marty Schnure | Maps for Good*

Damon Kessell led a handful of less experienced climbers to a ledge a third of the way up that wall before bailing. The first complete Daniels River wall climb wasn't done until last summer.

Why, exactly, three separate expeditions into hitherto untouched corners of the Big Wall Belt took place in a single two-month span in 2017, after receiving almost no attention during the three decades since John Clarke described them in print, is beyond me.

What I do know, after talking to the instigators of the other two expeditions last summer, is that there were certain immutable truths of climbing in the Big Wall Belt that we all experienced. There are grizzlies. There are bushy cracks. Rainstorms come in quickly and ferociously. The rock is impeccable. The walls are really big. We also came away from our journeys all parroting the same wide-eyed message: There are a hell of a lot more walls out there to be climbed.

Chris Kalman is an associate editor of the AAJ and author of the books As Above, So Below *and* The Index Town Walls: A Guide to Washington's Finest Crag.

Travis Foster starts the 25th and final pitch of Jungle is Massive, a wet, challenging corner that took hours to aid on the ninth day of the climb. *Drew Leiterman*

ANSWERING CLARKE'S CALL
THE FIRST ASCENT OF RED ALERT WALL

BY TRAVIS FOSTER

"Red Alert… Red Alert… Rock climbers: There's a 3,500-foot granite cliff on the south side of the upper Daniels. Go do it. Red Alert… This is not a drill."

That was the call to arms that John Clarke wrote nearly 30 years ago in the 1990 *Canadian Alpine Journal*. Yet, to our knowledge, the wall in question had seen only one attempt since then, in 1998, when Damon Kessell and a bevy of less experienced partners made it a third of the way up the face on two separate occasions.

In July 2017, Drew Leiterman and I decided to answer Clarke's call. After an exchange with some friendly loggers in a currency found most agreeable at the top of Powell Lake—a case of Lucky Lager beer—Drew and I were dropped off approximately 10 kilometers away from our soon-to-be base camp in the Daniels Valley by a lumberjack we took to calling "Steve: Man-of-the-Daniels." Steve told us that every now and then a grizzly will come over the ridge into the Daniels from the Toba Inlet and be "pissed right off" to find no salmon. He had found three dead black bears one year. Imagine our terror when, our very first night in the valley, a black bear came sidehilling through the alder with a full-grown grizzly thundering after him! Neither of them paid much attention to us, but we each slept with one eye open that night.

We spent a few days cutting trail and hauling all of our food and gear to the base of the Red Alert Wall, which faces west on the south side of the southwest-to-northeast-angling valley. The first 570 meters of our chosen line climbs what we called the Miami Slabs. (The name comes from a song by the band Against Me! that bears the same title and, more importantly, the same feeling.) It took us two long days to climb and haul these pitches. By 11 p.m. on the second night, we staggered onto a long bench we named the Halfway Highway (even though it's only about a third of the way up). The next morning, after a well-deserved sleep-in and a nice breakfast, we deliberated about what to do next. We decided to stash a bunch of gear here and continue, not exactly "fast and light" but at least a little less encumbered. We used the remaining daylight to fix ropes and prepare ourselves to launch the next morning.

For the first time since we arrived in the valley, the air felt heavy that night. Just to be safe, we rigged the portaledge's fly off a cam, but we left the ledge in its bag. Predictably enough, at some ungodly hour we woke to the rain, which seemed to be laughing at us. We dashed to the fly and wrapped ourselves in it like a blanket, passing the rest of the night trying to sit-sleep. As soon as it sounded like the rain had abated, we moved our condensation-soaked selves to action and rigged the portaledge properly. In the morning it was still raining on and off, so we took the opportunity for more sleep and woke

[Top] A 60km ride across Powell Lake is part of the approach to the Daniels Valley. [Bottom] Jungle is Massive (1,290m, VI 5.10 C2). *Drew Leiterman*

around noon. It was evening before things dried off enough to even think about climbing.

On the fifth day we woke early and jugged and hauled up to our high point. For nearly 400 meters we followed a massive right-facing corner system of mostly clean, mostly fun free climbing, and rigged camp at the top of the corner. The next morning we slept through our alarms, and once awake we agreed that simply to push our three ropes up would be enough to call the day a success. Ahead of us was the biggest question mark of the route, a section we called the Choss Band.

We spent the entire next day trying to surmount the Choss Band. Drew started aiding, sticking to the route we had planned from the valley, but it proved too wet and tricky, so he down-aided and decided to try free climbing up and left instead. From the top of his pitch, I continued on the same trajectory through fun and balancey face climbing, with thin protection in small cracks and flakes.

We started our seventh day on the wall with jugging to our new high point and then making a 70-meter, straight-right traverse across the top of the Choss Band. This was followed by another full rope length through easy terrain heading up and right. Figuring out how to haul these traversing pitches was interesting, to say the least. Eventually we were able to make our high camp underneath a pair of arches that looked like a great frown, just above the Choss Band. The next day we fixed our three ropes up the nearly vertical, 340-meter expanse of stone we named the Incredible Headwall. The top looked agonizingly close, but after some difficult free and aid climbing we elected to return to camp and blast for the summit in the morning.

At 7 a.m. on July 14, our ninth day on the wall, we were back at our high point and ready to fire to the top. We hoped to be back at high camp for lunch. Unfortunately, the Incredible Headwall had a different idea. What had looked to be cruiser climbing turned out to be more wet and thoughtful aid—the summit pitch took hours inside a saturated and mostly crackless left-facing corner. After some slimy small-nut placements and delicate hooks, I top-stepped on a perfect horn, grabbed some thick branches, and gleefully swam through the foliage to gain the summit at 5 p.m.

After our special bro moments on top, a bite to eat, and some photos for our moms we started to rappel. We hand-drilled a single-bolt rap route until the Halfway Highway, where we were able to continue on with the descent line installed by the 1998 party. It took us two days to return to the base.

I am under no illusion that this was by any means a world-class ascent, but it sure was a good time. And for two bush-league believers on their first big wall, we certainly impressed ourselves.

SUMMARY: First ascent of the Red Alert Wall in the Daniels River Valley by the route Jungle is Massive (1,290m, 25 pitches, VI 5.10 C2).

ABOUT THE AUTHOR: *Travis Foster grew up with Drew Leiterman in Cranbrook, BC, skipping classes to do kick flips then, quitting work to go climbing now.*

SACRED STONE
A JOURNEY INTO THE SUPER UNKNOWN

BY EVAN GUILBAULT

1995. POWELL RIVER climbing legends Rob and Casey Richards are deep in the Daniels River Valley doing forestry work. Soundgarden's "Super Unknown" blares from the speakers as they turn a corner 25 kilometers in. Out of heavy clouds, a giant appears. More than 1,200 meters of granite soars above them. Super Unknown, they agree, is a fitting name.

Rob and Casey were both in their prime at the time, but for reasons I still don't understand, they never attempted the wall. In fact, nobody did. In 2016, I made a recon mission with my friends Colin Landeck, Max Merkin, and Cameron Moustaffi to see the valley I had been dreaming of for three years. On that first trip, we did nothing other than clear out the old logging road that goes to the base of the Red Alert Wall. Filled with priceless beta, I returned to my home base in the Eldred for the remainder of the season. But the stage was set for Colin and my return the following year.

On August 4, we left the beautiful seaside town of Powell River, traditional territory of the Tla'amin and Klahoose First Nations, to venture deep into our backyard. Our friend Norbert and his wife ferried us across Powell Lake and left us alone with two bikes, 100 kilos of gear, and 25 kilometers of logging road to travel to access the Daniels. The first crux of our trip was simply figuring out how to get all of our stuff from point A to point B. For us, the answer entailed cutting down nearby alders to build a sturdy "rickshaw" with our mountain bikes.

With the gear hoisted between the two bikes,

[Previous page] A mountain bike "rickshaw" was used to haul equipment 16 kilometers en route to Super Unknown. [Above] Evan Guilbault returned to the Daniels after the first ascent to free the 10th pitch of Sacred Stone, an amazing 5.11b finger crack. *Robin Munshaw*

and Colin and myself jogging alongside the makeshift vehicle, we traveled 16 kilometers in four hours, which was far more efficient than we had hoped. Beyond there, the road became brushy, so we resorted to shuttling loads the final eight kilometers to Stokemaster Camp, directly beneath the improbably long, white tongue of granite that marks the base of the Super Unknown, which faces northwest on the south side of the valley.

By noon on August 5 we had all of our gear at camp. Organized and comfortably gawking from our hammocks at these stone sentinels, we began building the trail to the wall that evening. We macheted a path to the river, which was fast-moving but only calf-deep and easy to cross. The next day we made our way through the majestic groves of ancient cedars that led to the base of the wall: 400 meters of shimmering, glacier-polished slabs extending from valley floor to the base of our intended route and onward into the sky. With a glimpse from the toe of the wall, we headed home for a final dinner full of "who knows" talk.

By 8 p.m on August 7, Colin and I had lines fixed up to the slabs to our first bivy. Game on. In the morning, Colin wove up 120 meters of foreshortened slabs to the base of the Multi-Corners—six perfect corner systems all stacked atop one another. I took over, leading up and over the Gusher Gulley, which was as sweet as the fruit candies for which it's named, split by clean, impeccable crack and corner systems. We set up camp on top of pitch six, underneath a 300-meter-tall overhanging amphitheater of stone.

The south-side walls of the Daniels River Valley (left to right): Red Alert, Chico Flaco, and Super Unknown. Sacred Stone climbs the dark cleft on the right side of Super Unknown before moving to the right skyline. Chico Flaco awaits an ascent. *Robin Munshaw*

The next morning started mellow, but two pitches into the day I found myself pulling 5.10+ mantels above tiny cams and stoppers that probably would not have held a fall. Beautiful finger cracks took me to a tree belay 60 meters higher. Above us, a Jurassic mass of thimbleberries and devil's club clung to the cliff, 600 meters off the valley floor. Colin led a wild jungle pitch, slashing his way through head-high vegetation with an ice axe we'd brought specifically for this purpose.

Colin gently nailed his way up pitch ten: a flawless, 35-meter, off-vertical finger crack in a corner—perhaps the most beautiful pitch of the climb. Atop a comfortable belay pedestal, he handed me the rack as daylight disappeared. "It's 30 feet of 5.5," he told me, referring to the upcoming ledge system where we planned to bivy. What followed was a full 60 meters of jamming and stemming—more like 5.8. We finished the pitch by headlamp and began the night's gardening, hacking the devil's club out of our bivy for two.

As day three dawned, we found ourselves smack dab in the most intimidating section of the wall. Our water was running low, and we still had hundreds of meters of unknown technical terrain to cover. Surrounded by overhanging crack systems, we simply had to have faith and trust our abilities. We decided to leave our bivy gear and head out light and fast for a summit push.

The morning started with a pendulum into another steep corner system. Some bouldery moves off the belay connected beautiful features up to the Rickshaw Ramp, a third-class path right in the middle of intimidating steep terrain. The ramp was our salvation, taking us onto the Golden Headwall, where the angle of the wall eases and moderate corner systems appear by the dozen. The terrain all started to blend together as we swapped leads for 14 pitches, mostly clean, straightforward corner cracks, with a couple of steep bulges that were easily aided. We felt like we were flowing up this behemoth of stone, committed to the top.

Around 9 p.m. on August 10, just as the sky was lit on fire, Colin and I topped out the Super Unknown. We ecstatically embraced and ran to the true summit. We had just climbed a dream route: ground-up, no bolts, 27 pitches!

SUMMARY: First ascent of the northwest face of the Super Unknown formation in the Daniels River Valley by the route Sacred Stone (1,200m, 27 pitches inlcuding a 100-meter 3rd-class ramp, VI 5.10 A1). The crux 10th pitch was later freed at 5.11.

ABOUT THE AUTHOR: *Born in Vancouver, B.C. Evan Guilbault spends his summers in the Coast Mountains with his partner, Zoe, climbing walls, bushwhacking, and rambling on ridges.*

Chris Kalman forges up a vegetated wide crack, 800 meters up the Northwest Passage. *Austin Siadak*

THE DARK VALLEY
A THREE-WEEK TRIP DEEP INTO THE COAST MOUNTAINS

BY AUSTIN SIADAK

"That thing is taller than El Cap."

"Definitely."

Gulp.

During a late-night Google Earth binge, Chris Kalman had found a deep coastal valley filled with waterfalls and massive granite faces that had never been visited by climbers. Was I interested? Of course. We quickly added our friend and crack aficionado Miranda Oakley as a rope gun. In early July, we secured permission from the chief of the First Nation that presides over this land, but only on the condition that we not divulge the exact location. On July 9, on a gray British Columbia morning, we boarded a helicopter, bound for what we had come to call the Dark Valley.

Given the massive unknowns of new-routing in a remote valley where nobody had ever climbed before, we conservatively chose to climb in capsule style. We fixed 300 meters of rope on a day of clear weather and then returned a couple of days later with enough supplies for four days on the wall.

As Chris and Miranda pushed the rope up the wall, I took the lion's share of the big-wall toiling, jugging and hauling our packs up lines fixed by the other two, and building level sleeping platforms out of jumbled blocks and uneven ledges. The climbing was generally easier than we had expected, though often surrounded or covered by abundant shrubbery, especially on the lower third of the wall. At the end of our third day, we found ourselves perched on a beautiful bench system a little less than two-thirds of the way up the mountain, roughly 850 meters off the deck. We organized gear in the setting sun, enjoyed a small campfire on our ledge, and fell asleep beneath a billion stars twinkling above.

In the middle of the pitch-black night, I was jolted awake as raindrops hit my face. Within 30 seconds, a sprinkle turned into a torrential downpour and water cascaded down the rock all

around us. We sketchily stumbled up the slick stone to a protected bed of heather and huddled in a pile beneath a tarp, the only thing we had brought for shelter. I shivered uncontrollably as rain pelted down from above and we sipped hot drinks to warm our frozen cores.

We slept late into the next morning and spent hours drying out our soaked gear. By midday the weather seemed to have stabilized and I was getting antsy. It was very late to start a summit push, but the terrain above looked less steep—even 3rd class in parts. At the very least we could begin scouting.

Around 3 p.m. we headed upward. The ridge above our bivy was as easy as it looked, and we soloed long sections up to low 5th class, interspersed with steep heather and a healthy dose of vertical bushwhacking. Higher, we pulled out the rope and I led a few pitches up stepped buttresses, moving quickly in the waning daylight. Soon we were dodging snow-filled ledges and cracks, and I knew we must be close. We trudged up a long snow slope and could suddenly see down into the valley on the other side. We were on top. We hooted and hollered in disbelief and took a bunch of photos of the valley and the mind-blowing sunset light that filtered in from the west.

We made our way back to our bivy in twilight, mostly rapping from trees and bushes. When we finally settled in to sleep, exhausted from the day, we noticed a white glow to the north that seemed to be city lights. *Wait a minute*, I thought, pulling my sluggish brain through oncoming delirium, *there's*

The beautiful "Dark Valley." The Northwest Passage climbs Aurora Peak (front left) by the low apron leading to the right shoulder, then up the ridge to the summit. Mt. Shangri-La (front right) was climbed by the clean swath of stone cutting through the jungle on the right, then straight up to the summit. [Below] Chris Kalman braves the true crux of the mission: crossing what, in the Coast Mountains, passes for a "creek" in order to set up a Tyrolean traverse to access Shangri-La. *Austin Siadak*

no city to the north. We watched in awe as ghostly curtains of white light danced in the darkness.

With time waning in the trip, and Miranda sick, Chris and I summitted another unclimbed peak on the other side of the valley in a 20-hour push. The climbing was unremarkable, though not bad, as we mostly simul-climbed about 600 meters of 5.9 and easier to the top. The views were unparalleled. The descent was arduous, taking longer than the climb itself.

When we returned to civilization, I hopped on the Internet to try and confirm a hunch. Indeed, in July 2017 a rare meteorological event had sent an aurora borealis streaming as far south as Vancouver. We unanimously agreed on a name for the mountain: Aurora Peak, climbed via the Northwest Passage.

Summary: First ascent of the north face of Aurora Peak: Northwest Passage (1,430m, VI 5.11-R A0). The team placed one bolt and pulled on it for the sole aid move of the climb. First ascent of the east face of Mt. Shangri-La by Yacht Rock (ca 600m, IV 5.9).

About the Author: *Austin Siadak is a climber and photographer originally from Seattle, now based near steep walls and remote summits around the American West.*

SUNNY PATAGONIA?

CLIMBING IN A CHANGING CLIMATE

DÖRTE PIETRON

Life in El Chaltén, a small town in Southern Patagonia, revolves around the weather forecast. Waiting for elusive weather windows is an exciting and sometimes frustrating way to live.

When I first came to climb in El Chaltén, ten years ago, a friend taught me to interpret weather charts to make predictions for the next few days. Some years later, I started looking at Pacific Ocean weather maps to track weather systems coming toward South America, and at times I was able to forecast good weather as much as three weeks in advance.

Soon I wanted to know what the next season might be like, so I dove into the uncertain world of seasonal forecasts. Over time this took me even further, into trying to understand the bigger picture—how the climate has changed over the past decades and what to expect for the future.

In 2003, El Chaltén got Internet service for the first time, and soon Web-based weather forecasts began having a big impact on climbing in the area. Forecasts spared climbers the physical and mental energy of false starts and allowed them to choose objectives closer to the upper limits of their ability; it also encouraged them to take advantage of even the shortest weather windows. Along with increased climber visitation, a general increase in skill levels, and a wealth of communal know-how, the availability of weather forecasting could well account for the stunning jump in quality ascents over the last decades. And yet there seems to be something else going on.

A number of climbers that were active in the 1970s are convinced that today's climbers are also benefiting from better weather. Do they have a point? The Chaltén Massif was once known for its unrelenting bad weather. After yet another unsuccessful visit to the area, German alpinist Reinhard Karl famously wrote in early 1980, "Just as well I could hide inside my fridge at home and burn 100 Deutsche Mark bills." Then, sometime in the early 2000s, climbers started returning from Patagonia with tales of weeklong periods of good weather lining up one after the other.

There's no question that environmental changes in the Chaltén Massif in recent years have been dramatic and would seem to point to a change in climate. Glaciers are receding at incredible speed, moraines are collapsing, big rock features are falling off, and vegetation is advancing. Is the climate in Patagonia actually changing, improving the weather and making climbing easier?

To answer this question in a scientific manner, we first have to define "good" climbing weather in meteorological terms. The key variables are precipitation and wind. No long-term records exist for either of these for the Chaltén area. Luckily, however, in 1990 the U.S. National Centers for Environmental Prediction (NCEP) and National Center for Atmospheric Research

(NCAR) started the "Reanalysis" project to fill the needs of climate researchers for a retroactive record of global atmospheric circulation. It covers the period from 1948 to the present, combining observational data with state-of-the-art numerical models.

The NCEP/NCAR Reanalysis has some limitations. For the period before satellite observations started, in 1979, the Southern Hemisphere reanalysis results are less reliable because of insufficient observational data. Further, the project's 2.5° latitude/longitude grid lacks the precision to accurately deduce localized phenomena such as precipitation, which in the southern Andes varies dramatically in a very short distance. The most reliable data set that occurs on a big enough spatial scale and is a good indicator of regional weather is "sea level pressure." Relatively high atmospheric pressure at sea level is generally associated with little precipitation and wind. Pressure observations have been used for centuries to predict weather conditions.

From the NCEP/NCAR Reanalysis, I extracted the monthly mean sea level pressure (MSLP) and the "standardized monthly MSLP anomaly" since 1949 and analyzed the data. First, I wanted to answer one frequently asked question: Which is the best month to go climbing in the Chaltén Massif? Surprisingly, September is the month with the highest MSLP (suggesting likely good weather). In September, however, there is usually too much snow left over from the austral winter for good climbing conditions, plus it is very cold. During the summer season, the month with the highest MSLP is February, which usually also provides dry rock climbing conditions and higher temperatures.

Next I looked at long-term trends, using time series of both annual and summer (averaging December, January and February) data, focusing mainly on summer because of its greater interest to climbers and because, as I learned during my research, the relevant changes are most pronounced then.

CHART 1: SUMMER MSLP PER DECADE

(MSLP=mean sea level pressure; summer = Dec, Jan, Feb)

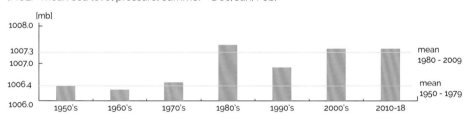

The summer MSLP shows a long-term trend toward higher values, with the strongest increases between the 1970s and the '80s—an increase in mean values of approximately 1 millibar (mb). (*See Chart 1.*) Although 1mb may seem like a small increase, its significance becomes more apparent when you consider the average summer MSLP in El Chaltén is approximately 1003mb to 1010mb. A rising average means high MSLP occurrences are more frequent. Could this explain the many dry summers we've experienced in recent years?

Next I looked at the "best" and "worst" summer seasons, those with the highest and lowest MSLP. To select them, I used +/-1.28 standard deviations as a threshold, to identify summers below the 10th and above the 90th percentile of the data distribution. Beginning again with 1949, I found eight "worst" and 11 "best" summers.

The first thing that stands out is that of those 11 "best" summers, nine happened in the last 30 years and only two in the 30 years prior. (*See Chart 2 on next page.*) Furthermore, seven have come since the year 2000. On the contrary, only one of the eight "worst" summers happened in the last 30 years, while the other seven happened in the 30 years before. This points to a marked trend toward more frequent "best" and less frequent "worst" summer periods.

CHART 2: "BEST" (RED) AND "WORST" (BLUE) SUMMERS IN EL CHALTÉN AREA
(Only summers exceeding +/-1.28 standard deviations are shown.)

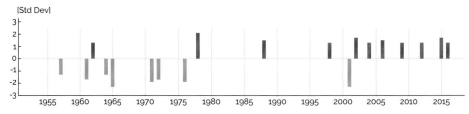

When comparing the "best" summers to a list of important ascents in the area, there appears to be a strong relationship. One notices a clear uptick of ascents during "best" summers after 1980, compared to average or "worst" summers. (This analysis applies also to the pre-forecast era, taking into account the number of climbers that visited the area at the time.) The "best" summers are related to long periods of good weather and thus favorable climbing conditions (dry, ice-free rock), which, for many objectives, can be as important as the weather for climbing success.

EL CHALTÉN IS located at 49°S, in the northern half of a zone of eastward-progressing low-pressure weather systems that travel around Antarctica and closely follow the westerly wind belt, with a quasi-stationary high-pressure system to the northwest. The north-south movement of the ring of low-pressure systems is poorly understood, but such shifts dictate the weather in this area. This north-south movement is described by an index called the Antarctic Oscillation (AAO). A positive AAO index corresponds to southward contraction of the low-pressure systems and favors good climbing weather. (In the last decades it has become fashionable to blame any weather pattern on El Niño or La Niña. Although their effects on the southern tip of the American continent are not entirely understood, it is safe to say that the AAO index is a far better indicator of the weather in Southern Patagonia than El Niño or La Niña.)

Since the AAO is the single most important influence on the weather in this region, I next looked at the AAO index provided by G.J. Marshall (1), derived from station data from 1957 to present. I observed a summertime trend toward a positive AAO index, strongly marked from the beginning of the 1980s (2, 4). In 13 of the 19 "best" and "worst" summers I found a direct relationship to the AAO index, while six occurred with a neutral AAO index. (Five of those six were high MSLP anomalies whose center was located too far south geographically for the AAO index to capture them.)

Since wind is such an important factor for climbing in this area, I also looked at the "zonal wind" (wind along latitudinal lines) at 850mb from 1949 to 2018. (Atmospheric pressure levels are often used to express elevation—850mb corresponds to approximately 1,500 meters, the average height of the Andes in this area.) I did not find an observable long-term change in wind speed. However, I did find that the "best summers" are associated with a negative (less than average) 850mb zonal wind anomaly, while the opposite is true for the "worst summers." Moreover, research suggests that in the Chaltén Massif, and generally south of 40°S, there is a positive correlation of 850mb zonal wind and precipitation in the mountain area (5). This means that a decrease in wind during the "best summers" is associated with a decrease in precipitation.

Together, these findings point to a shift in the climate between the mid-1970s and the 1980s, and an increased occurrence, especially in the last two decades, of high MSLP summer anomalies (characterized by below average winds and precipitation). This has profoundly benefited climbers. Although a multitude of factors have facilitated climbing in recent years, when average MSLP seasons occur hardly anything of note gets done. Conversely, the timing of previously unimaginable ascents seems to relate first and foremost to high MSLP seasonal anomalies. When climbers of old point out that climbing in the Chaltén Massif was harder in their time, they have a point.

So what happened at the beginning of the '80s that had such a big influence? Researchers agree that the recent changes of the AAO index can be attributed to the Austral summertime depletion of stratospheric ozone over Antarctica (the "ozone hole"), a phenomenon observed since the late 1970s, as well as the cumulative effect of the emission of greenhouse gases (from approximately the 1940s on). The long-term average of the AAO index is at its highest level for the past 1,000 years (2, 4).

State-of-the-art climate models predict that increasing greenhouse gases will lead to a continuing positive trend in the AAO index, dampened somewhat by the opposing effect of ozone hole recovery, initiated by the Montreal protocol agreement in 1987. This dampening effect is expected to end in midcentury with the healing of the ozone hole. After that, if greenhouse gas concentrations increase further, dramatic shifts in climate are expected for southern Patagonia (2, 3).

Regarding the wider arc of the Patagonian Andes, research suggests rather unequivocally that the surface air temperature is expected to rise over the entire area. There is less certainty regarding precipitation. During the summer months, the following trends are hypothesized: Precipitation increases are expected south of the center of the westerly wind belt, strongest at ~60°S but reaching northward to Tierra del Fuego; only slight precipitation changes are expected close to the center of the westerly wind belt, around ~52°S (just south of Torres del Paine); and precipitation decreases are expected farther north, strongest at ~45°S (around the northern Aysén Region) (5, 6).

Regarding the Chaltén Massif, its location just north of the center of the westerly wind belt means that, as the AAO index becomes more positive, we will see an increase in temperature and likely a general decrease in precipitation, again mostly during summer. Also, it seems reasonable to expect a continuation of the more frequent high MSLP summer events of the last two decades. These events result in long windows of good weather, paving the way for long link-ups and hard free climbing. However, as the last two seasons of poor weather have shown, this does not mean that El Chaltén will become a Caribbean beach and that every season will be "awesome."

Also, it's important to note that drier, warmer climate leads to a more unstable mountain environment, with more dangerous, difficult approaches and descents, and increased rockfall. The temperature will become a key variable for assessing objectives not only for the days of the planned ascent, but also in the preceding weeks. For example, in early 2016, after weeks of very high temperatures, a large piece fell off the Cerro Torre headwall, and, separately, a climber was killed by spontaneous rockfall on the east face of Cerro Fitz Roy. As often happens in life, when challenges diminish in one area, they increase in others. We won't get to have both sides of the coin.

ABOUT THE AUTHOR: *Dörte Pietron is a climber, physicist, and mountain guide, and is the trainer of the German Alpine Club's female young alpinists team. The author wishes to thank Dr. Panagiotis Athanasiadis, Kelly Cordes, Rolando Garibotti, Dr. Ricardo Villalba, Prof. Dr. Thomas Wagner, and Prof. Dr. Dave Whiteman.*

REFERENCES
1. Marshall, G. J., 2003: Trends in the southern annular mode from observations and reanalyses. *J. Climate*, 16, 4134–4143.
2. Thompson, D. W. J. et al., 2011: Signatures of the Antarctic ozone hole in Southern Hemisphere surface climate change. *Nature Geosci.*, 4, 741–749.
3. Gillett, N. P. & Fyfe, J. C., 2013: Annular mode changes in the CMIP5 simulations. *Geophys. Res. Lett.*, 40, 1189–1193.
4. Abram, N., 2014: Evolution of the Southern Annular Mode during the past millennium. Nature *Climate Change*, 4, 564-569.
5. Garreaud, R., P. Lopez, M. Minvielle, and M. Rojas, 2013: Large-scale control on the Patagonian climate. *J. Climate*, 26, 215–230.
6. Garreaud, R., M. Vuille, R. Compagnucci and J. Marengo, 2008: Present-day South American Climate. PALAEO3 Special Issue (LOTRED South America), 281, 180-195.

JEBEL MISHT

FORTY YEARS OF ADVENTUROUS CLIMBING ON OMAN'S MASSIVE LIMESTONE MOUNTAIN

GEOFF HORNBY

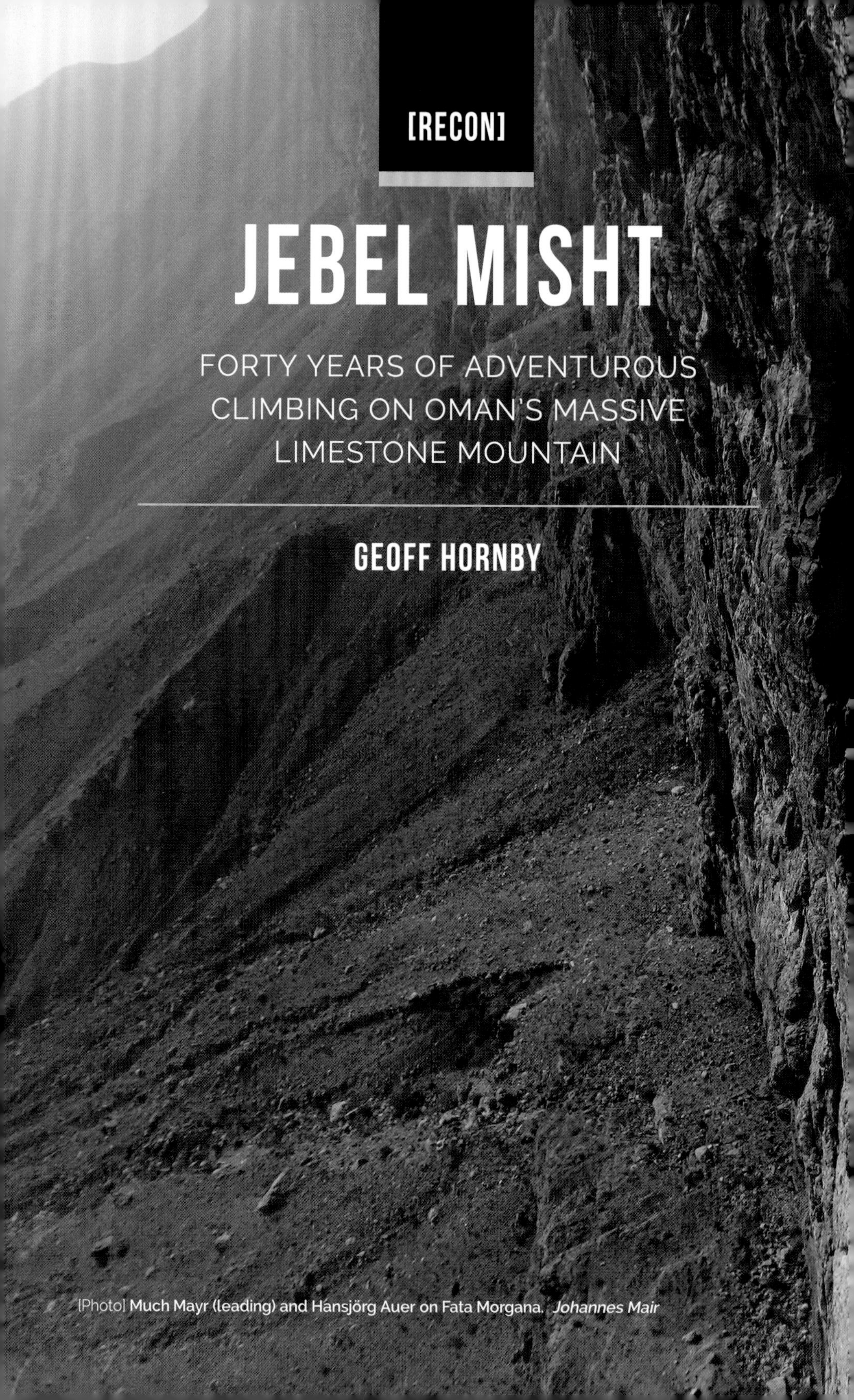

[Photo] Much Mayr (leading) and Hansjörg Auer on Fata Morgana. *Johannes Mair*

I was returning from a tough winter expedition in Nepal. It had been badly planned and badly executed, and all I had to show for it was some very cold bones. As I checked in at the Kathmandu airport, I asked for a window seat on the right side of the plane, as I fancied watching the sun rise as we flew along the southern coast of Iran. This was the pathway taken by Alexander's depleted army on its return from India.

I enjoyed that view, but my eyes really popped out of my head when we crossed the Strait of Hormuz and the plane banked over the Western Hajar mountains of Oman. In front of me unfolded a vista of limestone walls, thousands of feet high, as far as I could see.

Back home in England I started my research. This was 1999 and the Sultanate of Oman had thrown open its doors to tourists for the first time. By various means, a few climbers had made their way to the Western Hajar earlier, but the biggest walls had barely been touched. Eleven months after that plane flight, Susie Sammut and I flew into Muscat and started our own exploration. Over the next two years, we made repeated trips to Oman with British and American climbers and cherry-picked many of the obvious lines on the three great monoliths of the Western Hajar: Jebel Misht, Jebel Kawr, and Jebel Misfah.

These three peaks are comprised of a hard rock known as Exotic Limestone, eroded to produce complex mountain faces on all aspects. Kawr is nine miles long and three miles wide in places, with walls up to 3,000 feet, and Misfah has two long walls up to 1,500 feet high. But the jewel in the crown undoubtedly is Jebel Misht.

Misht is Arabic for "comb." As you look at the four-mile-long ridgeline topping Jebel Misht's southwest, south, and southeast faces, you cannot fail to notice the pinnacles running the length of the mountain—a ridge of comb teeth. The heights of these faces start at 1,600 feet, at either end, and top out just short of 4,000 feet in the central section.

I have always been a disciple of the great explorers of the Italian Dolomites—climbers such

as Ettore Castiglioni and Bruno Detassis, who roved across the range climbing up to three major new routes in a week. This was our opportunity to walk their path but in a newly developing, Dolomite-style range—and one with even more potential. The crown jewel of the Italian Dolomites, the Marmolada, is two miles wide, 2,600 feet high, and has well over 100 recorded routes. Jebel Misht is twice as wide and half again as high, and has fewer than half that number of routes. This canvas still has big spaces to be filled by those willing to brave the heat and unrelenting glare of the Arabian sun.

EARLY EXPLORATION

The French Pillar is the Nose of Arabia. A curving line that separates the two greatest faces of Jebel Misht, it was the target for a team of French guides led by Raymond Renaud in 1979. At that time, the French dominated climbing developments in the Sahara and the Middle East. The route was climbed over a three-week period with extensive use of fixed ropes and camps.

Other climbs in this period were made by climbers working or living in Oman. British climber Mike Searle spent his teenage years exploring both the Western and Eastern Hajar, making first ascents with whatever soldiers or oilmen could be persuaded to join him. After

Continued on page 104

The massive southwest, south, and southeast faces of Jebel Misht span about four miles. (A) The Towers sector. These formations and the Coxcomb to their west gave Jebel Misht its name—Misht means "comb" in Arabic. (B) South face, home to Fata Morgana (see previous photo) and many other serious routes. (C) Southeast face. The French Pillar tops out on the central prow. The steep face below is taken by Icarus, Shukran, Boys Don't Cry, and other major lines. The left side of the huge amphitheater at right is climbed by Physical Graffiti and Bayan Massir. The amphitheater's steepest face has never been climbed. (D) The Organ Pipes. *Will Saunders*

ICARUS

BY PAT LITTLEJOHN

THERE WAS STILL only one route up the center of Jebel Misht's highest face by March 2001 when Steve Sustad and I arrived in Oman, hoping to climb the very steep wall to the right of the original French route (1979). A 600-meter wall laden with overhangs leads to the base of the great pillar high on the cliff, which the French route skirts to the right. We reckoned that finishing directly up that pillar would give a great finale.

In Muscat we rented the cheapest 4WD vehicle we could find and headed straight for the mountains. The last 10 kilometers was a dirt track up to a farm, then it was real off-road over jagged scree and water-worn gullies to a camp spot just a couple of hours from the start of our intended line. On our first afternoon we lugged climbing gear to the base in ferocious heat and climbed through the first rock barrier to the base of the main face.

Studying the wall above, it seemed that all natural weaknesses were blocked somewhere by overhangs, so all we could do was pick the most promising line and give it a try. Once climbing, we were pleasantly surprised that the rock was basically excellent and well weathered, offering plenty of scope for natural protection and giving hope that even the more imposing sections might be climbable. Over two days we pushed the line for about 10 pitches. Looking ahead, there seemed to be a way around the left side of a huge roof 65 meters above us, as long as we could get to it. Feeling excited and optimistic, we abseiled off and walked back to camp in the dark.

Steve Sustad launches up 5.10 terrain on the first ascent of Icarus in 2001. *Pat Littlejohn*

Next day we needed to resupply, so we drove to the town of Ibri. We were back by the early afternoon and were invited into the farmstead below our camp to share their barbecue, a superb feast of roasted goat kebabs smothered in honey and butter and eaten with chapatis. It was the Muslim festival of Eid al-Fitr in Oman, and everybody was home with their families, having a good time. Fortified by this wonderful meal, we set off in the evening to bivouac below the face. We had three days of food and water with us and were going for the top.

An hour before first light, we forced down some bread and water and crossed scree to the start of the route. We climbed with packs because it was faster than hauling, but the extra weight made the pitches seem much harder, and it was after 2 p.m. before we reached our high point. Steve led off across an impressive wall, up some steep flakes to a stance in the middle of nowhere. The next pitch was clearly going to be harder, so I left my sack to haul later and set off across a compact wall. It was great limestone face climbing: little pockets and flakes with enough small wire protection to keep fear at bay. A hard groove led to the big crack system going round the overhang, and once there I knew the line was going to go.

Steve led a long, hard chimney while I looked nervously at my watch. By the time I was following the chimney pitch, it was dark. So far there hadn't been a single bivouac ledge along the route, and Steve's stance was no exception—just a couple of small footholds. To spend the night there would have been hell, so I grabbed the gear and led on through in more or less complete darkness. I was surprised how well you could get on by feeling all the footholds by hand, then using them from memory as you groped upward with your hands. Luckily it wasn't too hard, and by the time I was high on the pitch a big moon had come out and I was confident we could press on. By 9:30 p.m. we had reached the broken ridge taken by the French route, located a bivy site, and crashed out, exhausted.

Surprise, surprise, it dawned another fine day! (You get a lot of them in Oman.) The top didn't look far away, but this was the dreadful foreshortening of Jebel Misht. Three easy pitches took us to the base of the final pillar, a superb buttress more than 300 meters high. We considered different lines and opted for one that looked like it would have the fewest offwidth cracks. Some great pitches, mostly HVS/E1 (5.8–5.10), occupied us through the heat of the day, until about 80 meters below the top the rock got very compact. I tried to reach an obvious groove but ended up being forced left onto an open face. There was hardly any gear, and the climbing was sustained 5c (hard 5.10), but the pitch obviously had to go. It finished with a bold and airy section right on the crest. Steve got the last hard pitch, which also had its moments, and then we shot up easier ground to the wonderful summit plateau and—wait for it—a bloody great microwave tower!

We thought we were in with a chance of getting down by nightfall. The local farmer who had been so hospitable told us he had climbed Misht via a huge couloir system overlooking our camp. We figured if he could get up it, we could get down, especially with a few abseils. As we peered over the precipice, which was still well over 600 meters high at this point, we saw something moving at speed across the rocks. It was a tahr, a rare breed of mountain goat for which Jebel Misht is an important sanctuary. Now I've watched a lot of goats move on rock and a fair few chamois, but this creature was in a class of its own. It shot across 200 meters of terrifying terrain in a few seconds, then seemed to disappear into the mountain.

To cut a long story short, we tried every which way to get down the couloir and eventually gave up and settled for the long way home, down the north side and around the whole mountain. After another night out and six hours of trekking in crackling heat, we made it.

[Top] **Pat Littlejohn** starts one of the key pitches of Icarus: "little pockets and flakes with enough small wire protection to keep fear at bay." Night fell soon after Sustad followed the pitch. [Bottom] **Littlejohn** (left) and Sustad on the summit. *Steve Sustad*

Icarus was the first route to breach the steep left side of the southeast face. The 1,000-meter climb was graded E4 5c (run-out 5.10+/5.11-, more or less). Pat Littlejohn is a well-known exploratory climber and was the longtime director of the International School of Mountaineering, based in Leysin, Switzerland.

Arnaud Petit on the sixth pitch of Shukran, established in 2006 by Tyroleans Helli Gargitter and Paul Trenkwalder. With 1,000 meters of climbing and clean rock, the 5.10+ route is considered a modern classic. *Read Macadam*

Continued from page 101

graduating as a geologist from Oxford University, he returned to Oman repeatedly for work, and some of his climbs were the first forays onto the main faces on Misht. His 1983 route up the 4th Tower of the south face, climbed with Dan Coffield, Peter King, and Daniel Mithen, set a precedent for ground-up, single-push ascents that has largely been followed ever since.

In 1988, British desert climbing specialist Tony Howard received permission from the Omani government to carry out a mountain-tourism assessment project, and in the company of Alec McDonald he climbed the southeast pillar on Misht at 350 meters and 5.8. British expat Jerry Hadwin and Garth Bradshaw made the second ascent of the French Pillar in 1994, then added Southern Groove (1,100 meters, 5.9) up the right edge of the southeast face. This was the biggest route yet to be climbed ground-up and the first to breach the southeast wall.

These were the only lines climbed on Jebel Misht until just before the millennium.

GOLD RUSH

THE TEAMS OF British and American climbers that I lured to Jebel Misht from 1999 to 2001 were extremely productive, sometimes climbing several new routes in the same week, and always in a lightweight style relying on passive protection and no aid. More than a dozen long new routes were climbed over these three years.

During this period, the Cockscomb (southwest face) received its first attention, resulting in many free routes of 5.8 or 5.9 on a 500-meter wall. Easy access meant this wall became the place where many climbers would find their first footing on Misht.

These same teams climbed additional routes on the south face, with Threading the Needle (Paul Ramsden and Paul Eastwood), Madam Butterfly (Hornby and Aqil Chaudhry), and Snakes and Ladders (Hornby and David Wallis) weaving 700- to 750-meter lines among the broad towers on the upper face. Snakes and Ladders was named after Wallis was bitten on the ankle by a viper on the first attempt, while on the successful second attempt we were chased across slabs by vipers several times during the descent. During the first ascent of another route, Chaudhry and I had to dodge a large viper as it slithered down the crack we were jamming—a bit of a moment for both of us. If you climb here, you will almost certainly leave with your own snake story. My advice: Shout or sing to the cracks before you put your hands in them.

The pride of place in this period must go to the three imposing lines climbed on the 1,000-meter high southeast face. First blood went to Ramsden and visiting American Tom Nonis, in 1999, with Eastern Promise (5.10). Ramsden, Eastwood, and Chaudhry then produced the Empty Quarter (5.10). Not to be left out, Hornby and Wallis added the final obvious groove line of Intafada (5.9+). These same climbers also ascended the major pillars on neighboring Jebel Kawr during the same period.

MORE AND MORE CLIMBERS

THE PUBLICITY ABOUT these climbs in European magazines brought the first wave of interest from Swiss and Austrian climbers, initially organized by Oswald Oelz. He invited Albert Precht and Sigi Brachmeyer (both prolific developers of climbing in Wadi Rum in Jordan), and they climbed a number of new routes in late 2001. They in turn introduced Jakob Oberhauser, a young Austrian mountain guide, to the area. He fell in love with Oman, began working as a trekking guide, and became the driving force behind the next phase of development, eventually writing a guidebook to climbing in Oman, published in 2014.

Now the game shifted up a gear: harder grades, faster ascents, very bold leads, and eventually the introduction of a few pitons and bolts to protect the harder new routes.

In 2001 and 2002, two difficult routes went up adjacent to the French Pillar, incorporating steeper ground and more difficult climbing on the lower southeast face. The powerful British team of Pat Littlejohn and Steve Sustad climbed Icarus (1,000 meters, 5.10) over several days in March 2001, at the very hot end of the winter. Pat describes removing his rock shoes at every stance due to the heat being absorbed through the black rubber.

The next year, Oberhauser climbed his first major new route, the English Arête (5.10), with Brian Davison. It went up between the French Pillar and Icarus in an impressive 12-hour car-to-car blast up the highest part of the face. With the help of friends, they introduced a creative logistical tactic to deal with the 12-kilometer walk from the base of the north face descent back to the campsites on the south side: One team would drive a jeep and drop the climbing team off early in the morning and then pick them up on the north side at the end of the day. The next day the teams would swap roles. Oberhauser later pioneered a shorter descent between the southeast face and the Organ Pipes, but the north face remains the easiest way down in the dark. I've done it a dozen times, often hitchhiking back on school buses or other vehicles.

In 2003, a five-man German team led by Jens Richter produced a strong line up the southeast face with Make Love Not War (7b/5.12b). This was the hardest route on the mountain for many years and the first to make use of significant numbers of protection bolts, though the great majority of the pitches have few or no bolts.

Meanwhile, Oberhauser and Sepp Jochler were busy on the high right end of the south face, producing the very long Paradies der Fakire (1,500m, 5.10). The limestone here is so sharp that it cuts the hands, and leader falls could be a skin-shredding experience.

Three years later, in 2006, a pair of experienced desert climbers from Tyrol, Helli Gargitter and Paul Trenkwalder, added the modern classic Shukran (1,000m, 5.10+) up the middle of the southeast face. With clean rock and a logical, direct line, this is now the most commonly climbed route on the highest walls of the mountain—it has probably had 10 ascents to date.

In 2008 it was the turn of Slovenian climbers Pavle Kozjek and Dejan Miskovic, who raced up a new 5.10+, Yah-lah Sadikie, on the wall right of Make Love, reaching the summit in just nine hours—though they needed a full moon to make their way down the far side and back to camp. Miskovic then turned his attention, with Matej Knavs, to the big wall left of the French Pillar; they produced Kabir Hajar (5.11), topping out the 15-pitch route at 1 a.m., having used no hammered protection on either of the new routes.

Oberhauser had also tried a new route on the big face left of the French Pillar, climbing with Sepp Jochler; they reached a point about six pitches up in two different attempts, in 2003 and 2005. Oberhauser returned in 2008 and joined forces with Hansjörg Auer and Thomas Scheiber to complete the route: Flying Pegs (5.11+). Auer then came back the following year with Much Mayr and found a much harder route in the same area as Flying Pegs, starting farther left and finishing to the right. With two pitches of 5.13 (some bolt and piton protection but mostly trad), Fata Morgana is the mountain's hardest climb.

Jebel Misht seems to have the power to draw climbers back over and over again. In 2009, Miskovic returned to Oman and added two 1,300-meter 5.10s to the central part of the south face: Curry Power and Chilly Power, while Richter returned in early 2017 with Philip Flämig to climb Mitten ins Herz ("Straight to the Heart," VIII-/5.11c) through steep ground immediately left of Fakirs. Gareth Leah, who attempted a new route on the right side of the southeast face in 2010 but was badly injured by rockfall, returned in late 2017 with Sergio "Tiny" Almada to complete the line. Throughout this period, I joined Paul Knott and many others to add new routes to the various sectors of the mountain.

CLIMBING POTENTIAL

The four different faces of Jebel Misht are cut with grooves and hung with pillars that should provide new routes for the next two generations of climbers.

The very steep, roughly 300-meter section of wall that forms the right edge of the southeast face has been attempted several times by teams lacking the preparation or firepower to make the route. The first of these attempts resulted in the creation of Riddle in the Sands, a zigzagging line that was the logical escape from the difficulties of the unclimbed wall—and as a result has been repeated several times.

The broad 500-meter-high wall on the east face, above the village of Al Jil, has only eight routes in a mile width of rock. Known as the Organ Pipes, this is where some first-time visitors have added routes before stepping onto the mountain's bigger features. There is almost unlimited potential—enjoy the gaps at a grade to suit you.

For the 5.9 climber, there is a lot of potential for independent lines in the central and left-hand sections of the south face. The existing routes currently run to 900 meters and 5.8 to 5.10. Most routes follow logical grooves and crack lines, but there are many options for direct lines, as Tyroleans Simon Messner and friends discovered recently when they blasted a route straight

[Top] Sunrise at a no-shade campsite about two hours' walk from Jebel Misht's southeast face. *Simon Messner Collection* [Middle right] The author (lavender shirt) waits for sunset and *ifthar*, the evening meal that breaks each day's fast during Ramadan, with residents of the village of K'saw. *Geoff Hornby Collection* [Bottom right] The local water supply. *Lisi Steurer Collection* [Bottom left] Village elder in K'saw. *Geoff Hornby*

[Top] Twenty-one beehive structures line up in front of Jebel Misht's south face. Dated to 4,000 to 5,500 years old, they are said to be tombs, but no remains were found inside. [Left] Gareth Leah completing the new route Bayan Massir in late 2017, seven years after an attempt left him badly injured by rockfall. *Will Saunders*

DESTINY

BY GARETH "GAZ" LEAH

In 2010, I ATTEMPTED a new route on the southeast face of the incredible Jebel Misht. During the ascent, I was hit by rockfall, leaving me with debilitating injuries to my face and foot. My climbing partner, Hamza Zidoum, and I began a self-rescue that involved hundreds of meters of rappelling into the unknown. Then I crawled for hours through the desert until I was unable to continue. We sought help and I was eventually picked up by a military helicopter and airlifted to Ibri hospital.

I made a full recovery, minus an ankle that has since refused to bend up or down very much and a crescent scar across my left cheek, a constant reminder to live life to the fullest. Not being someone who gives up easily, I always dreamed that one day I would return to Oman and complete the route that had beaten me. In November 2017, I decided it was time to put my demons to rest. This time it would be with Sergio "Tiny" Almada, a climber with whom I've spent hundreds of days questing into the unknown on big walls.

The route we established started how we'd planned, but higher up it blanked out near the overhanging headwall on the right side of the face. Given our desire to complete the route in the purest trad style, we were forced to rappel and downclimb several hundred meters to a large ledge, where we spent a cold night. Having slept maybe two hours and shivered many more, we faced a difficult decision. After our retreat, we had only half our rack, plus some snack bars and half a liter of water each, with more than 700 meters of climbing to go. If we had to bail higher up, I didn't know if we could make it down with so little equipment.

One thing we did know was that in 2013 an Italian team had established a new route just a few meters to the left of our planned line (Physical Graffiti, Migliano-Schiera, *AAJ 2016*). With our options now limited, we decided we would cross their route, get around the roof that had forced us down, and rejoin our planned line higher up. We topped out just as the sun was setting, some 40 hours after starting, with no food or water. After another very cold night at the top, we walked down the back of the mountain in the morning. Our route shared a couple of pitches with the Italian line, but most of the way we deliberately climbed 5m to 10m away, following other crack features to keep it independent. Mainly, my goal was to complete the line that bested me, and I'm happy we succeeded.

The new route was named Bayan Massir ("Manifest Destiny," 1,045m, 5.11b X or E5 6a).

up the left end of the south wall in just seven hours.

There are a significant number of fierce pillars and headwalls in the mile-wide big wall between the French Pillar and Curry Power on the south face—in particular, the steep face and headwall right of Curry Power and the faces left and right of Kabir Hajar.

Perhaps direct lines on the southeast face, using a mix of trad and bolt protection, will be the new direction for harder lines on Misht. The Czech team that added Boys Don't Cry (1,000m, 7c+/5.13a) through the middle of the face in January 2016 showed the vision for a direct and independent creation, using 35 protection bolts in 21 pitches.

LOGISTICS

OMAN IS A stable and welcoming country. Indeed, the word "welcome" is probably the most commonly used in any meeting with Omanis. If you observe a polite dress code (long sleeves and pants in villages and towns) and behavior, refrain from overt use of alcohol, and follow low-impact approaches to camping, you will have no problems.

Commercial flights from any direction in the world will take you to Muscat, the capital of Oman. The city occupies a coastal strip that now extends for 50 kilometers, but your arrival into the international airport at Seeb places you conveniently at the start of the road to the interior.

Airport car rental agencies can provide both regular vehicles and 4WDs, while the adjacent supermarkets will provide all the food, water, and equipment you might need for extended camping. The nearest hotels to Misht are in Ibri and Bahla, about 50 kilometers away.

The road from Seeb travels over the Sumail gap, separating the Western Hajar mountains from the Eastern Hajar, before descending to the ancient interior capital towns of Birkat Al-Mauz and Nizwah and then passing Bahla. Provisions can be replenished in these towns. The road between Bahla and Ibri passes beneath the splendid walls and towers of Jebel Kawr before turning right into the valley of Al Ain. There's a stunning photo opportunity just as you pass the turning for Old Al Ain village as a line of 5,000-year-old beehive tombs provides a foreground image with Jebel Misht's south face in the background. Driving time from the airport is about four hours. Approaches from the United Arab Emirates can be made through Ibri.

All the faces on Misht are now accessible by paved road, but a 4WD will get you a couple of kilometers closer to the walls, which in turn allows you more privacy when camping. There are no regulations for climbing or camping in the area, nor is there any rescue service. Leave no trace practices should be the norm at the campsites and on the cliffs.

The climbing season is late November through late February, with December having the least chance of rain. All of the cliffs hold sun for hours—the southeast face starts heating up at the crack of dawn, while the southwest face catches the sunset's rays. Dealing with the heat and carrying enough water are significant challenges. My teams usually carry four liters of water per person, intending to finish the first liter before starting up the route. Start your approach two hours before dawn.

Climbing in Oman, by Jakob Oberhauser, includes descriptions and topos of all routes completed through 2013. The Oxford Alpine Club (*oxfordalpineclub.co.uk*) will producing a comprehensive guidebook to the limestone walls of Misht, Kawr, Ghul, and Misfah later in 2018.

ABOUT THE AUTHOR: *Geoff Hornby is a British adventure climber who has made 450 first ascents around the world, including 12 new routes on Jebel Misht. He splits his life between lecturing on safety engineering to universities and engineers in the U.K., working for the United Nations on specific projects, and living a mountain life in the Italian Dolomites.*

UNITED STATES

THE DRAWBRIDGE
A NEW ROUTE ON THE REMOTE NORTH FACE OF CASTLE PEAK

BY JASON SCHILLING

MORGAN ZENTLER IS a baller. Last year he finished the Bulger List, climbing Washington's 100 highest peaks, and his suffering knew no bounds. I've seen him pass out without a bug net or tent in a hideous swarm of mosquitoes, and I've picked him up after an epic Stehekin–Phelps Creek traverse that was the alpine equivalent of four marathons in a row.

Not yet satiated, Morgan set his sights on an extension of the Bulger List—the strictly defined Washington Top 100. [*Editor's note: The Bulger List generally employs a 400-foot prominence rule except in the case of volcanic subpeaks, such as Liberty Cap and Colfax Peak, where it uses an 800-foot prominence rule, and it allows some peaks with less than 400-foot prominence. The Washington Top 100 (P400) list employs a strict 400-foot prominence rule across the board. The two lists differ by seven peaks.*] We ticked Colfax Peak via the Cosley-Houston in May, and he followed that up with a rare ascent of Lincoln Peak, near Mt. Baker, several weeks later.

My tolerance for choss is limited, so it's infrequent that he and I can find overlapping objectives. But when he texted in late June and asked if I wanted to try a new route on the north face of Castle Peak (8,306'), I couldn't refuse. It was the last peak on his list, and I was due for a good North Cascadian adventure.

We approached from Canada via Lightning Lake in Manning Provincial Park, which involves climbing up and over Frosty Mountain. Encountering deep snow at treeline, we gained the crest just short of Frosty's summit and had our first views of Castle's north face. It was obvious that the face was snow-free enough for an attempt, so we descended into the States and the snowy Princess Creek basin before traversing up to the Princess–Crow Creek divide. Dropping into the Crow Creek drainage, we set up camp on the only dry spot on the ridge, two-thirds of the way down to the glacier at the base of Castle Peak's north face.

We scoped the face in the last few hours of light and worked out a reasonable line up the central north buttress. The first ascent of the north face proper was made in 1979 (Beckey-Nolting-Tindall, *AAJ 1980*). A formidable list of Cascade hard men and women have walked by this middle buttress over the past 30 years, and at least four more routes have been completed. We

The north face of Castle Peak in the North Cascades, showing the Drawbridge. The original route (1979) is just to the right. Three routes ascend buttresses to the left. Castle Peak is just one mile south of the Canadian border, and the easiest access is through Manning Provincial Park in Canada. *Morgan Zentler*

were curious why the plumb line below the summit remained untouched. We agreed on a safe and clean-looking line that would surpass the obvious roof that guards the lower third of the buttress.

The approach to the face at first light was easy, and we were climbing less than an hour from camp. Gearing up, we were paralyzed by the whizzing sound of falling and exploding rock. The first rays of sun had loosened choss on the upper slopes and sent down a barrage of stones, sailing overhead and cratering on the glacier. We hustled up easy fifth to get out of the firing line, setting up a belay at the base of an incredible-looking dihedral and multi-crack system.

Morgan took the lead on what would be the hardest pitch of the day. Encountering hard (possibly mid-5.11) climbing after 20m, he had to aid a short section. He traversed out of the dihedral on a tricky flake with thin pro and was soon at a flat belay ledge. I traversed left up a ramp and into a crack system that led into the roof, which was surmounted on fun but hard cracks and stemming. The pace slowed to a crawl as the next two pitches involved a lot of cleaning with a nut tool. Where there was moss, there was often hidden pro. At the top of pitch five, we did an obvious traversing pitch to the right to gain the ridge proper. With the exception of one short, harder hand and fist crack, the climbing was moderate and less stressful than the face below.

In typical Cascadian fashion, the last technical pitch involved dancing delicately around teetering blocks. After ten pitches, we emerged onto moderate snow slopes 400' feet below the summit and unroped for the 3rd- and 4th-class terrain to the top. We lounged on the summit, 14 hours after starting the climb, and took in the views of the Pickets, Hozomeen, and the lonesome peaks in the heart of the Pasayten.

The walk off the south side and east ridge was breezy, and we were back at camp as twilight faded. We celebrated with Scotch whisky and tunes on the speaker. Morgan had finished his P400 list in fine style and the walk out the next day felt entirely downhill.

Summary: First ascent of the Drawbridge (IV 5.10+ A1) on the north face of Castle Peak in the North Cascades.

Half Moon (7,960') showing the line of Uncle Wehrly's Toupee. The south face of Big Kangaroo is at far left. *Chris Mutzel*

WASHINGTON PASS, HALF MOON, UNCLE WEHRLY'S TOUPEE

IN JULY, CHRIS Mutzel and Jimmy Voorhis climbed a new line on the southwest end of Hai Tower, the right-most subpeak of Half Moon (as viewed from the highway), to the right of the route Digging for Dreams (*AAJ 2012*). The crux second pitch featured a gaping bomb-bay flare ("The Maw") that required horizontal stemming, crawling, and tunneling. Three more aesthetic pitches of finger cracks brought them to the top: Uncle Wehrly's Toupee (III 5.10-). An entertaining full account is at the AAJ website. 📄 📷

— INFORMATION FROM **CHRIS MUTZEL**

WASHINGTON PASS, LIBERTY BELL, LIVE FREE OR DIE!

IN THE PAST few years, the east face of Liberty Bell has seen several new variations and first free ascents added to the trio of original 1960s aid routes that evenly divide the wall. During a 2014 free ascent of Independence (5.12a, Bertulis-McPherson, 1966), I came across a beautiful two-pitch hand and finger crack that had recently been cleaned, and which featured bolted anchors and some protection bolts. These pitches were 700' up the wall and seemed to have been reached by rappel from other routes, as there was no obvious way to reach them from below. This crack is to the left of the Independence Route and to the right of Thin Red Line. Numerous inquiries failed to establish who had worked on these pitches.

Over July and August, Nathan Hadley and I used fixed ropes and top-down tactics to connect these crack pitches into additional terrain, yielding a continuous route of eight pitches up to M&M Ledge, from which four additional pitches to the summit are shared among other routes. We had originally hoped only to make a small variation to the Independence Route, but there kept being enough climbable features that we were able to construct a route sharing only 10–15m of

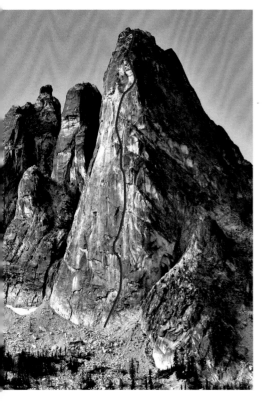

The east face of Liberty Bell, showing Live Free or Die! (5.12+), completed in 2017. Other routes on the face are not shown. *Blake Herrington*

climbing with the existing line. We called the route Live Free or Die! (1,200', 5.12+). It features mostly 5.10 and 5.11 thin face climbing, with a few short bouldery bits in the 5.12 range. The crux is a thin traverse that ends in a downclimb, with classically weird granite trickery. Independence also saw a couple minor hardware changes during this process: eliminating two hanging belays, adding hardware at two ledges (previously not used) for belays, and replacing a piton/copperhead combo with a bolt. These changes were made only after many days of climbing on the wall and out of desire to preserve the nature of the venue. 🔲

— BLAKE HERRINGTON

MORNING STAR PEAK, VEGA TOWER, WEST RIDGE, MARVIN'S EAR

DURING THE FOURTH of July weekend, a planned climb on Vesper Peak (6,214') turned into an alpine picnic due to my wife, Shelia, experiencing first-trimester morning sickness. But a piece of rock had caught my attention during our hike over Headlee Pass: Vega Tower (5,480'), a subsummit on the north ridge of Morning Star Peak (6,020'). [*Vega Tower is looker's right of Vegan Tower, another subsummit along the ridge that's home to the popular route Mile High Club (AAJ 2016).*] As best I could tell, the aesthetic west ridge appeared to be unclimbed.

A couple of weeks later, I returned with Imran Rahman. We scrambled up a gully to the right of our intended line and rapped down the crest, establishing the line from the top down. After a summer of hauling batteries and supplies, chucking choss, and dulling drill bits in the ultra-hard metaconglomerate rock, a seven-pitch alpine sport climb was ready for an attempt. On September 16, Shelia and I (along with our son now five months in utero) completed the first ascent of Marvin's Ear (800', III 5.10b). The route follows the skyline ridge of the tower, working through small roofs and overlaps and becoming quite exposed as it skirts over the north face near the top. Like Mile High Club, the climb is fully bolt-protected. In two of Tarantino's early films there is a Vega brother and a character named Marvin who loses an ear, hence the name. 📄 🔲

— MORGAN ZENTLER

SPEED RECORDS AND TRAVERSES

ON MAY 28, Andy and Jason Dorais set a fastest known time for Mt. Rainier's Liberty Ridge, approaching and climbing the ridge and skiing down the Emmons Glacier in 7 hours 7 minutes round trip from the White River Campground (5:57 to Columbia Crest). The Dorais brothers covered 21.3 miles and 11,222 feet of elevation gain. Just a few days earlier, Eric Carter, Nick Elson, and Colin Haley had set the previous FKT for the route, going 9:11 round trip.

Over the course of 34 days, from May 1 to June 4, longtime Cascade guides Trevor Kostanich and Forest McBrian skied from Snoqualamie Pass to the Canadian border through the heart of the North Cascades. Lowell Skoog Jr., chronicler of local ski mountaineering, called it "by far the most ambitious ski venture attempted in Washington's mountains, that I know of." The pair was joined for one week by a photographer and resupplied five times, but otherwise traveled self-supported. [*The Seattle Times published an excellent account, available online.*]

On August 7, Sean O'Rourke completed the Northern Pickets traverse (from East Fury to Challenger) in 28 hours 32 minutes round trip from the Ross Dam Trailhead. He estimated the total distance at 60 miles, with elevation gain over 15,000'. This was possibly only the third complete traverse of the Northern Pickets ridgeline and almost certainly the first in a push.

— ANDY ANDERSON, *COMPILED FROM VARIOUS SOURCES*

EL CAPITAN, THE DIRECT LINE

THE DIRECT LINE (39 pitches, 5.13+), a.k.a. the Platinum Wall, is a new, mostly independent free line up El Capitan. It begins just left of the Nose and continues up steepening blankness, following a circuitous path of 22 technical slab pitches before accessing the upper half of the Muir, either by the PreMuir or the Shaft. From where these two routes meet, it continues up the aesthetic upper Muir corner system to access wild and overhanging terrain on the right wall. Bolted pitches take you to the prow between the Muir and Nose, and the route finishes close to the original Muir.

In 2006, envisioning a possible variation to the Nose, Justen Sjong and I had explored multiple possibilities for exiting the Half Dollar on the Salathé Wall and finding some way to access Triple Direct Ledge, 80' below Camp IV on the Nose. Beginning in 2010, I picked up where we'd left off and began searching for the definitive free climbing path. During that hot and dry summer in 2010, it became clear there was a much more direct and independent way to climb the slabs to Triple Direct Ledge than using the Freeblast start to the Salathé. With that exciting realization, I just couldn't see finishing on the Nose, but instead envisioned a nearly independent route all the way up the wall. I took it on faith that there had to be a way to exit the Muir corner. Each tantalizing prospect on the upper wall would either yield a new approach or would clarify a dead end (which is also helpful). It never went as expected, but somehow different pieces of the puzzle started coming together.

Elliot Faber and I worked on the project from 2013 to 2015. We hand-drilled and established Standing Rock (5.13a), the first nine pitches that form the alternative to Freeblast. We also established the path of least resistance from Standing Rock to Triple Direct Ledge. We took turns catching long lobs into 3,000' of exposure, trying to unlock the beta for the last "hard pitch." In the early winter of 2015, we attempted a free ascent. The second free attempt was with Jay Selvidge in the fall of 2016, and it was then that I met Roby Rudolf (Switzerland), who joined me the following autumn for the send.

After hiking 30 gallons of water and 15 days of food to the summit and then caching it at ledges along the route, Roby and I began climbing on October 10 and spent 14 days on the wall, swinging leads and freeing every pitch. A one-day free ascent of the Direct Line is something I hope to witness in the next few years. [*An interesting description of Miller's tactics for climbing and hauling the route's middle section, which gains only 120m in eight pitches, is at Granitepage.com.*]

The Direct Line (39 pitches, 5.13+), left of the Nose on El Capitan. *Chris Falkenstein | Yosemiteprints.org*

— ROB MILLER

YOSEMITE VALLEY OVERVIEW

As usual, El Capitan saw considerable free climbing attention from an international cast. In the fall, Barbara Zangerl (Austria) and Jacopo Larcher (Italy) made the second free ascent of Magic Mushroom (VI 5.14a) in an 11-day push, while Hazel Findlay (U.K.) completed her fourth free route on the Captain with a send of the Salathé Wall (VI 5.13b). Keita Kurakama (Japan) made a nearly free repeat of the Nose (VI 5.14a), sending all of the pitches but returning to the ground for three days between climbing the two crux pitches, the Great Roof and the Changing Corners; he indicated he would return for a continuous free ascent.

In late October, Brad Gobright and Jim Reynolds snagged a new Nose speed record of 2:19:44, shaving nearly four minutes off Hans Florine and Alex Honnold's 2012 time. Honnold's article about his extraordinary solo of Freerider begins on page 12.

Nicolas Favresse (Belgium), with Alix Morris and Drew Smith, climbed Eye of Sauron (400m, 8 pitches, 5.13

Nicolas Favresse leading the wild crux pitch of Eye of Sauron, to the right of Ribbon Falls. The eight-pitch new route used no bolts. *Drew Smith*

a/b), a spectacular and difficult new trad line through a large cave just to the right of Ribbon Falls. The crux pitch is an overhanging elevator shaft out the roof of the cave that features three-dimensional climbing, thin laybacking, and splitter hand jamming for 40m. The route was done ground-up over two days without bolts, even for anchors.

In May, Bob Jensen and Josie McKee (with earlier help from Patrick Warren) completed a free variation to Hail to the Chief (V 5.9 A3 R, Bosque-DeWeese, 2016) on Lower Cathedral Spire. The new line, Long Live the Chief (10 pitches, 5.11 PG-13), climbs the first seven pitches of Hail to the Chief before branching left, eventually connecting with and freeing parts of the Upper North Face (Macdonald-Rowell, 1962). Steve Bosque and Kevin DeWeese, with help from Cameron Burns, finished a line on Higher Cathedral Rock called Generation Gap (5.9 A3) in June. The route starts on the first pitch of Wild Apes, then heads left and follows a sister system to the right of Learning To Crawl, before connecting to the last two pitches of Northeast Buttress. They suspect the route could go free with variations.

In May, Brandon Adams and Adam Ramsey climbed Make It So (8 pitches, V 5.8 A4) up the center of the Fifi Buttress, between Backburner (V 5.7 C3) and Final Frontier (V 5.13a/b). The route features extensive beaking.

Over 16 days in June, Jim Beyer soloed a new route on East Quarter Dome, Livin' the Dream (2,000', VI A5+). Beyer said the route bypasses good ledges and features huge runouts and beak belays; he placed no bolts, but the topo indicates a number of Zamac rivets. The route begins 300' right of Route of All Evil.

Vitaliy Musiyenko and Chris Koppl climbed two big new routes in Tenaya Canyon. Over four days in early September they started up Mt. Watkins' steep southeast face using a mix of direct aid and free climbing with difficulties to 5.10+/5.11. The route features extensive hooking, and blown placements resulted in several 50-foot whippers. The result was Cavity Dweller (VI 5.11- C4). They hoped this might be a start of a long free climbing project but concluded it's unlikely the line will go free.

Earlier, the two climbed Semper Farcisimus (IV 5.11) on Harding Tower. Musiyenko and Mark Westman made the first ascent of this slabby formation between Mt. Watkins and Yasoo Dome in 2016 (*see AAJ 2017*). On the new route, the two reported great slab climbing with intermittent cracks and flakes and zero loose rock.

– ANDY ANDERSON, *COMPILED FROM VARIOUS SOURCES*

CALIFORNIA / EASTERN SIERRA

DEER LAKES BASIN, NEW ROUTES

IN AUGUST AND October, Ray Eckland, Giselle Fernandez, and I established a dozen new climbs in the Deer Lakes Basin, south of Mammoth (John Muir Wilderness), an often-photographed alpine cirque at about 11,000', 5 miles from the road. All but one of our routes are found on the east face of Peak 11,600', a 150m escarpment of brilliant white Jurassic tuff rising directly above the south side of the uppermost Deer Lake. This broad feature is divided into three separate buttresses, which we named the Ivories for their abstract resemblance to a piano. We also climbed Slayer (170m, 5.10) on the northeast face of Peak 11,477'. A full report, including topos, is at the AAJ website. 📄 📷 🔍

– DEREK FIELD, *CANADA*

WHEELER CREST, NEW ROUTES

IN THE FALL of 2017, various partners and I established 10 new climbs, mostly six to eight pitches, in the steep canyons, cliffs, and towers of the Wheeler Crest. In general, we sought out the cleanest slabs and crack lines, as well as the few remaining unclimbed formations, including Sheepoopi Spire, Forgotten Tower, Torre Innominata, MOG Tower, and Haystack Needle. A full report with route descriptions and many photos is at the AAJ website. 📄 📷

– RICHARD SHORE

LONE PINE PEAK, BASTILLE BUTTRESS, BAD HOMBRES

ON APRIL 19, Myles Moser and I spotted an unclimbed snow and ice gully on the northeastern side of the Bastille Buttress, a 2,000' granite monolith that juts from the north ridge of Lone Pine Peak. With binoculars, we could see sections of thin ice connecting steep snow ramps in the deeply incised cleft. Increasing temperatures were forecasted, so we started from the trailhead at 3 a.m. the next morning.

We soloed the first few hundred feet of gradually steepening snow, which gave way to a section of WI2. Arriving at the base of a bomb-bay chimney at sunrise, we roped up for the crux pitch as meltwater droplets began to trickle from above. Myles gracefully led the physical, verglas-covered M4 chimney in crampons, scratching for holds with his ice tools. Above, easy snow ramps separated two pitches of thin and sun-rotted WI3. A final snow gully led to the end of the couloir, where two more pitches of mixed snow and decomposing fifth-class granite brought us to the summit. We were back at the trailhead by noon, and the temperature gauge in my truck registered 73° F. Most of the ice in the route had already fallen down.

The ephemeral 2,000-foot ice line Bad Hombres follows the obvious cleft to the right of the Bastille Buttress. Richard Shore and Myles Moser began the approach at 3 a.m.; by the time they returned to the car at noon, much of the ice was gone. *Richard Shore*

Having climbed many of the classic High Sierra couloirs, I feel that this is one of the very best. We felt like criminals for plucking such an obvious gem and narrowly escaping its collapse, so we named it *Bad Hombres* (2,000', WI3 M4). 📷

— RICHARD SHORE

LONE PINE PEAK, STONEHOUSE BUTTRESS, CREAM OF THE CROP

ON MAY 4, Myles Moser and I started a new route on the sunny south face of the Stonehouse Buttress, to the right of the Chimney Route (IV 5.8, Faint-Rowell, 1974). This formation in the Tuttle Creek drainage has largely been ignored after early ascents reported horrible rock quality. The fatal fall of a young woman here undoubtedly helped to seal its obscurity.

Amid the grainy choss, we found a clean section of good, varnished rock wandering up the central buttress. After breaking all of our drill bits and taking many big whippers from difficult hand-drilling stances on the first day, we retreated. We returned the next morning, armed with a beak that we used for aid while placing the free climbing protection bolts on the difficult second pitch—a long, left-leaning layback seam on a steep slab. A sustained 60m 5.10+ offwidth crack above guarded easier terrain that led to the top of a tower. Another pitch around to the right landed us at the base of our primary objective—a straight-in 5.11a thin-hands splitter on a grainy, vertical headwall. Halfway through our seventh pitch, we believe we joined the 1987 route Rots of Rock (IV 5.9 A2). We finished the climb in nine long pitches.

Amy Ness and Brandon Thau completed the second ascent that same day, hot on our heels, and we all rappelled the route together. Although we freed all the moves on the difficult second pitch, neither team succeeded in redpointing it. We believe this pitch will check in around 5.12. Our route linked some of the best rock and features on the formation, and we called it Cream of the Crop (1,200', IV 5.11+ A0). 📷

— RICHARD SHORE

Cartago Wall from the Crystal Geyser Crag, showing the line of Saddle Sores (1,600', IV 5.11a). Brian Prince and Richard Shore endured a five-hour bushwhack up Cartago Creek to reach the southeast-facing 1,600' cliff. *Richard Shore*

CARTAGO CREEK GORGE, NEW ROUTES

IN APRIL, THREE new routes were established on the large formations bordering the Cartago Creek Gorge, west of Highway 395 near the town of Cartago. On the 21st, Brian Prince and I hiked heavy loads deep into the gorge to the previously unclimbed Cartago Wall. This 1,600' southeast-facing cliff can be seen way back in the canyon from the highway. Much of the five-hour approach consisted of barefooted bushwhacking in the creek bed and polished fifth-class climbing around many waterfalls, all while being attacked by swarms of biting red ants. This approach ranks highest on my list of "Most Difficult and Unpleasant Hikes in California."

The following morning, Brian and I started up the logical and best-looking line, a crack system leading directly to the prominent northern subsummit of the Cartago Wall. We climbed the route in eight full 60m pitches, all of which were in the 5.10 range on high-quality granite, with a short 5.10+ offwidth crux at the start and a 5.11a roof at mid-height. We left no fixed gear on the climb and descended by scrambling down a ramp to the north and making many rappels off trees. An extra night's sleep and some pain meds were required before summoning the courage for the hike back down to the car. We called the route Saddle Sores (1,600', IV 5.11a).

On April 30, Peter Pribik and I climbed a new route on the Crystal Geyser Crag (a.k.a. Olancha Crag). This is the large formation visible from Highway 395 at the Crystal Geyser bottling plant in Olancha. Many buttresses or "towers" make up the cliff, and our seven-pitch route ascends the narrow buttress just right of the longest central one (also home to an excellent, unreported 11-pitch route called Hard Grit (IV 5.11 R), established by Myles Moser and Amy Ness in January 2016). Our line consisted of mostly moderate crack climbing on poor-quality, grainy desert granite. We called our route Sheriff Stanley (1,200', III/IV 5.10). After tagging the northern summit, we descended via double-rope rappels down a route on the buttress to the right. This line, Buckle Up Buckaroo (1,200', III 5.11), had been climbed just two weeks earlier by Moser, Ness, and Brandon Thau. In addition to the climbs mentioned above, four other unreported routes (both new and old, from five to eight pitches long) stretched across this broad formation as of early 2018. 📷

– RICHARD SHORE

MT. TYNDALL, JAHLOADA'S WITNESS AND CHORBLAMOS

IN MID-JULY, JON GRIFFIN, Gabriel Andres Mancilla Jipoulou, and I climbed two new routes in the Williamson Bowl of the Sierra Nevada. We first set our sights a prominent subpeak directly south of Mt. Tyndall (14,026'). We had dubbed this the First Pillar of Tyndall after the name of the only previous route on this feature, climbed by Urmas Franosch and Andy Selters in 2000. They had reported good climbing with a spectacular section of ridge up high. We planned to start up the buttress to the left and converge with their route at the stellar knife-edge. We climbed knobs and dikes to the base of a long right-facing dihedral (crux 5.10+), before extending up cracks and flakes to the magnificent knife-edge ridge, reminiscent of Wolfs Head in Wyoming's Cirque of the Towers. One last pitch up a small headwall at 5.9/5.10 brought us to the summit. We proceeded to the north, traversing the western slopes of Tyndall until we were able to descend the North Rib (third class) down to camp, completing Jahloada's Witness (8 pitches, IV 5.10+ R).

The next morning we returned to Tyndall and climbed a route up the far left buttress of the east face, between the East Gully route and the East Chimney (5.8). We climbed cracks and corner systems of all sizes to reach broken ledges leading to a chimney, which deposited us at the top of the face. After tagging the summit, we retraced our descent from the day before back to camp. The route is called Chorblamos (11 pitches, IV 5.10). 🖸

– TAD MCCREA

CALIFORNIA / KINGS CANYON NATIONAL PARK

CHARLOTTE DOME, DANCE OF DRAGONS

AFTER MAKING POSSIBLY the second ascent of Beast and Beauty (IV 5.11a), I returned to Charlotte Dome in July with Jeremy Ross because I'd noticed an intriguing set of parallel features to the left. The route we climbed turned out to be as good as all of the previous routes on this gorgeous alpine dome—stellar. Dance of Dragons (IV 5.11a) is close to 2,000' long with several pitches of varied 5.10 and a crux of 5.11a. The route mostly protects with natural gear in intermittent cracks, but also required several bolts to protect some difficult face climbing. 🖸

– VITALIY MUSIYENKO

NORTH COTTER, VERTICAL ILLUSION

A YEAR PRIOR to getting into technical rock climbing, I saw the sheer northeast wall of North Cotter (ca 12,560') while hiking to Mt. Gardiner and Clarence King. A few years later I saw Galen Rowell's 1973 *AAJ* report, describing the only known route up this remote wall. In the summer of 2017, I revisited the area with Chaz Langelier.

We approached from the Onion Valley trailhead, camped a short distance from the base of the wall, and chose a line left of the original route. The middle section didn't look rich with cracks, but it turned out that we were able to connect corners and cracks with a few sections of run-out low fifth class. Some of the best climbing on the route included a left-facing corner with a wild overhang and solid finger cracks up the red headwall on the last pitch. The steep, blank wall had only been an illusion—we found plenty of climbable features on Vertical Illusion (III/IV 5.9+). To descend, we scrambled down to a saddle and continued up the northeast ridge (varied 5th class) to the main summit of Cotter, then descended the eastern slopes. 🖸

– VITALIY MUSIYENKO

SPHINX LAKES, NEW ROUTES

IN EARLY AUGUST, Tad McCrea, Jon Griffin and I left Road's End and hiked into the Sphinx Lakes, where we established three new routes on various peaks in the area. After setting up camp at one of the upper lakes, we hiked up and over an unnamed pass east of Sphinx Lakes to

The Sphinxter (1,400', IV 5.10+) ascends the obvious sunlit arête on the north face of an unnamed peak above the Sphinx Lakes. *Whitney Clark*

reach the unclimbed northeast face of North Guard (13,327'). We followed a striking arête for eight pitches until we were able to gain a ridge that led to a final headwall. We named the route Jah Chosstafari (1,200', IV 5.10).

Getting off the peak was quite the challenge, as we had to scramble down thousands of feet to the south into a different drainage, walk a few miles west, and find our way up and over Sphinx Pass and back into the Sphinx Lakes basin. We descended a little too far in the dark, but luckily the moon rose full and we were able to find our way back to camp around 1 a.m.

After a rest day, we decided to climb a beautiful peak that rises directly above Sphinx Lake. Although the peak lies along the mile-long ridgeline west of North Guard's summit, it seems to have its own prominence. Our route followed an obvious arête, which led straight up the center of the north face, with some incredible climbing on corners and cracks up to 5.10+. We named the route the Sphinxter (1,400', IV 5.10+) and believe the peak was unclimbed. We walked off the backside and repeated the trek up and over Sphinx Pass to return to camp.

The following day we hiked over to Mt. Francis Farquhar (12,893') and climbed a new six-pitch route on the northeast face, starting with a tricky 5.10 face climbing to gain a splitter wide crack. We stemmed and groveled our way up until the crack narrowed to perfect fists for 50', then continued up along a shallow prow in the middle of the face to the summit: Only Cheese (800', III 5.10). 📄 📷

— WHITNEY CLARK

WALES LAKE PEAK, HIGH FASHION

IN LATE AUGUST, Jon Griffin, Tad McCrea, and I hiked into Wales Lake in search of steep unclimbed rock. We hiked via George Creek, which involves 6,000' feet of elevation gain to Vacation Pass and 2,000' down to Wales Lake. Our efforts were rewarded with a pristine lake, sandy beaches, and complete solitude for the four days we spent there.

On our first day, we attempted a 1,000' east-facing wall above Wales Lake via a striking crack that angled left across the face and up into steep dihedrals. We encountered great climbing up to 5.11 for six pitches before it got dark and we decided to rappel.

After a day of exploring the basin and relaxing on a white sand beach, we climbed the east side of an attractive peak to the left of the first line we attempted. We encountered continuous pitches of 5.10 climbing, following cracks and corners straight up the middle of the face. The route started with a beautiful right-facing dihedral, which slowly widened to offwidth. After a short leftward traverse, we followed a corner and chimney system all the way to the summit. We were glad to have two number 4s and a number 5.

Upon reaching the top, we found a tiny pill bottle stuffed with paper documenting two previous ascents of the peak. In the '70s (and later in the '90s), a team had walked up the backside and named the mountain Wales Lake Peak. We were likely the first to climb the technical east face, and we called our route High Fashion (1,000', IV 5.10+). [*These formations are part of the mile-long ridgeline extending northward from 13,494' Mt. Hale.*] 📷

— **WHITNEY CLARK**

MORO ROCK, METEORA

IN 2016, DANIEL Jeffcoach and I started a new independent line in the middle of the steep west face of Moro Rock. Due to sustained difficult climbing and the need to place several bolts, we could not finish the route in a day. The following day, we climbed the upper portion of the wall from the midway ledge but could not free several pitches of the route. Daniel was not so interested in working on the free ascent, so I returned a few times on my own, and then, in the spring of 2017, Brian Prince and I made a completely free ascent of Meteora (1,200', 8 pitches, IV 5.11c/d). The route has great climbing on exceptional rock, and most of the pitches are nearly 60 meters. 📖 📷

— **VITALIY MUSIYENKO**

Vitaliy Musiyenko traversing out steep slab during the first free ascent of Meteora (5.11c/d), a new independent line on Moro Rock. *Brian Prince*

CASTLE ROCKS, NEW ROUTES AND TRAVERSE

IN THE SPRING of 2017, Daniel Jeffcoach and I hiked out to climb the west face of the Fin, which to our knowledge had never been attempted. We took a wide system down and around the corner from the wide system of the North Buttress (IV 5.10). We climbed seven full 70m pitches up cracks of all sizes with good rock: The Cutting Edge (1,000', IV 5.9). This is now the easiest route up the Fin, and it does not involve run-out face climbing.

On the following day, Daniel and I traversed the Castle Rocks ridgeline from north to south. I do not know how many of the spires had previously been climbed via their northern ridges, but we summited all of the main formations and subsummits, including Amphitheater Dome and the Axe.

I returned to the Fin a few weeks later with Jeremy Ross and climbed a fun route that started up a steep crack system just right of the Cutting Edge. The route features quality face climbing and fun corner systems, providing a good mix of challenges, and we placed only three lead bolts. We called it Super Totally Trad (1,000', IV 5.11a).

After mentally preparing myself for a real battle, I was back in the late spring with Chaz Langelier to climb a direct line on the east face of the Fin. Tainted Love (IV 5.11a R/X) has more sustained and even higher quality face climbing than the classic Silver Lining (IV 5.10 R) to the right. Unfortunately, bolting on the lower route slowed us considerably, and I led the last three pitches of face climbing by headlamp, with only about six bolts remaining in our kit. This resulted in very run-out upper pitches, with potential for severe injury. I am planning to return to add bolts to the upper pitches and make this climb more manageable. 🖼 📷

— VITALIY MUSIYENKO

BEAU-TE CACHE DOME, FANTOMAS; HAMILTON DOME, OPHELIA

AFTER HIKING APPROXIMATELY 17 miles from Crescent Meadow, Chaz Langelier and I climbed Fantomas (1,100', III 5.8) up a previously unclimbed (to my knowledge) dome just west of Hamilton Dome. We called it the Beau-Te Cache Dome. This is an amazing moderate route with a mix of face and crack climbing, without huge run-outs. The following morning we got up half an hour before dawn and, after a quick breakfast, approached the southwest buttress of Hamilton Dome and climbed a new route with about 1,200' of stellar rock and a good mix of crack and face. Ophelia (III 5.9+) is named as a companion for the nearby Hamlet Buttress. 🖼 📷

— VITALIY MUSIYENKO

NEVADA / RED ROCK NATIONAL CONSERVATION AREA

MT. WILSON, TICKLED RIB

IN EARLY OCTOBER, Tom Bohanon and I spent several days climbing moderate classics in Red Rock Canyon. The rock climbing was exquisite, but the mountaineer in me yearned for something more adventurous. Bo was keen to travel new ground too.

On October 7 and 8 we climbed the prominent buttress to the left (south) of South Gully on the east face of Mt. Wilson's south peak. We started up a steep hanging chimney on the left side of the rib and climbed eight pitches up cracks, grooves, and chimneys to an easing where the rock transitions in color from crimson to yellow. We bivouacked on a good ledge and next day climbed eight more sustained and varied pitches to gain the south ridge. From there we scrambled up to and over Mt. Wilson's south and main peaks before descending First Creek Canyon. We called our 16-pitch route Tickled Rib and graded it 5.8+. 📷

— SIMON RICHARDSON, *SCOTLAND*

SANDSTONE CANYON, LONG NEW ROUTES

WHEN I ARRIVED in Red Rock in early October, it was still warm and I had trouble finding consistent partners, so on off days I would venture out in the canyons with a pair of binoculars to scout potential new routes. In Sandstone Canyon I found entire walls of mostly virgin crack systems. [*Editor's note: Sandstone Canyon lies between Black Velvet Canyon and First Creek Canyon and has long been overlooked due to the mouth of the canyon being owned by Spring Mountain Ranch State Park, which prevents access. Mountain Project lists several legal ways to access the canyon.*] I quickly made plans with Zack Lovell to check out a continuous line on one of the large north-facing walls near the mouth of the canyon that I dubbed the Wave. After about 750' of climbing we met up with a large fourth-class ramp system that we descended: Green Eggs and Sam (750', 6 pitches, 5.9).

With several different partners, I also put up a handful of new routes on and near the north-facing Gecko Wall, which is home to one of the few published routes in the canyon, the Golden Gecko (1,500', III 5.9). These routes included the Bolt (800', 6 pitches, 5.9), Jolly Roger (1,200', 7 pitches, 5.9), A Pirate's Life (500', 5 pitches, 5.11b), and Cthulu Rises (800', 6 pitches, 5.9). After climbing Chtulu, we topped out on the Gecko Wall and decided to continue up the summit ridge despite 60 mph winds. The final pitch went up the summit tower above the Wave, where we were a bit surprised and excited to find no evidence of previous traffic. The name Siren's Arete (600', 5 pitches, 5.8) seemed fitting.

I then set my eyes on a striking diagonal crack system that splits the intimidating upper wall on the Wave. To approach, Andy Stephen and I scrambled up the ramp Zack and I had used to descend from Green Eggs and Sam. From the top of that route, we traversed about 100' to the left to the diagonal cracks, which proved surprisingly moderate and continued all the way to the summit ridge: The Wave (1,000', 7 pitches, 5.7). If you link Green Eggs and Sam into the Wave you'll have a fun romp of about 1,700' of technical climbing.

– SAM BOYCE

MT. WILSON, AEOLIAN WALL, THE WICKED

IN THE FALL of 2016, Kyle Willis and I climbed the crack system to the right of the classic Inti Watana to create Dream of Wild Cheeseburgers (IV 5.9+, *AAJ 2017*). Still convinced of the potential on this wall, Kyle, Royal Magnel, and I decided to scope out the more difficult looking line to the left of Inti Watana. After climbing the first four pitches and experiencing a few close calls with loose rock, we decided to have a look at the upper part of the route before climbing it. We climbed Inti Watana, traversed into our route, climbed the last two pitches, and then established a rappel down the route using natural anchors and nuts. This gave us an opportunity to clean several death blocks.

At this point the route was primed for an ascent, with a sizable chunk that had yet to be climbed. But, as things go, both Kyle and Royal had to return to work. A week later I went back to the route alone. I rope-soloed the full route to the top of the wall, then spent the night scrubbing on rappel. The Wicked (1,000', 8 pitches, IV 5.11a) is a stellar and challenging natural line, and, as with Inti Watana, you can join Resolution Arête for another 1,500' of climbing to the summit of Mt. Wilson.

– SAM BOYCE

ARIZONA

SEDONA, VARIOUS NEW ROUTES

MOTIVATED BY THE vast potential for moderate traditional adventures and inspired by a solid group of like-minded partners, over 14 months I helped establish more than two dozen new routes, from one to four pitches, on and around the fantastic sandstone spires of the Sedona area. Most of these lines were done ground-up, employing a hand drill to install bolts where needed. Many were then retrofitted for future climbers. Topos and additional beta for all of these climbs can be found on Mountain Project, and a full summary is available at the AAJ website.

– DEREK FIELD, *CANADA*

Karl Kvashay climbing the first pitch of Morphology (IV 5.12+) on Tucupit Point in Zion's Kolob Canyons. *Brandon Gottung*

KOLOB, TUCUPIT POINT, MORPHOLOGY

THE DEVELOPMENT OF Morphology began in April 2015, when Karl Kvashay aid-soloed the first two pitches, following aesthetic thin seams, as a direct start to Tucupit occidentalis (800', 5.10+, *AAJ 2016*). The final version of that route started with the first two pitches of the old Forrest-March (5.8 A2, *AAJ 1982*). Karl and I later returned to his original start and added bolts to protect difficult face climbing while not significantly altering the natural aid line. We called these the Dimorph pitches—both eventually went free at 5.12, with bolt protection followed by thin wires and small cams.

Above this, Morphology follows the previously established Red Morph variation to Tucupit occidentalis for two pitches: a 60m 5.10 wide system and a beautiful 5.11 tips crack. I established the fifth pitch, dubbed the Geomorph, in spring of 2017, with Petrouchka Steiner-Grierson. I quickly realized it was beyond my abilities to free. However, after whipping around on some deeply set pins, I found just enough texture and one crucial bomber hold to warrant some drilling, and I placed three lead bolts. After the fifth pitch, the route links into the last pitch of Tucupit occidentalis.

After listening to me enthusiastically spraying about the high-quality rock on Tucupit for two years, Aaron Livingston finally rolled into Kolob in the fall to confirm. After climbing Tucupit occidentalis, he spent one day working the new route in a ground-up effort. I rushed out for my birthday to support him as he made the first continuous free ascent of this bold, direct line. With the Dimorph, Geomorph, and Red Morph pitches already named, we called the route Morphology (IV 5.12+)—six pitches of Tucupit goodness. 📷 🔍

— BRANDON GOTTUNG

KOLOB, TAYLOR CANYON, JUJ MONSTER

DURING A STRETCH of good weather in March, Mike Brumbaugh and I established a new route on the red sandstone of the North Fork of Taylor Canyon. I had been eyeing a potential line on a south-facing wall, just past the old cabin on the park trail, for a few years. It took us two days to climb seven pitches to the top, hand-drilling anchor bolts and about a dozen protection bolts. We came back in April to free the route. Two roof cruxes through extremely exposed terrain were the highlights of the climb: Juj Monster (7 pitches, 5.12). There was even a huge ledge at half height where we could stop, rest, and enjoy the views. 📄 📷 🔍

— ROB PIZEM

MT. KINESAVA, SLAM PANTHER!

IN APRIL, JONATHAN Schaffer and I climbed a ground-up new route on the north face of Mt. Kinesava. Slam Panther! (400m, 5.11) is a Zion adventure that takes an obvious line in the middle-right of the cliff. [*At least one other route has been completed by an unknown party on the north face of Kinesava, to the left of Slam Panther! Fasoldt also has attempted a prominent red pillar to the right, but was shut down by blank sections that would require a bolt ladder.*] The approach heads up a broad wash about an hour up the Chinle Trail—you are now officially in cougar country. After five minutes, a narrower wash leaves to the right. Rest assured that panthers notice your every step as you continue up this wash for about 35 minutes. [*Find more details on this approach at the AAJ website.*]

The route begins with a big, black left-facing corner. The first pitch, at 5.11, is likely the crux, featuring stemming and laybacking. If cleaned, it would go with less effort. From the ledge atop the first pitch, walk right for 30m to an obvious feature of cracks and corners. Some more shuttling up high leads to a run-out white face, which leads eventually to the top. We placed two protection bolts and left no fixed anchors. The easiest way down is the normal scramble on the east face (as for Cowboy Ridge).

– PETE FASOLDT

MINOTAUR TOWER, SUBURBAN BLONDES, FIRST FREE ASCENT

Suburban Blondes (IV 5.9 C2+) is a relatively obscure aid route up the 850' Minotaur Tower, which rises along the broad wall between Angels Landing and Moonlight Buttress. The route was established in April 1979 by desert legend Ron Olevsky and Scott Fischer.

On March 6, Caleb Lichtenberger and I crossed the freezing Virgin River and began working on a potential free ascent. With around 100' of simul-climbing, Caleb and I were able to link the first three pitches and free the route's first question mark, a C2 offwidth roof, at mid 5.11. At the start of the fourth pitch, we worked on a traverse into a thin crack system to the right, top-roping off the aid route's pendulum anchor, resulting in a few violent swings back into the main corner. Eventually we found a 5.12 face sequence and the following day added two bolts to protect this traverse (much lower than the aid traverse).

On March 8 we started early and soon were back at the ledge below what we hoped would be the crux. I was able to free the traverse and then the steep finger and tips splitter, a 5.12+ pitch. Caleb tried twice but was unable to link it clean, and we agreed I should try to finish off the next pitch (rated C2). This went at 5.11 R, and then Caleb led

Pat Kingsbury nears the end of the crux pitch during the first free ascent of Suburban Blondes. *Parker Cross*

a beautiful lichened dihedral (Caleb's Corner), also rated C2 and also around 5.11 R as a free pitch. A short, vegetated 5.8 lead with almost no pro brought us to the summit.

– PATRICK KINGSBURY

THE LABYRINTH: *Over the course of 2015 and 2016, Joel Enrico, Steffan Gregory, Ethan Newman, Alan Thorne, and Rob Warden completed a new line on Minotaur Tower that was not previously reported in the AAJ. The Labyrinth (6 pitches, 5.11 C1) climbs the north face of the tower and meets up with Suburban Blondes on the ledge below the summit block.*

THE WATCHMAN: SURF'S UP AND FREE ASCENT OF CRADLE TO GRAVE

In March, I finished a new free line on the west face of the Watchman called Surf's Up (1,000', IV 5.12-). Earlier, I'd spotted a striking splitter on an upper buttress that stares you directly in the face from the Central Pillar of the Watchman or the campground below. In October 2016, Ethan Newman and I started on a wide hand crack established by Brad Quinn and then climbed two more pitches to gain a large, vegetated ramp below the upper buttress. (We later learned that two parties had reached this same ramp earlier but hadn't climbed the upper wall; details are at the *AAJ* website). Ethan and I continued the route for seven more pitches. The headwall crack features a continuous splitter for 260', just barely wide enough to climb above the belay ledge. The middle of the crack opens to various sizes of splitter hands—second to none. We returned two more times that fall and freed all but the crux 20' of tips crack. In March, I redpointed this crux pitch at 5.12-.

Another line on the west face of the Watchman, Dave Jones and Brian Smoot's Cradle to Grave (10 pitches, IV 5.11 C2), had been on my to-do list for a long time, as this acclaimed duo has quite the reputation in Zion for quality routes. Armed with my friend Alan Thorne's motivation for wide cracks, we headed up on April 26 to give it a try. The route is quite wide and fun, with no shortage of Zion adventure climbing. Alan led the 5.11- offwidth in style, and I was able to redpoint the route's one section of aid, on the eighth pitch, on my second try (5.11+ R). This pitch hosts some very fun corner climbing, and the last 15' are a bit run-out without tiny wires or a red ball nut—exciting pieces for Zion sandstone, even in the best placements. 📄 📷 🔍

— STEFFAN GREGORY

JOHNSON MOUNTAIN, TRUE BELIEVERS

Over the course of several years, with myriad different partners, I established a new route on Johnson Mountain (6,120'), just south of the Watchman formation in Zion National Park. True Believers (800', III+ 5.11 C2) follows an obvious corner system on the mountain's north face and climbs 500' of technical terrain, with another 300' of scrambling to the summit. The name refers to a *Rock and Ice* article about Zion climbing written by Bryan Bird and titled "True Believers." 📄 📷 🔍

— STEFFAN GREGORY

VARIOUS FIRST ASCENTS AND TRAVERSES

Alone or with various partners, prolific Zion explorer Dan Stih made the first known ascents of more than 10 summits in 2016 and 2017, as well as several significant traverses. Space does not allow an account of all his activity, but a full report and photos will be found at the *AAJ* website. Highlights included the first ascent of North Bishopric, which required seven outings into the Zion backcountry and involved the likely first ascents of two other formations along the way. Stih also did the first known ascents of several Towers of the Virgin, north of the Altar of Sacrifice or Meridian Tower; these include Lancelot, Corbin Castle, Joyous Gard, and Sky Island. From September 15–18, he rope-soloed a new route on the southeast face of Cathedral Mountain: Iron Curtain (5.10 A3+), an add-on to a complex traverse around the formations surrounding the Emerald Pools that he had completed a month earlier. See our online report for details of these and other first ascents. 📄 📷 🔍

— INFORMATION FROM DAN STIH

MT. SPRY, HINTERSANDS

OVER MULTIPLE TRIPS from December 2017 to February 2018, I established and freed a new route on the steep southeast face of Mt. Spry. Hintersands (900', IV 5.12) is almost completely hidden from view on the tunnel road; I spied the line while climbing Lovelace (a.k.a. Fang Wall, IV 5.12+) on East Temple a year earlier. Over Christmas I found myself partnerless, and not wanting to waste precious days away from my desk-based career in Salt Lake City, I decided to head toward Zion alone. Over three days, I rope-soloed Hintersands ground-up at 5.10 A2, establishing three pitches per day and fixing back down to the ground each night. I aided or French-freed as necessary to get the rope up, while cleaning sand and trundling many blocks. Pitch three involved nailing a seam to hand-drill lead bolts; this is the only pitch with fixed protection,

Ethan Newman leads into the Flake Tunnel on pitch eight of Hintersands (900', IV 5.12). Brent Barghahn put up the route rope-solo over three days in late December 2017 and returned twice in early 2018 to free the line at 5.12. *Brent Barghahn*

and it now allows clean ascents. I left Zion suspecting my new line might just go free.

I piqued interest in my friend Andy Anderson for a free attempt. Our effort in mid-January left us exhausted, both physical and mentally. We found calorie-intensive wide climbing on every pitch, combined with challenging movement on friable holds. I freed up to the final pitch but only managed to one-hang this pitch's overhanging 5.12 laybacking to a horizontal roof, despite multiple tries. We drove home leaving Hintersands nearly free at 5.12- A0.

There was time for one final attempt before seasonal falcon nesting closed the wall. I teamed up with Zion local Ethan Newman, and we found the route surprisingly more stable than the previous attempt, as many of the most friable holds had peeled away.

I once again arrived at the last pitch with no falls. The first two attempts at the final roof ended when I was unable to keep tension on an undercling with opposing foot smears. On the third and final try for the day, I found myself at the marginal rest above the pumpy layback, staring across the roof traverse, trying my best to ignore the deep fatigue. I worked into a shallow stem and a thin hand jam, but I couldn't securely reach a jug around the roof. I wound up for a dramatic, feet-cutting deadpoint and stuck the jug, heel hooked the lip, and pressed out a bouldery mantel.

As a free climb, Hintersands presents a wild array of movement including multiple heel hooks and knee bars—unique fare for a Zion wall. All pitches have fixed anchors to rappel the route. 📷 🔍

— BRENT BARGHAHN

SAN RAFAEL SWELL, BROOMSTICK BUTTRESS, CROSSROADS

PROLIFIC UTAH ROUTE developer Bill Ohran recalls ripping down a dirty desert road in the San Rafael Swell in the mid-'90s, blaring Henry Rollins in his Chevy Nova. Unable to find a climbing partner, but with a strong desire to disconnect from the horizontal world, he went for the next best thing—aid soloing. On a distant buttress, a small seam led to an irresistible 125' fingers-to-hands crack, which Bill established as Disconnect (2 pitches, A2), though he stopped short of the summit, which was guarded by a long offwidth chimney.

Twenty years later, the music is different and the Chevy is a slight upgrade, but the charm of the Swell remains, drawing in a new crew looking to escape and explore. Mark Evans and I arrived at the 500' Broomstick Buttress (named for the broom-like pillar in the center) with the goal to create a free climb that incorporated the stellar corner on the second pitch of Disconnect and continued to the summit.

The initial attempts went ground up, mostly on good crack systems. However, virgin choss always has its exciting moments. I took a surprise rope-solo whipper while bolting a new traverse pitch into Disconnect. Later, after giving my partner a solid choss bath as I bumped a tipped-out number

Mark Evans finishing up the mega fourth pitch on the new route Crossroads (5 pitches, 5.11+). The route incorporates parts of two previous routes, creating the first free line on Broomstick Buttress. *Greg Troutman*

6 up the offwidth, I was disappointed to find the crack not only widened but steepened. A case of the "over its" kicked in—the ground-up attempts ended a mere 30' from the summit. However, while being lowered, I noticed the face to my left was full of solid edges.

A year later I hiked to the top and rappelled that upper face, discovering exposed gymnastic climbing on small edges. Even on rappel, bolting the path of most awesomeness was no easy task, as a desert storm and 40mph winds rolled in. This route didn't want to give it up easily.

Two years after our first attempt, Mark and I returned for the FFA of Crossroads (5 pitches, 5.11+). The name comes from the fact that we crossed or incorporated two other routes in the creation of ours (the first half of the first pitch is an unknown 5.10). It was also derived from our mind-sets at the time, after spending the winter wandering the jungles of Chile in search of large granite walls, with no real life goals except to continue upward. Perhaps Bill had a similar mind-set 20+ years earlier—a need to "Disconnect" from the horizontal world and all its expectations and obligations. [*The original Disconnect was later free climbed by Jon Winiasz and Evans. Notes on this and other new routes in the Swell are in the online version of this report.*] 🗒 📷

– GREG TROUTMAN

FISHER TOWERS, COTTONTAIL TOWER, LINE IN THE SAND

AFTER SHARING ADVENTURE stories and pictures of chossy towers one night in the fall of 2015 with the legendary Richard Jensen (of Wings of Steel fame), we envisioned a Fisher Towers climbing project that unexpectedly ended up spanning three trips over two years. In the spring of 2016 we met in the Fishers and selected a line on the east face of Cottontail Tower. Despite the lack of guarantee that we would be able to connect the dots and find a way up over 900' of rock—mud really—I gave up my annual Yosemite trip to begin the route that fall. Cam Burns joined us on all three trips for support.

We spent three weeks cleaning, jugging, engineering creative placements, and straining sand through bandanas covering our mouths to finish the first three pitches. Richard led the spicy first two pitches, the crux of the route, consisting of hooking on holes followed by traversing terrain with very little gear that could sustain a fall. I led the third pitch, which began with rock so hard it bent pitons. The layers forming the Fisher Towers change in density every 10' or so, from very solid rock to the consistency of kitty litter. The remainder of the third pitch featured crumbly knobs and irregular edges that I hooked with Richard's homemade hooks he calls "claws."

We returned in April 2017, and above our high point we faced a series of chandeliered mud curtains. There was nothing Richard could do but hack away and dig under these hanging horrors. As the 30- to 40-pound globs fell to the ground, they looked like meteors with a swirling plume of dirty smoke trailing all the way down. They exploded with a loud report, like mortar fire from an angry enemy. At the end of each day, Richard resembled a Virginia coal miner, only redder than a barn. We were shut down midway up the fourth pitch by Pacific North-west–style rain and agreed to come back in the fall.

Richard Jensen delicately mud-hooking in full Fisher Towers battle gear during the first ascent of Line in the Sand on Cottontail Tower. *Cameron M. Burns*

In October, Richard continued leading while I suffered through a bombardment of grape-fruit-size dirt clods and dust so bad I couldn't see or breathe. Pitch nine required going to the left to avoid a multi-ton, triangular-shaped detached flake that rang like a gong. Richard then suffered through an offwidth chimney, which he bolted with 3/8-inch bolts and hangers so that it could be free climbed in the future. The chimney leads to the shoulder of Cottontail, and Richard rewarded my suffering by letting me lead the summit pitch, the tail of the Cotton-tail, joining the route Brer Rabbit for the last 40'.

We named our 10-pitch route Line in the Sand. We decided to rate the route VI 5.8 BLT because all aid ratings are subjective, especially in the Fisher Towers, where the first ascent experience can't be replicated. If pressed, it would suffice to say the route is hard aid. 📷 🔍

— SCOTT "PLAID" PETERSON

NEW ROUTES IN THE MYSTERY TOWERS: *In the spring of 2017, Jim Beyer soloed two hard aid routes in the Mystery Towers, adjacent to the Fisher Towers: Let it Go (3 pitches, VI A6) on the northwest face of the Citadel, and Off the Rails (3 pitches, VI A5) on the north face of the Doric Column. The former route climbs thin, calcite-filled seams, and Beyer said it was his "hardest and best micro-beaking testpiece so far," with body-weight placements and groundfall potential for almost the entire first pitch. Some details are at Mountain Project.*

VALLEY OF THE GODS, NEW ROUTES

IN NOVEMBER, EMILY Reinsel and I completed a quest to summit all 22 freestanding forma-tions we identified in the Valley of the Gods (VOG) of southeast Utah. We completed our circuit just days before President Trump's administration announced reductions to the Bears Ears National Monument, stripping the VOG of its recently protected status. During our quest, we established nine new routes, including the first ascents of two buttes and the likely first free ascents of three other formations. Details on all of these routes can be found on Mountain Project, and a full summary is available at the AAJ website. 📄 📷

— TREVOR BOWMAN

OSTLER PEAK, SIREN SONG

THE SOUND ECHOED off the cliffs, intermittent yet consistent. I kept hearing it over and over but could not place it. Something natural yet foreign, like whales talking. I asked Matt if he heard the sound as well. Finally it dawned on me.

"It's the lake."

Amethyst Lake, more than 1,000' below, was just coming into the October sun. Partially frozen, the ice was reacting to the heat and starting to sing. The lake kept up its symphony for over an hour while we climbed.

A few days earlier, I had hiked 13 miles round-trip into Amethyst Basin to scout for ice. I'd long thought there might be something to climb on Ostler Peak (12,718'), but the gully systems on the northeast face were hidden from the road. At first, it looked like another long hike for nothing, but as I traversed the base I started to see corners where intermittent ice was flowing. It appeared a ledge would allow a traverse between two ice-filled gullies to create a very long, moderate line.

Matt Tuttle and I agreed to meet at 4:30 a.m. for the long approach. Reaching the base of the wall much earlier than expected, we built a campfire to stay warm while we waited for the sun to reveal our route. After a tedious hike up talus, we simul-soloed the first 400' of fun alpine ice in gullies and corner systems. We roped up when the ice became brittle, and I led a pillar on the left leading toward the traverse ledge. The first pitch of the second gully wasn't quite in, so Matt led a mixed variation to the right that looked like 5.2 or 5.3 on rotten rock but ended up more like 5.6/5.7 on *horrible* rock. After 100' back in the gully, a fun vertical pillar led to lower-angle ice and snow before a final ice step. We reached the summit ridge at almost exactly 12,000' and hiked up to the summit before heading down, having completed one of the longest alpine routes in Utah: Siren Song (1,600' climbing distance, WI4- M4 R/X).

– NATHAN SMITH

HAYDEN PEAK, THE KENNEDY ROUTE

LESS THAN A week after my friend Hayden Kennedy's death in October, I headed to the Uintas to scout for ice. It had been a good fall and I'd already climbed ice a few days in September. I've been watching Hayden Peak (12,479') for years, as there are many potential winter lines, but they come and go, sometimes within a few days' time. This time I was lucky to spot a series of smears that linked together for what looked to be around 900' of ice.

A few days later, Julien Baudrand and I were hiking in the predawn. Perfect temps and conditions made for fast hiking, and we were at the base in a little over an hour. The route unfolded with five pitches of moderate ice and M4 steps. Above this, I soloed another 200' of WI2 until it ended in talus above.

We were happy to have put together a fun alpine line on Hayden Peak, and it only seemed fitting to name it for a great American alpinist and friend—the Kennedy Route (900', WI3+ M4).

– NATHAN SMITH

[Below left] Julien Baudrand climbing the thin drips of the crux fourth pitch of the Kennedy Route (900', WI3+ M4) on Hayden Peak. The Uintas have been a popular summer cragging destination for years and recently have seen a surge in new ice and mixed routes. [Below right] Nathan Smith with a portrait of Hayden Kennedy during the first ascent of the Kennedy Route on Hayden Peak. The young climber's death, less than a week earlier, inspired the climb. *Nathan Smith*

MONTANA

BRIDGER RANGE, ROSS PEAK, BLUE PHOENIX

IN 2016, MY good friend Tony Chang mentioned that there was a lot of overlooked potential for long bolted limestone routes on the 1,000' northeast face of Ross Peak (9,003').

After a little research, it appeared that this expansive aspect of Ross had only two completed free lines, done between 2002 and 2006, in addition to the original ascent of the face by Gary Skaar and Jack Tackle, a climb that was done mostly with pins and required some aid (*AAJ 1977*).

Arriving in July with a haulbag full of ropes, bolts, bits, and batteries, I set off to scout the face. It soon became clear that I would need some help. I was able to rustle up the always psyched Matt Abbott to help develop Trial By Fire (9 pitches, 5.11) over the course of three days. Bolting entirely on lead from stances, we did our best to follow the style of those that had come before us.

The original plan that year had been to finish a route that was started by Tom Kalakay and Robert Mueller in 1996. They had only completed two pitches, but the full line would go directly up the center of the wall through a series of overhangs. I returned the following July to go to work on this direct line, which splits right from Trial By Fire after three pitches. As I knew that there would be at least one section of 5.12 or harder climbing, and there were essentially no opportunities to place natural gear for aid, I decided to bolt on rappel. I spent one night on a ledge about 250' below the summit, strung up in hammock between two trees that were much too close together, sleeping with one eye open as I watched an unexpected lightning storm miss me by about three miles. It was an adventure before the climbing even started.

The 1,000' northeast face of Ross Peak, in the Bridger Range, near Bozeman. (1) Unnamed (5.11-). (2) Trial By Fire (5.11). (3) Blue Phoenix (5.12). (4) The Fellowship (5.10c). In August 1975, Gary Skaar and Jack Tackle made the first ascent of the face via the Northeast Face Direct (IV 5.9 A4), which climbs a natural line between Blue Phoenix and the Fellowship, possibly sharing a pitch with the latter down low. *Ty Morrison-Heath*

The next day Matt helped me clean pitch five and put in a few bolts on pitch six. I came back a few days later to bolt the last pitch, and then returned again a week later with Tony Chang to complete the first free ascent of Blue Phoenix (8 pitches, 5.12), leading all the crux pitches. Overall the difficulties revolve around two 5.12- pitches (pitches 5 and 8) and a pitch of solid 5.12 (pitch 6), with fun 5.10 cruising in between. Every pitch is on high-quality gray, blue, and gold stone, with occasional patches of solid chert.

The second ascent of Blue Phoenix is worth noting: Bozeman local Inge Perkins was struggling to find a partner to try the route that September. Her boyfriend, Hayden Kennedy, who had recently had shoulder surgery, decided to jug along behind to support her, and Inge led and onsighted every pitch like an absolute badass. We tragically lost both of them in October 2017. They will be sorely missed.

– EVAN MATHEWS

BEARTOOTH MOUNTAINS, GLACIER PEAK, CATCH-A-SUNRISE

ON AUGUST 17, Elaine Kennedy and I set out from a bivy to climb the prominent Beckey Couloir (Beckey-Beckstead, *AAJ 1965*) on the north face of Glacier Peak (12,340'). Entering the small basin below the north face, I spotted an obvious couloir and we started up perfect 55–60° snow. However, as the couloir began to bend to the right after about 600', the snow ended and we hit rock sooner than expected.

Following our noses, we trended up and left. Fourth-class rubble turned into 5.7 face, followed by two pitches in a dirty, wet chimney, then some run-out 5.6 slab, followed by two more pitches of 5.7/5.8. At this point, we were pretty sure we were not on the Beckey Couloir.

The only feasible way ahead was a

The north face of Glacier Peak. (1) Beckey Couloir. (2) Catch-a-Sunrise (2,000', III/IV 5.9 PG-13). Elaine Kennedy and Matt Lemke completed this likely new route in August after intending to climb the Beckey Couloir but mistakenly starting up the Catch-a-Fire Couloir farther west, a line that fills with snow in winter and has been skied several times. *Matt Lemke*

scary 5.8 traverse to the right, followed by 200' of rubble-strewn 5.4. Elaine took the lead and attempted to attain the top of a rib to the left, following a ramp into a 5.9 dihedral with multiple microwave-size blocks teetering on the brink. She took a fall and was lucky to be unscathed. After some TLC, we were both above the looseness without knocking anything down. Searching for a way up the final 40', I rounded a large boulder with some serious air and found a bomber 5.8 hand crack. With darkness nearing, we did one more long easy pitch and found a place to bivy.

The morning sunrise behind Granite Peak was the perfect energizer, and we finished the climb with a fourth-class pitch to the summit plateau. After returning to civilization, we determined we had initially started up the Catch-a-Fire Couloir, which ends at a notch in the ridge and has been skied several times. We could find no history of summer climbing routes in the vicinity of the couloir, and we named our route Catch-a-Sunrise (2,000', III/IV 5.9 PG-13).

– MATT LEMKE

WYOMING / GRAND TETON NATIONAL PARK

DISAPPOINTMENT PEAK, KIM SCHMITZ MEMORIAL ROUTE

I HAD THE idea to put up a route in honor of Kim Schmitz well before he died. I would often spot him around Jackson at climbing events, films, and competitions in which he could no longer compete. Only a few of us knew that the old guy watching the comp possessed more skill than anyone on the boulders. I thought it would be great to actually honor a climbing legend before he died, and I had a line in mind on the southwest face of Disappointment Peak above Garnet Canyon. However, I had the toughest time thinking of a suitable name.

Many of the obvious lines in the Tetons were climbed long ago. But the range is by no means climbed out. If anything, the real adventure has just begun. New routes can no longer follow the path of least resistance or trace a weakness from bottom to top. The frontier now lies out on the faces and up the *direttissmas*. In order to establish these routes, climbers will need to change their perspective of what is possible.

The new route on Disappointment Peak starts to the left and uphill of the Whiton-Wiggins (II 5.9, 1981) and to the right of West Side Story (II 5.8, Hadley-Montopoli, 1977) and follows a prominent buttress between those two routes the entire way. The intention was to do this route in impeccable style, and the first attempt with Adam Fabricant started ground up, free, and onsight. We encountered difficult and poorly protected climbing right off the ground. During this attempt, I got more than halfway up pitch four, the Big Flake Pitch, to a smaller but much looser flake looming above me. Since the first rule of climbing is not to kill yourself, and the second rule is not to kill your partners, our attempt ended there. Our ideal style also ended there, because the only way the route would go is if we knocked off the death flake from above.

On the second attempt, Adam and I rappelled down the route off nut and pin anchors to launch the death flake. Even after seeing the upper wall, I had no idea if it would go. Climbing back up from the ground that day, darkness found us three pitches from the top. I was 15 feet left and level with my last gear, looking up at a blank arête, not knowing what was around the corner. We escaped right and up the Whiton-Wiggins in the dark.

Foreshortened view of the southwest face of Disappointment Peak in the Tetons, showing the line of the Kim Schmitz Memorial Route (1,000', IV 5.11d). The route took three attempts and was completed the day after Schmitz' death in September 2016. *Michael Abbey*

When I woke at 4 a.m. on the day of the final attempt in September 2016, I had one text on my phone. It was the news of Kim's death the day before. Unfortunately, now we had a route name.

Returning this time with Sam Macke, I re-led the first pitch (5.11d), which was mentally harder the second time because I knew how scary it would be. I think a bolt or two on this pitch would be appropriate. (This pitch can be bypassed by climbing ledges uphill to the left of the start.) The second pitch was also sketchy—hard climbing with difficult protection and ledge-fall potential. I suggested to Sam that he should take this pitch since I'd already freed it. However, with rule number two in mind, I first aided up the pitch and preplaced some critical gear for his lead. This started a trend of leaving critical nuts, pins, and even a Pecker on the route for future ascents.

The only other pitch that required aid was the arête that had previously stopped Adam and me. After aiding to a belay around the corner, we pulled the ropes and freed this pitch at 5.11c, ending in an amazing position on the upper headwall. A pitch of 5.10 R up this headwall led to a 4th-class pitch and the top.

The Kim Schmitz Memorial Route [1,000', IV 5.11d (5.10c R)] is an adventurous line up the most prominent part of the buttress. It's a little dangerous and requires a commitment to cast off into the unknown well above the gear. Like Kim, it doesn't take the easy path.

– **MICHAEL ABBEY**

Jesse Huey leading the crux pitch of Original Sin. *Austin Siadak*

ORIGINAL SIN

FREEING THE HISTORIC FIRST ROUTE ON MT. HOOKER'S NORTH FACE

BY MAURY BIRDWELL

GRAND OBJECTIVES within six hours' drive from your front door are still to be found.

In July of 1964, Dick McCracken, Charlie Raymond, and Royal Robbins spent four days making the first ascent of Mt. Hooker's (12,504') imposing north face, an audacious and groundbreaking climb—one of the first Grade VI walls outside of Yosemite Valley. To this day, the 16-mile approach is more than a step removed from El Capitan's roadside nature and full cell service.

As Jesse Huey and I searched for a worthy, achievable target for this year's "JTG" (Just The Guys) venture, we squinted at photos of the original Robbins line. In 1990, Paul Piana, Galen Rowell, Todd Skinner, and Tim Toula had completed a free variation called Jaded Lady (1,800', V 5.12-, *AAJ 1991*) that weaved right and left to avoid the central nose of the headwall, joining the original route about 800' up the wall. [*Several weeks before this ascent, Stuart Ritchie, Mark Rolofson, and Annie Whitehouse had spent 21 days attempting the first ascent of this line, freeing all but a short section.*] We wondered about the lower part of Robbins' route. Was it too chossy? Too thin? Or, hope against hope, just overlooked? In our tradition of plucking low-hanging fruit, we hubristically packed for a gentleman's adventure to see if we might garner a bit of glory ourselves.

On the morning of day one, we spent all of 20 minutes scoping the wall before affirming to each other that, yes, this was the line for us. Jesse went first, and after a fun initial pitch of 5.9, he found himself executing delicate 5.11 moves with poor protection on a variation to the original start. Not out to prove a point, we added our first bolt. Another 10 feet of solid 5.11 gained a thin corner leading to an alcove belay below the horrifying, "creaking flake" McCracken had written about in *AAJ 1965*. We debated the relative merits of climbing over or around the Volkswagen-size menace. Thankfully it didn't budge, and Jesse again executed some delicate face climbing to put us at the base of a gorgeous corner—my breakfast for the next day.

After ascending our fixed lines in the morning, I started up with solid pro and delightful edges, still rooted in the ideal that we might free each pitch onsight. A difficult bulge quickly dissolved that fantasy, but after a hang and inspection, I was finger-locking up glorious, clean rock. The corner melded into an arching roof with no perceptible weakness, but ten feet to the right was a tantalizing arête, and a little scrubbing yielded the right combination of holds for a 5.12 boulder problem to cap off the pitch. Wunderbar!

Next up was a hanging corner made of golden, glowing granite. A quick refresher on tenuous aid and beaking saw Jesse at the anchor; I foolishly tried to free climb on top rope before we had cleaned the flaky rock and lichen, practically destroying my only rock shoes in the process. We were now in 5.12+/5.13- territory for sure.

From here a small flake feature snaked out left for 15 feet, giving way to the horizontal line

The north prow of Mt. Hooker: Yellow line: Original Sin (2017), incorporating and freeing parts of the original route (1964), then following Jaded Lady (red line, 1990) to the top. Other routes not shown. *Austin Siadak*

of rivet bolts Robbins had used to traverse to a 5.10 chimney system. (Jaded Lady traverses higher up.) Jesse replaced the first three rivets with two shiny new badges of courage before launching into a bold 20-foot 5.11 runout to gain a Butterballs-esque crack that deposited us at the belay by Jaded Lady's crux traverse.

Now came a question: Should we take our win with six newly freed pitches and finish on Jaded Lady's final 1,000' of mostly moderate free climbing or chance it with a more direct line up the headwall above? Always tenacious, Jesse wanted a direct line, and I cautiously assented to what I thought might be a Sisyphean task.

After a rest day we headed back up. Spirits were high, but an entire day of effort found us only two pitches higher. On the second of these, using aid, Jesse surmounted a giant roof that would certainly not go free. Rapping straight down, he found a barely extant passage through a different section of the roof, with an obvious wide pitch below. Above the roof was one more 5.12 pitch through the featured headwall to join straight into the final crux of Jaded Lady and complete the plumb line.

Over the next few days we sussed the crux pitches and engaged in a heated debate about whether to add bolts to the route's crux fourth pitch. As it stood, the pitch had a couple critical cam placements but otherwise relied on six preplaced beaks for protection. We'd added some bolts to our new variations but not to the original route (except for anchors). We agreed to leave the pitch as it was, but Jesse would have to lead it in the condition he championed!

The final, single-day push felt almost anticlimactic. At the crux Jesse racked up a precise selection of gear—not terribly difficult since there were only a couple of nuts and cams in addition to the six beaks. He flawlessly executed the tenuous pressing, palming, and smearing, and erupted with excitement as he pulled onto the belay stance. Armed with the courage of a top rope, I managed to squeak by with a clean follow.

We flowed through the pitches above, our complete free climb nearly compromised as my foot slipped on the final new pitch of 5.12a on the headwall. Our power was winding down, but we each mustered just enough to put this one to rest and link into Jaded Lady with no falls. We still faced that line's upper crux, a 5.12 corner. It would be unfair to say this was inconsequential, but when you have a Huey on the rack that's just how it is. In exchange for his valiant cornersmanship, I led out the final 300' of meat and potatoes 5.9.

Staring out at that perfect cirque, on that perfect day, with our greatest rock climbing accomplishment below us, we each knew it would never get better than this. Until next year, that is.

SUMMARY: First ascent of Original Sin (1,800', V 5.12+) on the north face of Mt. Hooker in the Wind River Range. The route frees four and a half pitches of the original 1964 line (McCracken-Raymond-Robbins) and adds five pitches of new variations before finishing on Jaded Lady. 📷 🔍

MT. HOOKER, HOOTERS

IN MID-JULY, JEN Olson (Canada) and I embarked on the long, soggy, and yet stunningly beautiful walk into the Wind River Range with the idea of repeating Hook, Line, and Sinker (1,800', V 5.12) on Mt. Hooker (12,504'). This route was freed by Whit Magro and Josh Wharton (*AAJ 2015*), and our late good friend Hayden Kennedy had recommended it.

At the base, we worked out where the route apparently started, yet it looked very improbable. After a sketchy quest into no man's land, we realized the starting pitch had fallen down.

Without any topos for alternative routes, we discussed putting up a new line. The most obvious and easy grab with the single day we had left was a line on Hooker's northwest face that we eventually named Hooters (500m, III 5.9). This natural line is attractive in some ways—offering a summit route at a much lower free grade than its neighbors—yet it's also a little loose, mossy, and generally sloppy around the edges. Our favorite pitch, the crux, was a wet, intimidating 5.9 flare—the kind of pitch that is much better in retrospect. All in all, a fine outing with a great partner. ▣

– HAZEL FINDLAY, *U.K.*

CIRQUE OF THE TOWERS, WOLFS HEAD, BRASS MONKEY

THE SOUTH FACE of Wolfs Head, in the Cirque of the Towers, appears to have been scratched by the claws of a large creature, leaving gouges that look perfect for climbing. In 2012, I spotted a clean slab lacerated with discontinuous finger cracks. Above, a labyrinth of roofs crisscrossed the square arête leading to the summit.

The next year I convinced Paul Kimbrough to have a look. Amazed by the quality of the cracks, we chuckled our way up the moderate slab until we were dead-ended by incipient seams. Above us, several overhanging pitches hovered like a tsunami suspended in time. Our skimpy selection of hardware was reason enough to make a hasty retreat. We vowed to return.

In 2014, armed to the teeth with an arsenal of big-wall paraphernalia, we retraced our steps from the previous year. Higher on the line, substantial difficulties and unrelenting steepness forced us to pull on gear. While leading what would become the crux pitch, the rope was gobbled up by a flake and became hopelessly stuck. I lumped together some climbing tape and plugged the offending flake. This worked and we continued up, elated to be granted passage to the top but perturbed by the aid the upper route had required. Again we swore to return, intent on a free ascent.

Another winter passed, and in 2015 we once again queued up at the base and prepared for battle. Progress was smooth as we freed all of the pitches up to the crux. To our astonishment, many of the pins we had fixed for anchors had fallen out over the winter, but the plug of tape had held. Our new strategy for negotiating the rope-drag dilemma was to fold our rope in half and use a hodgepodge double-rope system that would utilize the left rope for the first half of the pitch and the right side for the top. From a bad rest at the tape lump, the left rope would be pulled through a Mini Traxion, alleviating any rope drag but consequently rendering it useless in the event of a fall.

Our knuckleheaded plan proved effective until a horrid burning pump welled up inside my forearms. Run-out above a single green Camalot clipped to the right-hand rope, I stabbed for a flaring jam, and then I was flying, finally coming to a halt level with Paul at the belay. We swapped rope ends. I clenched the rope, eagerly anticipating Paul sending the pitch. His

The south face of Wolfs Head. (1) Green Dragon (2017). (2) Brass Monkey (2017). (3) Red Cloud (Collins-Gust, 2012). (4) White Buffalo (Collins-McBride, 2005). (5) South Face (Beckey-Fuller, 1966). The classic East Ridge (Buckingham-Plummer, 1959) follows the right skyline. Other routes not shown. *Brandon Gust*

fate was the same. After dropping countless F-bombs we retreated down to our camp and the Cirque Lake Bar to wash down another failure and numb our bludgeoned extremities.

I was obsessed with the route and returned alone the following season, this time scrambling to the top of the line with heaps of static line. A case of steel brushes was obliterated as I cleaned lichen and scabby rock from cracks. I replaced the rotting tape nugget with a bolt, which would serve as a directional around the rope-eating constriction. (I had realized it made more sense to create a route that people would have fun repeating than to fuel our egos by pushing it ground-up.) Our work schedules only allowed for one real go that year. Wolfs Head came out on top, and again we went home empty-handed.

In 2017 more brushes were destroyed, more bolts were added, and I started to feel at home on the south face of Wolfs Head. The route began to seem more reasonable. Nevertheless, the X-factor persisted in the crux pitch. Over the course of the four years we had invested, both of us had redpointed every pitch save the crux. Now it was time to see if we could link all the moves, all the pitches, in one continuous flow to the top. At each belay our energy multiplied, but in no way was it in the bag until we sunk our mitts into the last splitter hand crack of Brass Monkey (III 5.12c).

Words are incapable of capturing the pleasure of completing a goal into which so much energy has been poured. Witnessing the transformation we both went through over the years to make this vision a reality, I realize that instant gratification is nice but the slow burn stays with you much longer. [*The climbers subsequently added another route to the left, Green Dragon (III 5.11 PG-13). The full story is at the AAJ website.*]

— BRANDON GUST

HAYSTACK MOUNTAIN, THE FAR SIDE, FIRST FREE ASCENT

"HERE ARE THE same pins and hammer we used to put it up in '96," Norm Larson said, handing over four pitons and a bright-red, lightweight wall hammer. "You should place a pin or bolt at the A2 crux on pitch five, and then I remember a knifeblade was particularly comforting on the last 10c pitch."

Armed with this trusty iron and a hand-drawn topo from first ascensionists Norm Larson and Lorna Corson, Madaleine Sorkin and I, along with photographer Henna Taylor, headed to the Far Side (IV 5.10 A2) of Haystack Mountain in the Deep Lake area of the Winds. On August 27, we racked up at the lowest point of the slabs on the southwest face of Haystack. [*The Far Side is the furthest route to the right on the peak's western exposure, to the right of the Jim Beyer route Southern Wall Right (IV 5.10 A1).*] We simul-climbed as a three-pack up the first three low-angle

Madaleine Sorkin placing a pin with Norm Larson's red hammer before embarking on the crux section of the Far Side (IV 5.12a). *Kate Rutherford*

pitches. One pitch of 5.9 brought us to a belay at an umbrella shaped roof, and from there we could see the angling finger crack that would take us all the way to the top.

Madaleine employed our borrowed hammer and placed one of Norm's pitons (which we left for future free climbing parties) and then freed the tricky A2 crux with powerful moves and technical footwork. Beautiful, thought-provoking cracks continued past mostly good rock (we trundled the really loose ones) to a stance below the second to last pitch.

The final 10c pitch still hosts a garden of lichen between finger locks and crimps. It angles up to the summit ridge with a striking V-notch to finish. We may or may not have shed a tear after forgetting the recommended knifeblade, but ultimately we hammered in a final pin, tiptoed past multiple #000 C3 placements on thin edges, and threw one last hand jam in the V-slot to gain the summit ridge. After one more short, slippery 5.8 step, we were scrambling to the summit.

The Far Side, which Norm and Lorna named after those kooky cartoons, is a beautiful route, but not for the faint of heart. The nine-pitch line now goes free at IV 5.11+ (if you're a 5.13 climber like Madaleine) or something more like 5.12a for mere mortals. 📷 🔍

– KATE RUTHERFORD

MONOLITH CIRQUE, DOGTOOTH PINNACLE, ONCE BITTEN

ON THE EAST-FACING aspect of the Monolith Cirque, the towering sub-buttresses of Dog Tooth Peak are stacked up like a row of teeth, impossible to ignore when walking in either direction along the North Fork Trail. Even though climbing history here stretches back to the 1963 first ascent of the Monolith's north face, I could find no record of activity on the cirque's next-most-impressive formation, the Dogtooth Pinnacle. Intrigued, my good friend Drew Smith and I loaded our packs at the end of July and made the 12-mile trek in from Big Sandy to have a look.

After establishing a cushy base camp in the talus near Papoose Lake, we spent a day glassing the wall and stashing gear at the base. The Dogtooth Pinnacle was as impressive in real life as it was in the pictures—a towering triangular face that appeared to be dead vertical for more

than 1,500 feet. We awoke early on August 2 for an attempt up the center of the steep and imposing southeast aspect.

After a long, moderate approach pitch, the wall reared up and Drew led an overhanging 5.11 stem corner with wild movement but less than desirable rock. I then quested up low-5.11 finger cracks through more questionable stone to reach a dirty, arcing splitter that I aided at C1. This pitch ended below a steep wall devoid of cracks. Drew led a traversing pitch leftward up a large, low-angle ramp. Above this, a muddy corner abruptly pinched off, and more leftward traversing looked to end in a large, blank wall.

Deflated by the crummy rock, dead-end cracks, and wandering nature of our line, we decided to bag it. Though a team with more time, bolts, and an arsenal of wire brushes might be able to forge a line up this impressive face, we found this aspect of the peak to be an unfortunate case of "good from far, but far from good."

The next morning, we decided to explore the buttress' only other obvious weakness: a large chimney that looked to lead onto the less-steep north face. Once Bitten (1,500', III/IV 5.10) begins in this obvious cleft on the lower right-hand portion of the southeast face.

Our route climbs flakes and cracks in and outside of the large chimney for three pitches of 5.10 to reach a spacious ledge on the northeast arête. From here, the route transitions onto the north face, climbing a spectacular 70m pitch (5.10) through an hourglass feature. The route trends generally right for three more long pitches, connecting intermittent systems with comfy belay ledges and generally good rock. The top of our sixth pitch brought us to a large, V-shaped gully. We put the rope away and scrambled 200m or so of low fifth-class to the summit of Dogtooth Pinnacle.

On our last day in the cirque, we repeated the northwest buttress of the Monolith (1,600', IV 5.9, Beckey-Fuller, *AAJ 1967*), which we found to be a wild and engaging classic that, in my opinion, surpasses the nearby northeast buttress of Pingora in both quality and adventure.

— ANDY ANDERSON

[Top] East face of the Dog Tooth Peak massif. (1) Dogtooth attempt (2017). (2) Once Bitten (III/IV 5.10, Anderson-Smith, 2017). (3) Infinite Jest (IV 5.11 C2, Barker-Daverin-Warren, 2016). This buttress had a major rockfall after the first ascent in 1980; Infinite Jest climbs new terrain down low and up high (see AAJ 2017). (4) A-Frame Buttress (IV 5.9, Metcalf-Thuermer, 1977). The second buttress from the right is possibly unclimbed. [Bottom] Andy Anderson engaging the high-quality "hourglass pitch" during the first ascent of Once Bitten on the Dogtooth Pinnacle. *Drew Smith*

Sam Lightner Jr. battles a steep corner on pitch 14 of Discovery (1,600', IV 5.12a C1). Lightner, Mike Lilygren, and Shep Vail made three trips into the Monolith Cirque to establish the route, freeing everything but 25 feet of desperate stemming they believe will go at 5.13a. *Shep Vail*

THE PREMONITION
A 30-YEAR DREAM COMES TRUE IN THE WIND RIVERS

BY SAM LIGHTNER JR.

"SAM, YOU NEED a copy of Bonney and Bonney's *Guide to the Wyoming Mountains*," said Paul Piana as we sunned ourselves on Vedauwoo's Clamshell boulder in 1986. "It's a rite of passage to becoming a Wyoming climber. You aren't worth your salt without that book."

I remembered those words the following spring when my friend Bill Walker offered me his old copy. "I'm kinda sick of this sport, and you're just getting going," he'd said. "I want this book to go to a good home." I thanked Bill profusely, drove straight home with the scruffy book, and began poring over its yellowed pages.

Originally published in 1960, Orrin and Lorraine Bonney's book held 702 pages of mountain info and wilderness know-how that any self-respecting Wyoming climber would want. The book was chock full of traditional bushcraft, like how to field dress a pronghorn so you preserved the most meat, or how to determine north with nothing more than a couple of twigs. It explained what mountain ranges hid the best amethyst crystals and dinosaur bones, and how to make a proper SOS distress call with a fading flashlight. It also had the established route information of every known peak, cliff, and crag across the Cowboy State. Sure, you had the well-documented Devil's Tower ascents and the very debatable 1872 ascent of the Grand Teton, but also mysterious and seldom-seen knobs and spires like the Boar's Tusk in the Red Desert and the Sitting Camel south of Laramie.

After only a couple minutes of page turning, there it was on page 498. The simple caption read, "*Monolith, N. face. Photo Arthur C.*" The black and white photo showed a granite buttress worthy of Yosemite, but deep in the Wind River Wilderness of my home state. The text claimed

Jessie Allen leading a string of pack horses into the camp below the Monolith (back left), the second-largest formation in the Wind Rivers, after Mt. Hooker. The east-facing buttresses of Dog Tooth Peak are on right, including the Dogtooth Pinnacle, the Wisdom Tooth and the A-Frame Buttress. *Sam Lightner Jr.*

only two routes had been completed on the mountain: the first ascent of the north face by Art Gran, John Hudson, and Doug Tompkins in 1963 and a Fred Beckey route on the northwest face in '66. Beckey claimed in his vague report in *AAJ 1967* that he had, "never seen better rock, anywhere." Strangely, neither party had chosen to scale the obvious and direct line up the central northeast face. "It must be damn hard," I thought. "I'll have to get better for that." Grabbing a pen from my book bag, I drew in what seemed to be the obvious line, folded the corner of the page, and turned to another chapter.

Fast-forward 28 years, past numerous chapters of my climbing life. Somehow trips to far-flung mountains in Asia, Europe, Africa, and South America had overshadowed my home range. So in the summer of 2015, my friends Shep Vail, Mike Lilygren, and I decided we would put together an expedition to the face I'd fallen for nearly three decades before, and we'd do it in style.

We invited a few friends along, noting it would be easier to handle the coming bills with more wallets. Our trip would be ten days, and the dinner menu contained things like boiled shrimp cocktail, beef tenderloin, fresh apple-strawberry pie, and of course libations to wash it all down. We threw in enough wall gear to get us up Great Trango, all of which added up to more than just a backpack of supplies. This led to a phone call to the Diamond 4 Ranch, which operates out of Dickinson Park, a mere 14 miles from the Monolith. The chief wrangler at the Diamond 4 is Jessie Allen, who not only was the 2014 Miss America contestant from Wyoming, but also sleeps under the stars for a third of the year, calms macho big-game hunters in grizzly country, and cares for a remuda of 75 horses and mules through the Wyoming winter.

Jessie hauled our base camp, climbing gear, and a half dozen other friends to a level site near Papoose Lake, about three miles east of Pingora. This gave our friends targets to tackle in the nearby Cirque of the Towers and on Dogtooth Peak, and the Monolith was only about two miles and 1,700' of elevation gain away.

Shep, Mike, and I attacked the line I'd drawn on the photograph so many years before and found that Fred Beckey had aptly described the granite. At the top of pitch two we found bail gear from a previous attempt by an unknown party. We pushed on, and about 500 feet above the talus, found what looked to be another party's retreat point below a bulging and blank stretch of rock. We could see two possible ways to tackle this headwall and decided on the left variation. It was the wrong decision, and to make a long story a few words shorter, we failed in 2015. Our tails tucked, we vowed to be back the following summer.

In 2016 we came in with determination to figure out the headwall and get into the splitter crack system above. We also brought more rope, less bourbon, and a designated cook, Elyse Guarino, to speed up the mornings and extend our climbing time. Coming in from the right and hanging on hooks, we managed to get in a few pieces of fixed gear and then free the blank bulge at 5.11d. The ledge above it, a beer cooler–size pedestal on flawless granite, showed no signs of human disturbance. Above was 200 feet of perfect hand crack that had obviously not been climbed, then a hard finger crack that led to the base of the overhanging upper wall.

After seven days of route-finding and cleaning, we made it 14 pitches into the sky but there ran into a problem. The climbing below was world class, but the easiest cracks through the upper headwall had been anything but stellar. We wanted this to be a classic but needed days more time to figure out a line that befit the rest of the route. With a severe thunderstorm and cold front approaching, we bailed again.

On a warm afternoon in 2017, four friends disappeared with empty backpacks down the western slope of Big Sandy Mountain toward the Big Sandy trailhead, and Mike, Shep and I were left alone on the summit of the Monolith. [*The plateau atop the Monolith is just north of Big Sandy Mountain (12,416'), which lies on the Continental Divide between the Monolith Cirque and Big Sandy Lake.*] Instead of the comforts of base camp, we now had a few packets of freeze-dried food, the necessary rack, two static lines, and only one bottle of bourbon for our summit camp above 12,000 feet. We would find the finish to this line according to quality, not ease, and it would be established moss- and choss-free to inspire future climbers.

In a matter of 50 hours we extensively cleaned and worked four pitches through the overhangs. We then rapped down and gave it our best. Sadly, 25 feet of pitch 12, a tips and stemming nightmare, did not go free on that try. It will likely go at 5.13a. We climbed this 25-foot section French free on microcams, with a 12a start and 11b finish. Another pitch of 5.11 face climbing on a mix of fixed gear and cams led to a large ledge, followed by a 5.12 pitch of fingers and hands that qualifies as the steepest crack any of us had ever scaled. One more 5.10 pitch and we were back at our summit bivy.

We made Discovery the focus of three years of climbing. Dozens of hours of cleaning and camouflaged, stainless-steel rappel anchors helped to make this a spectacular route. We will be back in 2018 to free that 25 feet of aid and climb the complete route in a push. Amazingly, it follows the exact line I'd drawn in the Bonney and Bonney guide, 30 years before.

SUMMARY: First ascent of Discovery (1,600', IV 5.12a C1) on the northeast face of the Monolith in the Wind River Range of Wyoming, by Mike Lilygren, Sam Lightner Jr., and Shep Vail.

[Top] The line of Discovery (1,600', IV 5.12a C1) on the Monolith. Previous routes lie around to the right. [Bottom] Sam Lightner Jr.'s original copy of Bonney and Bonney's *Guide to the Wyoming Mountains and Wilderness Areas,* which planted the seed for a new route on the Monolith nearly 30 years ago. The line Lightner drew in the late 1980s is a near perfect match of what ended up becoming Discovery, the first known new route up the northeast face of the formation. *Sam Lightner Jr.*

[Top] Hansjörg Auer working up the final steep pitch on his and Much Mayr's new route Mango Tango (5.11+ R/X), which they climbed ground-up in May 2017. *Elias Holzknecht* [Left] The Diagonal Wall in Colorado's Black Canyon of the Gunnison, showing the line of Mango Tango. The 600-meter new route is between Diagonal Will and Pathfinder. *Hansjörg Auer*

COLORADO

BLACK CANYON OF THE GUNNISON NATIONAL PARK, DIAGONAL WALL BUTTRESS, MANGO TANGO

ON MAY 4, Much Mayr and I completed a new route on the Black Canyon's Diagonal Wall, ground-up and in a single 11-hour push. This was my second trip to the Black Canyon, after traveling there with Ben Lepesant in 2011 to make the first free ascent of the historic Hallucinogen Wall (5.13+ R, *AAJ 2012*).

Mango Tango (600m, 5.11+ R/X) is on the right side of the Diagonal Wall, between the routes Diagonal Will and Pathfinder. The route's 18 pitches follow logical systems of cracks and corners, but also feature some spicy runouts through unprotected face climbing—like the third pitch, where falling is not an option. We left two pitons and one nut in situ. Although the Black Canyon is famous for poor rock, this new climb offers mostly the opposite. 📷 🔍

— HANSJÖRG AUER, *AUSTRIA*

UNAWEEP CANYON, UNAWEEP WALL, WINTERTIME JOY

ON A RAINY April day, Curtis Chabot and I carried 1,000' of static line and a double set of cams up the northwest arête of the Unaweep Wall, the largest cliff in the canyon (possibly establishing a new mountaineer's route in the process). By the time we reached the top and chose a line to rappel and fix our ropes, it was pouring rain, with the temperatures hovering just above freezing. It was a slippery rappel down the wall, but each turn, twist, and slam down the water-soaked granite unveiled climbable crack after climbable crack.

Matt Hurd joined me a week later to clean the line. After the 45-minute uphill approach in subfreezing temperatures, Matt tossed off loose rocks while I ascended the fixed lines and added anchors and the necessary bolts to allow a safe and engaging free ascent. The day ended with high winds and frozen hands but high psyche.

Jason Nelson accompanied me for the final day of prepping the route. Our goal was to get to the top, clean and bolt the highest anchors, and bolt a variation on a 40m granite tower one pitch from the top. I had told Jason to plan for an adventure, but he didn't bring boots or warm clothes—it was a miserable day for him. It began snowing hard as we hiked up to the base, then turned into a whiteout; post-holing up a gully to the top in waist-deep snow was grim. But at the end of the day, the route was finally ready to be climbed.

I returned a few weeks later with Mike Brumbaugh, and we freed the route on a perfectly sunny day. Wintertime Joy (8 pitches, 5.11+ with 5.12+ variation) was established through much pain, discomfort, and tenacity. I am so lucky to have such tough partners.

– ROB PIZEM

ROCKY MOUNTAIN NATIONAL PARK, AIGUILLE DE FLEUR, RUSSIAN TIES

MICHAEL GOODHUE AND Vincent Keller climbed a new line up the east face of Aiguille de Fleur on the west side of the Park in July. The six-pitch Russian Ties (III, 5.10 R) is in the center of the face, between the original east face route (Hodge-Trout, 1974, to the right) and Eastern Roofs (Kilgore-Sambataro, 2011).

– INFORMATION FROM MOUNTAINPROJECT.COM

SANGRE DE CRISTO MOUNTAINS, SEPTEM VIRTUTUM ANIMA MEA

OVER THREE STORMY days in July, Elisha Gallegos and Daniel Schuerch put up a long technical route up the north side of Challenger Point (14,081'). Septem Virtutum Anima Mea (1,500', 5.8+) ascends a clean shield of rock above the Willow Lake Campground, about five miles from the trailhead. The crux is found at roofs on the first pitch, and the first four pitches have bolted anchors. From the top of the technical climbing, it's possible to scramble off to the northwest or continue over a false summit toward Challenger Point and descend via the standard hiking route.

– INFORMATION FROM DANIEL SCHUERCH

ALASKA

Jessica Keil traversing the icy summit ridge of Australia after climbing the south face via the new route Ask and You Shall Receive (III 5.9), possibly the first ascent of the peak. *Alan Goldbetter*

BROOKS RANGE / ARRIGETCH PEAKS

AUSTRALIA, SOUTH FACE

ON AUGUST 6, under clear skies and with dreams of first ascents on remote peaks, Anina Friedrich, Tess Ferguson, Jessica Keil, and I flew into Gates of the Arctic National Park. Landing on a small gravel bar approximately 12 miles downstream from our climbing objectives, we spent the next five days carrying our 20 days of supplies up Aiyagomahala Creek to base camp.

Moments after reaching camp, we received a forecast showing 24 hours of good weather before ten days of solid rain. We departed immediately for an ascent of the west ridge of Shot Tower (IV 5.9 C2, Roberts-Ward, 1971), the most classic and popular route in this valley. Climbing through the night in two teams of two, we made a camp-to-camp ascent in 21 hours.

The forecast delivered as promised, bringing sustained wet and cold conditions to the range. During the entirety of our remaining weeks in the Arrigetch, we only were able to climb one more day. Splitting into teams of two, we attempted separate objectives. Tess and Anina attempted a new route on Battleship Peak, but after finding much loose rock, increasingly difficult climbing, and one near miss with a falling block, they chose to descend.

Meanwhile, Jessica and I ascended the previously unclimbed south face of Australia. Our route, Ask and You Shall Receive (150m, III 5.9), follows the face's obvious central line of weakness, over continuously worsening rock. It was completed in trying weather conditions and took over 20 hours, camp to camp. Once we reached the summit ridge, we cruised climber's left (west), hitting a number of the smaller summit blocks to be sure we reached the true high point. [*Australia lies along the ridge east of Badile, between Disneyland and Tasmania, both climbed in 1971 by a Hampshire College expedition (AAJ 1972). It is very possible the 2017 climb was the first ascent of Australia.*]

Only a few days later, with more snow coming, we began the hike out to the landing zone. In a process that always feels simultaneously too slow and too fast, we were dumped back into the civilized world on August 25.

— ALAN GOLDBETTER, *USA/FINLAND*

ALEUTIAN RANGE

KATMAI NATIONAL PARK TRAVERSE

LUC MEHL AND Josh Mumm completed a 200-mile, 15-day ski traverse through Katmai National Park, at the northeast end of the Alaska Peninsula, at the end of winter. On March 20, the two flew from Anchorage to Kamishak Bay in the northeast corner of the park. Their trip ended in the village of King Salmon on the west side.

Along the way, they climbed several volcanoes, including Mt. Douglas (ca 7,050'), where they used litmus paper to test the crater lake—it showed a pH of 1, the equivalent of sulfuric acid. They then climbed Fourpeaked Mountain (6,903'), which erupted in 2006, and skied down to the coast at Swikshak Bay. Turning inland, they continued southwest, weaving among numerous volcanoes. After dropping to the Katmai River, they followed a traditional native trade route over Katmai Pass, dropped into the Valley of Ten Thousand Smokes, sat out a blizzard in a USGS hut, and continued out flatter terrain toward King Salmon. Crossing Naknek Lake, they were able to use their "skickets"—snow pickets equipped with Nordic bindngs to double as ice skates. Thanks to a strong tailwind and generally good conditions, they finished the traverse on April 4—a week earlier than planned. An excellent video documenting this trip is at the *AAJ* website, along with a link to a report with many photos. ▶

– DOUGALD MACDONALD, *WITH INFORMATION FROM LUC MEHL*

CHIGMIT MOUNTAINS, DOUBLE GLACIER, VARIOUS ASCENTS

IN MID-JUNE, JAMES Kesterson, Paul Muscat, Glenn Wilson, and I spent eight days mountaineering above the Double Glacier, at the north end of the Chigmit Mountains. We had planned to visit the Neacolas, but bad weather forced us to make a spontaneous shift to the Chigmits. Poor volcanic rock keeps this region off the radar of climbers, although mountaineers and skiers are attracted by the heavy glaciation and high volcanic summits of Redoubt (10,197') and Iliamna (10,016'). Our unplanned visit exceeded expectations.

Double Peak (left) and Peak 6,402'. The latter was first climbed in 2017 by the south face and east ridge (hidden behind the col). *Joe Stock*

We landed on a glacial ridge at 4,400'. Our base camp location (approx. 60°44'28"N, 152°31'41"W) looked down to the oil and gas platforms in Cook Inlet and across to the Kenai Mountains. Surrounding our camp were numerous small summits, rising up to the area's high point of Double Peak (6,818'). Despite rain every day, we climbed so many peaks that we didn't count, mostly little bumps, all of them first known ascents. Our most significant climb was Peak 6,402', due west of our camp, accessed by its south slope and east ridge. On our last day we rose at 11 p.m. for a crack at Double Peak, first climbed from the south and west in 1973. We made it to within a few hundred feet of the summit on the northwest slopes. 📷 🔍

– JOE STOCK

REVELATION MOUNTAINS, FIRST ASCENTS ABOVE THE FISH GLACIER

CAN A PLACE be remote but accessible at the same time? Thanks to the impressive skills of our pilot, Paul Roderick, the south fork of the Fish Glacier in the Revelation Mountains turned out to be just that.

Ever since Clint Helander's article in *AAJ 2013*, we kept reading about the wild mountains, fickle weather, and good climbing in the Revelations. But as the years went by, many of the objectives identified by Clint were being ticked off. One valley, however, seemed to have been spared the attention: the south fork of the Fish Glacier (a.k.a. Fish Creek Glacier). Having checked the landing feasibility with Talkeetna Air Taxi, Frieder Wittmann (Germany) and I were soon loading a plane with food and fuel for three weeks. After a scenic roller-coaster flight, we landed in the soft snow with good-looking walls on one side and perfect ski slopes on the other.

The first day on the glacier, March 28, we climbed Peak 6,905', just to the east of our landing spot. We were able to ski to a col northeast of the peak, and a pleasant ridge with a few rocky steps got us to the top. The mountain has two obvious high points, and because we couldn't be certain which was higher, we tagged them both. We named the route It's A Girl! (PD). The long Alaskan day gave us some time to look at other objectives in the valley, and as the peak was such a great vantage point, we called it the Prophet for all the promises that it gave us.

On March 30, we picked a line on the east face of neighboring Peak 8,568', which we'd started calling Mephisto. Moderate névé led us to a pitch of ice climbing. As the ice thinned, a mixed pitch followed, which turned out to be a good workout. After wrestling onto the upper gully, more of the perfect névé led all the way to the top. We named our route Langstrasse (800m, WI4 M4) after the training venue in Zurich where we prepared for the trip.

After some forced rest due to snowfall, we set our sights on a rocky peak (ca 7,350') north of the Prophet. After a few recon trips, we decided to try its east ridge. It took us a couple of attempts, and we started calling the mountain the Charlatan by the time we went up there a third time.

The final part of the ridge turned out to be rockier than expected, with beautifully sculpted granite somewhat reminiscent of the climbing in Corsica. The Charlatan pulled one last trick before the summit, when I punched through a cornice. We summited on April 7 and named our route Piled Higher and Deeper (AD, WI2 M3) after the light, fresh snow we encountered— and because we were both set to graduate from our Ph.D. programs upon returning home.

A couple more days of sour weather followed, during which we scouted a potential gully route between the granite towers of the Obelisk (9,304'). The peak's southwest face was first climbed in 2015 by John Giraldo and Clint Helander (Emotional Atrophy, 1,000m, WI5 M6 A0, see *AAJ 2016*), but the southeast face, above our glacier, hadn't been attempted. Using binoculars and photos we took from the Prophet and the Charlatan, we pieced together a line of gullies cutting through the granite towers.

Our first attempt came to a halt as we retreated due to strong spindrift. After recuperating and allowing the snow to settle, we were back on April 11 for a second go. A gully with good névé led us to a series of mixed pitches that turned out to be the crux of the route, and we had to aid through a couple of sections. A snow ramp then led us to a pitch of ice that looked deceivingly fat, but the lower portion started disintegrating as we were climbing it. The remaining slopes went smoothly, and soon we were brewing coffee on the summit as the sun

[Above] Frieder Wittmann coming up to the summit of the Charlatan during the peak's first ascent, by its east ridge. The east face of Mephisto is behind on the left, and the southeast face of the Obelisk is on the right. Arrows mark the 2017 routes; much of the Obelisk line is hidden by a foreground ridge. [Right] Wittmann climbing an aesthetic ice gully midway up Alternative Facts (900m, WI5 M6 A1) on the southeast face of the Obelisk. *Gediminas Simutis*

was starting to hide behind other peaks. We named our line Alternative Facts (900m, WI5 M6 A1) for the times we are living in.

Despite the recent activity in the range, the Revelation Mountains still have many adventures to offer. In particular, we regretted not having brought our climbing shoes for the imposing rock buttresses, as well as more technical skis for the many steep snow descents. We would like to thank Paul Roderick for flying us into the valley and the Academic Alpine Club Zurich for generous support of our expedition.

— **GEDIMINAS SIMUTIS**, *LITHUANIA/SWITZERLAND*

The Salmon Shark in the Serendipity Spires of southwest Alaska, showing the line of Predatory Waters (1,200', 5.8) up the southeast face and ridge. The Serendipity Spires are located 100 miles west of the nearest road. Zach Clanton discovered this cluster of peaks while snapping photos from a bush plane's window far in the distance. *Zach Clanton*

SERENDIPITY
A STASH OF BEAUTIFUL GRANITE IN WILD SOUTHWEST ALASKA

BY ZACH CLANTON

From June 22 to July 16, 2016, Reese Doyle, James Gustafson, and I spent 25 days exploring an alpine rock climbing arena in southwestern Alaska that we are calling the Serendipity Spires. But the history and meaning of this adventure run much deeper than simply seeing a mountain on a map and going for it.

As Alaskan rock climbers, we have made it our goal to utilize the thriving bush plane culture to continually search the vastness of the Great State for quality stone on peaks with no previous climbing history. This simple prospect excites us to no end.

My first glimpse of the toothy Serendipity Spires was incidental. I snapped a photo of them from a great distance, purely by instinct, while flying to an entirely different destination. It wasn't until months later that I took a closer look at my telephoto images and started the investigation. I had to cross-reference the photographs' time stamps and approximate headings on the aviator's compass with Google Earth images and inaccurate topo maps. After the coordinates were certain, I still had no idea what the rock would be like or how to approach a base camp. I would have to wait another year to get in the plane once more.

When the day of departure finally came and our bags were packed, a floatplane carried us 100 miles west of the nearest road, in Nikiski, and settled into the choppy blue-green waters of Two Lakes, north of the Neacola Mountains and east of the Revelations. We then hiked five days through 16 brutal miles of thick forest, rushing waters, and sprawling tundra east of Two Lakes to a camp beneath the spires. Through tremendous effort, we had discovered our own version of paradise, where peaks remain nameless and even the USGS maps don't speak the truth.

By day eight of the trip we were ready to climb, and we set our sights on a beautiful peak we named the Salmon Shark. The clouds began to lift as we roped up, and pitch by quality pitch this ultra-classic route revealed itself, following the southeast ridge to an unclimbed coffee-table summit. Predatory Waters (1,200', 5.8) was one of the wildest adventures I have ever known. Some downclimbing and two long rappels brought us to a col from which we were able to hike back to camp.

After completing Predatory Waters, we turned our attention to a striking arête on unnamed formation near the Salmon Shark. Due to a full week of rain (luckily we brought whiskey), our first attempt was delayed until day 19 of the trip. Laden with bivy gear and multiple days of food and water, we got a mere four pitches off the ground.

On day 22, with supplies dwindling and a four-day hike out still ahead of us, we made our final attempt, going as light as possible. The arête featured laser-cut cracks one after another—an impeccable 5.11 second pitch gave passage to glorious back-to-back 5.10 splitter pitches above. The Finite Spur, as we're calling it, was a legendary climb in the making, but unfortunately cut short by lack of time and supplies. We were 10 pitches up but less than halfway to the top. If we continued, it would be at least another one to two days before we got back to camp, and as good as the climbing was, we had to think about our survival in this wild coun-try. As it turns out, we made it back to Two Lakes with only one salami left in our packs. Luckily, the plane was able to pick us up that same afternoon.

With tools like Google Earth and guidebooks documenting nearly every climb on the planet, it's easy for the modern climber to forget that unex-plored corners of the world remain. I go through the effort to do these exploratory trips not just because I believe the best rock climbs in Alaska are yet to be found, but also to show people an untamed world they never knew existed. Images have the power to spark the imagination. And the alpinist's imagination is the most fundamental tool we possess. 📷

SUMMARY: First ascent of the Salmon Shark, just south of the Hidden Moun-tains in the Alaska Range, July 2016, by Predatory Waters (southeast ridge, 1,200', 5.8). This trip was supported by the Copp-Dash Inspire Award and the Mazamas' Monty Smith Memorial Grant.

James Gustafson climbing low-angle splitters along the ridge crest during the first ascent of the Salmon Shark. *Reese Doyle*

"Hero ridge scrambling" partway up the south side of Mt. Russell (11,670'), high above the upper east fork of the Dall Glacier. *Freddie Wilkinson*

MODERN CLASSIC
THE SOUTH RIDGE OF MT. RUSSELL IN THE ALASKA RANGE

BY FREDDIE WILKINSON

DANA "MADDOG" DRUMMOND and I knew we were in for a good time when Paul Roderick admitted this was his first time landing on the East Fork of the Dall Glacier. Six miles up valley from our base camp lay the east face of Mt. Russell (11,670'), an impressive wall first climbed by Dave Auble and Charlie Townsend in 1989. Maddog's and my intentions were comparatively modest. Over the past decade, Russell's voie normale, the north ridge, first climbed in 1972, had become increasingly broken up and blocked by problematic crevasses. To the best of our knowledge, the mountain hadn't been summited in the last five years. We hoped to find a new and moderate line to Russell's elusive summit, and to make good on my promise to Maddog that we wouldn't get in over our heads, we had brought a spare selection of hardware, including half a dozen ice screws, a biner of nuts, and three pitons.

We left our base camp at 4,900' early on April 7 and headed for what we called the south face, a triangular feature bounded by two tributary spurs that rise to form the south ridge of the mountain. A line of steep snowfields led to the left-hand spur. Perfect granite gendarmes and hero ridge scrambling followed. Ten hours after leaving camp, we arrived at a snowfield a few hundred feet below the apex of the face and decided this was our best chance to dig a snow cave. After another three hours of aggressive chopping and man-labor, we had carved a ten-foot torpedo tube capable of housing us both head to toe.

The next morning we left most of our kit and set off for the summit. The weather seemed iffy but held enough promise of clearing to lure us on. Mellow ridge climbing led to a short corniced traverse before the ridge met with the final summit slopes. This last section of the ascent yielded otherworldly yet technically easy climbing as we navigated "Russell's Cheeks," a distinctive series of rime formations. On the summit we were rewarded with about five seconds of the lovely view looking north to Foraker before the approaching storm enveloped us for good. We carefully reversed the route to our cozy snow cave, where we elected to spend a fun-filled 36 hours snuggled together before returning to our base camp at a leisurely pace.

Although the first ascent of the Russell, accomplished in 1962 by a German and American team, is often described as having followed the south ridge, this is misleading. The party began their ascent on the Chedotlothna Glacier, to the north of the mountain, and followed a glacial route around its western flank to reach the col ("Bavarian Col") on the main divide between Russell and Point 9,803', southwest of the summit. From there, they ascended a 600' "steep ice ramp" on the west face to reach the south ridge. We surmise that they gained the south ridge just before or after the steepest section of corniced ridge we negotiated, approximately 1,500' below the summit. Given the overall length of the route and the fact that we followed the south ridge from its side of the divide, we feel confident saying ours was the first ascent of the south ridge. A better descriptor for the 1963 line might be the west face.

[Top] **The corniced and rime-laden upper south ridge.** [Bottom] Mt. Russell's south side, showing the line climbed in 2017. The "Bavarian Col" (left) was accessed from the north by the German team that did the first ascent of Russell in 1962. They climbed the face above the col to reach the upper south ridge and the summit. *Freddie Wilkinson*

The lighthearted spontaneity of our little adventure belies an incredible stroke of luck. I have no doubts that Maddog and I stumbled onto one of the best technical moderates in the entire Alaska Range. The south ridge of Russell could and should have been done a half century ago. It's every bit as classy as the west ridge of Hunter, the French Ridge on Huntington, or the Cassin on Denali.

SUMMARY: First ascent of the south ridge of Mt. Russell (5,000', AK Grade 4), April 7–10, 2017, by Dana Drummond and Freddie Wilkinson.

John Giraldo heading along the ridge between Mt. Gabriel and Mt. Laurens (directly behind) on day two of the traverse. Behind and right is Mt. Red Beard, first climbed in 2001 by Jim LaRue and Jamal Lee-Elkin. *Jason Stuckey*

MT. GABRIEL, FIRST ASCENT, AND MT. LAURENS, COMPLETE WEST RIDGE

FOR THE PAST year we had been planning a trip into the Revelations, for which we had won a McNeill-Nott Award. But after waiting almost a week to fly in, with low clouds sitting over some key passes, our pilot suggested an alternative destination: a seldom-visited area on the southwest side of Mt. Foraker. On April 4, Chad Diesinger, John "The Poodle" Giraldo, and I flew onto the Yentna Glacier and set up base camp at the edge of the wilderness boundary. The only signs of life we saw for the next 10 days were a couple of birds and two planes that flew over briefly.

After some scouting, we climbed a 3,000' route on an unnamed 8,535' peak above our base camp by the east face and north ridge. On the first day we simul-climbed snow and broken mixed terrain down low, roped up for some steeper rock pitches up to 5.7, put the ropes away for some moderate terrain in the middle of the face, and then roped up again when we joined the north ridge, where we encountered steep snow and ice up to AI3. We bivied about 600' below the summit.

The next day a series of gendarmes blocked our way. A rappel off the first gendarme put us at a notch in the ridge. At this point Chad wasn't feeling psyched, so he decided to downclimb a straightforward snow couloir below the notch and head back to base camp. The Poodle and I continued, with the plan of heading up and over this peak, down to a col below the west ridge of Mt. Laurens (10,042'), and then on to the summit of Laurens.

We traversed across rock and deep, unconsolidated snow for several time-consuming rope lengths before finally reaching the summit of the 8,535' peak. We continued toward Laurens along the crest of the ridge, curving around to the east and simul-climbing on moderate terrain. The Poodle suggested it might be faster to put away the rope, then quickly reconsidered as a giant piece of the ridge broke away at his feet. I was really happy we'd stayed roped up when I broke off an even bigger cornice about an hour later.

We bivied again on a broad snow shoulder about 1,500' below the top of Mt. Laurens. In the morning, after an incredible sunrise, we simul-climbed the ridgeline, which was heavily corniced and steep, to reach the summit plateau. From the central summit, we could see the east summit was a few feet higher, so we headed that way. About an hour later we were on top. Returning the way we'd come, we reached the col and then traversed to a large snow slope and down-climbed to our skis.

Once back in the world of computers, we contacted Steve Gruhn, an expert chronicler of Alaskan ascents. To the best of his knowledge, our ascent of the 8,535' peak was the first. We decided to name it Mt. Gabriel, in honor of a dear friend who had passed away a few weeks prior to our trip. The upper west ridge of Mt. Laurens had been soloed by Austrian badass Thomas Bubendorfer back in 1997, approaching via the north face. [*Graham Zimmerman and Mark Allen made the peak's second ascent in 2013 via the northeast buttress. The 2017 climb was likely the third ascent.*]

Mt. Gabriel (8,535'), showing the line of the Cleveland Steam (5.7 A0 AI3 60'). After making the first ascent of Gabriel, John Giraldo and Jason Stuckey continued left along the ridgeline to the summit of Mt. Laurens (10,042', out of frame), making that peak's third known ascent. The high peak in the background is Mt. Russell. *John Giraldo*

Overall, our climb was three miles from the bergschrund below Gabriel to the summit of Mt. Laurens, 2.5 miles of that being new terrain, with 6,000' of vertical gain. We called our route the Cleveland Steam (5.7 A0 AI3 60°). We'd like to thank the McNeill-Nott Award for the generous support they provided us on this trip. 📷

— JASON STUCKEY

DENALI SUMMARY AND SPEED RECORD

FORTY-TWO PERCENT OF climbers registered to attempt Denali reached the summit in 2017, the lowest percentage since 2014. More than 90 percent of the summit days were after May 30. No climbers succeeded on Mt. Foraker (Sultana).

In a difficult season on Denali, the highlight was a speed ascent by Katie Bono from Colorado, who left Kahiltna base camp at 6:01 a.m. on June 13 and followed the West Buttress Route to the summit in 14 hours 45 minutes. Her round-trip time was 21 hours 6 minutes. High winds caused drifting snow and whiteout, forcing her to break trail for two long sections of the route. Both the ascent and round-trip times are the fastest known for a female climber. Kilian Jornet (Spain) set the fastest ascent time (9:43) in 2014, using a variation to the West Buttress (*AAJ 2015*).

— DOUGALD MACDONALD, *WITH INFORMATION FROM DENALI NATIONAL PARK*

[Top] Looking down the crux of Colin Haley's solo route up Mt. Hunter's North Buttress, in the first rock band. *Colin Haley* [Bottom] Mt. Hunter's upper northeast ridge from the point where a prior party's tracks ended—the route ahead is obviously not a stroll in the park. In 2012, Haley soloed the North Buttress and climbed this ridge to within 100 meters of the summit before turning around due to exhaustion. *Colin Haley*

MT. HUNTER, NORTH BUTTRESS, FIRST SOLO ASCENT TO SUMMIT

IN MAY 2012, I attempted to solo Begguya (a.k.a. Mt. Hunter, 14,573') via the North Buttress, and in a state of extreme exhaustion I turned around only 100m below the summit. One hundred meters is not a lot of mountain, especially on a route that gains about 2,000m, with the steepest and most technical climbing in the first two-thirds. But since it was an objective that I really cared about, I knew I wouldn't feel satisfied with that near miss.

On May 12, 2017, I woke up around 4:30 a.m., skied up to the base of the North Buttress, and at a deliberately relaxed pace labored up to the bergschrund, which I crossed at 6:35 a.m. Through the first rock band, I climbed on essentially the same line that I had established in 2012. [*This line is well to the right of Deprivation (Backes-Twight, 1994).*] Once on the first ice band, I moved up and left to link up with Deprivation. There was dramatically less ice in the second rock band than in 2012, but fortunately the climbing remained easy.

At about 9 a.m., I began a long ice traverse to the right to join the upper portion of the Björnberg-Ireland Route (1980). In 2012, I had followed this route all the way to its junction with the original Japanese northeast ridge route (1971), at the top of the North Buttress, but then I had to spend perhaps an entire hour tunneling through the cornice. Knowing better this time around, I veered up and left, climbing the classic final ice slope of the Bibler-Klewin (1983) to gain the top of the buttress. I reached this spot, the "Cornice Bivy," at 11:53 a.m., about five and a quarter hours after crossing the 'schrund.

In four previous trips to the top of the North Buttress, I had only managed to reach Begguya's summit once, despite trying hard every time, and I knew to not underestimate the difficulty of the upper northeast ridge. Therefore, I was quite happy to see tracks in the snow from another party. After a quick break to eat and drink, I started up the ridge, looking forward to cruising along a trail. A couple of minutes later, the tracks came to an abrupt end. After feeling briefly disheartened, I continued on my way, and the crazy purist inside me felt a little relieved that I would have to "earn" my solo ascent all on my own.

There were just a few short steps of AI3 along the route, and after some short pockets of calf-deep trail breaking, the snow became pleasantly firm. I pulled out my iPod and enjoyed the non-technical cardio exercise, except for one section of crevasses where I turned off the music and carefully picked my way through.

I arrived on Begguya's summit at 2:22 p.m., 7 hours and 47 minutes after crossing the bergschrund. After more food and water, I started down. Once back at the Cornice Bivy, I down-climbed most of the top ice band on the North Buttress and rappelled the rest of the wall. Descending 1,500m of steep terrain with a single 80m rope makes for a lot of rappels, and I would guess that I did 40 to 45 raps. However, rappelling is faster alone than with a partner, and by 9:53 p.m. I was below the bergschrund. (I had preplaced a few anchors low on the Bibler-Klewin during a "cragging" day with Mikey Schaefer a week earlier, the biggest concession of style on my solo.) At 10:20 p.m., I was back in Kahiltna base camp, 17 hours and 13 minutes after leaving.

I think that my solo on Begguya set various speed records. However, much more significant and meaningful to me is how much faster I was able to climb compared with my attempt in 2012. That year I took 15 hours and 10 minutes to climb from the bergschrund to the Cornice Bivy—nearly three times as long!

I was faster in part due to better conditions, better weather, better and lighter equipment, and wiser strategy. This time I free soloed everything, while in 2012 I had self-belayed a few short bits. I saved time by not carrying a stove for melting snow and eating; I brought only bars and gels, plus four liters of water insulated with bubble wrap. Strategy aside, I have become a better technical climber and have greater cardiovascular fitness compared with 2012. Those personal improvements, and the very direct, quantitative evidence of them, are the most satisfying aspect of my solo ascent. 📄 📷

— COLIN HALEY

RUTH GORGE, NEW ROCK ROUTES

DESPITE BEING ACCOMPANIED to the Ruth Gorge by the all-star team of Alex Honnold and Renan Ozturk, conditions and motivations didn't align for a big adventure. Instead, we made two minor first ascents on the sunny side of the gorge.

On June 17, Alex and I climbed a new line on the buttress immediately north of the Stump. This route began with a 5.11 fist crack through a roof, followed by an impressive 400' 5.10 offwidth (thanks Alex!) before relenting to simul-climbable terrain. We called it the Alaskan Monster (1,000', 5.11).

On June 20, Renan, Alex, and I climbed a probable new line on the southeastern aspect of the Stump. From below the start of Goldfinger, we hiked east toward the Eye Tooth for 15 or 20 minutes to reach the start of our route. It had a few OK pitches, but the rock paled in comparison to the nearby Goldfinger (McNamara-Puryear, 2004). We named this one the Stump Rider (1,500', 5.11). 📷

— FREDDIE WILKINSON

Alex Honnold slays the Alaskan Monster (5.11) in the Ruth Gorge. *Freddie Wilkinson*

SAVAGE BEASTS
BEAUTIFUL NEW ROUTES ABOVE THE BUCKSKIN GLACIER

BY WILL SIM

IN EARLY MAY, Greg Boswell, Lindsay Yule, Paul Prentice, and I (all from the U.K.) flew to the lower Buckskin Glacier with food for three weeks. It was a trip with no set objectives but with lots of ideas and flexibility in mind. Aware that we had flown in during a huge high-pressure system, we set about climbing immediately. Over the next 10 days, Greg and I climbed two new routes, including the first ascent of a mountain.

Our first objective was the obvious huge fault line splitting the southeast face of the Bear Tooth. The first day we climbed a couloir and thin connecting ramp that bypasses a dangerous icefall below the chimney. This made the route safer and better than running the gauntlet under seracs. [*Editor's note: In 2007, Jesser Billmeier, Zach Shlosar, and Jared Vilhauer climbed directly up this icefall and connected into a couloir system to the left of the chimney climbed by Boswell and Sim. The 2007 ascent ended just below the cornice on the southwest ridge.*] We then had a luxury

Will Sim leaves the chimney feature on the Bear Tooth's southeast face, hoping to outflank a rotten and overhanging section of the chimney. Sim and Greg Boswell climbed 30 sustained pitches and topped out their new route Beastiality (1,400m) after three days of climbing. *Greg Boswell*

bivy on the lip of a crevasse on the hanging glacier, beneath the 900m headwall.

Day two was slow, absorbing, and stressful as we navigated up and around the fault line. Rotten and blank rock forced us out right onto the face for eight or nine pitches. This felt a bit like climbing on El Cap in crampons, but was extremely fun and engaging—the whole time we were unsure if it would be possible to re-enter the chimney.

A make-or-break last lead of the day saw me up a nerve-wracking pitch to a point where I reckoned we could access the chimney again. I fixed a line so we could lower to the only bum-seat bivy in sight, and then we had an uncomfortable few hours of continually slipping off the ledge in our sleeping bags.

On day three we miraculously managed to re-enter the chimney and had one of the most amazing days ever on sustained, sometimes thin, five-star ice, all the time pinching ourselves that the route was actually going. We topped out into a windless sunset, strolled to the summit, and bivied again. The next day we rappelled the line, which surprisingly went without a hitch! Beastiality (1,400m) had roughly 30 sustained pitches, with some of the best and most continuous technical climbing I've ever done on a big route—it was simply Alaskan perfection.

After two days of rest, there was no sign of the good weather leaving us, so we decided to try a smaller but very technical line up the center of an unnamed pyramidal mountain directly across the glacier from the east face of the Bear Tooth. We were unsure what tactics to employ, but in the end it did require a bivy, despite only being about 600m and 15 pitches.

All the pitches had some spice: scary, thin ice, snow mushrooms requiring careful clearing, and just hard climbing. As on Beastiality, we were blown away by the quality of climbing—the kind of route where you lean back on the belay after leading and can't stop smiling about how outrageous the last 40m had been.

We named the route Shark Fishing (600m), as the colors and shapes of some of the granite features resemble the markings of a great white shark. We found some tat from a previous attempt at the top of pitch two, but nothing above. To our knowledge, this peak was previously unclimbed, and we gave the mountain the unofficial name of Shark Tooth, keeping in line with the local animal and dental names.

We haven't put any grades to either of our routes, as we felt like it wouldn't enhance our experience, nor do the climbing justice. One person's M6 is another's M9; one season a granite seam is a streak of ice. I don't think I have ever done a mountain route where a number has done a good job of explaining the difficulty. Both of our routes featured sustained ice and dry tooling, and all of the climbing went free.

I hope that in years to come, when people

[Top] Greg Boswell climbs a spectacular steep ice runnel on the new route Beastiality (1,400m) on the southeast face of Bear Tooth. Boswell and Will Sim spent three days on the route, bivied on the summit, and rappelled on the fourth day. *Will Sim* [Bottom] A foreshortened view of the Bear Tooth, showing the line of Beastiality (1,400m, 2017). The route House of the Rising Sun (Billmeier-Shlosar-Vilhauer, 2007) climbed the icefall directly and continued up the obvious cleft to the left of Beastiality as far as the southwest ridge. The prominent buttress to the right of Beastiality is the southeast pillar, climbed in 2002 by a Polish expedition. Other routes ascend the faces to the right. At far right is the southeast face of the Moose's Tooth. *Greg Boswell*

are climbing incomprehensibly hard, routes such as Arctic Rage and NWS on Moose's Tooth, and Bear Skin and Beastiality on Bear Tooth, will be often-repeated classics, so that more people can see the incredible quality of climbing on these walls. 📷

A Chelatna Lake Lodge plane heads over the rainbow, with the Dogtooth in the background. The peak is close in geographic space to the end of the lake, but not close in real time. *Zach Clanton*

THE RAMPARTS, FIRST ASCENT OF THE DOGTOOTH

NEVER HAVE I sandbagged my friends or myself so hard. I convinced my poor unsuspecting victims, Reese Doyle and Robin Miller, to take a lovely flight out to my friend Matt Bertke's lodge at stunning Chelatna Lake, a little over 40 miles west of Talkeetna. We would then enjoy an eight-mile, beer-in-hand jet-boat cruise across the lake to a picturesque white-sand beach, where we would begin a three-mile approach hike. The objective was an unclimbed granite pinnacle known locally as the Dogtooth. At the southern gateway to the Ramparts, this peak rises sharply above a jungle of alders, just west of the toe of the famed Kahiltna Glacier.

The struggle began almost immediately. We spent two days just trying to make it to base camp, which was still far from the climbing. We fought like hell with heavy packs, sometimes waist-deep in moving water, through 15-foot-tall alders so dense and disorienting they blotted out the sun.

In all, this first attempt lasted five days, just to be stormed off the mountain at the base of the first pitch. But nobody had it worse than Titus the dog. In a single hour, he got porcupined in the face and had a standoff with a bear and her two cubs. The logical thing would have been to write off this peak and move on. But the prospect of such an incredible-looking unclimbed mountain within sight of Matt's sauna deck was just too much for me.

After we dried out our piles of soaking clothes and gear at the lodge and had a good night's rest, Reese and I loaded up the jet boat with chainsaws. Our aim was to tunnel a trail through the alders for Matt's guests at the lodge and other adventurers (including us). After three days of hard manual labor, we had built a proud one-mile trail to the Denali National Park boundary, where game trails led farther into the park. A section of approach that had taken us nine hours on our first go would now take less than two. But the weather was closing in and my friends had to get back to their jobs in Anchorage.

A week later, my next victim, Travis Powell, and I cruised the approach to base camp, a.k.a.

Swamp Camp, where water squirts up between your toes when you step out of the tent onto the tundra. Above Swamp Camp the alder jungle rises for 3,500' to reach the real climbing, with relentless steepness and slick rock slabs. With lighter packs and lessons learned, however, we were much quicker than before, and in less than five hours we were standing on the wildly exposed southeast ridge of the Dogtooth.

Here, our incredible effort was finally rewarded, as a classic ridge climb unfolded into 1,200' of 5.6 glory. The climbing was so fun and solid that we simul-climbed the entire route, only stopping to belay when we wanted to give each other the thrill of leading new terrain. After a close call with a thunderstorm that snuck up on us, we reached the summit. I had contacted Matt at the lodge via InReach when we got close, and now he buzzed us with his Super Cub eight times. We named our route Eye Level for the airplane that buzzed us at eye level, the lightning bolt that had appeared at eye level, and because Travis had gotten stung between the eyes by a wasp on the approach.

Partway down the long descent, we couldn't bear the thought of steep downhill bushwhacking in the dark, so we found a grassy spot to lay our heads, put on our mosquito nets, and passed out. Deep satisfaction saturated us to the bone, and we didn't wake up until nine hours later, when it started to rain. Then the real saturation began.

— ZACH CLANTON

COAST MOUNTAINS

DEVILS THUMB, NORTH PILLAR, SECOND ASCENT (SOLO)

I ARRIVED IN Petersburg, Alaska, at the end of July, about six weeks after setting sail from Port Hadlock, Washington, in *Ember*, my Freya 39 sailboat. I was keen to get off the boat for a while, and a long walk to a big mountain seemed like just the thing. The normally soggy weather gave way to sunshine, but the locals remained pessimistic. The forecasters didn't know it yet, but nearly two weeks would pass before the next rainfall. I headed off to try the North Pillar of Devils Thumb (VI 5.9).

From my sailboat anchored in Scenery Cove, I rowed up Thomas Bay in my 8' dinghy *Scrounge*. Floating slush thwarted easy access to the Baird Glacier, so I had to tackle it from its heavily crevassed

Cole Taylor at his spectacular sitting bivy partway up the North Pillar of the Devils Thumb (VI 5.9, Plumb-Stutzman, 1997). Taylor's ascent was the second (and first solo) of the route, which he accomplished in a nine-day round trip from his boat in Thomas Bay. *Cole Taylor*

central toe. I progressed in stages, reconnoitering unburdened then doubling back for my gear, until I gained a convincing spine. A mile of crest walking up a network of ice ribs brought me to a buffed path of ice winding up the center of the glacier.

Arrow marks the North Pillar of Devils Thumb. Unwilling to climb beneath the dangerous northwest face, Taylor approached via the south side of the peak (hidden), from right to left, then traversed past the classic east ridge and northeast face (left) to reach the pillar. *John Scurlock*

The first ascent of the North Pillar, made by Bob Plumb and David Stutzman in August 1977, began on the left side of the 6,000' northwest face of the Thumb. Starting directly up the face, they were persuaded by rockfall, a running waterfall, and technical difficulty to traverse into the icefall on the left. They had to bivouac in the icefall before reaching the main pillar. That whole business looked terrifying. I dodged into the south arm of the Witches Cauldron, aiming to traverse around the peak to reach the upper 3,000' of the pillar.

The inner Cauldron is a mash of quarry-fresh talus blanketed across dwindling ice, and I had some spooky close calls on the unstable terrain. Climbing the south icefall felt wild and inadvisable—4,000' of things you should never do unroped. Six days after leaving Petersburg, I reached the southern shoulder of Devils Thumb. It's an unlikely place to make acquaintances, but Mike and Tyler were already there, cozy in camp, having choppered from town a couple of hours earlier to climb the classic east ridge. They delivered a dream forecast, and we spent the evening ramping stoke for the mountain above.

In the morning I left the tent pitched below the southeast face and continued my slow spiral up the mountain. I crossed the eastern shoulder of the Thumb and traversed beneath the northeast face over frightening, snow-covered crevasses. It was a relief to finally reach the solid rock of the pillar. The first few hundred feet is the steepest part. I self-belayed two pitches, then, once on easier terrain, I free soloed as much as possible (pack on my back, trailing my lone 7.7mm rope, and wearing my boots to avoid carrying them), occasionally pulling out a tool to deal with snow and ice. I stopped in a notch roughly midway up the pillar and spent the night seated on a small ledge.

The next day I climbed some dandy cracks in the morning sun, eventually reaching the long snow band that Plumb and Stutzman had traversed leftward to join the upper east ridge. Plumb had told me about a possible direct finish he'd seen around to the right, but by then I'd spotted Mike and Tyler high on the east ridge, and it seemed a sure thing I'd catch them in time to join their descent if I blasted across the snow. But soon I was puckered up, excavating a path through sugar snow across the top of the snow band. I had to back off a couple of moves to regroup. Then I pulled off a handhold and wavered for an instant on the brink of destruction.

I couldn't shake the gut-sick feeling until I'd anchored securely at the far side of the traverse and led a pitch of wet rock, for which I was too flustered to remove my crampons. One more pitch brought me to the east ridge, and soon I caught Mike and Tyler on what passes for a summit up there—a fin of boulders cantilevered into space, 9,077 feet above my boat at sea level. After a proper sky-lounge, we made our way down the southeast face, returning to camp in the moonlight.

First thing in the morning, the boys disappeared in a helicopter and I began the long retreat alone. The glaciers, ever changing, surprised me with fresh hazards. There were some doubtful moments, but I made it safely down the south icefall, out the Witches Cauldron, and back down the Baird Glacier to my dinghy in three days, ending a nine-day round trip.

– COLE TAYLOR

Luke Holloway starting the upper headwall on the first free route up Tara Tower, a neighbor of Lotus Flower Tower in the Cirque of the Unclimbables. *David Allfrey*

THE SOURCE

A BOAT-AND-CLIMB ADVENTURE IN THE NORTHWEST TERRITORIES

BY DAVID ALLFREY

THE TRIP STARTED as a 10-year-old dream of Luke Holloway's, one of my longest climbing partners: Boat the Little Nahanni and South Nahanni rivers to Brintnell Creek, hike into the Cirque of the Unclimbables, then boat the Nahanni for another 100 miles to the Unesco World Heritage Site at Virginia Falls. Luke used to be a river guide and had always dreamed of combining boating and climbing. I signed on immediately because it sounded like a great adventure.

Luke, Carmen Cross Johnson, Colleen Weeks, and I got dropped off by floatplane at Flat Lakes, on the west edge of the MacKenzie Mountains, on July 28. It had rained every day of the month, and the river was nearly at flood stage. We inflated our 11-foot white-water raft and put in. Over the next four days, we boated 90 miles of amazing class 4 white water down the Little Nahanni. Another day of flat water on the South Nahanni River, with a sweet downriver wind, deposited us at the inflow of Brintnell Creek, 140 miles from where we had started.

We packed up the raft (it weighed about 85 pounds), picked up our gear, and hiked six miles through shin-deep bog and moss to Glacier Lake—one of the longest six miles I have ever done. We shouted and talked the whole way for fear of spooking a grizzly in the thick bush. At Glacier Lake, the usual drop-off point for visitors to the Cirque of the Unclimbables, our friend Pat Goodman joined us with the climbing gear and the ladies flew out and began their journey home. Pat, Luke, and I then spent about four weeks exploring the Cirque of the Unclimbables.

[Top]. **Holloway, a former river guide, led the first raft descent of Brintnell Creek to depart the Cirque of the Unclimbables.** *David Allfrey* [Bottom] **The southeast face of Tara Tower. (1) Loeks-Putnam, 1975. (2) The Source (13 pitches, V 5.12, 2017). (3) Eric Weinstein Memorial Route (1984).** *Pat Goodman*

After repeating a few routes and enjoying some welcome rest days due to rain and snow, we all started exploring Tara Tower, the tower immediately to the left of Lotus Flower. It held two old aid routes and hardly any recorded history. We began working on free climbing the tower whenever weather permitted. We had a mix of conditions, but over the next few weeks, climbing in poor and cold weather, we managed the first free ascent of the Tara Tower, establishing a new route that deserves to become a classic: The Source, 13 pitches, V 5.12. Our line starts on the original route up the southeast face (Loeks-Putnam, 1975, VI 5.9 A3) and then breaks after a couple of pitches and climbs independently to the top. [*The other route on the face, the Eric Weinstein Memorial Route (Austrom-Down, 1984, VI 5.10 A3) is farther to the right.*] The team spent four days working on the route; we freed all the pitches but ran out of time before making a continuous free ascent. We placed six protection bolts and bolted rappel anchors.

In early September we broke camp, shouldered 100-pound loads, and hiked back to Glacier Lake. Pat flew out of the mountains with our climbing gear and another team. The next day Luke and I paddled across Glacier Lake and dropped into Brintnell Creek for 10 miles of serious class 5 white water. The boating starts with back-to-back big drops (10 and 25 feet) that you have to run in sequence, as there is nowhere to stop between them. With just the two of us and a single boat, it made for a very serious day. I was fully trusting Luke with my life, and he was trusting me to hit my strokes and stay in the boat. We managed to stomp the lines and complete the first raft descent of Brintnell Creek (it had been kayaked at least once, in 2001, by Will Gadd and team).

Finally we joined the Nahanni once more and continued south for 100 miles to Virginia Falls. We arrived only to find out that plane troubles would not allow a pickup for an additional two days, so we rationed our food and spent a hungry couple of days waiting for our ride and enjoying the massive and unique waterfall.

THUNDER MOUNTAIN, WEST FACE TO NORTH FACE

TWO YEARS AFTER first attempting the unclimbed 1,000m west face of Thunder Mountain (Mt. Nirvana, 2,773m, *AAJ 2016*), Dave Custer, Eric Gilbertson, and Susan Ruff returned in 2017. Their first try was up a buttress just left of their 2015 line, starting from a camp halfway up the face, during which Ruff injured her ankle. After two more attempts, they decided to shift focus to the left side of the face. Their new line started near Trident Col and moved rightward across the west side of Scylla and Charybdis (the two peaks north of Thunder Mountain), then followed a gully to steep cracks below Thunder's northwest ridge. After an attempt on August 6 that ended at a cold bivy below this headwall, Custer and Gilbertson started again early on August 10, completed the steep pitches to the northwest ridge, then moved onto the north face and angled toward the summit, likely above the line followed by Bill Buckingham and Lew Surdam for Thunder's first ascent in 1965. A little under 24 hours after leaving base camp, they reached the top. Their route up the west and north faces of Thunder Mountain involved 30 pitches plus scrambling (1,000m, 5.9). A full account is at the *AAJ* website.

– *INFORMATION FROM* **ERIC GILBERTSON**, USA

SPLIT MOUNTAIN, NORTHEAST FACE, ISENGARD

THE NORTHEAST FACE of Split Mountain, near Terrace, presents an outrageous prow of granite rising out of the mist from a deep, narrow chasm. (This formation is just south of the Skeena River at 54°22'19.00"N, 128°59'37.57"W.) Nick Black, Gary McQuaid, and Tim Russell worked out an approach and established the initial pitches on this feature in 2013 and 2014. The following year, Tyler McDivitt and I joined Tim for an attempt to climb the prow over eight days in capsule style. We were forced to retreat from high on the wall by a storm.

In August 2016, Tim, Tyler, and I made our way back to Split Mountain and retraced our previous route, including the two crux pitches (5.11+ and 5.11). On the third night on the wall, we received a forecast for a storm. The next day we climbed past our 2015 high point into steep, uncertain terrain. Tim led the final pitch of run-out slab and a 5.10+ roof before pulling a dicey mantel onto the flat summit just as the daylight died on August 10. Ten minutes later, we found ourselves in the lashing rain of a cold West Coast storm. An epic descent of stuck ropes and shivering got us back at our portaledge camp, soaked to the bone, at 2:30 a.m. We named the route Isengard (450m, 5.11+ A1) after the fortress from *The Lord of the Rings*, as we felt it captured the hostile nature of the wall and the primordial feel of the area.

– **GRANT STEWART**, CANADA

THE MADELINE WALL, KIDS IN THE HAUL: *One week before completing Isengard, Grant Stewart and Tim Russell teamed up with Laurent Janssen and Gary McQuaid to finish a multiyear effort on a 700m route up a big south face near the junction of Madeline Creek and the Ecstall River, a tributary of the Skeena River. They called their route Kids in the Haul (VI 5.10 A1), and the cliff the Madeline Wall. The full story of this ascent is in the 2017 Canadian Alpine Journal.*

KING LINE

THE SOUTHWEST FACE OF MONARCH IN THE COAST MOUNTAINS

BY SIMON RICHARDSON

How a Scottish-German climbing team came to know about one of the finest unclimbed features in western Canada requires some explanation. My fascination with Monarch Mountain (3,555m), the second-highest massif in the Coast Mountains, began 20 years ago when Dave Hesleden and I traversed the Serra Group in the Waddington Range. As we tussled with the jagged crest, Monarch stood out like a sentinel 70 miles to the north. With a prominence of 2,925m, there is no higher peak until you reach Mt. Fairweather, a thousand miles up the spine of the coastal range. I was smitten by Monarch's dominance and resolved to climb it.

The Coast Mountains had got under my skin, and I made two further trips to the Waddington massif, a couple to the Pantheon Spires, and one to the difficult-to-access Mt. Gilbert to the south. During this time I became friendly with Don Serl, who had made five visits to Monarch, culminating in the first ascent of the stupendous pinnacled north ridge in July 2000 with Bill Durtler and Bruce Fairley. This was the fourth route on the mountain, and it seemed unlikely that Monarch would yield any further major lines. [*Monarch was first climbed in 1936, by the east ridge, by Hans Fuhrer and Henry S. Hall Jr.*]

In April 2007, mountain photographer John Scurlock set off from Seattle in his home-built airplane, bound for the Monarch Icefield. During a circumnavigation of the mountain, he photographed the rarely seen southwest face with its compelling central spur. This unclimbed 1,250m line prompted awe and excitement in equal measure—a veritable Walker Spur leading directly to the summit. John published his photos on the Internet, where Don and I saw them. We considered making an attempt on the stunning feature, but our expedition failed to materialize. Don later made plans without me, but these also fell by the wayside. Other teams considered the route, but nobody made a serious attempt. Later, Don retired from climbing and one of the unclimbed jewels of the Coast Mountains lay almost forgotten and untouched.

My interest in Monarch was rekindled when Micha Rinn and I climbed a 1,600m new route on the south side of the Grandes Jorasses, in July 2016. The Diamond Ridge was a logical and proud line, never very difficult but long and committing. We were looking for a similar objective for 2017, and I suggested Monarch.

On July 28, we helicoptered to the col between Monarch Mountain and Page Mountain at the head of the Empire Way Glacier. Two days later, we warmed up by climbing Peak 2,625m from the north and then descending the south ridge to the col separating the Empire Way Glacier from the Monarch Icefield. There was a cairn on top, and we presume the peak had been ascended by the rocky south ridge from the col. On August 1 we climbed the Broda-Dudra route on the west face of Monarch, a substantial climb on rock, mixed, and snow. This was the second route up the mountain, climbed in 1953, and had only seen a handful of repeats. It provided an interesting and somewhat demanding mountaineering route (D) and would be our descent route if we were successful on the southwest spur.

After a reconnaissance, we started up the southwest face at 6 a.m. on August 4. Our ascent was delayed by high winds and low cloud, and for the first time on the trip the air was full of smoke and ash from the forest fires raging that summer

[Top] **Micha Rinn traversing the summit ridge of Monarch Mountain after climbing Game of Thrones on the southwest face. The Waddington group is visible in the distance.** *Simon Richardson* [Above] **Route line for Game of Thrones (1,250m, ED2 5.10a) on the southwest face of Monarch Mountain.** *John Scurlock*

Micha Rinn on day two of Game of Thrones, the first ascent of the southwest face of Monarch Mountain. The compact, metamorphic rock was difficult to protect. *Simon Richardson*

in British Columbia. We convinced ourselves there was no harm in just "having a look." After an initial loose pitch, the rock improved and we committed ourselves to the ascent. We had seen from the west face that the lower half of the spur is comprised of a series of very steep towers, so, rather than follow the crest, we climbed a more direct line to its left before bivouacking at the foot of the impressive upper spur at half-height on the face.

The climbing had become gradually more difficult during the first day and was particularly challenging on day two as we climbed the crest of the upper spur. Unlike the Waddington Range, which is mainly comprised of excellent granite, Monarch's rock is a metamorphosed volcanic variety. Although this was very solid in the upper half of the route, the rock was compact with few protection possibilities, and the holds sloped downward rather alarmingly. We had numerous long runouts, and at times were worried whether the route would go, but fortunately we were always able to find a climbable line.

At the top of the upper pillar the ridge provided easier climbing and we were able to simul-climb for about 200m. We bivouacked for a second time 70m below the summit ridge. Our ledge was cramped and exposed, and it was cold in our thin sleeping bags, but it was one of the finest bivouacs I've ever enjoyed. Below us lay 1,200m of challenging alpine ground, and all we had to do the following morning was to climb a couple of mixed pitches to gain the summit ridge.

We were on the summit early on August 6, enjoying a surreal view of the tops of the surrounding peaks rising above a layer of light gray smoke. The descent of the west face went smoothly, and we arrived back at our tent late that afternoon.

We called our route Game of Thrones and graded it ED2 5.10a. As expected, it was similar in difficulty and scale to the Walker Spur on the Grandes Jorasses, but more serious. We would not have been able to descend from above half-height because the compact rock would have quickly exhausted our rack.

After a day's rest lounging around at base camp we made the first ascent of the Sugarloaf (2,620m) on August 8; this is the highest peak on the pinnacled ridge running north from Peak 2,625m. Although not technically difficult, this proved to be almost a climb too far, as it traversed over six summits and we soon realized we were still very tired after our Monarch ascent. We flew out two days later. 📷

SUMMARY: First ascent of the southwest face of Monarch Mountain by Game of Thrones (1,250m, ED2 5.10a), by Simon Richardson (U.K.) and Micha Rinn (Germany), August 4-6, 2017. The two also made the first ascent of the Sugarloaf (Peak 2,620m) and climbed Peak 2,625m from the north.

HOMATHKO ICEFIELD, PEAK 9,331' AND OTHER NEW ROUTES

I FIRST LAID eyes upon the beautiful northeast face of Peak 9,331' while walking across the Homathko Icefield in 2016. Upon returning to the frontcountry, I was excited to find that the peak had not been climbed. Later that summer, I asked Fred Giroux if he would be interested in a mostly human-powered mission to the area. We spent the winter planning and training.

On May 15, Fred and I began our epic journey out to the Homathko Icefield. We took a water taxi up Bute Inlet to Homathko Camp, then trekked across the Teaquahan Valley to the Galleon Valley. For four and a half days we slogged through the bush, skied, and were tossed around by our packs until we reached a campsite half a kilometer from Mt. Grenville (10,001'). We hadn't weighed our packs, but we did decide to name them: Fred's was Soul Crusher, and mine was Suffer Sack. We estimated them at around 85 pounds each.

On May 25 we headed to the northwest face of Mt. Grenville. The face had been climbed in September 1991 by Michael Down and Alan Fletcher (on a heli-supported expedition), via a snow slope of about 50°. To the right is a gorgeous steep face of snow, ice, and rock. We ascended a mostly iced-up line on that face to an upper right-trending ramp. After pitching out the crux headwall, we simul-climbed the ridge to the summit. We named our new line (as we did with all the routes on this trip) after a character or place from Gabriel García Márquez' *One Hundred Years of Solitude*: Melquíades (350m, AI4 M4+).

The next day we were up early and descending to the base of the northeast face of Peak 9,331'. We moved quite quickly and climbed this route in 2.5 hours from base to summit, ascending steep snow to a 75° ice step on the west side of the glacier. There was significant overhead hazard on this route, so moving fast was essential. We named our route Remedios the Beauty (600m, AI3). On the summit we honored my friend Cory Hall by spreading some of his ashes; Cory passed away in 2014 while climbing in Peru.

After climbing these two fine lines and skiing the north ridge of Mt. Grenville, we decided to head back to the toe of the Bute Glacier and try the north side of Mt. Bute via a potential new line. But with warm temperatures and constant snow movement, we decided instead to ramble our way up the south side of Galleon Peak. We mostly scrambled on dry rock, roping up only for four pitches of fun climbing. We called this route Macondo (600m, 5.10). This was possibly the second ascent of Galleon Peak, which was first climbed by Coast Mountain legends John Clarke and Jeff Eppler in September 1988.

With weather moving in, we decided to retreat. After six and a half hours of shwacking, linking the strands of flagging tape that mark the route, we made it back to Homathko Camp on June 1. Our trip was supported by the John Lauchlan Memorial Award.

– MAX FISHER, *CANADA*

Remedios the Beauty (600m, AI3) on the northeast face of Peak 9,331'. *Max Fisher*

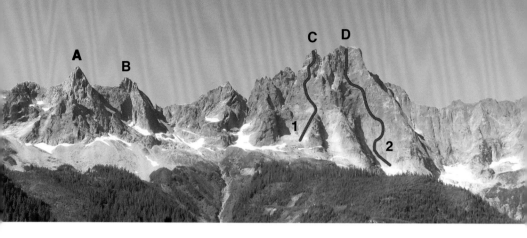

The Slesse group from the east, showing (A) Labour Day Horn, (B) Station D, (C) South Peak, and (D) Slesse Mountain. The 2017 traverses spanned the full massif from left to right. (1) Approximate line of Navigator Wall. (2) Approximate line of 2017 free variation to the east face of Slesse. *Steph Abegg*

SLESSE SOUTH PEAK, NAVIGATOR WALL, FIRST WINTER ASCENT

MARC-ANDRÉ LECLERC HAD told me about a winter project he had been dreaming of on Slesse Mountain. "Dude, it's awesome! I reckon there's a new line! It's so steep, I think you'd need a portaledge," he said. When I arrived at the start of January 2018, the forecast showed a couple days of good weather and Marc was psyched—a theme which would continue throughout my trip. In the haze of jet lag, I found myself agreeing to all plans and suddenly was surrounded by stoked Canadians, skiing up to Slesse. Marc had organized a helicopter to fly supplies to our "base camp," thus allowing us to utilize the good weather for climbing rather than load carrying.

Marc's "Mega Proj" wasn't fully formed—ice is required in the lower third. And so we settled for a consolation prize: the first winter ascent of the Navigator Wall on Slesse's South Peak (700m, 6b M7+ R; the climb was first done in 1987 and is rated ED1 5.10+ in summer). Marc had free soloed the route in 2014 during a linkup of three big solo routes on Slesse in one day.

The climbing was on mostly good rock and was either dry-tooling, mixed, or ice. In some places, we had to climb with bare hands and crampons. The wall was in the sunshine for about an hour in the morning, but then went into the shade, which made the bare-hands climbing quite problematic at times. A couple of harder pitches in the M7 or Scottish VIII/IX region proved interesting. The rock was at times sub-optimal, and there were some quite serious runouts too. We skipped the final two headwall pitches of Marc's summer ascent as it was dark. Instead we decided to follow the scrambly terrain up and left, which seemed more logical. 🗒 📷

— TOM LIVINGSTONE, *u.k.*

LABOUR DAY BUTTRESS AND STATION D, FIRST WINTER ASCENTS AND NEW ROUTE: *While Leclerc and Livingstone were climbing Navigator Wall on Slesse Mountain, Kieran Brownie and Brette Harrington made the first winter ascent of Labour Day Buttress (D- 5.7/5.8), which is the northeast buttress of Labour Day Horn, the peak at the south end of the Slesse massif. They then traversed the ridge line to Station D, which they climbed by its east face, just right of the east ridge, making the first winter ascent of that peak. Returning for a three-day trip in February 2018, Harrington, accompanied by Leclerc, led the first ascent of Jupiter Shift (200m, M5+ 85°), a striking gash on the north face of Station D.*

COMPLETE SLESSE MASSIF TRAVERSE

AT THE END of August, Nick Elson and Julian Stoddart (Canada) did a one-day car-to-car traverse of the Slesse Mountain group, from south to north, completing a linkup that may first have been attempted by Coast Mountains legend Don Serl and Rob Nugent in 2006.

Elson and Stoddart began at 4:45 a.m. on August 29 and started climbing with the south ridge of Labour Day Horn, then continued over Peak 5 (Station D), Peak 4, and Peak 3. They rappeled off Peak 3, then simul-climbed to Slesse's South Peak (the crux of the traverse, with some off-route climbing on bad rock) and rappelled off the far side, before climbing the west side of the main summit. After negotiating the Crossover descent route, they were back at their truck 15 hours after leaving.

Just one day earlier, Jenn Carter and Wayne Wallace (both USA) finished a nearly complete traverse of the same group over three days, starting with the northeast buttress of Labour Day Horn. They bivouacked on this summit and on the top of Slesse before descending, having tagged all but Slesse's South Peak, which they bypassed on the west side.

— DOUGALD MACDONALD, *WITH INFORMATION FROM JULIAN STODDART AND WAYNE WALLACE*

SLESSE MOUNTAIN, EAST FACE, FIRST FREE ASCENT

AFTER FIVE TRIPS with four partners over two seasons, I completed the second ascent and first free ascent of Slesse Mountain's east face, climbing with Jacob Cook (U.K.), via a six-pitch variation to the original route (1997, Easton-Edgar, ED2 VI 5.9 A3).

I made my first mission with Ian Strachan in July 2016. The goal was to climb an indirect line, traversing right from the top of the lower spur of the East Pillar into the upper half of the face. Familiarity with the upper route would prove to be a strategic advantage for an eventual direct ascent, especially if benighted. Ian and I completed two new free pitches branching off from the East Pillar before a barrage of rockfall and the ensuing nerves prompted retreat. The progress was hopeful.

A few weeks later, another Squamish local, Paul Cordy, was game to see it go to the summit. We succeeded in establishing the East Face In-Direct (5.10d) in a long day.

Tony McLane starts the "glory layback" of pitch four on the east face of Slesse. McLane and various partners worked out many variations to free the 1,000-meter east face. *Jacob Cook*

Paul followed almost the entire route with two broken fingers after a fall from a committing position low on the climb.

The next obvious step, in the summer of 2017, was to attempt the direct east face, loosely following the Easton-Edgar route. My friend Will Stanhope was interested. We climbed seven pitches before turning back, disheartened at the wetness, loose rock, and difficulty.

Later that summer, Jacob said he was fired up for an attempt. We made the now-familiar journey to the mountain, intent on establishing a new variation that would end where Paul and I had joined the original route with the East Face In-Direct. Hauling a power drill and full bivy kit gave us plenty of opportunity for exploration. The thick forest-fire smoke provided some respite from the morning sun while Jacob mused over the possibility of his van catching fire.

The first day went smoothly, as I had done the first five pitches with Will previously. We climbed mostly moderate terrain with a crux up to 5.11b, eventually stopping to bivy at some spacious ledges about 600' up the wall. The next day we started up unclimbed terrain to the right of the Easton-Edgar. After two dead-ends, five bolts placed, and all the moves freed, our variation brought us to within 30m of our goal of a complete free route. However, since we had not freed the route entirely in good style up to that point, we decided to call it and return to the ground.

With the path now clear, the urgency to return for a single-push free ascent weighed heavily. Happily, the weather was dry and in our favor. Our chance came in early September.

Jacob's extensive background on sketchy British face climbs showed in his speedy confidence. We used double ropes in the traditional way Jacob is accustomed to. Without tagging a line or bag, we moved quickly. Around mid-height, the day's closest call occurred when a large rotten section of the corner I was following collapsed under my weight, luckily not hitting me as I swung into a 90° barn door. After almost coming off, I swung back and clutched a newly exposed edge. Jacob, out of sight, heard the carnage and then me shouting, "I didn't fall! I'm sending!"

The knowledge we'd gained and bolts we placed earlier were instrumental in making the ascent go smoothly. Once on the upper wall, which I'd climbed before with Paul, I took the lead as Jacob and I simul'd through several pitches with minimal or no gear between us. We unroped for a couple hundred feet of easy terrain, content that we'd make the descent in the daylight. We stopped briefly on the summit, in a cloud of mosquitoes, to make a short entry in the summit register: Welcome to the Wack, 1,000m, 5.11d.

It may be a bit surprising how long it took this wall to get a second complete (and first free) ascent. Neither the grade nor the approach is that difficult by modern standards. I don't imagine the route will ever get much action, but it's a big, fun climb on pretty decent stone. It still awaits an onsight. ▤ ▣ ▶

– TONY MCLANE, *CANADA*

CHEAM RANGE, LADY PEAK, NORTH FACE

ON MAY 7, Brette Harrington and Marc-André Leclerc climbed the north face of Lady Peak (2,178m) in the Cheam Range, near Chilliwack. This was likely the first ascent of the face, whose steepest section gains about 500m and is comprised of loose but compact volcanic rock. The two spent 13 hours on the climb, which involved thin ice and technical dry tooling on slabs, often with marginal protection (11 long pitces, 5.8 M4 80°). They topped out at sundown and scrambled to the summit before descending easy slopes to the west. In January 2016, the same pair made the probable first ski descent of the northeast couloir on Lady Peak. ▤

– DOUGALD MACDONALD, *WITH INFORMATION FROM MARC-ANDRÉ LECLERC*

DEEP IN THE WILD

THE FIRST SOLO ASCENT OF MT. GEIKIE'S NORTH FACE

BY TONY MCLANE

I SAT BENEATH a clear, calm sky sipping coffee. The warm beverage soothed my apprehension, which had been building through a long, restless night below the north face of Mt. Geikie. The Lowe-Hannibal Route—750m of beautiful quartzite topped by 450m of icy mixed ground—loomed above. My nerves began to ease as I sat on my pad and watched the sun lift over the horizon. It was August 8. With such fine weather, I was soon more afraid of squandering a great opportunity with a premature retreat than I was of soloing the enormous face.

I packed my bag: two ropes, a light rack, a stove, an ice screw, an ice tool, crampons, an inflatable pad, a day's food, and two days worth of coffee. Harnessing up, I began the approach, eyes enthusiastically soaking up the details of the wall above. I roped up for the bergschrund—getting from the snow to the rock had some tense moments with sandy, loose insecurity. For the next few hundred feet, wearing rock shoes, I free-soloed sustained 5.8, with occasional sections of 5.10, up cracks, chimneys, and open face. The pack was on my back, and I tagged a rope behind me. Every so

The north face of Mt. Geikie (3,298m), rising about 1,400 meters above Tonquin Creek. (1) Hesse-Shilling, 1994. (2) Hudson-Robbins, 1967 (the original route up the face). (3) Dougherty-Sevigny variations, 1988. (4) Hannibal-Lowe, 1979. (5) McLane variation, 2017. (McLane followed the Dougherty-Sevigny line at the start.) (6) Shaw-Simper, 1996. A true wilderness wall, the north face of Geikie is about 15 miles from the nearest highway. *Marc Piché*

often I'd pull up the rope and pile it on a ledge. I hung on a couple of cams in this section for rests, but did not use any protection to aid in upward progress.

Eventually, about 500m off the deck, the buttress steepened and I decided to belay a couple of pitches. The first of these (5.11a, according to the guidebook, but felt more like 5.10c) I freed with a proper solo belay. At the second pitch, the route took an abrupt turn to the right. Here, I made a tension traverse off an old piton, which was followed by free climbing. This section took a considerable amount of time and effort. It was tense work to climb, reverse, and clean the gear. The rock on this part of the wall was of excellent quality: dark, purple, and with ample opportunity for good protection.

At the end of this traverse, I found myself on a large ledge and took off my harness for a rest. Taking stock of the terrain above, I began to doubt if I'd make the top before night-fall. I discovered water and happily sat and drank, soaking in the spectacular surroundings. I reached for my camera but discovered it was gone; the strap must have broken in one of the chimneys below.

The next section passed with less effort and brought an end to the real difficulties. I swapped back to boots and scrambled through a few hundred feet of sandy ledges strewn with running water and patches of snow. At this point, the remaining daylight looked favorable, but I had already covered 900m and fatigue was building noticeably. I started to become concerned that I might make a weakness-induced mistake.

The Lowe-Hannibal continued above through a maze of rock and ice couloirs, but I took aim for a broad buttress to the left. Though this was unclimbed and unknown terrain, it promised a tantalizingly dry rock passage to the summit. I didn't get far before I came upon an amazing flat ledge, and the decision to spend the night there was easy. I ate the rest of my food and settled in for a sleepless night without a bag. Squats and jumping jacks helped keep the cold at bay.

I welcomed the morning sun with black coffee and rising spirits. The summit was only a couple of hundred meters away. The final pitches wove a convoluted path through an unnerving world of dubiously stacked blocks and wet patches. I climbed onto the summit and stood there for a brief moment, then immediately lay down in the hot morning sun and brewed what I would later discover, to my chagrin, was my last coffee packet.

Descending the west face required several tiring hours of rappels (about eight, mostly setting my own anchors), downclimbing, and scrambling down a ridge from the bottom of the west face back over to the north side. I breathed a sigh of relief as I walked down the final scree slope leading to the valley, its grass and water as welcoming as ever. As I walked away, I couldn't help feeling like I had gotten away with something. Like I had prodded a great beast and slipped away unnoticed.

SUMMARY: The north face of Mt. Geikie (3,298m) is in the Tonquin Creek drainage of British Columbia, about 15 miles from the nearest road. Tony McLane (Canada) left Highway 16, west of Jasper, in midafternoon on August 6 and returned to the highway around noon on August 10. The route he followed, the Lowe-Hannibal (George Lowe and Dean Hannibal, August 1979), was the second route up the north face of Geikie and is believed to have been repeated only a handful of times. The 1,200m route is graded ED2 5.11a; the route was free climbed in 2006 by Steve Holeczi and Mike Verwey, with crux pitches of 5.11a and 5.10c R. For his new variation, McLane traversed up and left to join the face's original route near the top; that route was first climbed by John Hudson and Royal Robbins in 1967 (5.9 A3).

MT. PROTEUS, SOUTH FACE

STANDING PROUD AS the tallest peak in the Battle Range, Mt. Proteus (3,198m) has a striking south face that just begs to be climbed. Yet no direct route had been completed up this rock face. The surrounding glaciers, along with deep and steep valleys choked with alder, devil's club, and impressive rock slabs, make any approach on foot rather daunting. We chose to use a helicopter, thanks in large part to a grant from the MEC Expedition Fund. [*Editor's note: The south face of Mt. Proteus is a big rock wall on the left flank of the peak's very prominent eastern buttress, the right flank of which was climbed in 1988 (Tempus Fugit, D+ 5.8, Allen-Horvath).*]

The south face of Mt. Proteus, showing the route line for the B-Team (500m, TD- 5.10a). on the south face of Mt. Proteus. The 1988 route Tempus Fugit (D+ 5.8) starts off-picture to the right and angles left across the slabby east face to the same finish. *Alex Geary*

We flew to Houston Lake in smoky but sunny skies on July 18. After a reconnaissance of the broken Moby Dick Glacier, during which we found a reasonable approach route with our non-technical crampons and single ice axe apiece, we left at sunrise the next day. We were able to step fairly easily over a small bergschrund and onto the south face, where we climbed six pitches of high-quality granite, with a mix of sustained 5.8–5.10a crack and face climbing, before reaching the blocky east buttress. From here, the angle eased off and another six pitches of moderate climbing (up to 5.8) and scrambling brought us to the top. Several pitches on this ridge followed the 1988 route. We called our route the B-Team (500m, TD- 5.10a).

– MADELEINE MARTIN-PRENEY, *CANADA*

BUGABOO SPIRE, NORTH FACE, TUTTI-FRUTTI SUMMER LOVE

IN EARLY AUGUST, Tom Schindfessel (Belgium) and Vlad Capusan (Romania) climbed a long new route on the north face of Bugaboo Spire. After a couple of warmups on established routes, the duo approached the north face and began climbing on August 8. They simul-climbed up to a large ledge and then traversed left of the ledge for 50m to reach a steep and surprisingly clean section of overhanging flakes. Here, they climbed a couple more pitches, fixed ropes, and returned to the ledge for the night.

During their second day on the wall, the team was confronted with dirty offwidths and some aid climbing. They eventually reached a second ledge, more than halfway up the wall, where they spent the night. Running low on water and seeing no options to fill up or melt snow, the pair decided to go light on the third day and push for the summit. According to

The north side of Bugaboo Spire. (1) North Face (Kor-Suhl, 1960). (2) North Face Direct (Robinson-Ehmann). (3) Tutti Frutti Summer Love (Capusan-Schindfessel, 2017). The classic northeast ridge route is mostly hidden behind the left skyline. *Marc Piché*

Capusan, "The upper part of the wall was full of terrifying large blocks that looked as though they could fall at any moment, but we walked like cats and passed them safely."

The pair reached the north summit of Bugaboo Spire at 7 p.m. and began rappelling toward their stashed gear on the second ledge. The descent went slowly, including a few stuck ropes. By the time they reached the ledge, they had been out for 19 hours. In the morning of the fourth day, Capusan and Schindfessel returned to the Vowell Glacier.

"We named our route Tutti Frutti Summer Love (610m, 17 pitches, 5.11+ A3)," Capusan said, "after a famous song that inspired us on the wall. We enjoyed every pitch, and the remoteness of the Vowell valley was outstanding. It was an amazing adventure from one end to the other."

The new route stays mostly to the right of the North Face (Kor-Suhl, 1960) in its lower half, then climbs directly to the north summit, left of the 1960 route, on the upper wall.

— CHRIS KALMAN, *WITH INFORMATION FROM VLAD CAPUSAN, ROMANIA*

Craig McGee on the first pitch (5.11+) of the Beckey-Mather Route on the east face of Snowpatch Spire in the Bugaboos. *Tim Banfield*

SNOWPATCH SPIRE, BECKEY-MATHER, FIRST FREE ASCENT

AFTER MORE THAN 20 seasons in the Bugaboos, and suffering from some lingering injuries, I wasn't sure how much energy I had to devote to my beloved backyard spires. But thanks to my uber-psyched girlfriend, Michelle Kadatz, we found ourselves camped at Applebee in late July as usual. Our original plan had been to go into North Howser, but with a change in the forecast we needed something less committing and decided to check out the original 1959 line up the face by the legendary Fred Beckey and Hank Mather.

Amazingly, this route had somehow escaped the free climbing fiesta of recent decades on the rest of the east face. We cleaned heaps of wet moss with nut tools on the way up, but the line was totally free climbable. After three pitches of climbing and prepping, a fast-approaching storm forced our retreat.

The following weekend I was back with Tim Banfield, We climbed the first four pitches, bolted three anchors, and gave the route a quick scrub with wire brushes. Craig McGee met us that night, and the next day he and I climbed from glacier to summit, rappelled the west face, and made it back to camp in about 14 hours for the route's first free ascent.

We used a left variation on pitches three to five, ascending a long right-facing corner to rejoin the line in the guidebook at the roof. This exceptionally fun variation clearly had been climbed before, as there were rusty pitons and a couple of old bolts on it. We thought the route as a whole was superb, with the crux on the first two pitches (11+ and 12-), followed by three 5.10 pitches and then another eight rope lengths of fun 5.7–5.9 choose-your-own-adventure terrain.

Word quickly spread and the "new" Beckey-Mather received another five or six ascents before the season was done. The route is a significantly easier free climb than anything else on the east face of Snowpatch.

– JON WALSH, *CANADA*

LEANING TOWERS, THE PULPIT, EAST FACE

OVER THE COURSE of 10 days in August, Ian Dusome and I aimed to climb the east face of the Pulpit, a striking subsummit of Hall Peak in the Leaning Towers group. Early on August 3, we shouldered heavy packs and began the march along the Dewar Creek Trail into the Purcell Wilderness Conservancy. By that evening we had made it to a large boulder below the Leaning Towers, where, thankfully, the ropes, rack, and some camping gear we'd cached two weekends earlier were still hanging unscathed from the boulder.

We moved all of the climbing gear up to the base of the Pulpit and scoped the face. The line up the white upper headwall seemed relatively straightforward—a long stretch of wide cracks split the wall vertically— but there were two very prominent obstacles. The large roof that caps the wall didn't appear to have an obvious solution, and a 20m blank section on the gray lower apron looked nearly impossible to protect without bolts. (We would later discover a line of bat-hook holes up the slab just left of where we ended up climbing, most likely from an initial foray onto the wall in 1975 by Joanna McComb and Joe Meyers. They were part of a group that may have made the first ascent of the Pulpit, that same year, by the easier western slabs.)

The next day we worked on the blank slab. After I'd turned back at a small overlap, Ian took the sharp end and quested upward successfully, leaving a few small cams crammed into a flare under the overlap. I took the next pitch and climbed up into a beautiful stem corner, occasionally aiding when gardening for gear place-

The first route up the Pulpit's east face started left of the snow patch and fired up the prow of the white headwall. Hall Peak is behind. *John Scurlock*

ments was necessary. (Our nut tools were sharp by the end of the trip.) We pushed a few more pitches up to the top of the gray apron and fixed lines, and on a rest day halfway through the trip, we hauled a portledge, food and water, and our gear to the midpoint of the wall.

We climbed the main crack system over two days, finding mostly chimney and offwidth cracks. After some searching below the roof at the top of the wall, we found a wide crack through the huge, 45° overhang; Ian aided this at C1, and I tried desperately to free it while following but had to resort to aid. This topped us out just north of the summit of the Pupit, with only a short scramble to the top.

In addition to the bat-hook holes, we found signs of a previous attempt up to our fourth pitch (possibly as new as summer 2016), but there were no signs of travel or retreat on the upper white headwall. We called our route Preaching to the Choir (400m, 10 pitches, 5.11 C1), and we have hopes to return and climb the route free in a single push.

– KEVIN MARTIN, *CANADA*

BRITISH COLUMBIA / SOUTHERN SELKIRKS

Mt. Dag from the northeast. (1) Ankles Me Boy... (2000). (2) North Face Direct (2000/2001) (3) Sweet Judy Blue Eyes (1971). (4) Riding Skinfaxi (2002). *David Lussier*

VALHALLA RANGES UPDATE

OVER THE PAST few years, Valhalla Provincial Park, about 100km southwest of the Bugaboos, near Nelson, B.C., has seen an explosion in activity, spearheaded by local guide David Lussier, who is working on a guidebook to the area. On August 22, 2017, during their second attempt in two years, Lussier and Vince Hempsall linked the 13 peaks of the Valhallas surrounding Mulvey Basin, from Dag to Gladsheim, including an ascent of the south ridge of Gimli (III 5.10a). "The route involves about 12km of linear distance and 2,300m of elevation gain," Lussier wrote. "There are numerous single-rope rappels required, endless 4th-class scrambling, and multiple pitches of simul-climbing up to 5.10a."

Also in August, Caton and Shute achieved possibly the second ascent of the 2002 Lussier and Alan Jones masterpiece on the north face of Mt. Dag: Riding Skinfaxi (950m, VI 5.11d). While they did not free the entire route (they climbed it at 5.11c C1), Caton still considered their three-day effort "one of the most physically and mentally difficult climbs I have ever done." [*The first ascent of the north side of Dag's north buttress was in 1971 by Roy Kligfield and John Roskelley: Sweet Judy Blue Eyes (5.9 A2). A direct route up the north face and a line up the northeast face were climbed in 2000.*]

The most notable climb of 2016 was Lussier and Jonas Furger's first ascent of the south face of Wedge Peak (1,100m, ED1 5.10), from August 23 to 25. In all, Lussier and various partners climbed half a dozen new routes in the Valhallas in 2016; see the 2017 *Canadian Alpine Journal* for details.

In 2015, Lussier and Stephen Senecal climbed 520m of new terrain en route to the first ascent of the complete north ridge of Little Dag via their route Huckleberry Start (950m, TD+ 5.9).

The accessible and relatively popular south side of Mt. Gimli has seen a number of new five- or six-pitch routes in recent years; see the online version of this report for details.

– **CHRIS KALMAN,** *WITH INFORMATION FROM JASMIN CATON, DAVID LUSSIER, STEVE OGLE, AND CAM SHUTE*

CANADIAN ROCKIES

ICE AND MIXED ROUNDUP

IN 2017 THE focus for activists in the Canadian Rockies seemed to shift away from alpine routes and toward ice and mixed cragging in the winter and new bolted rock routes in the summer. A striking exception—and by far the biggest news in alpine climbing this year (and perhaps for many years to come)—was the first solo ascent of Mt. Geikie's north face in August (*see page 173*), which shocked the few who had previously made ascents of this face, one of the biggest in the range.

In a more traditional alpine vein were new routes by Bow Valley climbers such as Hiding in Plain Sight (600m, M5 AI5), climbed by Alik Berg and Quentin Lindfield Roberts in May. The route follows moderate ground and steep ice pillars on the east face of Mt. Tuzo to the south ridge and on to the summit, all visible from Moraine Lake. Kris Irwin and John Price climbed Remembering Fred (330m, M6 WI5) on October 30, the day Fred Beckey died, above O'Brien Lake. It climbs the north aspect of an unnamed peak south of Mt. Bell, featuring quartzite dry tooling, no major avalanche hazard, and a walk-off descent. On the north side of Storm Mountain, Noboru Kikuchi and Toshiyuki Yamada climbed Full Moon Corner (400m, WI4 R M6).

[Top] Kris Irwin starting the crux pillar of Remembering Fred (330m, M6 WI5) on the north aspect of an unnamed peak south of Mt. Bell, above O'Brien Lake. The route was climbed on October 30, the day Fred Beckey died. *John Price* [Bottom] The route line for Hiding in Plain Sight (600m, M5 AI5), climbed by Alik Berg and Quentin Lindfield Roberts) on the east face of Mt. Tuzo. *Alik Berg*

The Storm Creek Headwall, showing (1) Scar Tissue and (2) Ikiru. Both routes are about 160 meters. *Niall Hamill*

Multipitch ice routes were established in bunches where new low-hanging danglers formed. In Field, right of the ice route Twisted, Michelle Kadatz, Sebastian Taborsky, and Jon Walsh opened Nasty Habit (four pitches, M6 WI5—not to be confused with Nasty *Habits* on the Upper Weeping Wall) at the end of January. The line climbs a previously unformed pillar to a bench and then bolt-protected dry tooling to a thin drip. Soon afterward, Sarah Hueniken and Raphael Slawinski found a yet more improbable line just to the left: Blob Blob Blob (two pitches, M6+). The first pitch followed a line of surprisingly solid blue blobs pasted to an arête, while the second pitch was more conventional edgy dry tooling with bolt protection to a dagger top-out.

Protection Valley, north of Castle Mountain, came into form early in November. Though visible from the TransCanada highway, it was seldom visited before. New routes starting right of the existing Superlight (230m, 5.10 WI5+) include: Mix Fix (150m, M7, Walsh and Jeff Mercier) in a deep cleft; Paradise City (110m, M6 WI4, Walsh and Jon Sims), near the unformed Paradis Perdu; Grab the Cupcakes (310m, M6 WI4+, Kris Irwin and Jay Mills), engaging a gully/chimney with thin ice; Dirtbag Dreams (210m, WI4+, Walsh, Landon Thompson, and Paul Taylor); and Safe Space (7 pitches, M7 R WI4, Berg, Steven Kovalenko, and Slawinski), which ended prematurely, with ice and cracks above, because the seconds didn't want to follow on a poor anchor. With the power of the Internet, this previously quiet hanging valley became a regular cragging venue for numerous parties.

Tom Ballard paid a visit to the area from the U.K. and surprised many with his onsight of the dry-tooling testpiece Nophobia (5 pitches, M10), which was lacking the key exit ice. With Slawinski, he completed the FFA of Tupperware Tea Party (2 pitches, M8+), an old Dave Thomson project next to Stairway to Heaven on Mt. Wilson. The most hard-fought new drytooling route was Gord McArthur's Storm Giant (80m, rated D16), which took him three years of work before sending in August. Established near Fernie, B.C., in a style similar to Nophobia (drilled pockets, holds ticked with paint and tape), the grade unfortunately will be difficult to corroborate as the climb is closed due to access issues.

In the Ghost, Berg established Ophidiophobia (140m, M7 WI4+) with Maarten Van Haeren. In Kananaskis Country, Berg also climbed the Man Hole (300m, M5) with Slawinski. This is the obvious gash on the north face of the Fist; the first pitch had seen previous attempts—and a ground fall—but was tamed in the end with the ubiquitous bolt.

In December, about 200m down and right of Saddam's Insane on Mt. Kidd, Ryan Patterson and Paul Taylor claimed Insane Alligators (150m, M6), rap-bolting the route in six pitches, and adding a bolt to the previously climbed first pitch (Axes of Evil) in the process. Much to Slawinski's chagrin, he found their bolts while leading what he thought was a ground-up first ascent with Henriquez. The two continued onto Alligators, calling their variation Tasty Texting (40m, M6+ WI5).

In February 2018, at the Storm Creek Headwall, Niall Hamill, Jeremy Regato, and Taylor established Ikiru (160m, M7+ WI5+). In March, Hamill and Walsh completed a more direct line, Scar Tissue, on the same wall. *The online version of this report has information on additional new routes and repeats.* 📄 📷

— IAN WELSTED, *CANADA*

MT. HECTOR, SOUTH RIDGE, APOLLO

LOCAL GUIDE MARK Klassen spearheaded the first ascent of the south ridge of Mt. Hector (3,394m), above the east side of the Icefields Parkway. Klassen noticed the stepped ridgeline while working at nearby Lake Louise ski area in the late 1980s, and he climbed the first four pitches in 2015. Over three summers, he completed the route with various partners: Apollo (10 pitches plus scrambling, 5.9). A detailed description and topo are at Tabvar.org.

— DOUGALD MACDONALD, *WITH INFORMATION FROM TABVAR.ORG*

ALBERTA / BOW VALLEY

GOAT BUTTRESS, FLUFFY GOAT BUTT-FACE

ABOUT 20KM EAST of Canmore is one of the most impressive rock features in the Bow Valley: the Goat Buttress sector of the Goat Wall. In morning light the buttress appears almost like a spire, towering 1,800' above the trees and scree below. Although the buttress and the Goat Wall share a col with the famous Yamnuska, they lack the popularity of that wall.

The eponymous Goat Buttress route was first climbed in 1977 by Chris Perry and Trevor Jones. Their climb is bold and old-school, marred by loose rock and featuring tricky or poor protection, with a run-out 5.10d crux. I consulted Peter Gatzsch about other routes on the Goat Wall, since he helped put up the majority of them. Gatzsch's lines tend to be rated 5.9, hard 5.9, and f'n hard 5.9—with obligatory runouts of up to 120' on "easy" terrain. According to Peter, many await second ascents.

It became clear that if I wanted to climb a safer-feeling route in this area, I would have to establish it myself, using a lot of bolts. After chatting with Peter, Andy Genereux, and other new-route activists, it was apparent that nobody would mind if I did precisely that.

I'd spent many hours gazing at the walls with binoculars and always found myself fixed on one sector: the stark and beautiful face immediately right of the Goat Buttress route. My longtime friend and climbing partner Mark Carlson began work on the project in March

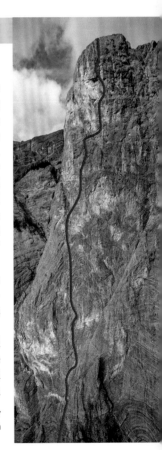

The Goat Buttress and the line of Mark Carlson and Tyler Kirkland's new route Fluffy Goat Butt-face (21 pitches, 5.11). A few pitches are shared with an earlier route, Gatzch Your Goat (2001). *John Price*

Mark Carlson nearing the summit on the 20th pitch of Fluffy Goat Butt-face (1,800', 5.11b) on Goat Buttress. *Dan Kim*

2016. There is no easy, non-technical way to the top of the buttress, so we were forced to establish our line ground up. We began the route leading with a rack of nuts, cams, and bolting gear—free climbing while drilling protection bolts from natural stances. We eventually stopped bringing the nuts and cams, since each pitch of steep, compact rock offered little in the way of trustworthy natural protection. After 25 days of effort and 500-plus bolts, on July 1, we topped out our route. We celebrated reaching the summit, but much work still remained.

That summer in Alberta was rainy, keeping us away from the face until fall. In mid-September we were back to work, crowbarring off death blocks and replacing aid bolts with permanent 3/8-inch stainless steel; we added enough protection bolts to bring it into proper "sport" condition. The route was ready for a redpoint attempt just as winter arrived.

After a winter of fantasizing and two months of climbing in the U.S. in the spring, we returned to our route in June, jugging up to give redpoint burns on the most difficult climbing, which was at my limit. On June 20 we started up the route at first light for a full free push. We finessed our way up the cryptic dance of sidepulls, underclings, and laybacks with big smiles on our faces, redpointing pitch after pitch while savoring the results of nearly 40 days of effort. We stood atop the buttress nine hours and 45 minutes later, cheering and yodeling.

At 21 pitches, Fluffy Goat Butt-face (1,800', 5.11b) is one of the longest sport climbs in Canada. We hope such accessible pleasure will draw some attention to this beautiful wall. [*Editor's note: Fluffy Goat Butt-face shares the first, second, and part of the seventh pitch with Peter Gatzsch and Andy Genereux's possibly unrepeated route Gatzsch Your Goat (2001, 550m, 5.12a or 5.11a/A0).*]

— TYLER KIRKLAND, *CANADA*

HEART MOUNTAIN, HEART LINE

HEART MOUNTAIN IS a very popular scrambling peak just an hour's drive from Calgary. I'd often wondered whether a worthwhile line could go from Heart Creek at the base all the way to the summit. There had been activity on the middle portion of the line I envisioned (Black Roll Over, 5.6, MacLeod-Sampson, 2002) and on the attractive upper headwall (St. Pierres' Summit, 5.7, DeMaio–St. Pierre–St. Pierre, 1995). There had also been an attempt at a traditional ascent of a full-length route by Dwayne Congdon and partner in 1995; they made it up to the midpoint of the second step before bailing. In the end, these routes were integrated into less than 10 percent of my line.

I started working on the route in earnest in March 2017, carting ropes and gear up the Heart Mountain scramblers' trail and then working from the top downward, with many long days of labor. Chris Perry and I finally made the first ascent in June 2017. The full route is called the Heart Line (1,100m, 17 pitches plus scrambling, 5.9 C1) and requires only quickdraws and slings for a rack, with some long runouts on easier ground. The only aid is a six-bolt swing up what I dubbed the "unclimbable wall;" we guess it might go free at 5.13.

— CHAS YONGE, *CANADA*

BRITISH EMPIRE RANGE, MANY FIRST ASCENTS NEAR BARBEAU PEAK

OUR CANADIAN AND American team of Brian and Laura Friedrich, Serge Massad, Len Vanderstar, and myself hoped to ascend Barbeau Peak (2,616m), the highest mountain in Nunavut, as well as unclimbed peaks nearby. On June 17 we flew in a ski-mounted Twin Otter from Resolute to the ice cap. We then pulled sleds for several hours to a campsite just east of Barbeau.

Peak 2,258m, very close to camp, was unclimbed, so after dinner Brian, Laura, Serge, and I climbed snow and then hard ice to reach the top. We returned to camp around 11 p.m., and Brian and I decided to hit one more peak under the midnight sun. Over the next few hours, we ascended the previously unclimbed east ridge of Griper (2,417m), a knife-edge with terrific exposure on both sides, with amazing rock gendarmes. We continued down to the Barbeau-Griper col, then up the north ridge of Barbeau, reaching the summit at 3 a.m. and staggering back into camp at 6 a.m. The full team climbed Barbeau that same day via the north ridge, and Len became the first Canadian to reach the high points of all 13 provinces and territories, a tough, decade-long endeavor.

Peak 2,359m. *Laura Friedrich*

On June 19, Brian and I made a long loop to the east of camp, traversing over several unclimbed peaks, starting with the pyramidal summit of Peak 2,359m. We then crossed the Henrietta Nesmith Glacier, climbed Peak 2,016m, and headed back west along the ridge toward camp. We passed over many minor peaks before climbing steeply up to Peak 2,254m, which was flanked by a huge rock cliff and a hanging glacier. After a few more hours we reached our last summit of the day, Peak 2,246m. After a scary slip on powder-covered ice, we arrived back at camp, exhausted, at 2:30 a.m.

We all then headed south down the Adams Glacier, bagging unclimbed Peak 1,893m along the way. We exited the glacier above Atka Lake and trekked to Tanquary Fjord for our flight out on June 30. [*Barbeau Peak was first climbed in June 1967 and the north ridge in 1982. A 1996 expedition made the first ascent of Mt. Woodmont, the only significant peak known to have been climbed before in the area east of Barbeau where this expedition focused its time.*] 🗎 📷 🔍

– **ERIC GILBERTSON**, *USA*

HEIM PENINSULA AND SYDKAP ICECAP, VARIOUS ASCENTS

AFTER TRAVELING TO Grise Fiord, Greg Horne and Louise Jarry (Canada) were dropped by snowmobile at the head of Harbour Fiord, from which they made a counter-clockwise ski loop onto the Sydkap Icecap. The two ascended Glacier 17 onto the icecap to a high point of 1,265m, then descended southward to Glacier 179, from which they skied up three nearby peaks, ranging from 875m to 936m. After exiting the glacier, they continued down toward the Heim Peninsula, detouring to the southwest for a long day tour to a 788m summit overlooking South Cape Fiord. They then skied back to Grise Fiord, three weeks after departing. A map at the AAJ website shows the route and peaks climbed, all believed to be first ascents. 🗎 📷 🔍

– *INFORMATION FROM* **GREG HORNE**, *CANADA*

THE SHIP'S PROW
TWO SOLO NEW ROUTES ON BAFFIN'S SCOTT ISLAND

BY MAREK RAGANOWICZ, *AS TOLD TO EARL BATES*

THE VISION FOR an expedition to Baffin Island had crystalized in April 2016, during a solitary walk near the base of Mt. Dickey in Alaska. Severe conditions had forced Marcin "Yeti" Tomaszewski and me to retreat from the east face. Waiting for the air taxi back to Talkeetna, my thoughts went back to my 2012 expedition to Baffin Island with Yeti, to the state of mind and evolving harmony that allowed us to achieve the first ascent of Superbalance (VII A4 M7+) on Polar Sun Spire. Walking back to camp, I perceived the need to return to the lonesome granite of Baffin Island. An ancient primal nature was calling me.

In February, Yeti and I flew to Ottawa, then far north to Clyde River, on the east coast of Baffin Island. Here we met up with our Inuit friend, the trusted outfitter Levi Palituq. We packed the cargo sled and snowmobiled five hours to the base of the huge, unclimbed Chinese Wall, at the mouth of Sam Ford Fjord. We were prepared for typical winter temps of -30°C, but instead encountered -50°C (-58°F) and ferocious winds that made walking almost impossible. After ten days with no improvement, we knew there was no chance for an ascent. Yeti's portion of the expedition had come to an end, but I planned to stay. He was reluctant to leave me in these hazardous conditions, but I told him not to worry. I had planned the second part of the expedition to be solo, and I was already centered on being alone.

We called the outfitter for a pickup, and Yeti returned to Clyde River with our sat phone and broken photovoltaic charging system. I realized, *OK, now I am really alone, no chance to communicate with anyone.* No imagining that I could call for help if attacked by a hungry polar bear. I became very calm, it was simple. I felt a wave of freedom.

Levi returned three days later, on March 14, with a new sat phone. We snowmobiled another 40 miles to the north and west to Scott Island, deep into polar bear territory. Levi explained a few techniques on how to avoid becoming lunch. "If you try to run from a bear, he will catch you in a second, you would have no chance," he said. "You need to show him you are brave and ready to fight." It was scary, but I was calm because there was no choice.

Levi motored the snowmobile eight hours back to Clyde River, and I was left to make camp on the frozen sea at the base of the north face of Ship's Prow. Temperatures had warmed to -35°C (-31°F). Stillness permeated everything. *This is the place,* I thought. *I don't need to meditate, I am in the meditation, just being here.*

For days I examined the north face of Ship's Prow. The severe low temperature prevented climbing. I didn't want to wait,

The route line for MantraMandala (450m, VI A3+), the first ascent of the east face of Ship's Prow on Scott Island. *Marek Raganowicz*

[Left] The north face of the Ship's Prow. (1) The Hinayana (600m, VI 5.8 A3+, Mike Libecki, 1999). (2) Secret of Silence (600m, VI A4, 2017). [Right] On Marek Raganowicz's seventh day on Secret of Silence, this rock came flying through the fabric of his portaledge. *Marek Raganowicz*

but nature asked me. So I ventured out on walks, studied the east face of Ship's Prow, and found it was warmed by some direct sunlight, enough to climb there for three or four hours per day.

While searching the east face, I discovered a possible break in the wall's defenses, saw my chance for an attack. I realized I was still thinking like a man from civilization, mistakenly seeing the wall as something to be conquered. As my vision opened, the big wall became an association of intriguing granite, concise sunshine, steady gravity. Nature offered an ancient earthly rhythm, allowing me a chance to play my improvisation.

I made a plan to climb with no fixing to the ground, no returning to camp. Only the essentials, the nature of the wall, a couple of haul bags, me and my mind. After 17 days I'd finished the route MantraMandala. I climbed in capsule style, without fixed lines to the ground or bolts, rivets, or copperheads. I needed to drill six holes for bat-hook placements.

Standing atop the Ship's Prow, my thoughts were already fastened on the north face route. I returned to the snow and sea ice at the base of the east wall and found polar bear prints all around my sled. I walked back to camp at the base of the north wall. Paw prints again, all around my tent, but nothing was disturbed. Not even the food. The next day, I carried the second bag from the wall back to camp, then I took two days for sorting food and gear and repacking.

Still snowy, windy, temps of -35° C. I decided I needed to fix the first few pitches for the longer, more technical route on the north face. Bears investigated my camp again. I scared them away, but they were back in a few hours. The bears carried off a bag and a rope that night; the next day they played with the fixed line hanging down from the wall. I kept my rifle next to me in the tent and tied it to the end of the rope when jugging the fixed line.

I spent nine days on the north face route. I used a full assortment of beaks, cams, and nuts. No copperheads, no drilling. Secret of Silence is my cleanest line. [*Secret of Silence is to the right of the Hinayana, climbed by Mike Libecki during his solo first ascent of the north face of Ship's Prow in the spring of 1999.*]

The experience of silence in Baffin Island was deeper than anything I'd experienced before in my life. Beyond normal understanding or description, beneath the stillness I sensed a secret. Seven weeks of immense solitude—I had become a bit of the wild of Baffin Island.

On May 3, Levi arrived along with a group of trekkers and a friend of mine. I heard names, shook hands, smiled for photos. Culture shock on the sea ice. Two weeks later, I was sitting by the warm fireplace at home in Inverness, Scotland, attempting to assimilate. 📷

Summary: First ascent of the east face of Ship's Prow by MantraMandala (450m, VI A3+). New route on the north face of Ship's Prow: Secret of Silence (600m, VI A4). Both climbed solo by Marek Raganowicz from Poland.

CLYDE INLET, UMIGUQJUAQ WALL, MAROONED AT MIDNIGHT

THE TWO OF US had been dreaming of an expedition to Baffin Island's big walls ever since we started climbing together in 2013. With the help of Live Your Dream grants from the American Alpine Club, we finally made it happen.

With hopes of going to the Sam Ford Fjord by boat and climbing the Chinese Wall, we arrived in Clyde River in early August. Our outfitter, Levi Palituq, informed us that the sea ice had not broken up enough to allow travel to the Sam Ford region. After studying some maps, Levi agreed to take us into Clyde Inlet. He believes we may have been the first to climb here. We inspected several good-looking walls before getting dropped off at the base of Umiguqjuaq Wall at midnight. This wall (69°59'21"N, 69°49'56"W) is located on the peninsula where the Cormack Arm splits to the west while Clyde Inlet continues to the south. The Inuit name for the formation roughly translates to "pubic mound," as the wall bears some resemblance.

[Top] A lone iceberg passes by the "Turret Wall," a large unclimbed formation along the southern coast of Clyde Inlet. *Ryan Little* [Bottom] Foreshortened view of Marooned at Midnight (700m, VI 5.11a A3) on the southwest face of the Umiguqjuaq Wall. The climbers descended the large gully on the left of the photo. *Sam England*

Seeing very few crack systems on the face, we chose a line on the southwest buttress that would link several corner systems. Blessed with good weather, we averaged about two pitches per day. As we moved up the wall, the climbing continually unfolded along a natural line, with much transitioning between aid and free. After eight days of climbing, we reached a large, talus-covered ledge at the base of the 500' summit block. With an early start the next morning, we abandoned our haul bags, free climbed to the summit, and returned to the ledge. The next day we walked off the talus ledge and descended the large gully to the west of the wall. This involved 16 hours of long rappels and dragging haul bags down the steep, talus-filled gulley.

We named our route Marooned at Midnight (700m, VI 5.11a A3), as this best described how we felt upon being dropped on the isolated shoreline in the middle of the night.

When Levi picked us up three days later, he told us he planned to spend the next two days hunting in Clyde Inlet. After exploring other possible climbing objectives, he dropped us below a formation he called "The Mitten," with hopes of making a push-style free ascent of "The Thumb" spire. We climbed 10 pitches through very featured terrain up to 5.10a, making it about 75 percent of the way to the summit. We retreated when we could no longer find a reasonable free climbing line. [*The online report includes photos of unclimbed walls in Clyde Inlet.*]

– SAM ENGLAND *AND* RYAN LITTLE, *USA*

AUYUITTUQ NATIONAL PARK, MT. ASGARD, RATATOSKR

DMITRY GOLOVCHENKO AND Sergey Nilov from Russia climbed a new route up the northwest face of the south tower of Mt. Asgard in August. They climbed a prominent pillar on the left side of the face, well to the left of Sensory Overload (2012, Lavigne-Papert-Walsh).

The two men climbed and fixed the bottom of the route on August 7 and 8, before establishing their first wall camp on August 9; they continued capsule-style to the top. The crux of the climb came on pitches 10 to 12 (the first three pitches of the headwall), where shattered rock created difficult climbing and poor protection. In all, they climbed 28 pitches (1,265m climbing distance, with 765m on the steep upper wall), reaching the summit on August 21. They named the route Ratatoskr (Russian 6B VI A3), after a squirrel in Norse mythology. *More details and a complete expedition report (in Russian) with photos and topos are available online.*

— DOUGALD MACDONALD, *WITH INFORMATION FROM DMITRY GOLOVCHENKO, RUSSIA, AND RUSSIANCLIMB.COM*

NEWFOUNDLAND / GROS MORNE NATIONAL PARK

WESTERN BROOK POND, DREAMLINE AND PSYCHO KILLER

ON FEBRUARY 21, Will Mayo, Anna Pfaff, and Joe Terravecchia (all USA) completed Dreamline, a huge "spray ice" route to the right of Pissing Mare Falls. Terravecchia, one of the main developers of ice climbing in Newfoundland, had been eyeing this line for about two decades. He and longtime climbing partner Casey Shaw had camped on top of the cliff for a week before Mayo and Pfaff arrived, waiting for a break in the weather that never came.

After Shaw's departure, Mayo, Pfaff, and Terravecchia snowmobiled to the top of the falls before dawn, downclimbed a snow gully to the shore of Western Brook Pond (a fjord that rarely freezes, preventing an easier approach from below), and began climbing around 9 a.m. After hurrying up an approach gully threatened by falling ice, they simul-climbed a 500' ramp leading to the main icefall. Above, five pitches of very steep ice and frozen spray gained the top: Dreamline (1,260', WI6+).

Joe Terravecchia starts the overhanging crux lead of Dreamline above Western Brook Pond. *Will Mayo*

Less than a week later, Mayo and Pfaff climbed Psycho Killer (650', WI7+ M9) above Bakers Brook Pond. The traditionally protected route concluded with an overhanging rock corner leading to a huge ice roof.

— DOUGALD MACDONALD, *WITH INFORMATION FROM JOE TERRAVECCHIA*

GREENLAND

Unclimbed walls of Kangeq, to the south of Anchor Wall. Bob Shepton inspected these walls from his boat in 2010, during the time an American-Belgian team was making the first ascent of the nearby Impossible Wall, but subsequently the team decided to head for Cape Farewell. The walls are estimated to be 800 to 900 meters high. *Marcin Tomaszewski*

WEST GREENLAND

AGPAD ISLAND, EUROPA WALL; AKULIARUSEQ ISLAND, ANCHOR WALL

BETWEEN JUNE 28 and August 6, Wojtek Malawski, Konrad Ociepka, and I visited the Uummannaq and Upernavik regions aboard the yacht Berg. We flew to Illulisat on Greenland's west coast and then sailed north for a few days to the Horn, a 1,000m wall on the northeast spur of Upernavik Island (Upernavik Ø), first climbed in 2013. However, we found the wall unattractive, with no logical or fine-looking lines on solid rock, and decided to change our plans.

We moved south and the next day reached Agpat (Agpad or Appat) Island, where we discovered the Sleeping Man (a.k.a. Old Man) Range at the western end of the island's south coast. It comprised seven 800m faces that had seen no previous climbing. Standing above these cliffs is the Old Man of Saatut (70°53.9'N, 52°06'W); the only recorded route to the summit was completed in 2010 by Matthew Budekin, Sam Doyle, Miles Hill, and George Ullrich (U.K.), with mostly scrambling on poor rock and a section of British HVS 5a. The main cliffs looked technically difficult, with hardly any continuous features.

We selected a face that we named Europa Wall (70°53'4.37"N, 52°7'54.81"W), and after reaching the base in a dinghy, we fixed ropes on the first four pitches. We soon found chossy rock on our chosen line, so we changed tactics and opted for an alpine-style ascent along the easiest and most logical route. On July 7, after one day of rest, we ascended our fixed ropes and 18 hours later reached the top of the wall. (The true summit proved to be too dangerous to climb, being a tower of rubble.) On the penultimate pitch, rockfall cut our two lead ropes into five pieces. Fortunately, we had a spare rope, and this allowed us to rappel to the base of the wall, 26 hours after starting. The route was named Rollingstones (850m, 6c). One bolt was placed by hand.

We spent the next two days resting in the town of Uummannaq. The following day, two hours into the voyage toward our next destination, a pressure cooker exploded in my face, causing severe skin burns. We returned to Uummannaq, where I had my face treated and dressed in the hospital.

On July 12 we reached Sortehul Fjord and the Impossible Wall and Red Wall, climbed by an American-Belgian team in 2010. Although these looked like exceptionally beautiful objectives, they also appeared to be quite grassy, and there was snow on the tops, meaning that potential routes would likely be wet. We moved on, and on the 13th discovered an area of virgin 800m to 900m walls on Akuliaruseq Island and the Kangeq Peninsula. Both sets of walls lie above Angmarqua (Ammarqua) Strait. On Akuliaruseq (72°33.54'N, 55°20.50'W), we knew of no named walls nor saw any traces of climbing activity.

Over 10 climbing days, during the period from July 14–28, we put up a new route on what we dubbed the Anchor Wall, on the northwest tip of Akuliaruseq Island. We first located a descent route on the opposite side, then fixed a few ropes on our chosen line so we could work several difficult pitches, and subsequently we committed to the wall, reaching the summit on the July 26. We descended partway on the far side to collect some food, returned to the summit, and bivouacked for two nights. On the 28th, Konrad and Wojtek rappelled the headwall and started freeing the difficult sections, with Konrad leading the key 7c+, 7b, and 6c+ pitches. That evening, we made 5.5-hour descent to the coast, where we were picked up by our yacht at 2 a.m. on the 29th.

We named the route Nightwatch (700m, 7c+, three bolts and two rivets), and we have called this region Bergland after the name of our vessel and its captain Artur Bergier, without whom the expedition never would have happened. 🖸

– MARCIN TOMASZEWSKI, *POLISH MOUNTAINEERING ASSOCIATION*

Nesting Birds: *AAJ 2013 included a note on regulations governing access to certain seacliffs in Greenland during bird-nesting season. Available at the AAJ website, this note provides information and contacts helpful to climbers who want to learn more about these regulations.*

[Top] **Rollingstones (850m, 6c) on the Europa Wall of Agpat Island.** [Bottom] **Anchor Wall on Akuliaruseq Island and the line of Nightwatch (700m, 7c+).** *Marcin Tomaszewski*

[Top] **The footprints of the Sequoia Spire Route—and some lovely ski tracks on the descent—are visible on the west-southwest face of Sue's Spire, above the Bjørnbo Glacier.** [Bottom] **Looking southwest over the melt streams of the Bjørnbo Glacier during the failed attempt on Peanut Peak. Many, but certainly not all, peaks visible in this photo have been climbed.** *British 2017 Stauning Alps Expedition*

STAUNING ALPS, SUE'S SPIRE, WEST-SOUTHWEST FACE; BOUGHFELL, SOUTHWEST FACE

DURING APRIL, JESSE DUFTON, Alastair Everett, Oliver Mentz, Jennifer Roberts, and Molly Thompson (expedition leader) completed a self-supported expedition to the southern Stauning Alps. We aimed to rekindle the link between science and mountaineering, and our objectives included repeating glacial measurements taken during the 1970s and installing a network of ablation stakes in the Roslin Glacier to observe the impacts of climate change. Our expedition also had an inspirational aspect: Team member Jesse Dufton suffers from rod-cone dystrophy, a genetic disorder that has affected his eyes in a degenerative manner since birth, leaving him severely sight-impaired.

On April 8 we were transported from Constable Pynt to the bottom of the Roslin Glacier by snowmobile; from here, each member pulled a pulk containing team kit and scientific equipment. Once on the Roslin we established a network of ablation stakes, each placed at 150m to 200m elevation intervals, with additional stakes placed to replicate cross-glacier lines monitored during the 1970s. We also collected snow pit data, including temperature and density measurements, at 12 locations. We aim to collaborate with future expeditions that return to the area and are interested in taking further measurements.

We then spent four days (with one day tent-bound due to poor weather) crossing two steep cols to reach the upper Bjørnbo Glacier. On the 22nd we climbed our first peak. In sunny weather with light wind, we climbed from the west-southwest to summit Sue's Spire (2,237m, 71°47'46.99"N, 25°11'52.35"W) via the Sequoia Spire Route (ca 800m, PD). Most of the climb was done unroped, but we needed to tie in for a loose, rocky section about 100m below the summit.

We rested next day and then, on the 24th, made the first ascent of Boughfell (2,191m, 71°45'16.69"N, 25°4'46.35"W) from the southwest. It gave 1,100m of ascent (AD), and our route was named Katalice.

Moving farther down Bjørnbo Glacier, on the 26th we attempted a third summit, which we dubbed Peanut Peak. We reached the base of a large couloir on the southwestern flanks that we had expected to give a practical ascent of about 900m. However, it was much warmer than on previous days and avalanches were releasing on the surrounding mountains. We decided to go no further. The summit is at approximately 71°42'51.6"N, 24°50'00.7"W, and from digital elevation models we estimate the height to be 1,777m. We were collected by skidoos from the bottom of the Bjørnbo Glacier on May 2. A comprehensive report is available at the AAJ website. 📄 📷 🔍

— JENNIFER ROBERTS, U.K., ON BEHALF OF THE BRITISH 2017 STAUNING ALPS EXPEDITION

STAUNING ALPS, OXFORD GLACIER, HISTORICAL FIRST ASCENTS

IN APRIL AND May of 2013, Neil Mathews and I made first ascents of three peaks from the Oxford Glacier in the southern Staunings. We used snowmobiles for two days (212km) from Constable Pynt and then skied up Oxford Glacier for three days.

On April 26 we climbed what we called Island Peak (1,960m, 71°35' 09.44N, 25°13'02.22W), a distinctive triangular mountain just north of the point where the Oxford Glacier makes a major division into east and west branches. Our approach on skis from the east branch was circuitous because of crevasses. At 1,500m on the east face, the slope steepened to about 45°, so

Island Peak from the southeast and the 2013 route of ascent. *Mark Aitken*

we continued with crampons and ice axes, climbing deep, unconsolidated snow to a long, rocky summit ridge and the top. We took seven hours up (PD+) and a further four hours for the descent.

On the 28th and 29th we explored the eastern glacial valley opposite Island Peak. At the end of the valley, a slope of 35° led to a pass between two peaks (PD). We climbed both: Snow Dome (2,030m, 71°34'15.72N, 25°08'12.28W) and Isikkivinginner (Panorama Peak, 2,040m). These peaks had appeared rocky and difficult from the Oxford Glacier, but the eastern valley gave us an easy route to both tops (F from the pass). The round trip from base camp was 11 hours. 📄 📷 🔍

— MARK AITKEN, U.K.

GRUNDTVIGSKIRKEN, HISTORICAL FIRST ASCENT BY SOUTHWEST FACE

IN 1999 A Norwegian-Swedish team climbed the south ridge of Grundtvigskirken (1,977m), thinking they were making the first ascent. Although this route had been attempted previously to around half height (most likely by the British military in 1978), the peak was not known to have been climbed. However, when one of the Norwegians scrambled to the north top, he discovered a cairn and rappel slings. We can now confirm what is thought to be the first ascent of Grundtvigskirken.

In 1989 a Belgian expedition (Nunatak 89) left Amsterdam and set sail for Ittoqqortoormiit (Scoresbysund) on a 17m yacht. One of their goals was to climb an impressive rock tower on Renland that had been identified in 1985 by a previous Belgian expedition.

Jean-Marc Piron and Luc Reginster first explored the east face of the tower (climbed 21 years later by a Swiss-Italian team, *AAJ 2011*), but found it to be too serious for two climb-

The southwest face of Grundtvigskirken and the line of the 1989 Belgian route, the first known route up the tower. Luc Reginster, one of the climbers, cannot remember whether their exit was to the left or right of the summit, but either way the two Belgians reached the top via the east face. *Ian Browns*

ers with neither portaledge nor bolt kit. So they moved to the opposite side of the mountain and climbed the southwest face. This started up slabby terrain to reach a bivouac below the 550m headwall, which they climbed the next day in 10 hours, via a prominent crack system in the middle of the face. The rock was excellent and the difficulties 5c–6a. Finding no evidence of a previous ascent, they built a cairn on a big block at the top and rappelled the route of ascent.

The 1985 Belgian expedition had dubbed the peak Penguin Tower, and the first ascensionists decided to stick with this, unaware of a previous name. [*Editor's note: Grundtvigskirken was named in the 1930s after the famous Grundtvig Church in Copenhagen, whose tower the mountain strongly resembles. Search "Grundtvigskirken" at the AAJ website for two reports describing the history of this name and other place names in Greenland.*]

– LINDSAY GRIFFIN, WITH INFORMATION FROM LUC REGINSTER, *BELGIUM*

INUGSUARMIUT FJORD, PLAN B TOWER

KEITH LADZINSKI, ANDY Mann, Ethan Pringle, Connor Seibert, and I hired a boat from Tasiilaq for the ca 500km journey south to Inugsuarmiut Fjord, an area I had visited several times before (see *AAJ 2017*). After being stuck in sea ice for 10 days, we shuttled loads and endured rain and dangerous glaciers for another eight days or so in late July and early August, getting into position to attempt a route on huge Granddaddy Tower. We retreated after about 300m of climbing, when we realized we didn't have time to complete the approximately 1,200m line. This peak remains unclimbed.

We quickly changed objective to Plan B Tower (approximately 63°27'27.15"N, 41°59'10.71"W). Its northwest face had a straightforward lower section that would allow us quick access to a steep headwall.

Ethan and I did the leading down low. We took two days to establish a camp 550m up the face. To this point the climbing was easy (4th class) but quite dangerous, with huge choss ramps leading toward the headwall. Andy, Ethan, Keith, and I then took two days to climb from the top of the ramps to the summit. The headwall gave eight proper pitches, with four of these dead vertical or slightly overhanging. I led the first and Ethan onsighted the rest, with sections of 5.12 R and one pitch of 5.13 where his wizardry and badassery were put to the test. The entire route was onsight free climbed, and it was impressive seeing Ethan pull this off, given the loose rock in parts. It was an honor to share this adventure with my friends, to stand on the summit together, and to come home safely.

– MIKE LIBECKI, *AAC*

Ethan Pringle leading one of the 5.12 R pitches on Plan B Tower, near Inugsuarmiut Fjord. Pringle onsighted seven pitches in a row on the steep headwall, including a 60-meter pitch of 5.13. *Keith Ladzinski*

TASERMIUT FJORD, RDVN, WEST FACE, NOT MY PRESIDENT

ON JULY 1, Diana Wendt and I were dropped off at Tasermiut Fjord. Our first couple of weeks in the area were rainy, and patience was tested while waiting out storms in camp. We used brief spells of dry weather to climb the lower half of War and Poetry on Ulamertorssuaq, the Swiss Route on Ketil Pyramid (completed during an optimistic half-day window that found us summiting in a snowstorm), and two attempts on the British Route on Nalumasortoq. The weather then improved, allowing us to complete War and Poetry with two bivouacs.

The last four days of the trip were sunny—the longest window of fine weather we encountered in over 30 days. On July 28 we decided to attempt the unclimbed west face of RDVN (1,499m). The rock was chossy, with loose flakes and vegetation, but there were several clean 5.10 roofs and a perfect 5.11a corner. The leader made all the moves free but in a few places hung on gear to rest or clean the route; the second ascended the rope for speed. We placed natural anchors and used no bolts.

Not My President on the west face of RDVN. The original route on this formation (French, 1975) climbed the left skyline ridge. *Ben Peters*

Nightfall arrived before we topped out, so we endured an uncomfortable bivouac on a narrow ledge, then continued at first light, joining the northwest ridge for the last three pitches to the knife-edge summit. [*RDVN was first climbed in August 1975 via the northwest ridge (TD+*

and sustained) by the French Pierre Chapoutot, Bernard Gorgeon, and Jeff Lemoine, approaching from the south]. We named the route Not My President (ca 600m, 18 pitches, 5.11a) in honor of the times and the poor rock that will probably keep this from becoming a classic. Nonetheless, we were excited and more than a little surprised to have put up our first new route. We rappelled the northwest ridge, first following an existing rappel line and then leaving our own anchors 70m apart. *This expedition was supported by two AAC Live Your Dream grants.* 📷 🔍

– BEN PETERS, *AAC*

BLACK BALL, FIRST AND SECOND ASCENTS: *The American team encountered a few other parties in this area in July, generally repeating established routes. One of these comprised two Slovaks, who likely made the second ascent of Black Ball (400m, nine pitches, 6a+), a previously unreported route climbed on August 1, 2016, by the French Aurele Bremont, Benjamin Bouissou, Léa Dupery, Lucia Favard, Chloé Jaspers, Clothilde Morin, and Antony Ventura. This route ascends a black triangle of rock down and to the left of Nalumarsotoq; it follows a crack system that is clearly visible from the approach valley. Bolts were placed, but a selection of nuts is essential. A few days later in the French expedition, on a large boulder or pinnacle below Ulamertorssuaq, Bouissou opened the 15m Master and Commander (8b trad).*

TASERMIUT FJORD, NALUMASORTOQ, PEDO DE PLACER; ULAMERTORSSUAQ, QUJANAQ

IN JULY 2016, Georg Hoedle, Martin Lopez Abad, and I disembarked in Tasermiut Fjord with food and provisions for one month. The day after we arrived there was a two-day weather window, during which we climbed War and Poetry (5.12c) on the west face of Ulamertorssuaq in alpine style. We sent the entire route except for a 5.12b slab high on the wall. After three days of rest, we set our sights on a mountain in the back of the valley behind Nalumasortoq. However, the rock was poor and there was a lot of lichen. After three pitches, we abandoned this project.

We took a rest day and then attempted a new route on Nalumasortoq, almost in the center of the wall, in alpine style. The line began with a roof and was almost entirely comprised of hand and finger cracks. Just 150m from the summit, the haul bag with all our supplies came unclipped from the haul line—I had attached it using a non-locking carabiner—and it plummeted into the void. We decided to bail.

After three days of bad weather, we returned to our high point and finished the route, continuing up cracks to the right of the large detached block from which we had bailed before. On July 26 we climbed the whole route in four hours; we believe this will likely be the easiest route on the wall. We named it Pedo de Placer (550m, French 7a) and descended via the Spanish route to the left.

After two rest days, we started up an obvious line on the southeastern pillar of the north peak of Ulamertorssuaq. [*This pillar is just to the left of a separate pillar or fin climbed in 1998 by Ian Parsons and Tony Penning: the James Hopkins Trust Buttress (British E4 5c).*] We took the most natural route up the center of the wall, finding exceptional rock quality throughout the climb, and a mix of good face and crack climbing. With bad weather coming, we rapped back to the ground after climbing about half of the pillar.

We waited out a week of bad weather and then returned to our high point and finished the route. All of the pitches were opened ground up. We placed 20 protection bolts as well as a fully bolted rappel line. We named the route Qujanaq (700m of climbing, French 7a), which means "thank you" in the local language. The route is similar to War and Poetry but easier. 📷 🔍 ▶

– CARLOS "CARLITOS" MOLINA, *ARGENTINA, TRANSLATED FROM SPANISH BY CHRIS KALMAN*

MEXICO

PICO DE ORIZABA AND ITZACCIHUATL, NEW ROUTES

IN MAY, MAX Álvarez and Diego Montaño climbed a probable new route on the northwest face of Itzaccihuatl (5,230m), Mexico's third-highest peak. The climb involved two steep mixed pitches, followed by a stretch of alpine ice (AI3) leading to a glacial headwall and the summit. They named the route La Hernia (WI4 M4 AI3), as it marked Montaño's first serious climb after surgery.

The new line is not far to the right of Directa al Pecho, a difficult route up the northwest face climbed by Fernando "La Araña" Lipkau and Lenin Zabre Ramírez in 1955, when a larger glacier covered much of the face.

Álvarez and Daniel Araiza also explored the

[Top] The west side of Pico de Orizaba (5,636m) showing the line of the Serpent's Tail. The arrow at far right marks the approximate location of the Serpent's Head (Barrons-Blanchard, 1988). [Bottom] La Hernia on the northwest face of Itzaccihuatl (5,230m). *Diego Montaño*

west side of Pico de Orizaba (5,636m), the third-highest mountain in North America, in October, finding a new route on the icy flanks of the Sarcófago, the rocky peak north of Orizaba's summit. Their line ascends three pitches of steep, thin water ice through a rock band before angling left across mixed ground to reach the top of the face just north of the Sarcófago.

The new climb was named the Serpent's Tail (WI4/5) after a route on the west face called the Serpent's Head, climbed by Wink Barrons and Barry Blanchard in January 1988. The earlier climb was far to the right of the 2017 route.

Montaño said that water ice routes on both peaks are rarely in condition and that both the new climbs had "sketchy" ice and loose rock.

In September, Montaño, Sergio "Tiny" Almada, and Carlos Petersen climbed a three-pitch rock route on the north side of Nevado de Toluca (4,680m): Mata y Patata (5.11 X A1).

— **DOUGALD MACDONALD,** *WITH INFORMATION FROM DIEGO MONTAÑO*

COLOMBIA

El Abrazo de la Serpiente, the first route up the northwest face of Cerro Pajarito, as seen from Cerro Diablo. With 660m of climbing, the route links large huecos and run-out slabs. *David Allfrey*

CERRO PAJARITO, NORTHWEST FACE, EL ABRAZO DE LA SERPIENTE

ON FEBRUARY 1, 2018, Dave Allfrey (USA), Kieran Brownie (Canada), and Paul McSorley (Canada) completed a route up the previously unclimbed northwest face of Cerro Pajarito, one of the Cerros de Mavecure (also spelled Mavicure) monoliths in Guainía. This region in the far east of Colombia is home to the Puinave people, who have lived along the banks of the Río Inírida for millennia. Local legend tells the story of Princess Inírida, who soloed the four major formations of this area (Mavecure, Mono, Diablo, and Pajarito) during a rampage fueled by a magical love potion. She is said to reside in the south wall of Cerro Pajarito and can be recognized by a large white streak in the otherwise monolithic black slabs.

This climb was two seasons in the making: Brownie and McSorley climbed six pitches in February 2017, but then ran out of hardware. Returning a year later with Allfrey, they climbed to the previous high point and continued to the summit after fixing three ropes the previous day. Characterized by large huecos and run-out slabs on textured granite (the Guiana Shield has some of the oldest rock on Earth), the route is 660m long and rated V 5.11c. Though it is entirely bolt protected, there are serious runouts, and several pitches have an R or X rating. All pitches were established ground up and onsight.

Aside from the remoteness of this area, the intense heat proved to be a crux. Climbing in the midday sun was nearly impossible on the black granite, which was intensified by daytime highs averaging 47°C (117°F) during the climb and reaching up to 53°C during their visit. The Canadian-American team began their days around 2 a.m. and benefited from the "super blue blood moon" at the end of January for added light. Their route is called El Abrazo de la Serpiente ("Embrace of the Serpent"), inspired by Colombian director Ciro Guerra's film of that name, whose powerful imagery of the region prompted Brownie and McSorley to explore the area's climbing potential.

Two parties are believed to have climbed this formation before. An unknown German team climbed the smaller east or northeast face in 1992, linking run-out slabs between trees. Damian Benegas (Argentina) and some locals ascended a similar line in 2015, reporting eight long pitches up to 5.10b, with no protection other than trees.

— **PAUL MCSORLEY**, *CANADA, WITH ADDITIONAL INFORMATION FROM ALPINIST.COM*

CHICAMOCHA NATIONAL PARK

SUJETANDO AIRE

IN THE WINTER of 2017-'18, I spent two months in Colombia exploring different areas and climbing a few new lines with various partners. Since climbing has been banned in the popular El Cocuy National Park (*see note below*), climbers have been forced to explore smaller walls in outlying areas. The best of the new routes I did was in Chicamocha Canyon, a steep-sided sandstone canyon in the Santander Department, northeast of Bogotá.

Jorge Garzon and I opened this route on a southeast-facing wall 1km west of the entrance of Chicamocha National Park, near the Mesa de los Santos cable car site. Sujetando Aire ("Holding Air") is a 150m route that was established ground up, at a grade of 7a A1, with a mixture of bolts and traditional gear. The crux pitch is a 4m roof in bad rock that is expected to go at 7c+ but

Sujetando Aire (150m, 7a A1), the first known multi-pitch route on Chicamocha Canyon's sandstone, takes the obvious dihedral in left center. *Jens Richter*

has yet to see a redpoint. There is lots of potential nearby for good, steep climbing on walls up to 300m, but access is via private land. Visitors must seek permission from the farmer who lives beneath the walls and speaks only Spanish.

— **JENS RICHTER**, *GERMANY*

EL COCUY ACCESS ISSUES: *The Sierra Nevada del Cocuy, rising to over 5,300m in northern Colombia, has a long climbing history on tropical glaciers and rock walls up to about 500m. But El Cocuy National Park was closed in February 2016 because the local indigenous people felt visitors had behaved disrespectfully on snowfields and glaciers they consider sacred. In April 2017, park officials reopened a few sections of the park, allowing a limited number of people per day, accompanied by a local guide. However, snow and glacier travel is still forbidden, limiting climbing opportunities. No solution for climber access had been reached as of the spring of 2018.*

PERU

Manu Ponce on the wild first pitch of an attempt on the lower wall of Gocta Falls. *Al Aire Films*

AMAZONAS REGION

GOCTA FALLS, YAKU MAMA

Pedro Galán cleaning the second pitch of Yaku Mama by Gocta Falls. *Pou Collection*

IN JULY WE spent a month in Peru with our climbing partners Pedro Galán and Manu Ponce, along with Luis Rizo and Lina Schütze as cameraman. We first visited the Chachapoyas province of Amazonas, in northern Peru, where we established a beautiful route next to the upper waterfall of the two-tiered Gocta Falls. The approach to the waterfall takes approximately two to three hours from the village of San Pablo de Varela. Although our initial plan was to start climbing beside the lower falls, decomposing rock there led us to focus on the wall by the upper falls.

On July 3 we opened Yaku Mama ("Mother Water," 185m, 7a+). The route ascends just left of the upper falls, offering adventurous traditional climbing up variable-quality sandstone cracks and face climbing for six pitches. For repeat ascents, we would recommend a machete, two sets of cams, and two ropes to rappel the route. 🖼 🔍 ▶

— IKER POU AND ENEKO POU, *SPAIN*

CORDILLERA BLANCA

PUCARASHTA CENTRAL, SOUTH FACE

AN EXPEDITION OF the Female Mountaineering Team of the Spanish Federation of Mountain Sports and Climbing (FEDME) visited the Cordillera Blanca from June 5 to July 12. The team included Diana Calabuig, Ruth Craven, Fátima Gil, Esther Simón, and Vicky Vega, led by Marc Subirana and accompanied by guide Oriol Baró and doctor Augusto Covaro. After acclimatizing outside of Huaraz, the climbers packed into the Santa Cruz Valley and split up to make ascents of Alpamayo's Via Ferrari over three consecutive days.

After this, the team of Craven, Simón, and Baró focused on opening a new route on the south face of Pucarashta Central (5,450m). This peak is northeast of Alpamayo and southwest of Pucahirca Oeste. On June 18, they climbed a right-trending route up demanding mixed terrain and around seracs: Para Casa de Zarela (600m, MD+). According to a route line in the Scottish guidebook *Climbs of the Cordillera Blanca of Peru*, by David Sharman, the Spanish route may coincide in the middle of the face with a 1991 route (graded TD-) opened by Mick Davie, Phil Moorey, and Steve Di Ponio; however, that line is not precise enough to be sure (*see AAJ 1992, where the mountain is spelled "Pukarashta"*). 🔍

— SEVI BOHORQUEZ, *PERU, WITH ASSISTANCE FROM ORIOL BARÓ, SPAIN*

HUANDOY NORTE, NORTHWEST FACE, SOLO VARIATION

ON OCTOBER 18–19, Nathan Heald (Peru) soloed a variation to the 1959 Swiss and 1985 Mexican routes on the west-northwest face of Huandoy Norte (6,395m). Starting at 10:15 p.m., he took a direct line up the snow and ice face leading to the broad summit plateau, left of the 1959/1985 routes and right of the rock rib that divides the northwest face. Heald reached the summit at around 8:30 a.m. Approximately one-third of the route is believed to be new, and he graded the 1,200m climb TD. He descended by the same line. 📷 ▶

— ERIK RIEGER, *WITH INFORMATION FROM SEVI BOHORQUEZ AND NATHAN HEALD, PERU*

NEVADO HUANTSÁN, NORTHEAST RIDGE, ALPINE-STYLE SECOND ASCENT

ORIOL BARÓ AND Marc Torrales (Spain) completed what's likely the second ascent and first alpine-style ascent of the northeast ridge of Huantsán (6,395m). The two climbed the 1,700-meter route from June 4–8, finding mostly snow and ice, with sections of rock. Baró described long sections of poorly protected climbing and frightening aid using snow pickets. They rated the route ED+. The pair descended mostly the same way, making occasional detours onto the north face, with 20 rappels and downclimbing. They returned to the base on June 9.

The northeast ridge was the object of intense focus in the early 1970s, with attempts in 1971 and 1973 and the first ascent in 1974. (This formation has been described as the east ridge in previous AAJs; it faces generally east-northeast.) In 1973 a French team fixed ropes extensively on the ridge and climbed to around 6,000 meters. A year later the French were back, and they encountered an international expedition with the same goal. The two teams, totaling 20 people, joined forces and sieged the ridge using 7,000 feet of fixed rope and four camps. On August 17, Marc Batard and Michel Parmentier reached the top, followed by five other climbers over the next several days. A month earlier, an American team had attempted the same route, climbing mostly alpine style, with Bill Lahr and Rick Ridgeway reaching a point just 150 meters below the top.

— DOUGALD MACDONALD, *WITH INFORMATION FROM DESNIVEL AND THE AAJ*

QUEBRADA RUREC, FIRST FREE ASCENT AND NEW ROUTE

AFTER OPENING THE new route Yaku Mama at Gocta Falls, in Peru's northern Amazon, with Pedro Galán and Manu Ponce (*see report earlier in this section*), our team traveled by bus for 24 hours to reach Huaraz in the Cordillera Blanca. Our biggest problem now was arriving in a high mountain range with sleeping bags and clothing designed for the jungle. Without big boots, ice axes, or crampons, we focused on rock climbing. Cold was a constant during the rest of our expedition.

From Huaraz we traveled through the village of Olleros to Quebrada Rurec, a beautiful place where the climbing is all above 4,000m. We first focused on free climbing Qui Io Vado Ancora (originally graded 7b A1, see *AAJ 2007*), on the beautiful spire of Chaupi Huanca (5,179m), a route established 10 years prior by climbers from the famous Ragni di Lecco group of Italy. After camping at the base for three days, we spent two days sleeping on the wall (July 11–12), making the first free ascent at 7c+/8a-, with all pitches climbed onsight. This excellent route is one of the most difficult alpine rock climbs yet free climbed in Peru (585m, 7c+/8a-).

[*Editor's note: Chaupi Huanca was called Punta Numa in some past AAJs. It is located between the wall Itsoc Huanca (called Punta Ayudin in past AAJs) on the left and an unnamed wall to the right, where the Spaniards established their next route, Zerain. These northwest-facing walls are all at the head of the valley, located along the flanks of Cerro Pumahuagan-*]

[Top] **Pedro Galán leading pitch four of Qui Io Vado Ancora.** [Right] **Looking up the Quebrada Rurec to Itsoc Huanca and Chaupi Huanca.** *Al Aire Films*

gan (5,138m). The route Qui Io Vado Ancora does not reach the top of Chaupi Huanca; it finishes at a junction with the much longer route Caravaca Jubilar (1,000m, 21 pitches, VI 5.11 A4, Gallego-Gallego-Sandoval, 2003).]

After this climb, we returned to Huaraz for two days of rest and then hiked back into the Quebrada Rurec. We spent six days (July 17–22), including three nights sleeping on the wall, opening a route up the wall just right of Chaupi Huanca, which we called Zerain (860m, 7a+ A1). The route is dedicated to our partner Alberto Zerain, who disappeared that summer while attempting Nanga Parbat's Mazeno Ridge.

Although we did not have time to free three of the route's 20 pitches (pitches 9–11), the climb is one of the most significant of our careers, because of the elevation (the route tops out at approximately 5,200m), the size of the wall, the quality of the route, and its difficulty (we estimate 8a once it is freed). Of the pitches we did not redpoint, pitch nine involves a long rightward traverse on small crimps (about 7c+); pitch ten goes up a crack and very steep, beautiful corner that is a little dirty and about 8a; and pitch 11 continues up the corner at about 7b. 📷 🔍 ▶

— **IKER POU** *AND* **ENEKO POU**, *SPAIN*

NEW ROUTES IN QUEBRADA RUREC

OUR EXPEDITION (WWW.ARRAMPICANDE.IT) was the initiative of Pietro Rago, who first visited the Quebrada Rurec in 2005 and wanted to establish new routes with two professional athletes with disabilities: Silvia Parente, a skier who is blind, and Kevin Ferrari, a triathlete with an above-knee amputation. The team included Peruvian mountain guides (who got their first experience working with disabled climbers) and numerous climbers from Italy.

The group made their base camp at the beginning of August, directly under Chaupi Huanca (a.k.a. Punta Numa). From here, the team climbed three new rock routes, on both sides of the valley, from four to nine pitches. (See the online report for details.) The routes mostly follow slabs, so much of the climbing was bolt-protected. 🗎 🖾

– MIRKO SOTGIU, *ITALY*

CORDILLERA HUAYHUASH

SIULÁ GRANDE, EAST FACE, ATTEMPTS

IN LATE JULY, Tito Arosio, Matteo Bernasconi, and I traveled to the Cordillera Huayhuash with high hopes of climbing the impressive limestone wall in the center of the east face of Siulá Grande (6,344m). We had a little information about the place from Max Bonniot, who did the first ascent of the east face the year before with Didier Jourdain, via a line up the east pillar (*AAJ 2017*). The central wall rises in a high cirque above a large, steep icefall. In the first days of August, after establishing base camp at Laguna Siulá (4,300m), we determined that the only viable way to reach the main wall was from the right, by climbing some easier terrain and then crossing the glacier below the face.

On August 11 we left base camp and climbed 500m of moderate rock (up to 5c), plus two short ice pitches on seracs, before reaching the upper part of the glacier. [*This line was well to the left of the 2006 Italian route to the summit of the same formation (ca 5,550m), which they called Siulá Antecima; see AAJ 2007.*] Now we could see it would be too dangerous to approach the main face from this point, because of the terrible condition of the glacier. The following day we attempted to climb a snowy ridge on the right, hoping to traverse all the way to the rock wall. Unfortunately, after about 150m, we got shut down by long sections of inconsistent steep snow.

We changed plans and decided to attempt an independent line on the east pillar climbed by Bonniot and Jourdain in 2016. [*The Italians' attempt began well to the left of the French line.*] On August 18 we climbed the first 200m of the pillar, with difficulties up to 6a. After a good bivy, the following day we climbed some 200m of really compact limestone, with limited protection. Luckily, when the wall began to steepen, we joined a perfect ice runnel that led to a good bivy ledge. From here we moved right and joined the French route, continuing to the base of their crux rock pitch (6c), from which we fixed our two climbing ropes and rappelled to the ledge to bivy.

Up to that point we had climbed 550m to 600m, with difficulties up to 6c and WI4+. The next morning we woke under 20 cm of fresh snow and decided to retreat. I went up to retrieve the ropes so we could rappel.

The limestone in this little portion of the Cordillera Huayhuash is incredible: extremely solid, sharp, and compact, similar to what you find in the Rätikon or Wendenstöcke. The main wall in the east face of Siulá Grande is a challenge with top-notch technical difficulties on rock, plus a complex and committing approach, and surely will make for an intense alpine adventure. 🖾

– MATTEO DELLA BORDELLA, *RAGNI DI LECCO, ITALY*

CORDILLERA CENTRAL

NEVADO TUNSHO SUR, SOUTHEAST FACE (NOT TO SUMMIT)

In July, Peruvian IFMGA guide Victor Rímac traveled with Greg Meyering and Susie Young (both USA) to Reserva Paisajística Nor Yauyos Cocha, east of Lima. From the village of Pacha-cayo, they hiked to Lago Azulcocha (4,400m) and camped for five days to acclimatize. They then made their way to the base of their objective, Nevado Tunsho Sur (5,420m), and camped at 4,600m for two additional days.

On July 17 the three climbers started their ascent at 5 a.m., following a left-angling snow ramp on the southeast face. For the first 200m, they ascended snow slopes of 40–50°. After this, they followed mixed terrain up to 70° to reach a shoulder along the peak's south ridge, approximately 100m below the summit and at least 300m away horizontally. From this high point, they descended the west-southwest face by rappels. Their route is (400m, D+ 70°).

[Editor's note: Nevado Tunsho (11°53'46.37"S, 75°59'17.35"W, also spelled Tunshu) has three summits oriented in a southwest-northeast chain. The main summit is 5,730m, the central summit is 5,565m, and the southern summit is 5,420m. The main and central summits were first reached by a German expedition (AAJ 1968). To add further precision to reports about Tunsho in AAJ 2012 and 2015: The central summit was climbed via its south-southwest face in 2011 by Rolando Morales and Beto Pinto (both from Peru), and the south summit was first reached by a route up its west-southwest face, in 2014, by Guy Fonck (Belgium) and Beto Pinto.] ▣

— SERGIO RAMÍREZ CARRASCAL, *PERU, WITH INFORMATION FROM VICTOR RÍMAC*

NEVADO PARIACACA SUR, NORTHEAST FACE AND RIDGE

In August, Peruvian IFMGA guide Marco Jurado, along with Frank Huamán and Misael Mendoza (both Peru), made camp at 5,070m at a small lake under the northeast side of Nevado Pariacaca Sur (5,750m), which is the main summit of Pariacaca. On August 8 they started climbing at 6:30 a.m. After crossing a glacier, they started up the lower northeast face with two pitches on rock, following cracks. They reached a snowy shoulder and followed this to the final knife-edged north ridge. Mendoza waited here while Huamán and Jurado continued up the final 100m to the summit, with a serac and some crack climbing.

The three descended the east side of the mountain and reached base camp again at 6 p.m. Their route is Wanka Ñan (650m, AD+ UIAA V+ M3). Its upper portions are likely similar to the 1972 route and possibly the 1938 route; certainly snow and ice conditions have changed considerably since those earlier ascents.

[Editor's note: Nevado Pariacaca (also spelled Pary-aqaqa or Pariakaka, and also known as Tullujuto

Ascending the northeast ridge of Nevado Pariacaca Sur. *Marco Jurado*

or Tulluqutu) has two summits; both were first reached by American expeditions led by T.A. Dodge—the north (5,730m) in 1936 and south (5,750m) in 1938. The only known route on Pariacaca's steep south and west aspects is Peru 6 Mil, a very difficult route climbed by Diego Fernandez and Guillermo Mejia on the southwest face of the south peak (AAJ 2006).]

– SERGIO RAMÍREZ CARRASCAL, *PERU, WITH INFORMATION FROM MARCO JURADO*

Una Realidad Diferente (800m, MD M5) on the south face of Nevado Paca. *Pablo Maximiliano Laumann*

NEVADO PACA, SOUTH FACE

AFTER SPENDING THREE weeks in the Cordillera Blanca in July, Argentineans Nehuen Conterno and Pablo Maximiliano Laumann visited the Cordillera Central near Lima. On August 4, they ascended Tatajayco (5,342m) to gain a better vantage on the south face of Nevado Paca (5,600m, 11° 53′44 S, 76° 03′55″ W). [*The first documented ascent of Nevado Paca was from the northwest in 2006. See AAJ 2016 for more information, including a downloadable map of the peaks in this area.*]

On August 5 they began their ascent of Nevado Paca, climbing a direct line below the summit seracs. They climbed 300m unroped up a couloir feature before reaching the real difficulties. With poor snow and ice conditions, they took seven and a half hours to climb the next 500m of steeper terrain. At times they reported using a snow stake to help advance through bottomless snow. Moving slightly right near the top of the face, they gained the corniced southeast ridge near the summit. Only Conterno, who weighs 15kg less than Laumann, could reach the true summit; Laumann said the snow collapsed horrifyingly underneath him.

Their descent was down the north face; they returned to base camp at Laguna Rinconada 16 hours after they began. They called the route Una Realidad Diferente (800m, MD M5). Because of the poor conditions, they did not attempt other mountains in the zone.

– MARCELO SCANU, *ARGENTINA*

CORDILLLERA VILCABAMBA

NEVADO HUMANTAY SOUTH, SOUTH AND EAST FACES

AT THE END of October, Jark Barker and Emil Tjonneland, two spritely 18-year-olds from Maryland, and I left Soray Pampa, along the popular Salcantay trek to Machu Picchu, with a couple of horses carrying our packs, aiming for Nevado Humantay South (5,459m, Peruvian IGN map 2344). The Nevados Humantay are on the ridge extending west and north from Nevado Salcantay (6,264m); I led a group that made the first ascent of the north peak of Humantay in July 2014 (*AAJ 2015*). Taking our packs from the horses, the three of us hiked up

steeper terrain to a camp perched on a rock tower at about 4,900m, below the south face.

Leaving camp at 2 a.m. on October 31, we climbed the south face, crossed over the southeast ridge at its top, and finished on the east face, reaching the summit at 9:30 a.m. (500m, AD). Emil's watch altimeter read 5,455m. We rappelled the northeast face (opposite where we started), making the final rappel with one core-shot rope just after dark. We set the tent among the moraine and fell asleep at about 9 p.m. Over the next couple of days we descended the Ahobamba Valley to escape the mountains.

The line of the first ascent of Nevado Humantay South (5,459m), west of Nevado Salcantay. High camp is marked. The climbers finished on the upper east face and descended the northeast face into the Ahobamba Valley. *Nathan Heald*

— **NATHAN HEALD**, *PERU*

CORDILLERA URUBAMBA

NEVADO CHICÓN, SOUTHWEST FACE OF SOUTH PEAK

ON JUNE 3, Andres Putallaz (Argentina) and I left Urubamba at noon and traveled up the Chicón Valley. Climbing up the east side of the valley brought us to the glacier below the south peak of Nevado Chicón (5,526m), where we set a bivouac at 7 p.m. [*The north-south ridgeline of Chicón spans about 2 km. The southern summit is approximately 5,380m.*) At 3 a.m. we crossed the glacier, passing some crevasses, and started up the southwest wall. After about four rope lengths of climbing we arrived at the ridge leading to the south summit. We descended the same route, arriving back at the bivy at 4 p.m. and continuing to Urubamba that evening. 📷

— **COQUI GALVEZ**, *PERU*

TERIJUAY MASSIF, TERIJUAY GRANDE, SOUTH FACE

IN MID-AUGUST, MANOLO Urquizo, Coqui Galvez, Andres Putallaz, and I met in Calca and took a shuttle van to Lares on the northeastern side of the Cordillera Urubamba. From there we took a 4WD vehicle to the village of Cachin in the hills above. Very few tourists come to this area, and the villagers were surprised and wary of us when we arrived. After signing their community journal, as requested, we shouldered packs and headed up the valley westward before they could make any objection.

After a couple of hours, we crossed Paso Yanacocha and descended to Laguna Yuraccocha. From the lake we could see the Terijuay massif above. The approach continued up a craggy hillside, and we stopped below the crest to camp as nightfall and rain ensued. At camp we heard the song of a woman grazing her alpacas below, surely to ward off the bad spirits she assumed we were.

The next morning we topped the crest and headed toward the small lakes at the base of

The new route (400m, AD) up the south face of Terijuay to the west summit (5,330m), first climbed from the west in 1963. The rocky central summit, "Quelcanca," is just to the right. *Nathan Heald*

Terijauy's south aspect. We soon encountered a group of 12 locals who had hiked up on a trail from the village of Quelcanca. They were waiting for us—a couple of them wielding machetes—and demanded we descend to their village for a community meeting where they would decide if we had permission to make our ascent. We stood our ground, and after an intense discussion where we had to threaten to get the police involved, we were allowed to go on our way.

Entering the moraine, we crossed between a few small lagoons and set camp at the foot of the south face, where there is a large glacial basin formed by the three highest summits of the Terijuay massif. Terijuay Grande, first climbed by Italians in 1963 from the east (*AAJ 1964*), was said to be the tallest summit, reported at 5,380m; however, there are two other summits east of this, the middle of which may be taller. Oddly for August, the weather was cloudy and snowy.

We left camp late at 5:30 a.m. on August 17. Our navigation through the lower serac barriers was slow. We reached a point approximately 150m below the two highest summits but could not tell which was higher, so we picked the western, ice-covered one, Terijuay Grande. After reaching the summit just before noon, we glanced at the rocky summit to the east through the clouds; it appeared this peak, "Quelcanca," climbed by the Italians in 1963, was a couple of meters higher. Our ascent gained 400m and was graded AD, and we estimate the summit to be 5,330m.

The clouds thickened on our descent and we arrived at the tent with only an hour of light left. It snowed throughout the night and continued the next morning, so we descended promptly to the village of Quelcanca before the storm could trap us. Heavy snow prevented car travel, so we spent the night at the community town hall. The next day we hiked seven hours with all our gear to the village of Patacancha and took a car to Cusco.

After reviewing all the reports I could find about this area, I found that another subpeak of the Terijuay massif, located further west along Terijuay Grande's west ridge, was called Gatuyoc (5,303m, also spelled Gatuyoq). Gatuyoc was first climbed in 1970 by a New Zealand expedition that ascended its west ridge and upper southwest side; this route was likely repeated by German climbers Christoph Nick and Frank Toma in 2001. Both expeditions approached from the north-northwest. (*See AAJs 1964, 1971, 2006, and Alpine Journal 1969.*)

– NATHAN HEALD, *PERU*

Aaron Zimmerman finishing the 5.10a pitch on the summit block of Gabaratti during the first ascent of the peak, by a route mostly on the south face. *Derek Field*

GABARRITI, INCACCAPAC, AND OTHER ASCENTS

AFTER A FRUITFUL trip to the Cordillera Carabaya in 2016 (*see 2017 AAJ*), I returned to the area in June with Aaron and Jeanne Zimmerman (USA) for more adventure. Our primary goals were two unclimbed summits: Gabarriti and Incaccapac (labeled on the 1967 map by Salomon Nuñez Melgar and reproduced by Michael Cocker in 2007). We were an economy-level expedition (no mules or porters) but enjoyed ourselves thoroughly.

On June 10 we traveled from Cusco by *colectivo* to Macusani, capital of the Carabaya province. Despite boasting a wealth of cultural and natural wonders, this region of Peru has seen minimal tourism; the sight of toothy-grinned North Americans strolling around the markets in bright, puffy jackets succeeded in capturing the attention of every villager.

Our first objective was Incaccapac, a mostly rocky, fortress-like peak, most significant of the unclimbed Carabaya summits. (This peak is called "Incaccapac C1" on the Melgar map, though we could find no similar local name. The only known previous attempt was by a 1968 British expedition, which ended up making the first ascent of Chichoccapac (5,120m), a subpeak on the east ridge of Incaccapac.) On June 11 we took a *combi* toward Ayapata, disembarking in Escalera, a 400-person village located about 1,400m below Incaccapac. Hiking west, we walked around the north shore of a large lake that locals call Laguna Humanccaya (3,800m). At 4 p.m. we made base camp below Incaccapac's east face in a lovely, protected bowl within the lower moraine at 4,300m, a few hundred yards from a gushing spring.

The next day, intermittent rain made everything difficult. After a late start, we climbed the lower cliff band on the face by a 100m corner with damp rock and copious moss (Peachy Corner, 5.9 C2). We rappelled three times down an adjacent crack system. The rain was so intense that we spent the following day drying out. At 12 a.m. on June 14, we left our tent and headed back up under clear, starry skies. We first climbed the crack system we had rappelled (3 pitches, 5.8). This brought us to a 100m wall in the back of a cleft, which we surmounted via two excellent

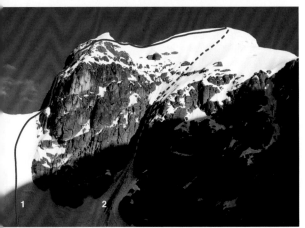

[Top] The line of Ruta Escalera (500m, D+ 5.8 M3) on the east face of Incaccapac (5,292m GPS). [Middle] Allinccapac II (5,809m) from the west. (1) North buttress (2017). (2) Approximate line of "northwest face" route (1960). [Bottom] The south face of Gabarriti (5,209m). The first ascent climbed the glacial slopes in center, then a crack system on the left (west) side of the summit block. *Derek Field (all photos)* -

crack pitches (5.8). Opting to attack the upper cliff band on its left (west) side, we traversed third-class slabs and eventually discovered a ledge system tracing its way up the south ridge. We followed this for two easy pitches until a dead-end, then rappelled 15m to a ledge and adjacent snow gully that regained the ridge. By 1 p.m., snow flurries had begun to fill the air. Two pitches of mixed left us with only a short, snowy scramble to the top. A momentary break in the clouds allowed us to verify that we had indeed reached the highest point; the GPS recorded 5,292m (174m higher than the elevation shown on the 1967 Melgar map). Our route is called Ruta Escalera (500m, D+ 5.8 M3).

As the sun dove for the horizon we frantically scoured the summit ridge for a bivouac site. Eventually we found a tiny rectangular nook where the three of us endured a 10-hour night sharing one bivy sack. The next day we descended the same route we had climbed.

After a rest in Macusani, we headed back out to the mountains on June 18, taking a taxi 45 minutes north to the head of Valle Antajahua, the base of Allinccapac's south face. With packs loaded with ten days' worth of supplies, it took us two hours to reach the bottle-ridden shores of Laguna Allinccapac (4,960m), where we set up our first camp. Two days later we had established a high camp at 5,500m, with five days of supplies, on the west shoulder of Allinccapac I. We spent the next day climbing two towers flanking the north ridge of Allinccapac II, accessed from the swooping saddle between Allinccapac I and Huaynaccapac I. [*Details of these and other ascents are at the AAJ website.*] On June 22, from the same high camp, we made the fifth recorded ascent of the west shoulder on Allinccapac I, finding it to be an enjoyable route to the highest point in the range (5,837m GPS).

On June 23 the three of us climbed the north buttress of Allinccapac II, a massive red-rock escarpment. We reached the base of this buttress via a 60° snow couloir. Hand cracks and an uncomfortable 5.7 squeeze chimney brought us to sun-drenched snow slopes leading directly to the corniced summit ridge. Standing a few meters below the summit in fear of the unstable cornice, our GPS recorded an elevation of 5,807m. Our new route was 200m, AD 5.8 60°.

The following day we descended from our high camp. It was June 24 and inhabitants of the Carabaya region had gathered to celebrate Allinccapac Raymi, the most important festival in honor of the *apu* (mountain spirit) of Allinccapac. It was quite a sight to see thousands of people sliding around playfully on the enormous, crevasse-ridden glacier below us. We headed down Valle Pacaje and camped that night at the gorgeous turquoise lake at the foot of Gabarriti. (This is the name given on the Melgar map. Ronald Gutierrez, former Carabaya governor, noted that it may be a misspelling of Ccapac Riti, which means something like "the prosperous snowy mountain.") After dunking in the frigid water at 4,700m, we kicked back and admired the marvelous south face of Gabarriti, the only remaining virgin peak labeled on the 1967 Melgar map.

We left the tent at 5 a.m. on June 25. Carving a line up the left side of the glacier, we climbed 60° ice onto a narrow hogback ridge just below (south of) the major saddle between the north and central summits. A full rope length of AI3 ice and a half rope of mixed climbing brought us to the saddle. The final 100m summit tower was steep on all sides. A left-trending ledge on the tower's west face, a 5.7 chimney, and a poorly protected mantel brought us to the final pitch: a perfect 35m dihedral (5.10a). We scrambled the narrow summit ridge to the highest point and recorded a GPS elevation of 5,209m. Our route is the south face (300m, D AI3 5.10a). When jungle clouds started to roll in, we started down, rappelling the upper route.

On June 27 we descended the remainder of Valle Pacaje, a long and twisting gorge cut by a tributary of the Río Gabán. After reaching dense cloud forest at 2,800m, we caught a glimpse of the highway below. Not long after, we were soaking in Ollachea's natural hot springs.

– DEREK FIELD, *CANADA*

CORDILLERA VOLCÁNICA

COROPUNA MASSIF, VARIOUS ASCENTS

COROPUNA (6,425M) IS the highest volcano in Peru. Located approximately 150km northwest of Arequipa, it has six glaciated summits higher than 6,000m, and the massif covers 83 square kilometers. During June and July, Julieta Ferreri (Argentina) and Marcelo Motta Delvaux (Brazil) opened possible new routes on the massif from the northwest and northeast; the standard approach is from Laguna Pallacocha to the southwest.

From June 13–19, approaching from the northwest, the pair ascended the west summit, Nevado Pallacocha (6,171m), and the north summit, Coropuna Casulla (6,377m). They used four camps between 5,000m and 6,000m, and their northwest approach was new until 6,020m, where they switched to established routes. During July 2–8 the same pair ascended Coropuna Este (6,305m), entering by its northeast glacier and making four camps between 4,875m and 5,537m. The final part of their route up the northwest face is new.

– MARCELO SCANU, *ARGENTINA*

BOLIVIA

Antoine Trichot on the summit ridge of Chearoco. Behind is the rocky ridge traverse over the Picos de la Vuelta, which the French climbed after the possible first ascent of Pirámide Ayamara (the sharp peak behind the snow point). In the far distance is Lake Titicaca. *Elsie Trichot*

CORDILLERA REAL

ILLAMPU, CHACHACOMANI, AND CHEAROCO GROUPS, VARIOUS FIRST ASCENTS

From May 25 to June 25, my husband, Antoine Trichot, and I climbed seven routes in the Cordillera Real, most of them new and a few to summits that may have been previously unclimbed. For me, first ascents had long been a dream.

Only 48 hours after arriving in La Paz, we headed for the Chachacomani region, where we discovered several lines we had not seen on Google Earth during our planning. Our first objective was a long rocky crest, the northwest ridge of Peak 5,600m (16°1'35.38"S, 68°21'39.94"W). On June 1, from a camp at 4,750m, we approached the crest from the south, then for the next six hours followed it on mostly quality granite to a finish over steep snow and mixed terrain. From the summit we descended north into a different valley, lost time trying to find the best way through moraine, and only made it back to the tent after dark. We named the peak Cerro Llama Blanco y Negro and graded our route D- F4+.

Our next objective was the magnificent south ridge of Jakoceri (5,910m), which at the time we believed to be unclimbed. Leaving from a high camp at 5,250m on June 3, we followed the ridge from its very beginning. [*Previous ascents, reported in AAJ 2017, gained the ridge higher up from the west.*] We reached the south top at 4 p.m., 10 hours after leaving the tent, and followed the elegant, sharp ridge to the north summit. From there we continued down to the Jakoceri-Chachacomani col, then more easily southwest down the glacier to our tent. We graded our first integral ascent of Jakoceri's south ridge TD- 4+ M5.

We then moved to Cocoyu in the northern Real, and after two days of hiking up boulder fields and glacier, established a base camp at 5,350m on the east side of the Illampu massif.

Our plan had been to try a new route on the east face of Illampu, but we were drawn to an elegant 700m line up the southeast face and pillar of Pico del Norte (6,050m). Ice too thin to protect, run-out dry tooling, strenuous climbing, nerve-wracking gusts of wind, and a long and complex descent in the dark—it was a climb we'll remember well. [*The French climbed the first half of the 1972 Mesili Route (Arias-Bathelemy-Grange-Khern-Mesili, 1972, TD) and the upper half of the classic Bettembourg Pillar (Bettembourg-Chaud-Mesili, 1982, D+); they graded this combination TD+ WI4 R M5+ and took 12 hours to reach the summit on June 11.*]

After a day in camp sitting out a windstorm, we headed for the beautiful east-southeast ridge of Pico Esperanza (5,760m). It soon became difficult: mixed climbing to one side of the crest, fine dry granite on the other. While examining the route with binoculars, we had spotted a 25m wall on the crest that obviously looked difficult. When we arrived beneath it, we found a vertical compact wall with a single thin crack. With our small rack this was impossible, and after exploring both left and right we had no option but to rappel to the glacier on the north side. We regained the ridge crest somewhat higher and followed straightforward terrain to the summit. The climb had taken eight hours from the foot of the ridge, had a vertical gain of around 250m, and was D 4+ M4.

After two days' rest on the shores of Lake Titicaca, we embarked on our third trip into the mountains, making a two-day approach (with the help of mules and porters) to the glacier that runs up the west side of Chearoco (6,104m). On June 18, from our camp at 5,200m, we started up a west-facing rock pillar leading to a 5,870m shoulder on the normal route up Chearoco. We climbed this 370m pillar at 4+. We decided to continue by downclimbing to the left to reach a glacier terrace at 5,720m, below the southwest face of Chearoco. At first we struggled in deep snow, but once we climbed onto the steeper southwest face, conditions were close to perfect. The 300m face (45–60° M4) led to an exposed snow arête and finally the summit. Overall, our route combination was D+ and took seven hours from the start of the rock pillar to the main summit. [*Their upper southwest face line is likely to have been climbed before. See notes in the online report.*]

On June 20 we aimed for a sharp, east-facing granite ridge rising to a pointed summit opposite the west

The southeast face of Pico del Norte. The yellow line is the route combination climbed in 2017: the first half of the 1972 Mesili Route and the second part of the Bettembourg Pillar (1982). The red lines show the start of the Bettembourg Pillar and continuation of the Mesili Route. *Elsie Trichot*

Elsie Trichot on the east ridge of Pirámide Aymara.
Antoine Trichot

face of Chearoco. It gave high-quality rock climbing to the summit (350m, D/D+ 5, five hours), which we measured at 5,750m and named Pirámide Aymara. Steep downclimbing of the southwest ridge led to a col from which it was possible to return to base camp or continue south along the ridge. We chose the latter and crossed several tops, for which we propose the name Picos de la Vuelta, before finally descending snow slopes to the east.

The following day we climbed the central pillar on the south face of a peak we dubbed Pirámide Santos, lower down the valley (15°58'49.98"S, 68°25'37.16"W). The difficulties proved higher than anticipated, both on rock (we used rock shoes for the first time on the trip) and mixed. It took eight hours to reach the summit, which we measured at 5,570m. The 470m pillar was graded TD 5 M5. The descent, via a couloir to the east, was easier than expected—a good thing, as it was once again dark before we reached camp. *[Whether these peaks west of Chearoco were previously unclimbed is difficult to say. In 1978 a team of Italians climbed five summits in this group, but it has not been possible to ascertain the exact location of any of them, reported at the time to be between 5,350m and 5,520m].*

More effort was required of us next day, as for six hours we carried our gear across the glacier and up scree to meet our muleteer. This brought an end to our most intense alpine experience. When can we come again?

— ELSIE TRICHOT, *RÊVES ALPINS, FRANCE*

HISTORICAL NOTE ON ILLAMPU'S WEST FACE: *New information has surfaced on the history of the 850m west face of Illampu (6,368m), including the true first ascent of the face (1978, by a Spanish team) and a previously unreported route in the center of the wall (1986, Slovenian climbers). A comprehensive report by Lindsay Griffin will be found at the AAJ website.*

HUALLOMEN, SOUTHWEST FACE, VIA DEL QUERUBIN

ON THE FIRST day of May, Pacifico Machaca (Bolivia) and I climbed a partial new route on the impressive southwest face of Huallomen (a.k.a. Wyoming, 5,463m). *[This face has a complex, somewhat obscure history, and, as the editor's note below outlines, two separate lines may have been climbed for the first time in 2017.]* Because of recent snowfall, we stayed in the refuge that locals recently have built at Chiarkhota base camp. We left around 3 a.m. and started our approach through about 20cm of new snow, reaching the southwest face at dawn.

In the initial section of the central gully we struggled through short sections of knee- to hip-deep snow, which slowed us considerably. Crossing the first rock band was harder than expected—we overcame this by a short, flared, slightly overhanging crack. After two much easier pitches of snow climbing, we finally reached the steepest section of the gully. Unfortunately, the snow from the rainy season had not transformed into solid ice and I was unable to find safe placements for ice screws. I therefore decided to continue up to the right, hoping for easier terrain. Given the wintry conditions and the bad quality schist (the strata on this face is downward sloping, making the cracks poor for nuts or pitons), I had a hard time finding good protection; the cruxes were dry tooling on mostly bare rock.

After nine pitches we reached the shoulder (ca 5,400m) south of the summit and descended from there along the normal route on the opposite side. It was already dark and my dear partner was in a hypoglycemic state. (I felt only partially responsible for this—Pacifico carried an entire cheese to the top, forgetting he had it.) We named our new finish Via del Querubín ("Cherub Route," TD+), referring to the existing route Canaleta del Angel and the fact that, despite poor pro, everything went well. 📷

— ALEXANDER VON UNGERN, *ANDEAN ASCENTS, BOLIVIA*

HISTORICAL NOTES AND ANOTHER NEW ROUTE ON HUALLOMEN: *On September 15, 1976, according to Alain Mesili's 1984 guidebook,* La Cordillera Real de los Andes-Bolivia, *Mesili climbed the route shown as (2) on the photo below; he graded it D (400m, 60° with short steeper sections). The relatively uniform snow/ice couloir that diagonals left to the summit is very visible under good snow cover, and at the time of Mesili's claimed ascent a broad snowfield led to the start of it. Since then, glacial recession has made the route harder, and Yossi Brain, who marks the same*

line in his 1999 guidebook, estimated the difficulties at ED1 UIAA V+ 85°; it definitely has been climbed since Mesili's claimed ascent.

Subsequently, in his 2004 book The Andes of Bolivia: Adventures and a Climbing Guide, *Mesili marks his 1976 line farther to the left, taking a much harder gully system that he called Canaleta del Angel (marked 1 in the photo). It is believed that the line Mesili claimed in 1976 actually was the easier one to the right. The harder line (1) was finally climbed in late July or early August of 2017 by Alex Albornoz, James Baragwanath, and Mati Korten (Argentina and Chile). They completed the route in a 25-hour day, rating it ED1+.*

The southwest face of Huallomen (5,463m). (1) Route climbed by an Argentinian-Chilean team in 2017. This line was dubbed Canaleta del Angel by Alain Mesili in his 2004 guidebook, but is believed to have been unclimbed before 2017. (2) Mesili Route, claimed in 1976 and definitely climbed later. (3) Via del Querubín. The peak's normal route is on the far side. *Alexander von Ungern*

CUCHILLO KHUNO, SOUTHWEST AND EAST FACES

IN MID-JUNE, WHILE guiding in the Condoriri area, Cecilio Daza and I decided to use part of a rest day to explore the southwest face of Cuchillo Khuno (ca 5,300m, a peak on the ridge northeast of Pico Austria. We approached the face directly from base camp, then slanted up left to the southwest ridge (between Cuchillio Khuno and Austria) to avoid sections of knee-deep snow. We followed the ridge over a little summit and rappelled to a col at the bottom of the upper southwest face. A vertical rock barrier shortly above the col provided the climb's main difficulty. After 250–300m of unroped climbing we reached the west summit and then descended the same way, as we could find no better route off the mountain.

After climbing Cabeza del Condor with my client Michael Ellis (USA) the following day, I wanted to return to Cuchillo Khuno, this time on the opposite side. Michael and I left high camp, crossed the ridge north of Cuchillo Khuno, and dropped to the start of a gully on its east face. From here we climbed to the east summit in four 70m pitches. We then rappelled twice on the northern side of the mountain before scrambling down scree to return to high camp.

Even though Cuchillo Khuno is located in one of the most visited mountaineering areas of Bolivia, we could find no record of these lines, nor any cairns or other signs of previous passage, perhaps because the area has many more attractive objectives for those visiting for their first time. 📄 📷

— ALEXANDER VON UNGERN, ANDEAN ASCENTS, BOLIVIA

CHARQUINI, EAST FACE, JUNTOS AL PUMA

ON MARCH 12, I circumnavigated Charquini (5,392m) on skis and spotted interesting steep granite on the "hidden" east face. While this face is visible from the popular Choro Trail (an ancient paved Inca road), most people are descending the trail at this point and Charquini is behind them. Most climbing activity in the broad Charquini massif is on the southwest and south faces. As far as I know, the rocky east face was unclimbed.

Sergio Condori and I returned on May 16, leaving the car at sunrise at the Eco Albergue of Pampalarama, southeast of the mountain. The approach took longer than expected, but we were happy to spot fresh puma tracks on the disappearing glacier between Wila Manquilisani and Charquini. We started climbing around 9 a.m. The first pitch was the crux (6a+) and also provided the worst rock of the route. The next three pitches, still steep and sustained, were really enjoyable, with solid protection.

Sergio Condori high on Juntos al Puma (6a+), the first route up the east face of Charquini. *Alexander von Ungern*

As the slope eased, we decided to head for the eastern summit, at roughly 5,300m, by a combination of short-roping and quick belays on steeper sections. After a brief picnic on top, interrupted by the threat of lightning that caused my trekking pole to "sing," we rappelled the snow-covered south face. 📷

— ALEXANDER VON UNGERN, ANDEAN ASCENTS, BOLIVIA

HAMPATURI GROUP, SERKHE VALLEY, THREE PEAKS TRAVERSE

ON MARCH 19 my wife dropped me at dawn at the "road head" (ca 4,800m) a little short of Serkhe Lake. I first climbed the southwest face of what some call Serkhe Negro (5,460m), descending the far side. After fixing a broken crampon with some cordelette, I continued onward to climb Serkhe Khollu (5,546m) via the easy northwest ridge. The descent, slanting down and across the southwest face, was a different matter: difficult, steep, and scary. I used my 35m rope to rappel short vertical sections.

After a break on the valley floor, I continued to Peak 5,540m (16°24'40.09"S, 67°56'51.80"W), which is sometimes referred to as Khasiri or Qasiri, though this name is also given to a peak farther south. I climbed a steep, snow-filled gully on the north face to the summit, arriving in midafternoon. Once again, the descent—along the northeast ridge—was more difficult, and I rappelled several short sections. I bivouacked beside the shore of Serkhe Lake and left the next morning. As is often the case in Bolivia, this adventure was wild, beautiful, and astonishingly close to civilization. 📄 📷 ▶

— ALEXANDER VON UNGERN, *ANDEAN ASCENTS, BOLIVIA*

CORDILLERA QUIMSA CRUZ

CUERNOS DEL DIABLO, SOUTHWEST FACE, DON RAYO

IN APRIL A group of aspirant guides underwent UIAGM training in the mountains of Bolivia, during which they spent nearly two weeks visiting the Quimsa Cruz. They repeated several lines, and the Bolivian instructor Roberto Gomez, along with guide candidates José Miguel Rosen and Cristobal Señoret (both from Chile), put up the new route Don Rayo (named after their cook) on the left side of the southwest face of the Cuernos del Diablo (5,271m).

The sunnier northwest face of this fine rock peak has been well-developed since the first route in 1987 (see, most recently, *AAJ 2017*), but the southwest face has seen very little exploration. After walking 2.5 hours from base camp to the foot of this wall, the trio chose a 350m line left of the monolithic steep slabs that characterize this aspect of the mountain. Difficulties were 6b A0 and almost entirely in cracks. A section of face climbing near the top of the route led to a 10m offwidth chimney, followed

Cuernos del Diablo from the west with the line of Don Rayo. The steep, slabbly northwest face at far left is home to many routes from 220m to 270m. Don Rayo appears to finish up the last section of the 2011 Condori-Daza route Inti Wiracocha (six pitches, 6b+). *Gregg Beisly*

by a completely run-out 15m section of 5+. Descent was by four rappels down the northwest face. The climbers feel this area still has extensive possibilities for new routes.

— LINDSAY GRIFFIN, *FROM INFORMATION SUPPLIED BY CRISTOBAL SEÑORET, CHILE*

The northwest face of Gran Muralla (some routes not shown). (1) Traditionally marked as a route climbed by a strong German team in 1987. The five-pitch route was climbed in 2015 by Juvenal and Sergio Condori at 6c. (2) Espiritu Vertical (200m, 7 pitches, 7a+), climbed in 2016 by Sergio Condori and Rolando Tarqui. (3) German route from 1987, reported to be around 6a. (4) Chabert-Labaeye (200m, 4 pitches, 6b+, 2006. Re-equipped for rappel descent in 2015). (5) Kamasa (6b A2, Acuna-Camargo-Rainone-Rosso, 2017; part or all of the top section may coincide with an established line). *Enrico Rosso*

GRAN MURALLA, NORTHWEST FACE, KAMASA

I SET OFF from Italy with Giovanni Penna and Marco Rainone to achieve two goals: working with the Università Campesina and attempting a new route on the south face of Illimani. Università Campesina is a project run by Antonio "Topio" Zavattarelli, a priest and mountaineer who, through his missionary at Peñas, is training Bolivian high school pupils to become tour guides. The best may even progress to become mountain guides.

During the first part of our stay, we held a series of lessons with the students in the classroom and at the crags close to Peñas, after which we completed the program by climbing Chachacomani (6,074m) and Condoriri (5,648m).

Abundant snowfall and unsettled weather in May, coupled with high winds, had created unstable conditions, so we decided not to attempt Illimani and instead opted for the Quimsa Cruz. On June 18, Marco, Topio, and I, along with three young climbers connected with the mission at Peñas—Rosmel Varillas Acuna (24), Ronaldo Choque Camargo (19), and Davide Vitali (26)—headed for the small village of Viloco. After establishing base camp at 4,500m in the Kuchu Mocoya valley, we chose as an objective the northwest face of Gran Muralla (a.k.a. Grosse Mauer, ca 5,100m). Rising 200–250m, this face is certainly one of the most beautiful rock formations in the cordillera.

Our climb focused on a series of cracks on the right-hand side of the face [*well right of a route climbed in 2006 by two aspirant French guides*]. We completed the climb in eight hours, using mostly cams and nuts, along with some pegs. We rappelled the face from existing anchors on the wall to the left. [*This rappel route, established in 2015 by Juvenal and Sergio Condori, generally descends along the French route from 2006 (Chabert-Labaeye), but these cracks have "gone back to nature" and are choked with dirt.*] We called our route Kamasa (250m, 6b A2), which means "courage" in the local Aymara language.

In both of its phases, the expedition was very positive. The Università Campesina project offers a bright future for the younger generation on the Bolivian plateau. 🄾

– ENRICO ROSSO, *ITALY*

CORDILLERA DE COCAPATA

PICO TUNARI, SOUTH FACE, PIPPO

FROM JUNE 21-22, Rodrigo Lobo and I made the first ascent of the south face of Tunari (5,035m), a long escarpment clearly visible from Cochabamba, Bolivia's third-largest city. Rodrigo's parents live in Cochabamba, and we spent the night at their house before driving to the north side of Tunari and hiking up to a small lake below the main summit, where we camped.

Since a direct approach to the south face looked too complicated, we walked up the north slopes to the summit and then descended steep, snow-covered terrain to the south. At the base we traversed along the steep south face. It had an intimidating aura, which almost made you want to quit before starting.

We headed for a dihedral, invisible from a distance, which rises to the main summit. We first climbed 100m of hard snow/ice, which, as we were wearing running shoes, proved dangerous; I used two stones as ice axe substitutes. We then simulclimbed to the dihedral, which we climbed via a steep pitch in loose metamorphic rock at 6a+. The face above was consistently hard, 6b+ to 6c+, on far from sound rock. Snow on the face and a temperature of -5°C didn't make the climb any easier. Close to the summit, we were stopped by a difficult pitch that we spent hours unsuccessfully trying to surmount. We

[Top] The Cordillera de Cocapata and high camp on the north side of Tunari. From here, Rodrigo Lobo and Robert Rauch crossed the mountain and descended the far side before making the first ascent of the south face. [Bottom] The south face of Tunari. The first ascent followed a route a little right of the fall line from the summit, then moved left near the top, eventually reaching the summit from the left. *Robert Rauch*

had to spend the night on a poor ledge with rudimentary bivouac gear.

At 8 a.m. the following morning, we began again. Rodrigo managed to climb above our high point and found a cam placement. We both took a deep breath. He continued and then, almost in despair, found a fixed anchor placed by two climbers who had rappelled the face some time ago. He belayed there. From his cam, 15m of unprotected traverse on tiny holds separated me from Rodrigo. I switched mentally to solo mode and made it—the crux pitch.

We traversed left beneath huge loose overhangs and discovered a vertical, loose chimney. This led to easy ground, our first rays of sun for 26 hours, and the summit. What a route! We named our line Pippo (500m climbing distance, 7a+) after a friend of Rodrigo's who had died while trying to traverse all the main summits in the range. 📷

– ROBERT RAUCH, *BOLIVIAN TOURS, RAUCHROBERT@HOTMAIL.COM*

PIRHUATA, SOUTHEAST FACE AND SOUTH-SOUTHWEST RIDGE

AFTER MAKING THE first ascent of the south face of Pico Tunari in June (*see report above*), Rodrigo Lobo and I decided that we simply had to climb the three most significant rock walls in the extensive Cordillera de Cocapata: Tunari's south face, the southeast face of Pirhuata, and

the west face of Hatuncasa (Jatúncasa). Due to a little frostbite sustained on our ascent of Tunari, we decided to wait for the warmer spring temperatures of November.

We joined the fearless Carlos Regalsky from Cochabamba and James Monypenny from the U.K., who was on a 10-month climbing trip through South America. From Cochabamba, a friend drove us two and a half hours to a spot below the southeast face of Pirhuata (ca 5,060m, 17°12′50″S, 66°24′0″W), about 8km north of Pico Tunari. We traversed below the entire southeast face and found it extremely intimidating, with large overhangs that looked impossible to breach. We started at 7:30 a.m. next morning, Rodrigo and I aiming for a weakness in the center of the southeast face, Carlos and James for the long but reasonable-looking south-southwest ridge.

Our start was loose 6b+ with only sporadic protection. We then simulclimbed 150m to a dihedral

[Top] Looking across the extensive southeast face of Pirhuata from the new route Las Tortugas Tambien Vuelan. [Bottom] Traversing below the southeast face of Pirhuata while prospecting for climbable lines. *Robert Rauch*

that led to large overhangs in the upper half of the face. The rock was not sound, but the day was warm and we climbed in T-shirts. We found a wild crack through the overhangs. The next pitch was easier, but then we were hit by a violent thunderstorm with hail. After a couple of cold hours, Rodrigo pulled off a fine lead with stiff fingers on the pitch above. One more pitch led to easier ground, which we simulclimbed for 150m. At 4:30 p.m. we hugged like grizzlies on the summit.

We named our route Las Tortugas Tambien Vuelan ("Even Turtles Can Fly," 6c+). Carlos and James completed the south-southwest ridge (which James called Bolivia's chossiest cliff). There were two hard pitches of around 6b, and the rest rather easier. They were also pinned down by the scary thunderstorm on the final ridge, and Monypenny's fingers sparked with electricity. It had been an intense day for both teams. 🖹 📷

— ROBERT RAUCH, *BOLIVIAN TOURS, RAUCHROBERT@HOTMAIL.COM*

SOLO ASCENT OF ILLIMANI SOUTH FACE: *While in Bolivia, James Monypenny made what's probably the first solo ascent of the south face of Illimani (6,439m) in the Cordillera Real. He climbed the route claimed in 1978 by Alain Mesili (with Christian Jacquier), descended below Nido de Condores along the normal route—all in a 31-hour push—and then flew down from there using a lightweight paraglider. This was probably the third ascent of this line.*

ARGENTINA-CHILE

VOLCÁN INCAHUASI, NEW ROUTE, AND OTHER ASCENTS

INCAHUASI IS A 6,638m volcano on the border between Chile and Argentina whose name means "Inca house" in Quechua. The world's second-highest ruins, an Incan temple, are found near the summit. In January 2018, Diego Cavassa (Argentina) climbed a new route up the steep, rocky slopes of the northeast face, left of the normal route.

Also in early 2018, Argentine climbers made a rare ascent of the large glacier on the south side of Volcán El Muerto (officially 6,488m, but maybe higher), northeast of Ojos del Salado. This route was possibly first climbed in 2005 by Janne Corax (Sweden) and Nadine Saulnier (France). In December 2017, Andrés Fabeiro and Marcelo Scanu climbed the northeast ridge of Cerro de los Caranchos (4,225m), one of the highest unclimbed mountains in the Chaschuil zone, as condors flew a few meters overhead. More details on these climbs are at the AAJ website. 📄 📷

— MARCELO SCANU, *ARGENTINA*

FAMATINA RANGE: PEAK 5,849M; NEGRO OVERO, SOUTHEAST FACE

DURING JULY 2016, an Argentine team (Lucas Alzamora, Juan Guerra, and Roberto Rivas Jordan) climbed a new route up the southeast face of Negro Overo (5,780m) in La Rioja Province, a mountain first climbed by the Incas. The new route ascended a snow couloir (average 45°), with a final stretch of 55° snow.

In September 2017, Alzamora teamed up with Argentine Diego Nakamura to climb the highest virgin summit of this massif. They reached the summit (5,849m) on their second attempt by the east-southeast face (45–55° snow). The only previous recorded attempt was by the east ridge and ended 100m short of the top. These mountains are along the ridgeline to the north of Cerro General Belgrano (6,097m), high point of this range. 📷

— MARCELO SCANU, *ARGENTINA*

QUEBRADA CHORRILLOS: CERRO 34 LEGUAS AND EXPLORATION

GLAUCO MURATTI HAS been exploring the mountains of Mendoza Province, near Aconcagua, for years. In February 2018, he joined another Argentine, Lisandro Arelovich, and headed to the remote Quebrada Chorrillos, a valley with many obstacles that has left it little explored.

On February 7 they departed from the town of Punta de Vacas (2,400m), southeast of Aconcagua, trekking south along the Tupungato River and then west up Chorrillos Creek, crossing the Paso de los Guanacos (4,200m, with some difficult steps) and the Paso Modesto (4,200m) and then descending to the south branch of the Chorrillos, a route that was certainly previously untrodden.

On the fifth day of their expedition the pair summited a virgin 5,150m peak (33°06′28.72″S, 69°55′02.24″W) by its north ridge with some delicate steps and rotten rock. They named it

Cerro Tito Magnani from the south. The peak was first climbed from the north and east in 2016. *Glauco Muratti*

Cerro 34 Leguas because of the long journey to reach it. On the way back they returned to Paso Modesto, then traversed directly to Paso de los Guanacos, ascending Cerro Horqueta (4,565m) by its virgin south face, with some grade III rotten rock. (This peak was first climbed from the northwest in 2016; see *AAJ 2017*.) They descended to the Valle de las Huellitas and then crossed over the Cordón de Clonquis to reach Quebrada Potrero Escondido before exiting to Punta de Vacas. The round-trip journey took eight hard days.

— MARCELO SCANU, *ARGENTINA*

NORTHERN PATAGONIA

CERRO KURALEMU, EL CAMINO DEL PUMA

THROUGH OUR CONSTANT search for overlooked places in our majestic backyard cordillera, Max Didier, my brother Diego Señoret, and I found a large granite wall in Chile's Parque Nacional Puyehue (*Puyehue means "stone forest"*) on Google Earth. The landscape here is full of rivers, dense vegetation, and burned forest from the last time the Puyehue stratovolcano erupted. It looked like an adventure just to get there.

We set out on March 12, packing for a five-day trip. The hike was 56km in each direction.

Drying gear on the shore of Lago Gris with Cerro Kuralemu rising in the background. After walking in for 56 kilometers, the team used a tiny inflatable boat to ferry three people and gear across the lake, making two trips to reach the wall, which they climbed in a single push. *Juan Señoret*

There were no signs of humans but plenty of puma tracks. I've lost count of the number of rivers we had to cross and the struggles we had in the dense forest. It's just a nice memory now.

Our chosen wall rises from the north shore of Lago Gris, a few miles west of the border with Argentina. We carried one really tiny inflatable boat to reach it. With only an 80kg load capacity, we had to do two trips across the 3km lake, dangerously surpassing the raft's capacity each time.

Once we had everything below the wall, we began climbing almost immediately, around 1 a.m. on March 14. Our line connected crack systems before reaching a headwall, which had a few more demanding leads. The climbing was incredible. We reached the summit at 9:45 p.m. after a single 20-hour-push, climbing 15 pitches of high-quality granite.

It took approximately eight hours to descend back to our boat, which we reached at 4:20 a.m. We waited until dawn to paddle back across the lake. We called the mountain Cerro Kura-lemu (1,705m) and our route Camino del Puma (700m, 7a).

– **JUAN SEÑORET**, *CHILE*

CERRO PANTOJO, NEW ROUTES

IN OCTOBER 2017, Ian Schwer and I completed two new routes on the south face of Cerro Pantojo (2,027m). This mountain is the heart of an extinguished volcano near the Paso Cardenal Antonio Samoré between Argentina and Chile. The normal route runs through the central gutter of the southwest face of the tower and is a moderate climb in summer (200m, 5.7). In winter, the same route gets more interesting, about 80° and M4.

We left Bariloche and approached on skis for about three hours to a good bivy close to the south face. There, we met a frustrated soloist, Chilean Jorge Rosas,

The south face of Cerro Pantojo. (1) Por Hongos y Por Honguitos. The normal route (descent route) is just to the left. (2) Supercanaleta del Pantojo. *Ian Schwer*

who ended up joining us for our climb of a spur on the left side of the south face, which was plastered in rime. For the descent we used the normal route, which has recently been retro-bolted (despite existing without these bolts since the 1930s), creating a mess but also a fast and safe way down. We named the route Por Hongos y Por Honguitos (220m climbing distance, M3 80°).

Ten days later, all the rime had fallen when Ian and I returned to tackle the center of the south face via a big couloir that we dubbed Supercanaleta del Pantojo. This time, we crossed the border as soon as the immigration office opened, approached on skis, climbed our route, and made it back to the immigration office about 10 hours later, just before it closed at 6 p.m. Going nonstop is lighter, but you are bound to descend the west side in the afternoon, which becomes a giant waterfall on warm days. This route was about 270m and M4 85°. There is still some virgin space on the right side of the south face: steeper and longer but also more fragile than the routes we climbed.

– **MATI KORTEN**, *ARGENTINA*

Inti Mellado leading the second and crux pitch of Arrayan on Trinidad Sur. *Clinton Leung*

COCHAMÓ, TRINIDAD SUR, ARRAYAN

IN FEBRUARY 2017, Trevor Boley, Kyle Kent, Rhane Pfeiffer, Cooper Varney, and I completed a new route on Trinidad Sur. I first spotted this line while climbing the neighboring route Alendalaca (450m, 5.12b) in December 2016. From that vantage, I became enthralled by a headwall splitter to the left and with finding a way to reach it.

My original plan was to climb the flat, forward-facing buttress of Trinidad Sur and traverse leftward onto the upper headwall. However, Rhane suggested we explore the inner gully between Trinidad Sur and Trinidad Central. On a recon trip in January, we accessed the gully via a quality 5.10 corner. We knew then that we'd found the start of our route: Above us stood a stupendous steep, leaning, 60m 5.12 splitter.

We started the route on January 17, climbing ground-up and siege-style, fixing lines as we pushed the high point. Some days we spent cleaning and bolting the pitches we had fixed to prepare them to be free climbed, and other days we spent pushing the route higher via aid.

We surmounted many challenges—including some harrowing aid, a 5.11 R/X pitch led by Cooper, as well as multiple core shots in our fixed lines. That final headwall splitter turned out to be an incredibly pleasant 60m 5.10b thin hands to hands crack that leads right to the top of Trinidad Sur.

We topped out on February 17. With an impending storm and the season ending, we did not manage to redpoint the entire route. We called the route Arrayan (8 pitches, 400m, 5.11 A2+); it's an open project with a proposed grade of 5.12+. 📷 🔍

— CLINTON LEUNG, *CANADA*

COCHAMÓ, ANFITEATRO, WALL MAPU

IN MARCH, MAXIMO Fernandez (Chile), Lucas "Turco" Dahir (Argentina), and I finished a project we started a few years ago on the east face of Anfiteatro, beginning partway up the gully that separates Walwalun from Cerro Anfiteatro. The seven-pitch route mostly follows corners with difficulties to 5.10c (a number 5 cam is recommended for the final pitch), after which 300m of scrambling leads to the summit.

We called the route Wall Mapu after the Mapuche people who lived here before the Spanish invasion. With this name we hope to remind climbers that these ancestral lands are still threatened by mega-projects that do not respect the environment. We are very worried over the future of Cochamó, and are ready to defend this mythical valley of the south. 📷

— JOSÉ DATTOLI, *CHILE*

TURBIO VALLEY, CERRO MARIPOSA, PRODUCI CONSUMA CREPA

Paolo Marazzi and I (both Ragni de Lecco members) traveled to Argentina in February with the goal of climbing Cerro Mariposa. In Bariloche, local alpinist Sebastián de la Cruz helped us with logistics; as he's one of the few who knows much about the remote climbing in the Turbio Valley. We waited in Bariloche one week while heavy rains flooded the area. Then we had to wait two additional days for the Rio Turbio's water level to drop.

On February 25, we managed to cross the river with horses and start our approach up the valley. After eight hours of riding, we reached the first of two cabanas, a luxury shelter in the woods at the entrance of the Turbio Valley. (Sebastián joined us to this point). From there, in one day on foot, we arrived at the second cabana, a small hut in a flat area close to the walls. It was a nice place, but this marked the beginning of 20 days of rain and rare moments of sun.

Looking up valley at Cerro Mariposa from the top of La Blanca. (1) Approximate location of La Vuelta de los Condores (2014). (2) Produci Consuma Crepa (2017). If there are completed routes on the walls farther up the valley, they are undocumented. *Luca Schiera*

Our primary goal was to climb the main northeast face of Cerro Mariposa, to the right of the tower ascended by La Vuelta de los Condores (Leclerc-McSorley-Stanhope-Van Biene, 2014). We went to the base three times, always with a single-day window—not enough for this climb.

We also attempted a nearby 800m wall, where, a few pitches from the top, we retreated due to vegetated and muddy cracks. This wall is up the left (south) branch of the valley, just before a lake. We also simul-soloed a nice route on a wall left of the Oreja, which we called Margherita (900m, low fifth class) for a friend of Paolo's who had died in an avalanche one month before. (This could be the same as the 2011 route Earlobe.) The elevation of the summit is 2,100m.

After two weeks we carried most of our extra equipment back down the river, hoping this might save us time at the end of our trip, in case of a possible window for Cerro Mariposa. We kept only the essentials for a fast alpine climb and were lucky enough to catch four sunny days at the very end of our stay. After a failed attempt due to strong wind, we crossed the lake at the base of Cerro Mariposa again with our packrafts. During the prior days it had snowed at least a meter on the summit, and the wall was completely wet. But it was our only chance. We fixed a rope on the first pitch and slept at the base that night.

The next day we started at dawn. The temperature was nice, but a couple of big rockfalls kissed us, just a few meters away, forcing us to choose a more sheltered line. By the evening we arrived at a big ledge two-thirds of the way up. Above us were wet roofs capped by a headwall. Sleeping there didn't seem safe, so we kept on in "night mode." Climbing the roofs in the dark was pretty relaxing, and later on, we had a nearly full moon. With some free climbing and some aid, we reached the top of the wall at 1 a.m. We continued to the summit by easy rock scrambling and snow walking. One hour later, we found a good bivy spot close to the summit.

The following day we rappelled our line, and the same evening we were back at base camp. The following day we descended to the lower cabana with our equipment, loaded our packrafts with 50kg of gear, and descended the Rio Turbio until Lago Puelo. We called our route Produci Consuma Crepa (900m, 6c A2). 📷 🔍

— LUCA SCHIERA, *ITALY*

Josie McKee jungle climbing on the third pitch of the Christmas Wall. *Jared Spaulding*

LA JUNGLA

NEW CLIMBS AND EXPLORATION IN THE RÍO ALERCE VALLEY

BY JARED SPAULDING, *USA*

FROM LATE DECEMBER 2016 through early February 2017, Josie McKee and I spent just over four weeks exploring and climbing in northern Patagonia's Río Alerce Valley. This region is 20–30km southwest of Chaitén, Chile, and east of Parque Nacional Corcovado. We were inspired to visit this relatively unknown (climbing-wise) region by hours of cerveza-fueled Google Earth searching. Photos from a local woman who had backpacked far up the valley eventually pinned down our choice.

On December 17, after securing a boat ride across the formidable moat of Río Yelcho, we tracked in a southwest direction along the Río Alerce, wading rivers and bushwhacking through dense jungle, braving the ubiquitous leeches and frequent (and fierce) flash floods, until we were able to establish a base camp below several 600m-plus walls.

We explored west to the headwaters of the Río Alerce, poking our noses up various side valleys. We found classic *siempre verde* forests with thick stands of *colihue* (bamboo) and ferns under moss-draped canopies of beech trees and old-growth *alerces* (larch) along with the everpresent *nalca* (a giant rhubarb plant) poking out into the sun-bathed areas. Higher, we found classic alpine terrain of meadows, tarns, glaciers, and snowfields.

This valley plays host to countless craggy peaks, ridges, and canyons, which together could be said to contain a lifetime's worth of quality stone, graced with splitter cracks, featured faces, and excellent friction. Many of the lower portions of these cliffs, however, are cloaked in jungle, thus necessitating navigation over mossy, slick slabs, vegetation-filled cracks (usually good when gardened), and through dense brush, most of which can seemingly hold body weight. We believe the rock to mostly be diorite, with bands of whiter-colored granite showing up throughout the area. Regardless of elevation, the granite-like stone appears not to hold as much vegetation as the diorite does.

We established two new routes of insignificant proportions. One ascends the northwest face of what is locally called El Trono (1,527m). [*This formation's very large east face was climbed in 2007 by Mariana Gallego, Luis Molina, and Martin Molina, after an earlier attempt in 1999, and then soloed by a new route in early 2012 by Sílvia Vídal. She called the approximately 1,000–1,300m face "Serrania Avalancha" in her 2012 AAJ report, though this may refer to a broader ridge, range, or the nearby Río Avalancha to the south. It is accessed via a valley to the east of the peak, starting from Lago Yelcho.*]

Our new route, Well, Here We Are (250m, 5.9+), mostly involved linking ledges and wandering up slabs to the north shoulder of the peak.

Our second foray into the vertical yielded a possible first ascent of what may be called Cerro Desnudo (1,458m). We ascended a wandering linkup of slabs, jungle climbing, walking, and alpine bouldering on the left side of the southeast face— Pollos de Selva (1,358m, V 5.7 JC1 J5 V0). What do those grades mean? JC1: Clean jungle aid (with straightforward slinging and weighting of suitable, secure vegetation). J5: Steep jungle free climbing (compared with, for example, J2, which is rough jungle-y trail).

We also made a spirited, though unsuccessful, attempt at a route up what we dubbed Christmas Wall, as it was the wall that we first saw close up on Christmas Day. It cemented our desire to return and further explore the valley. Our attempt was ultimately thwarted by lack of gear, time, and incoming weather. We climbed terrain with difficulties up to 5.10+ JC3.

In the classic Patagonian style of "it ain't over till its over," we ended our expedition with a one-day load carry back to Río Yelcho, followed by a second day of bushwhacking another mile down the river in order to flag down a boat from the other side. After the boat ride, we hitchhiked back to Chaitén, reaching town on February 5. 📷 🔍

[Top] **Looking southward up the Río Alerce Valley from the summit of Cerro Desnudo. The Christmas Wall, attempted in early 2017, is on the right.** [Bottom] **Josie McKee wading up Río Alerce.** *Jared Spaulding*

The northern Cordón Aysén as seen from the summit of Cerro Enroque during the first ascent of the peak by Camilo Rada and Natalia Martínez. The two climbers referred to the sharp peak in center as Cerro Alfil ("Bishop"); behind, barely poking trough the clouds, is the top of Cerro De Geer. *Camilo Rada*

CORDÓN AYSÉN: EXPLORATION AND FIRST ASCENT OF CERRO ENROQUE

DURING A 23-DAY expedition in the austral winter of 2017, Natalia Martínez and I accessed and explored the remote Cordón Aysén in Chilean Patagonia. The Cordón Aysén is a 30km mountain range on the western edge of the Northern Patagonian Icefield, 16km northwest of Cerro Arenales. It is dotted with beautiful and challenging summits, almost all of them believed to be unclimbed prior to our expedition. The exception is a minor peak at the range's northern end, Cerro Margarita (2,236m), which was climbed by Sir Crispin Agnew as part of the British Joint Services Expedition of 1972 (*Alpine Journal 1974*).

Other than Cerro Margarita, named after the British princess, the only other named feature until recently was Cerro De Geer (2,520m), likely the highest summit of the range. It was named by Otto Nordenskjöld and his expedition's geographer, Hugo Pallin, in 1921 (*Alpine Journal 1933*). To date, Cerro De Geer remains unclimbed, along with many extraordinary peaks to its south (*see "Climbing Potential on the North Patagonian Icefield" below.*)

Natalia and I started by boat from Puerto Bertrand on July 24, heading toward the outlet of the Soler River. From there we walked 21km to El Palomar, a rudimentary wooden shelter owned by Patagonia Adventure Expeditions and part of the impressive Aysén Glacier Trail. Our loads arrived at El Palomar on pack horses; from there, following Romero Creek, we carried three sets of loads to the Nef Glacier.

On July 30 we started crossing the glacier using sleds. A very broken-up area of the glacier forced us to camp and explore the crevasse field for a feasible route. The following day we started to carry loads through the maze. During this time we experienced an extreme rain event, where many crevasses turned into lakes and our camp was spared from flooding only by some channels we carved in the ice at the last minute.

On August 4 we accessed the Northern Patagonian Icefield by a 1,690m pass between Cerro

Cachet and Cerro Largo. (*In 2007, Nicolas Von Graevenitz and Camilo Rada made the first ascent of Cerro Largo; see AAJ 2008.*) We were most likely the first team to use this pass after the New Zealand expedition of 1971 (*AAJ 1973*). After traveling west, we established our advanced base camp on August 6 at 1,509m, at the foot of the Cordón Aysén, completing our 12-day approach.

At noon on August 7, taking advantage of a sudden break in the bad weather, we initiated the ascent of an unnamed peak that we later named Cerro Enroque (2,466m, 47°04'03"S, 73°34'25"W). From camp, we approached on skis for 5.7km, gaining about 760m up a glacial ramp on the north side of the peak. This brought us to the upper pinnacle of the mountain, where we crossed a bergschrund and cramponed up snow slopes for approximately 120m. Once the terrain steepened, we first attempted a direct route up the east side of the summit tower. Eventually, we wrapped from west to east around the tower, climbing two pitches of ice (about 80m) up to 70°. We reached the summit at 6 p.m. After two rappels, we enjoyed an extraordinary ski descent under a full moon. The ascent was D-.

On the morning of August 9, we launched an attempt on Cerro De Geer, but we were thwarted by thick fog and high avalanche risk. We started toward home on August 10 and arrived back in Puerto Bertrand on August 15.

[Top] **The east side of Cerro Enroque. The summit is the tower on the far right-hand (north) side. The climbers ascended a ramp (mostly hidden) on the north side before tackling the final pinnacle; only the very top of their route can be seen.** [Middle] **The southern Cordón Aysén as seen from the summit of Cerro Enroque. The sharp peak on the left is Cerro Aguila.** [Bottom] **Natalia Martinez on the icefield with the formidable west face of Cerro Cachet behind.** *Camilo Rada*

See next page for a map of the area and more information on climbing potential.

— CAMILO RADA, *CHILE*

The Northern Patagonian Icefield, showing approach from Puerto Bertrand to the Cordón Aysén used by Natalia Martínez and Camilo Rada in July/August 2017. (Yellow line: boat travel; blue: foot travel aided by horses; red: foot travel and climbing.) Martínez and Rada made the first ascent of Cerro Enroque. Other peaks climbed in early 2018: (1) Cerro Fantasma. (2) Punta Pantagruel. Cerro Chueco and Cerro Puño (see p.232) are in lower right. This is a simplified version of a map under development by the Uncharted project. Peak names and locations differ from other sources, including official maps, but the mapmakers have strong historical evidence to support the naming. Maps and more information can be requested from natalia@unchart.org. *Camilo Rada / UNCHARTED*

CLIMBING POTENTIAL ON THE NORTH PATAGONIAN ICEFIELD

THE NORTH PATAGONIAN Icefield has enormous potential for exploration and mountaineering. The area can be divided in three zones: The northern section is mostly within the basin of the San Rafael Glacier and is dominated by Monte San Valentin (4,032m), the highest peak in Patagonia. (The official elevation of San Valentin is 3,910m; however, a research team doing ice coring near the summit about a decade ago measured the elevation with a geodetic GPS and obtained a result of 4,032m, as reported in a paper published in 2008.) The natural longing for the highest summits has drawn most mountaineers to this area, and most of the summits have been climbed, but only San Valentin has more than one route.

The southern section of the icefield, corresponding mainly to the basin of the Steffen Glacier, has the highest unclimbed peaks, which have been defended by difficult access.

The central section, visited by several expeditions in 2017–2018, including ours, is comprised of the basins of the San Quintín, Colonia, and Nef glaciers, and offers the largest concentration of unclimbed summits and a range of difficulties and terrain types, from big peaks that could be climbed on skis to sheer granite walls. On the west side, all of the Cordón Aysén peaks offer about 1,000m of elevation gain from the plateau. Cerro De Geer and the mountains in the southern extreme of this group present beautiful climbs without much technical difficulty aside from crevasse fields and an eventual bergschrund. But the ones in the center, such as Cerro Aguila and Cerro Alfil, have no straightforward routes.

On the east side, the horizon is dominated by the peaks Largo, Cachet, Nora East, and

Nora West, all of them flanked by vertical granite and ice walls. They were first surveyed and named by Juan Waag around 1898, as part of surveys made for the British arbitration that defined the border between Chile and Argentina in this area. Waag worked for the Argentine government, which supported a boundary that followed the highest summits, forcing the surveyors to explore deep into uncharted sections of the maps. Chilean surveyors worked far to the east, tracing the limits of the basins that eventually drain into the Pacific Ocean (the criteria supported by the Chilean government to trace the border). So, paradoxically, each survey commission was exploring the land that would end up in the territory of the other.

A hundred and twenty years later, Nora East and West remain unclimbed. The first, while not extremely difficult, could offer an epic ski descent. Nora West is defended by 1,000m faces on its north and south aspects, and steep and narrow arêtes on the east and west. Cerro Cachet was climbed in 1971 by the only route that bypasses the sheer granite walls that surround most of the mountain. Largo was climbed in 2007; however it offers many other routes and is surrounded by other summits that rise abruptly from the ice, with sheer granite walls up to 900m tall. Cerro Gargantua was climbed in 1971, but has a striking unclimbed wall, and Punta Pantagruel was just climbed last season, along with a couple of smaller summits. Many other peaks are yet to be named or climbed. *The online version of this report includes many photos of peaks in the area.* 📷

— CAMILO RADA, *CHILE*

NORTHERN PATAGONIAN ICEFIELD, PUNTA ANNA

IN LATE 2017, my guides Gabriel Fava and Joaquin Gomez (both Argentina) and I traveled to the central-eastern part of the little-visited Northern Patagonian Icefield. From Puerto Bertrand, a village of 50 inhabitants, we traveled west by boat across the Bertrand and Plomo lakes. We then walked three days, crossing the Soler and Cacho rivers by riding our packhorses— to reach the eastern bank of the Nef Glacier. We crossed this 4km-wide and very crevassed glacier to establish a camp at 966m on the moraine of the glacier's west bank.

On November 17, after six days of storms, Gabriel and I ascended to a

Southeast side of (A) Punta Pantagruel, showing the 2018 route, (B) Punta Anna, and (C) Cerro Gargantua. Cerro Gargantua was climbed in 1971–1972 by a New Zealand team, following a snow ramp on the north side. The face seen here is about 300m. *Camilo Rada*

1,616m col, from which we reached the icefield. In front of us was our objective, an unclimbed mountain called Pantagruel (2,537m). Unfortunately, we found our planned route up its north face covered with dangerous, wind-affected snow. As a consolation, we climbed a non-technical snow ramp up a peak just to the north, situated between Pantagruel and Gargantua, which we called Punta Anna (2,365m). A storm arrived that night, just as we finished the 10km hike back to our tent. [*The report at the AAJ website contains excellent photos of nearby peaks.*] 📄 📷

— HENRY BIZOT, *FRANCE*

[Above] Panorama south and west across the Northern Patagonian Icefield from the summit of Pantagruel. (A) Cerro Cachet. (B) Cerro Nora Oeste. (C) Cerro Arenales. (D) Cerro Garcia. (E) Cerros Silvia and Buscaini. (F) Cerro Aguila. (G) Cerro Enroque. (H) Cerro Alfil. (I) Cerro De Geer. (J) Cerro Fantasma. [Bottom] Approaching Cerro Fantasma before the first ascent by the southwest face. *Willy Oppenheim*

NORTHERN PATAGONIAN ICEFIELD, PUNTA PANTAGRUEL AND CERRO FANTASMA

ON FEBRUARY 10 and 11, 2018, Felipe Cancino (Chile), Max Fisher (Canada), and I reached the summits of two previously unclimbed peaks on the Northern Patagonia Icefield (Campo de Hielo Norte). The first, Punta Pantagruel (2,410m), had already been named and was attempted as recently as 2017 (*see report above*). We managed to climb it via a route on its east face that we dubbed Brisa Suave (350m, M6 C1 70°). The name means "soft breeze," which is what the weather forecast called for on a night when the winds almost snapped our tent poles! The second peak, Cerro Fantasma (2,252m), was not previously named, and in fact did not even appear on the official map of the area —hence the name, which means "ghost peak." We climbed Cerro Fantasma via its southwest face (300m, AI4).

In total, our expedition lasted 16 days. After months of planning, we convened in Coyhaique in late January and drove south to Puerto Bertrand. On February 1, we received a boat ride across Lago Plomo from Tyo, a Bertrand resident and an old friend of Felipe's, and then we started walking up the Soler Valley toward the Nef Glacier. We were very grateful to walk with light packs on the first day while Ramón, a local *poblador*, carried our gear and food on several horses and met us about 20km up the valley, near the edge of the Nef.

We were self-supported from that point onward and spent the next eight days ferrying loads westward across the Nef and then north up the moraine and up a small glacier to establish a high camp just south of Pantagruel. During this time we encountered some challenging

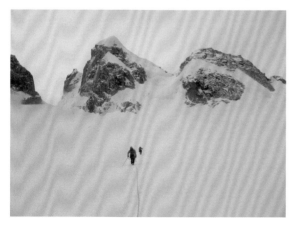

weather and almost watched the expedition fall apart when one of our boot liners took off in a huge gust of wind in the middle of the night. Fortunately, we recovered the liner and managed to reach our high camp during a snowstorm on February 9.

The next morning dawned cold, clear, and with minimal winds, and we giddily took off for Pantagruel. We reached the summit under a cloudless blue sky. From there, we got our first

glimpse of Cerro Fantasma to the north—a peak that is indistinguishable on earlier maps of the icefield but had been brought to our attention by Camilo Rada and his inspiring Uncharted project. We decided to attempt it the next day and left camp only eight hours after returning from Pantagruel. The climbing on Fantasma was more straightforward than Pantagruel, but with more challenging conditions: By the time we reached the summit ridge, we were climbing in wind, rain, and low visibility. We reached the summit in whiteout conditions. After a few rappels and some downclimbing, we were back on the glacier in early evening—wet, cold, and happy!

We were prepared for an expedition of 20 days, but on February 12 we received a forecast via InReach that predicted serious winds and significant precipitation starting the next morning and continuing into the foreseeable future. We considered trying to squeeze in one more climb, but ultimately decided to be grateful for two days of fantastic climbing. And so much is like this: knowing when to push hard and when to ease off. We headed down that afternoon, reaching Lago Plomo again on February 15 and getting picked up by boat the next day.

We felt proud that our expedition had made a small contribution to Camilo Rada's growing storehouse of knowledge about this incredible area. We also benefited tremendously from attentive weather forecasting by Frank Preston, generous sponsorships from NOLS and Patagonia, and unfailing hospitality from residents of Puerto Bertrand and the surrounding areas. We humbly look forward to continuing to explore the vastness of Campo de Hielo Norte. 📷

— WILLY OPPENHEIM, *USA*

CERRO CASTILLO NATIONAL RESERVE, CERRO SAHNE NUSS

IN NOVEMBER 2017, Pedro Binfa and Joan Marc Henares climbed a new route on the south face Cerro Sahne Nuss (2,237m). They began by ascending snow slopes that led to the glacier that divides Cerro Palo and Sahne Nuss. Their route begins looker's right of Las Vueltas de la Vida (Bieger-Bifna, 2015) and La Invernada (Bifna-Mascareno, 2015) and ascends mostly steep snow with a few sections of ice and mixed terrain, including a thin 20m section of difficult-to-protect M4. Once the top was reached, they continued along the normal route to the summit. They called the climb El Camino del Arriero (360m, WI4 M4 90°). 📷

— *INFORMATION FROM* PEDRO BINFA, *CHILE*

SOUTH AVELLANO TOWER, EAST FACE

BRITISH CLIMBERS RUTH Bevan, John Crook, John McCune, Will Sim, and Paul Swall spent several weeks in the Avellano Towers, north of Lago General Carrera, in early 2018. The climbers made several first ascents, notably the east face of South Avellano Tower (about 1,000m of climbing), which Crook had tried twice before. *A full report was not available by press time but will be found at publications.americanalpineclub.org and in AAJ 2019.* 📄 📷

Puño Este (ca 2,050m) from the southeast. Half-Cocked (600m, 5.9+) follows the curving granite ridge that forms the left side of the prominent east face. The peak was first climbed by Chileans in 2014, following the glacier to mixed ground on the summit tower. *Tad McCrea*

PUÑO ESTE, HALF-COCKED

In January 2016, Jim Donini and I climbed a new route on Puño Este (ca 2,050m), a peak just east of the Hielo Continental Norte in Chilean Patagonia. We base-camped at Jim's house by the shores of Lago General Carrera, and when the weather cleared, Jim's wife, Angela, drove us up a long, winding road in the Rio de la Colonia glacial drainage. During the drive we caught a glimpse of a glowing granite spire with a sizable east wall. We aborted plans for our initial objective and diverted our attention on sight.

For the approach, we forged a path up rocky dikes and through dense bamboo and lenga forest to a beautiful hanging lake. This "infinity pool," with its stunning view of Monte San Lorenzo to the east, served as high camp.

The next morning we approached the impressive east face of Puño Este up a broad shoulder above the lake. With limited time, we chose to ascend the scenic southeast ridge. The climbing involved eight pitches up to 5.9+ and several hundred feet of 4th- to low 5th-class scrambling. We descended the rear of the peak by low-angle slopes to a rocky arm. Here, we made one short rappel to the glacier and traversed back to camp. Our route is called Half-Cocked (600m, 5.9+).

Unbeknown to us at the time of our ascent, Puño Este was climbed in December 2014 by Chileans Armando Montero and Juan Ruiz, who ascended a route (6 pitches, mixed to 60°) that we followed in part during our descent. We encountered a small cairn and later unearthed an online story *(find the link at the AAJ website)*, in which the climbers refer to the peak they climbed as Cerro Puño. 📄 📷 🔍

— TAD MCCREA, USA

CERRO CHUECO, FIRST ASCENT

In early 2018, Tad McCrea and I made the first ascent of Cerro Chueco (47°13'46.7"S, 73°02'34.4"W, *see map on page 228*). Clearly visible west of the Carretera Austral (highway), Cerro Chueco rises above a sea of glaciers and lush forest. Though not a giant, even mountains of 7,100' (ca 2,164m) entail real climbing in an area where glaciers come down to the sea and treeline is 3,500'.

Approaches in Aysén can be trying. Fortunately, the forest below Cerro Chueco was relatively open and blessed with an intermittent, overgrown gaucho trail. After scoping the peak from the road and deciphering the approach with my wife, Angela, I made two solo trips to establish a cache of gear just above treeline and directly below the peak.

Jim Donini on the north side of Cerro Chueco during the first ascent. *Tad McCrea*

On February 1, Tad and I drove to Los Leones, located on a side road about 25km south-west of the Carretera Austral, where we would begin our hike. Next day, in clear weather, we did the seven-hour approach to my cache. On February 3 we ascended several hundred vertical feet of easy slab to reach the base of the glacier. Another 1,500' of unroped glacier travel and snow slopes brought us to the northern ridge of the peak.

We soloed the first couple of hundred feet of easy terrain until the route steepened. Nine belayed pitches (up to 5.9+) on good quartzite, interspersed with sections of choss, led us to the top. Our route had approximately 300m of vertical gain.

We were loathe to rappel the circuitous ridge we had climbed, so we were pleased to find a direct rappel line down the west side. Four 60m rappels got us down to a short traverse across a glacier to a col that brought us back to our approach and down to base camp. [*This climb was featured in episode five of the AAJ's Cutting Edge Podcast.*] 📷

Cerro Chueco (ca 2,164 meters) from the east. The first ascent weaved up the right-hand (northern) ridge. The climbers rappeled the far side (west face) to descend. *Tad McCrea*

— JIM DONINI, USA

CORDÓN COCHRANE, CERRO CREMILDA

IN DECEMBER 2015, Marissa Bieger and Marcelo Mascareño made the first known ascent of Cerro Cremilda (1,980m), the northern point of a chain of rocky spires northwest of Monte San Lorenzo. They approached via old horse trails, following the river valley to the south of the peak, and established a high camp on moraine below the mountain. The climb followed steep snow on the south face, a mixed gully, and sections of exposed fifth-class rock on the southwest ridge (580m, 5.3 60°). They named the tower in honor of a settler of the region, Cremilda de la Cruz. 📷 🔍

— INFORMATION FROM PEDRO BINFA, CHILE

SOUTHERN PATAGONIA

CHALTÉN MASSIF AND TORRES DEL PAINE: SEASON SUMMARY

THE SOUTHERN PATAGONIAN season was marked by very unstable weather. This prevented any groundbreaking ascents, but a good time was had by most, and for the first time in years there were no serious accidents. If bad weather is what it takes to accomplish that, let's hope it continues. There has been far too much death in our community of late.

In the Chaltén Massif, the big news was the change of ownership of around 8,000 acres on the south side of the Río Eléctrico Valley, which gives access to the northern flank of the massif via Piedra Negra, one of the most popular advanced camps. The land was purchased with funds provided by the Wyss Foundation, from Swiss-American philanthropist Hansjörg Wyss, with hopes of donating it to Los Glaciares National Park. The NGO Banco de Bosques is in charge of the land for now and unfortunately has decided to keep charging the access fee that

Cerro Chaltén
Cordón Marconi
Chile
Parque Nacional
los Glaciares
Piedra Negra
Piedra del Fraile
"Los Huémules"

The northern part of the Chaltén Massif, seen from the east. The land purchased with Wyss Foundation funds, slated to be donated to the national park, is highlighted in red. (Borders are approximate.) El Chaltén is to the south, 10km left of the edge of the photo. *Rolando Garibotti*

the previous owners had in place. (During the second half of the season, the concessionaire, a third party, decided to stop charging climbers.) To become part of the national park, the land first has to be transferred from provincial to federal control. The proposal that was presented to the provincial legislature includes several other national park expansions, totaling over one million acres. Such a vast land transfer has resulted in strong opposition from farming (livestock) and mining groups, and an agreement seems improbable.

Another concern with the land purchase is that Banco de Bosques, with funding from American Richard Butler has taken a rather unexpected turn in Perito Moreno National Park, near Cerro San Lorenzo. They have installed five new huts in what was an otherwise pristine area, which until now received only 800 to 1,200 visitors per year. The fear is that Banco de Bosques might intend to install similar levels of infrastructure along the Río Eléctrico. In Argentina there has been an 80-year debate regarding the management of wilderness areas, between the non-interventionist model copied from North America and the much heavier-handed European vision of the outdoors. There is also a proposal to place a hut below Cerro Colorado (Apidame), a pristine climbing destination outside of Chile Chico in the Aysén Region.

There are now two private helicopters stationed in El Calafate. Although unable to perform technically difficult rescues (such as long-line recoveries), they should be able to retrieve injured climbers from most valley bottoms or glaciers, saving precious time and effort. Insurance coverage for rescue costs in excess of US$10,000 is essential. (Rescue insurance is mandatory in Torres del Paine National Park.) The standard AAC membership benefit of $7,500 is not sufficient, so either pay for added coverage from Global Rescue or consider joining the British section of the Austrian Alpine Club (aacuk.org.uk), which offers coverage for quite a low fee. Go Fund Me campaigns are not the way to pay for rescues.

In the Chaltén Massif, the following new routes were climbed, listed in geographical order, from south to north along the west side, and back south along the east side. [*The online version of this report includes additional new routes.*]

Two lines got climbed on the southwest and west faces of Cerro Solo: French Connection (600m, WI4 M6 A0) by James Monypenny (U.K.) and Austin Siadak (USA), and Los Gringos No Comen Llajua (600m, 5.8 90°) by Monypenny and Rodrigo Lobo Villarroel (Bolivia). On the north face of Punta Filip, Jonathan Griffin and Tad McCrea (both USA) climbed Espera que te Pegue (10 pitches, 5.10+ C1) to join Amigos Perdidos, retreating without continuing to the summit.

In early September, Markus Pucher (Austria) did the first solo winter ascent of Aguja Guillaumet via the Amy-Vidailhet couloir. Unreported last season, Seán Villanueva and Siebe Vanhee (Belgium) did the first free ascent of Disfrute la Vida (Pitelka-VonBirckhahn, 2009) on the west face of Guillaumet, now 5.11. On the east face of Aguja Val Biois, Lutz Zybell,

Felix Getzlaff, and Tom Ehrig (German) climbed La Torcida (350m, 5.11+ M4) to the junction with the first-ascent route, from where they retreated.

On Cerro Chaltén, Colin Haley (USA) and Austin Siadak repeated the classic French Northwest Ridge route (a.k.a. Afanassieff) in 10 hours 37 minutes, taking 23:57 round-trip from Piedra Negra, descending via the Francesa. On Aguja Poincenot, Villanueva and Vanhee free climbed all the crux sections of the unrepeated Whisky Time (Eggler-Pitelka, 1994), originally A4, now 5.11+. The second crux was climbed via a variation, traversing left into an offwidth crack right from the belay. Unfortunately, with only three easier pitches left, high winds forced them to retreat.

Very little got done in the Torres del Paine massif. Aleta de Tiburón was the most visited feature, with more than 30 parties attempting it this season, out of a total of 45 climbing permits issued for the entire massif. And for good reason: The French 1981 southwest face route offers 10 pitches to 5.8 on good rock and in one of the most stunning settings one can possibly fathom.

Cerro Solo from the southwest. (1) Los Gringos No Comen Llajua. (2) French Connection. (3) Chosspotamia (AAJ 2017). *Colin Haley*

Climbing out of the Bader Valley on the east face of Aguja Desconocida (the north summit of La Máscara, a feature originally called the Thumb), Villanueva and Vanhee climbed El Matédor (500m, 5.11c), a new line just to the left of Chi Dorme non Piglia Pesci (Amore-Angelini-Polacci-Vietina, 2002), with which it shares a couple of pitches in the upper section. A Catalan team made a valiant attempt to repeat the South African Route (1,200m, 5.12d) on the east face of Torre Central, but were forced to retreat one or two pitches shy of the summit ridge. 📄

— ROLANDO GARIBOTTI

CERRO RISO PATRÓN SUR, FIRST ASCENT BY SOUTHWEST FACE

IN FEBRUARY 2018, Matteo Della Bordella (Italy) and Silvan Schüpbach (Switzerland) approached Cerro Riso Patrón Sur (ca 2,350m), on the west side of the Southern Patagonian Icefield, by paddling 100km from Puerto Eden in kayaks. They then made the first ascent of the peak by its southwest face: King Kong (900m M7+ 90°) and returned to Puerto Eden by kayak. It was not possible to prepare a first-person report by press time; *the full story and photos are available at the AAJ website and will be seen in AAJ 2019.* 📄 📷 🔍

CORDILLERA SARMIENTO

PUNTA SATYA, ESTOY VERDE

IN MARCH, JON Griffin, Tad McCrea, and I traveled to the remote western side of the Cordillera Sarmiento and spent two weeks exploring the area. Previously, the majority of the few climbing expeditions to this range have accessed the peaks from the narrow Fiordo de las

[Top] **During the approach to Punta Satya the climbers discovered a glacial lake they called Lago Arco Iris.** [Bottom] **The west side of Peak 1,444m, just west of Punta Barlovento in the Cordillera Sarmiento. Punta Satya is the blocky summit on the left, and the route Estoy Verde (200m, M6) ascends the obvious corner system.** *Whitney Clark*

Montañas on the east side of the cordillera.

We departed Puerto Natales in a fishing boat on March 3, first crossing Golfo Almirante Montt, then heading west and eventually north up the Estrecho Collingwood, east through the Paso Cubillos, and south down the Seno Taraba. The 12-hour boat ride deposited us in an unnamed bay in the central part of the Seno Taraba. (*This bay is directly west of Cerro Cinco Amigos and north of the smaller bay Seno Agujas, which was used to access Cerro Caprichoso on the 1992 expedition led by Jack Miller; see AAJ 1993.*) As far as we know, no one had ever set foot in this area of the range, leaving us to discover waterfalls plunging into aqua blue lakes, unnamed glaciers, and virgin peaks.

By the time we anchored night was falling, so we slept peacefully on the boat and waited until morning to search for a place to establish base camp. Finding dry ground proved to be a challenge, but eventually we built a nice little house using small trees, plastic, and other supplies we'd purchased in Puerto Natales, including old crates for tables and wooden pallets for seats

Once camp was established, we hacked a trail through dense jungle toward the high mountains above. On our first day of good weather, we left camp at noon, after the rain stopped, and made our way up the jungle trail, eventually gaining a steep ridge that led us to a glacier. We navigated up the glacier and climbed a nearby peak with a striking mixed line gutting the center of the southwest face.

We began climbing around 8 p.m. and encountered mixed terrain up to M6 for 200m. The summit ridge was perfect névé. The moon cast shadows of towering giants nearby, only increasing our wonder. Our rappels began around 2 a.m., and we were caught in a storm on the descent. Howling wind and sideways rain pelted our faces, making it challenging to find our passage off the glacier. Eventually, we made it safely back to solid ground, and at 7 a.m. we set up the tent and crawled inside to dry off.

We named our new route Estoy Verde (M6) after the green rock we encountered while climbing the mountain, for which we adopted the name Punta Satya, given by the party that climbed the same peak later in the season from the east (*see report below.*) According to our GPS, the summit is 51°52.39.20S, 73°23.23.90W. On the map produced by Camilo Rada, Punta Satya is the northern and highest summit of the 1,444m peak just west of Punta Barlovento. (*See this map in the online report, as well as in AAJ 2014.*)

After a few rainy days, we ventured out to attempt unclimbed Alas de Angel Sur. We retraced our steps through the jungle and onto the glacier, then over a col to reach the east side of the range. We spent almost six hours searching for a way to access the peak, but as dark clouds began to swirl and the wind began to blow we began the journey back to camp.

Two days later, our boat arrived on schedule, bringing with them bottles of wine and wide smiles. We celebrated with our friends, toasting to adventure and relishing in those last moments deep in the Patagonian wilderness. 🔲 🔍

– **WHITNEY CLARK**, USA

CERRO GALLIE, NORTHEAST RIDGE, AND OTHER ASCENTS

Approaching Cerro Tigreli (above the skiers) from the east. Punta Satya is the knob on the left. *Julian Casanova*

IN THE AUSTRAL spring of 2017, Tomy Aguilo and Julian Casanova (guides), Sebastian and Stephen Gallie, and I took a four-hour boat ride from Puerto Natales to the Canal de las Montañas on the east side of the Cordillera Sarmiento. We landed at the valley south of Glaciar Bernal and spent our first day finding a way through dense vegetation to the glacier that leads toward Punta Barlovento.

Once on the glacier, we skinned up to around 600m, where we could then walk with skis until the col between Cerro Tigreli (1,626m) and the small summit south of it. We left the skis at the col and climbed 60° rime to the summit. We also quickly climbed the little summit on the south side of the col. [*Cerro Tigreli was climbed and named a year earlier by a party following approximately the same route—see note below.*]

We then skied down to the flat plateau at around 1,200m and skinned up to the south toward Point 1,444m, which had a little section of 80° rime climbing to get to the summit. We called it Punta Satya, later learning that a previous expedition had already climbed it from the west.

We slept on the boat and the next day got dropped off in the dark a bit north of Fiordo Hermann. The vegetation was not dense here, but we had to navigate a system of slabs and some steeper scrambling to get to the snow at around 600m. We skinned south to gain a snow ridge and then traversed north on a glacier with big crevasses, for which we had to rope up and travel in crampons. We had to fight very strong winds but still made it to the col northeast of our unclimbed peak.

We climbed the northeast ridge with some snow and rime up to 80°. Not knowing which was highest, we climbed all three high points of the summit ridge. We reversed back down to the col and skied from there to the end of the snow. We called the peak Cerro Gallie (1,596m) after Andrew Norie Gallie, who migrated to Punta Arenas in 1904. 🔲

– **CARO NORTH**, GERMANY

CERRO TIGRELI, FIRST ASCENT: *On October 23 and 24, 2016, David Sanabria, Jacob Slot, and Cornelia Zamernik made the first ascent of Cerro Tigreli (1,626m) in the Cordillera Sarmiento. The trio took a boat from Puerto Natales into the Fiordo de los Montanas, where they were dropped off about 1km south of the Bernal Glacier. They cut their way through the forest and camped at the edge of the glacier. The next day they skinned up the glacier and the peak above until the terrain steepened below the final summit mushroom, which they climbed on good rime, reaching the top 6.5 hours after they began.*

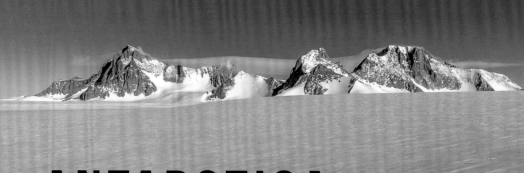

The isolated Pirrit Hills from the northwest. The three main peaks are (left to right) Tidd, Turcotte, and Goodwin. "Hills" is a bit of a misnomer: The peaks rise about 1,000 meters above the ice cap. *GMHM*

TOUR DE FORCE
THE FIRST TECHNICAL ROUTES IN THE REMOTE PIRRIT HILLS

BY DAMIEN GILDEA, *WITH INFORMATION FROM DIDIER JOURDAIN*

IN JANUARY 2018 a team of six from the elite Groupe Militaire de Haute Montagne (GMHM) visited the Pirrit Hills, an isolated group of sharp granite peaks, around 13km in length, sitting on the icecap around 160km south of the Antarctic Logistics & Expeditions (ALE) base at Union Glacier. Arnaud Bayol, Antoine Bletton, Jean-Yves Igonenc, Didier Jourdain, Seb Moatti, and Dimitry Munoz had planned to visit the Organ Pipes in the Transantarctic Mountains, but, upon learning another team would be going there, they sought an alternative objective.

The Pirrits (81°08'S, 85°28'W) have been visited several times over the last few decades by geologists and others working with national science programs. However, they had never seen a party of technical climbers. Mt. Goodwin was summited by a pair of geologists in November 1992. Mt. Axtell, a subpeak of Mt. Tidd, was climbed in 2013 from the east during geological sampling. In the 2015-'16 season, Mt. Tidd itself was climbed from the south up an easy snow slope, after approaching relatively high on snowmobiles.

The GMHM have an impressive history in Antarctica, with a fast, unsupported ski to the South Pole in 1996, the third ascent of Mt. Tyree (4,852m) by a new route in 1997, first ascents and new routes in the Sentinel Range, and technical rock routes in Queen Maud Land.

This season, after flying to the range with ALE, Bayol, Jourdain, and Munoz started things off on January 12 by taking on one of the most distinctive features in the range: the Tafoni Pillar (as they called it) on the east face of Mt. Turcotte (1,959m). A remarkable feature of granite faces in this range and elsewhere in Antarctica is the *tafoni:* hollowed-out sections creating climbable scoops and edges of all shapes and sizes. (*See a spectacular photo of these formations on page 4.*) These features are created primarily by differences in salinity and temperature that cause the rock to weather this way, more so than the incessant winds that strafe the range. The French trio named their route Corrasion (600m, TD, 40° snow ramp to seven pitches of rock up to 5c). From the summit, they made a rappel descent of the north face and traversed through a col back to the east side.

Also on January 12, on Mt. Tidd (2,244m), Bletton and Moatti worked their way up ice runnels and mixed ground in the broad couloir on the left side of the north face, creating Coming in from the Cold (800m, TD WI4 M4). The next day the pair returned to make a 1,000m ski descent (up to 45°) of the southwestern side of the mountain; part of this descent followed the line of the first ascent in 2013. On the same day, the other three repeated Coming in from the Cold.

On the 15th, Bayol and Munoz put up an easier route on the right side of the north face of Tidd, named ARDI (800m, D), while on the same day, over on the northeast side of Mt. Goodwin (2,181m), a ramp and slanting gully system was climbed by Bletton, Jourdain, and Moatti to give Three Little Birds (700m, TD WI4 M4).

On the 18th, Bletton and Moatti took an easier way up Mt. Turcotte, climbing the straightforward north face by a route they named Paradis Blanc (450m, D+ 70° snow and ice). As a final effort, on the 19th, Jourdain and Munoz ventured up Mt. Tidd once again, attempting one of the most attractive features in the range, climbing to just under half-height on the left pillar of the north face.

The French then returned to the ALE base at Union Glacier by kiting, benefiting from the prevailing southerly winds that blow toward the Ellsworth Mountains. By choosing areas suitably oriented to the usual winds, future climbing teams may be able to undertake expeditions that would be prohibitively expensive using aircraft access—another example is found in the Trans-Antarctic Mountains report below. However, in addition to the extra skills and risks of kiting in Antarctica, such expeditions will need to take into account fickle winds, unpredictable routes, and time lost accordingly.

The GMHM trip to the Pirrit Hills was a gem of an expedition—skilled and experienced alpinists climbing interesting new routes up impressive peaks, in a beautiful and stark area most people had never heard of. They made the most of their short time, on a budget far less than it could have been, and ended on a note that should point the way to future adventurous, low-impact expeditions on the continent.

ABOUT THE AUTHOR: *Damien Gildea, from Australia, is author of* Mountaineering in Antarctica.

[Top] **Munoz and Bayol on the Tafoni Pillar, with the fantastic weathered rock called "tafoni" waiting above. (See also page 4.)** [Middle] **The north face of Mt. Tidd showing, from left to right, the north pillar attempted by Jourdain and Munoz, Coming in from the Cold, and ARDI.** [Bottom] **The line of Corrasion (600m, TD) on the Tafoni Pillar of the east face of Mt. Turcotte.** *GMHM*

THE SPECTRE, VARIATION TO ORIGINAL ROUTE; ALPHA TOWER, FIRST ASCENT BY NORTH FACE

THE SPECTRE, REMINISCENT of Fitz Roy, is located at 86°12.255'S, 148°28.294'W, in the Gothic Peaks (named by American scientist and mountaineer Ed Stump). The closest human habitation is the U.S. base at the South Pole, 440km away, while the closest logistics hub is the Antarctic Logistics & Expeditions (ALE) Union Glacier Camp and blue-ice runway 1,060km away.

Although it would be possible to fly directly to the foot of the Spectre, the distance from ALE's fuel depot at Thiels Ski-way would make additional flights necessary, and the whole undertaking would become prohibitively expensive ($500,000+). After extensive research and study of Antarctic wind models, Jean Burgun (France), Mark Sedon (New Zealand), and I developed a strategy to limit the interior flight time to a minimum by utilizing the revolutionary tool of high-aspect-ratio power kites to tow skiers and sleds. These enable long-distance travel at high speed with great loads.

On November 15 we were dropped 220km from the South Pole at 88°S, 135°W (3,000m above sea level). This marked the point of no return from the Thiels Ski-way for a Twin Otter carrying our team of three with 65 days of supplies and equipment for snow kiting, traditional man-hauling, polar survival, and alpine-style wall climbing (total weight 650kg). We intentionally omitted to pack a drill.

It was -37°C and clear with a light easterly, but within hours the weather deteriorated into a full-scale blizzard, with wind of 40+ knots and wind chill below -60°C. We were tent-bound for four days.

Once moving, our objective was to kite-ski 300km downwind before descending to the Trans-Antarctic Mountains along the massive and heavily crevassed Scott Glacier. We then had to reach and climb our intended goal, the spectacular south spur of the Spectre, return upwind to our drop-off point via a combination of man-hauling and upwind tacking by kite, collect cached food and equipment, and kite downwind 1,100km to the Union Glacier Camp.

Each phase posed a formidable challenge. The initial journey to reach the Spectre was hindered by unusually strong wind and poor visibility. These factors, combined with the expected extreme cold, pushed us beyond the limits of safe kiting with 180kg loads, and the journey took far longer than anticipated.

The only previous technical climbing in the Gothic Peaks took place during four science expeditions led by American geologist Edmund Stump, backed by the huge resource of the U.S. government. Stump and his brother Mugs, who acted as field guide on two of the expeditions, completed several very impressive climbs, including the intimidating and massive east face of Grizzly Peak (2,200m) and the first ascent of the Spectre (2,020m) by an impressive 750m route up the north face and northwest ridge.

On December 7, within days of our arrival, all three of us summited the Spectre via an unintentional variation to the Stump route. We found cruxes up to Scottish VII, 7—difficulties far in excess of those described by the Stumps. These were due in part to our taking a different route and also to different conditions. On top, feeling that we were the most isolated people on Earth, we made a hasty and thankfully uneventful retreat as a storm approached, reaching the tents 24 hours after leaving. Within an hour the wind was blowing 30 knots.

Due to the length of our journey, we hadn't brought a portaledge or enough gear for a full big-wall ascent, and, on closer inspection, the elegant 720m south spur of the Spectre appeared far more "big wall" in nature than anticipated. This, together with the ferocious wind we experienced, led us to decide against an attempt—an easy decision for those who value their toes and futures.

Instead, Jean and I attempted to traverse the Organ Pipes, a series of towers running east to west, with Spectre being the highest. We began on December 11 with the north face of the most westerly peak, which we dubbed Alpha Tower. Once again we found far steeper and more difficult terrain than expected, including a desperate 15m ice-choked offwidth and unconsolidated snow gullies with sustained difficulties of Scottish VII, 7. We summited in sublime conditions, then made a committing rappel descent to the col on the far side, down the most compact granite I've encountered.

To that point it had taken us 14 hours and the way ahead looked of a similar nature. We opted to escape down snow slopes on the north side of the col. Once again, severe winds struck just a few hours after we regained camp.

The outbound journey proved to be far less brutal than the approach, and our high-performance kites and skis performed far better than hoped for upwind travel, reducing the total man-hauling distance to just 60km. Toward the end of the journey, beneficial wind allowed us to cover 650km in just four days, reaching Union Glacier after 51 days in the field.

We believe it would be possible for a skilled team to travel overland and unsupported for the entire approach and return from Union Glacier. This would add 1,000km to the journey, upping the ante a big notch and creating a truly "by fair means" approach to one of the great remaining alpine prizes. 📷

— LEO HOULDING, U.K.

[Top] Jean Burgon on the summit ridge of Alpha Tower during the first ascent. (A) Mt. Griffith (3,095m). (B) Scott Glacier. (C) Grizzly Peak (2,200m). (D) Zanuck (2,525m). (E) Zanuck East (2,380m). (F) Sanctuary Glacier. Zanuck was first climbed in 1987 by Paul Fitzgerald and Ed Stump. Zanuck East was climbed by the 1970 New Zealand expedition—they also may have climbed the peak immediately to the right. Grizzly Peak was named after Mugs Stump, who climbed it twice, though the official version is that it was so named because it bristles like a bearskin. Mt. Griffith is unclimbed, though in 1987 the Stumps reached quite high on the mountain. *Leo Houlding* [Bottom] Kite skiing in front of the Organ Pipes. The lowest and most westerly of the towers, dubbed Alpha Tower, lies above and slightly left of the skier and was climbed from the far side (north face). The Spectre, two towers to the right, is the highest peak in the group, with the elegant, unclimbed south spur falling 720m directly to the glacier. *Mark Sedon*

HERITAGE RANGE

LARSON VALLEY ASCENTS

THE LARSON RIDGE is the name given to the east-west-oriented crest that borders the northern edge of the Larson Valley. On January 12, 2018, the American-led team of Christine Amour-Lavar, Claire Floriet, Patricia Jones, and Sandra Marichal-Ragot, with guides Chelsea Bomba and Yoshiko Miyazaki-Back, made the first ascents of the central (1,879m) and west (1,861m) summits on the ridge. The east summit (79°29.779'S, 83° 53.519'W) had been climbed in December 2013 by Nick Lewis and Rob Smith.

Floriet, Marichal-Ragot, and Miyazaki-Back then made the first ascent of the south face of West Pyramid, a little to the east of Larson Ridge. The three climbed slightly right of a prominent U-bend of geologic folds in the rock face, then exited left up a snow ramp to gain the southwest ridge. The route was named Infinite Curves (PD, 5.7 M4- 45°). Descent was along the southwest ridge and west face, more or less following the route of the first ascent in December 2012. 📷

– NICK LEWIS, *ANTARCTIC LOGISTICS & EXPEDITIONS, USA, SUPPLIED BY DAMIEN GILDEA, AUSTRALIA*

QUEEN MAUD LAND

ULVETANNA, STETIND, FENRIS, AND MANY OTHER PEAKS

FROM DECEMBER 1–17 our team of seven climbers, ranging in age from mid-20s to mid-50s and comprising Jimmy Chin, Savannah Cummins, Pablo Durana, Alex Honnold, Anna Pfaff, Cedar Wright, and me, visited the Fenris Kjeften (Wolf's Jaw). We flew from Cape Town with Antarctic Logistics Centre International (ALCI) to the Novolazarevskaya ice runway but were delayed five days leaving South Africa and four days once on the continent due to inclement weather. We accessed base camp at 71°51.3357'S, 8°17.4213'E via a Twin Otter flight.

We then split into three climbing groups: Alex and Cedar, Anna and Savannah, and Jimmy and me. Pablo was key in documenting the expedition, which was commercial in nature, with support from the North Face, National Geographic, and CBS. In total, the team reached 15 summits, including two probable first ascents, up to ten new routes, and several first free ascents.

Alex and Cedar, building on the speed climbing techniques they have perfected in Yosemite, were able to climb many summits in single pushes from base camp, among them Fenris, Hel, Thor, Odin, Long Worm, Midgard, Stetind, and Kinntanna. Stetind's east pillar was notable for the level of onsight climbing—5.11 in cold and wind. A light and fast style of climbing is well suited to peaks in this range. By staying in motion, one stays warm.

Anna and Savannah climbed Philiptanna, Annatanna, and the Chimney, with the last two being likely first ascents. [*Many of these peak names are still unofficial.*] Anna, Savannah, Alex, and Cedar made the first ascent of the Penguin, a small rock tower, via the north ridge. The same four climbers also repeated Skywalk on the north ridge of Holtanna (450m, 10 pitches, 5.10-, Huber-Huber-Reichel-Siegrist, 2008) in a 16-hour round trip; the climb was reported to have bolts and rappel anchors, but only two bolts and a few other fixed pieces were found.

Taking a more traditional approach, Jimmy and I climbed Ulvetanna (2,931m)—the highest peak in the range—via a new route on the west buttress and south ridge. We were stuck in our aiders and not able to free climb due to the steep and wide climbing. Jimmy and I summited

Seen from the west: (A) Philiptanna, (B) Fenris, (C) Thor, and (D) Odin. (BC) Base camp. (U) Ulvetanna. (H) Hel. (S) The Sandeggtinde Massif (3,053m). Arrow marks the dihedral climbed by Conrad Anker and Jimmy Chin to start their ascent of Ulvetanna. (1) South ridge, first climbed from its base in 2014 and followed to the summit by Anker and Chin. The original Norwegian route (1994) ascended snow/ice slopes toward the left edge of this face and then rock above (UIAA VIII A2). *Jimmy Chin*

in -30°C, and it took all of our effort to maintain warmth. This was the seventh overall ascent of the peak, and as of the 2017-'18 season, Ulvetanna has yet to be climbed in alpine style. [*The peak was first climbed in February 1994, via the northwest face, by Robert Caspersen, Sjur Nesheim, and Ivar Tollefson; the south ridge from its base (27 pitches) was first completed in early 2014 by a British-Norwegian team after previous attempts by three different parties.*]

The granite we encountered varied from solid and well bonded to loose and friable. Our greatest challenge was rope awareness and management; the coarse rock eats rope. The team did not place any bolts or pitons and rappelled from standard gear and natural features. With a small window of time, the team was active almost every day. The midnight sun compensated for the sharp, loose rock, biting wind, and constant freezing temperatures. We made the most of the hand we were dealt. [*This expedition was featured in an interview with Anker on episode four of the Cutting Edge Podcast.*] 📷

— CONRAD ANKER, *AAC*

ANTARCTIC PENINSULA

WIENCKE ISLAND, MONTE PIZDUCH, BLOODY NOSE

IN 2014 I climbed the south face of an unnamed peak on the east coast of Anvers Island, which I named Monte Samila (64°38′56"S, 63°12′59"W). It gave a 1,500m ascent with difficult ice and unstable snow (WI5). Afterward, I sailed south to nearby Wiencke Island. On that occa-

Monte Pizduch, the most southerly peak of the Wall Range, and the line of Bloody Nose on the south-southwest face. *Mira Dub*

sion the weather was not on my side, but some of the island's virgin summits registered indelibly in my mind.

In late December, Mira Dub and I sailed from Tierra del Fuego and anchored on January 5, 2018, at Port Lockroy, Wiencke Island. Next day a dinghy took us to shore and we skied toward the southernmost peak in the Wall Range, at the end of the ridge that extends southwest from Mt. Wheat. At 2:30 p.m. we started up steep névé at the base of a narrow couloir on the south-southwest face leading directly to the unnamed summit (64°50'0.18"S, 63°23'53.56"W). Near the top was a vertical section below a huge summit cornice. How we would overcome this was an unanswered question from the very beginning.

In late afternoon the sun reached the face and small amounts of rock and ice began to fall. One stone found Mira's nose, but fortunately there was only a little blood. At around 11 p.m. we reached the vertical section. The ice was aerated, and I had to climb an entire 30m pitch without being able to place any screws. The following pitch involved mixed climbing on broken granite with collapsing powder snow. Finally I stood below the cornice. I went for the least overhanging part of this formation of inflated cotton wool. It was a terrible experience—I had the feeling that neither axes nor crampons would hold.

At 2 a.m. we were both standing on the nameless summit, watching the mist roll in. We made tea and pitched a small tent, though we had no mats or sleeping bags. Four hours later the mist broke apart and we walked east-northeast along the corniced ridge, in the direction of Mt. Wheat. We couldn't see any suitable descent and in the end were forced to traverse four tops before we could head in a more easterly direction down a wild glacier. Thirty-three hours after setting out, we regained the coast and were picked up. We named our summit Monte Pizduch (1,000m) and the climb Bloody Nose (850m, ED+ WI5+ M4 95°). 📷

— **MAREK HOLECEK,** *CZECH REPUBLIC*

ANVERS ISLAND, UNNAMED PEAK, SOUTHWEST RIDGE

IN JANUARY 2016, Robert Catton, Mike Jaques, Paul Kutarski, Jim Searight, and I made the first ascent of the southwest ridge of an unnamed summit immediately southwest of, and lower than, Shewry Peak (1,065m) in the southern part of Anvers Island. We ascended glaciated terrain and gained the col at the foot of the ridge, where we left skis. The ascent from here, passing large snow obstacles, was PD+ Scottish II. A small vertical ice wall was outflanked via a fluted and difficult-to-protect couloir. During the descent, we rappelled the ice wall from a snow bollard. [*This peak was climbed on January 17, 2015, via the northeast ridge, starting from the col between it and Shewry, by the Chinese guide Daliu (Liu Yong) and a Chinese client (part of an expedition reported in AAJ 2015). They nicknamed the peak Mini Rat, having misunderstood the name of the nearby peak Minaret. This is not official!*] 📷

— **TIM BLAKEMORE,** *FRANCE*

NORWAY

Storskiva and its east buttress, showing the approximate line of the first ascent (2016), above the Bunesstranda beach. The climbers continued to the main summit. *Jonathan Crison*

MOSKENESØYA, VARIOUS NEW ROUTES

CATALAN CLIMBERS GUILLE Cuadrado, Gerber Cucurell, Jordi Esteve, Pau Gómez, and Felix Queipo established multiple new routes in the Lofoten Islands in the late spring and summer of 2016 and 2017. The team completed all routes in alpine style and followed a strict ethic of no bolts, pins, fixed ropes, or portaledges.

In June 2016, on the west coast of the island of Moskenesøya, Cuadrado, Esteve and Gomez made the first ascent of the east shoulder (Point 551m) of Storskiva. The climbers followed obvious crack and corner systems up to 6- (5.10a) until they were forced into a rightward traverse under a roof before continuing up the wall. They descended to the southeast along a ridge. [*One year later, Elise Crison, Adrien Gilbert, and Jonathan Crison from France climbed a nearly identical line, thinking it was a first ascent. They climbed 13 pitches and rated their route Norwegian 6 or F6a+.*] The Catalans also climbed two 400–450m new routes on the south face of Marklitinden, near Kirkefjorden. Details of the routes are at Escaladatradicional.com.

In May 2017, Cuadrado, Cucurell, and Esteve returned to Lofoten and attempted the possibly unclimbed southeast face of Moltbaertinden, also above Kirkefjorden. Connecting features up seemingly blank slabs, they encountered an eight-meter vertical step halfway up the wall, which they were unable to protect clean. Above the slab, they could see a crack system, but rather than use bolts, they decided to rappel in hopes of returning stronger—mentally and physically—for a future attempt in clean style.

A few weeks later, the trio established a difficult new route on Merraflestinden. This peak overlooks the northwest side of Kirkefjorden, and at the time they believed it had only two routes: Kor e Hammaren Edvard and Borr i Bekkmortna (both by Storvik-Tetlie, 2002). [*See note on more routes below.*] The Catalans' new route, Syg Veggen (480m, 7+), follows a crack system for most of its 11 pitches, including a 30m 5.11d offwidth that they climbed without any wide gear. (A number 6 cam would be required for future parties wanting to protect this pitch.) The route has a few other sections of bold climbing, surmounting roofs and on slabs with sparse pro. The last two pitches follow easy but delicate ramps covered in moss to reach the flat-topped summit.

Cuadrado and Esteve also climbed the "North Dihedral" [450m, 7 (5.11) A1] on Moltbaertinden but are uncertain if it was a first ascent—they found a fixed piton halfway up the wall. 📷 🔍

– WHITNEY CLARK, *WITH INFORMATION FROM GERBER CUCURELL, BARCELONA*

MORE NEW ROUTES ON MERRAFLESTINDEN: *In 2016, British climbers Rob Lamey and Mike Wolf put up several new routes in this area, including two on Merraflestinden. The eight-pitch Bilberry Meadow (7+), climbed on July 28, is just to the right of the new Catalan route, with excellent rock and a crux in a technical, shallow groove protected by micro-wires—a test of nerve. On August 4 the two returned to climb Indiana, farther left on the face. The route starts with the first four pitches of Borr i Bekkmortna (7- A0, Storvik-Tetlie, 2002) before moving right to an open groove. The crux ninth pitch of this 10-pitch line climbs a perfect hand crack in a smooth wall (7). The route rejoins Borr i Bekkmortna near the top. An independent start may be possible but was wet at the time. See the AAJ website for a full report from these two climbers.* 📄 📷

BREIFLOGTINDEN, EAST FACE, ARCTIC ODYSSEY

FROM JULY 20 to 22, Anar Demirov and Andrey and Dmitriy Panov from Russia made the first ascent of the main east face of Breiflogtinden via Arctic Odyssey (950m of climbing, 20 pitches, 7a A3). Breiflogtinden (750m, approximately 68°0'22.07"N, 12°58'47.49"E), on Lofoten's westernmost island of Moskenesøya, is visible from Reine, looking north up the Kjerkfjord. The left side of the east face is bounded by the damp depression of Reicht Rinne (ca 18 pitches, Norwegian 4/5, 1972). Around to the left on the southeast face are more demanding routes such as One Hundred Years Later (N7+, 2013) and Permit to Asgard (N7, 1997).

In 2016 the Panov brothers and Vanya Cherkashin climbed the first nine pitches of the east face but were rained off. The face can be divided into three sections: a 70-80° slab, often with very poor protection; five pitches of vertical or overhanging terrain that was mainly A3 (estimated to go free at around 7c); and then much easier climbing (one pitch of 6b+) to the top. Pitch four (6a+) has no natural gear placements, and in 2016 Andrey led this 60m pitch with no protection. In 2017, Dmitriy placed two bolts. The team climbed the route with a portaledge, and on the last day made a 24-hour push to reach the top. 📷

– LINDSAY GRIFFIN, *WITH INFORMATION FROM ELENA DMITRENKO, RISK.RU*

LYNGEN / ULØYA ISLAND

BLÅTINDEN, NIGHTWATCH PILLAR

IN SEPTEMBER I sat in my house in Uløya in amazingly stable weather. Finally, I couldn't bear the pressure any more and set out to free solo the southeast pillar of Blåtinden (1,142m, 69°50'39.80"N, 20°36'37.28"E). I climbed the left flank of the 250m pillar in 45 minutes—most of the route was UIAA II and III, but there were three sections of IV+. This was the first route on the entire Blåtinden wall. Although the rock on the eastern aspect appears damp and slimy, in fact it is clean and very sound. My route, which I named Nightwatch Pillar, was absolutely solid from bottom to top—amazing for mountain terrain that has never been climbed. 📷

– ARTUR PASZCZAK, *POLAND*

The north side of the Sakran Range, rising to nearly 3,500m, from Choman (about 10km away). *Jan Bakker*

HALGURD, FIRST SKI DESCENT

IN LATE FEBRUARY, in partnership with Dutch guide Jan Bakker, I led a small team of American skiers on what we believe to be the first ski ascent and descent of the highest mountain lying fully in Iraq: Mt. Halgurd (3,606m, 36°44'27.75"N, 44°51'42.20"E). Three members of our team had served in Iraq during our time in the U.S. Army.

Halgurd is close to the Iranian border, and in darkness we could see lights from Iranian border posts on ridges and mountaintops. We accessed the peak from the south via a dirt road outside the small Kurdish town of Choman, a place that, given its proximity to incredible mountain recreation opportunities, we nicknamed "Chomanix." When the road became too choked with snow for our two 4WDs, we skinned about 11km up the rest of the road, then further on to base camp. We were careful to stay on the trail at all times, wary of land mines from the Iran-Iraq War (1980–1988).

Once on Halgurd, some skiers might opt to rope up for the final climb to the summit ridge; crampons and at least one ice axe felt like essential gear. [*The mountain was climbed from the southeast to gain the north-south-oriented summit ridge (snow/névé to 45°, with a little mixed terrain). Halgurd has two summits, with the north slightly higher.*] There are two couloirs below the summit that give steep skiing options; we chose the one on skier's right. Robin Brown, Matt Griffin, Max Lowe, and I skied from the summit, while Jan climbed up and down on foot.

The real skiing gem of the region appeared to lie above Sakran, a summer herding village about 30 to 40 minutes' drive southeast of Choman. The culminating point of the Sakran (a.k.a. Hassar) Range rises to 3,458m (approx. 36°32'49.52"N, 44°55'34.36"E). In the right conditions, likely to be found in late January or early February, it would provide fantastic opportunities for ski mountaineering and winter climbing. However, the angle of the north-facing slopes (largely 35–45°) makes the area quite prone to avalanches.

During our two-week visit to the Kurdish Autonomous Region of Iraq we also saw numerous opportunities for rock climbing and other mountain sports. Despite at one point being only 40km from where the Iraqi government, with support from the United States, started the decisive battle to drive ISIS from Mosul, we never felt unsafe. [*This climb is featured in the film* Adventure Not War, *which can be seen at the AAJ website.*] 🗎 📷 ▶

— STACY BARE, *AAC, WITH ADDITIONAL INFORMATION FROM JAN BAKKER*

SOUTH SINAI, NEW ROUTES

WITH THE HELP and encouragement of Dave Lucas, a British guide, Kyle Duba, Kyle Elmquist, Micah Rush, and I—all Wyoming boys—pulled off a one-month climbing expedition in South Sinai in November. Near the village of St. Catherine (site of a nearly 1,500-year-old, still-operating Christian monastery), Rush and I put up a new line on the west face of Jebel Safsafa, naming it the Muezzin Calling (8 pitches, 5.11). On Jebel Batta, also near St. Catherine, we freed two three-pitch aid routes, Dire Straights and Tachtonie HaShahar. Dire Straights, which had been described as an "unprotected 5.12 offwidth," went clean at Wyoming 5.10 with good gear. Rush freed HaShashar with a crux of 5.12+ flared fingers.

[Top] Micah Rush frees HaShashar (5.12+) on Jebel Batta. [Bottom] The village of St. Catherine, surrounded by rock. *Kyle Duba*

With support from two Bedouin guides, Salim and Ragab, and camels, we then walked for a day through stunningly beautiful desert, northwest of St. Catherine, to reach the west face of Jebel Naja. Here, three nine- to 11-pitch routes had been completed, starting in 2007, two of them by Lucas. He also started the central line on the face, but was stymied by a 100-foot blank section. He encouraged us to give it a try. While Micah and Kyle worked on hand-drilling three bolts in this blank section, Duba and I put up a seven-pitch 5.11 route to the left, naming it Jamel Bahr ("camel shit") for the frighteningly crumbly rock up high. On November 23 our party of four climbed the central line, naming it the Sheik (10 pitches, 5.11 C1 or 5.13b).

After this we continued to travel by camel to several gorgeous crags, including Jebel Umma H Shaur, east of St. Catherine, where we repeated a number of routes put up by Lucas. I can't say enough about the hospitality of the Bedouin people. Without their kindness and guidance, this expedition would not have been possible. [*Editor's note: In January 2018, Russian climbers Mikhail Khomenyuk and Vladimir Moroz added Egyptian Executions (350m, 9 pitches, 5B) to the southwest face of Safsafa. A route photo is at the AAJ website.*] 📷

— MARK JENKINS, *AAC*

UNITED ARAB EMIRATES

CLIMBS IN WADI NAQAB AND WADI GHALILAH

FROM 2009 TO 2011, Peter Thompson completed two notable routes in the limestone Hajar mountains, which extend from Oman into the eastern UAE. Thompson and Andrew LaBonte climbed the first route in Wadi Naqab: Vertical Vice (187m climbing distance, E3/4 6a) on the Red Wall. In Wadi Ghalilah, Thompson and various partners made three trips to the Stairway to Heaven area, eventually completing the longest route in the UAE: Black Dog (16 pitches, E1 5a or TD VI). Details and photos are at the AAJ website. 📄 📷

— *INFORMATION FROM* PETE THOMPSON, *ALPINE CLUB, U.K.*

Alexander Huber leading the third 5.13 pitch of La Grand Rouge on Tadrarate in Morocco. This 40-meter pitch (8a /5.13b) has only two protection bolts. *Heinz Zak*

TAGHIA GORGE, TADRARATE, LA GRAND ROUGE

IN SEARCH OF new projects, Alexander Huber and I were drawn to the deep and impressive Taghia Gorge, especially to the Tadrarate, a 500m wall of beautiful red limestone. We first visited the Taghia in October 2016. As always, Alexander was psyched, because the cliff was steep and difficult, and this was a country he had never visited. The charm of the mountains, the intense red colors of the landscape, the green columns of the poplars, the hospitality of the Berbers, and the decelerated life without the slightest sound of a motor—these alone are worth a trip.

The southeast face of the Tadrarate holds an unfinished project of Arnaud Petit and friends. Farther to the left is a mostly bolted Polish route, Widmo, first climbed in 2004 and then redpointed with a hard direct finish in 2015 (Opozda-Samitowski, 8a). A quick check of the wall showed us that it would be very hard to open a direct new route ground-up in our chosen style. We prefer to follow the line of least resistance, using all the weaknesses a wall offers to us, with a minimum of bolts.

So we decided to start up Arnaud's project and then strike out on our own. The first ascent of our route, La Grande Rouge, took four climbing days. Once we left Arnaud's line, part-way through his sixth pitch, protection became scarce and long free climbing passages became obligatory. Especially in the heart of the route, there was hardly a possibility to use trad gear—our only chance was to run it out, always in the hope of finding a placement for the skyhook in order to drill another bolt. The last six pitches (up to 7b) offer two bolts in total for protection; the rest has to be protected by yourself. These pitches show that the grade is not everything. Here you will see that style matters!

Exactly one year after the first ascent we were back in order to redpoint our project. Including travel days we had only two weeks, so there was no time to waste. We understood that we would have to climb all the crux pitches in the shade, before the relentless yellow star killed our plans with its heat. Therefore, we started at first light in order to have perfect sending conditions in the core of the route.

The sixth pitch is the first 8a, followed by an easier (7a) but almost featureless pitch that traverses straight left for roughly 25m, with only one cam as protection—as challenging to second as to lead. Our line then goes straight up again on an 8b pitch that is beautiful to climb and has a pretty challenging runout at the finish. The final difficult pitch (8a) is the ninth, with long runouts and, in the middle of the pitch, a dynamic move that is very exciting.

Although the upper six pitches are no more difficult then 7b, they are serious and we had to stay focused. Meanwhile, the sky was totally covered in dark clouds. It was almost ridiculous after all the merciless hot and dry days on the wall—exactly on the day of our redpoint, it started to rain! But we had no choice, we had to finish. At 3 p.m. we were on top of La Grand Rouge (15 pitches, 8b), as proud of our route as we were happy about the amazing time we'd spent in the High Atlas. 📷 🔍

– FABIAN BUHL, *GERMANY*

ANTI-ATLAS, TAFRAOUT AREA, MANY NEW ROUTES

DEVELOPMENT OF THE quartzite crags in Morocco's Anti-Atlas Mountains has continued at a steady pace during the last few winters, with several hundred routes being added to crags across the Jebel el Kest and Jebel Taskra massifs. These are described in a new guidebook to the area, *Moroccan Anti-Atlas*, published by the Oxford Alpine Club in March 2017. (*See AAJ 2016 for an introduction to this area.*) Of particular note were free ascents of a number of difficult crag routes up to E7 6b in difficulty.

This area is also known for its long traditionally protected climbs, and several noteworthy new routes have been completed. Aguila (Broatch-Mortimer-Widowson, 335m climbing distance, HVS 5a) ascends the full height of Anergui's impressive Upper Crag. Anti-Atlas regulars Graham Everitt, Bruce Kerry, and Ian Wilson made the first ascent of a very remote crag above Ameln's Lion's Face via the Lion's Tail (200m, HVS 5a). Also of note is the region's longest climb to date: Millennium Ridge (1,500m climbing distance, V-Diff) on Upper Prophet Peak, by Lina Arthur and Steve Broadbent in January 2018.

Considerable development also has taken place on the granite tors around Tafraout, which now boast a large variety of crack and slab climbs, as well as a number of fully bolted sport crags. A new guidebook, *Tafraout Granite*, is due for publication by the Oxford Alpine Club in summer 2018. [*Additional new climbs are described at the AAJ website.*] 📄

– STEVE BROADBENT, *U.K.*

KENYA

SAMBURU REGION, MT. OLOLOKWE, 100 PERCENT NOT LOSING

THE BEST BEER in Kenya is served at a place called Sabache Camp, tucked into a lush valley on the northeast flank of Mt. Ololokwe. It serves up ice-cold (sometimes frozen) tall-boy Tuskers on 100°-plus days. I imagine it was the enchanting contrast of hellish, thorny, heat-stroke-inducing approaches and cold beer that brought Brittany Griffith, Kate Rutherford, and Jonathan Thesenga back to Mt. Ololokwe for a second year in a row in February 2017. That and

[Above] **The east face of Mt. Ololokwe, showing the line of 100 Percent Not Losing (1,300', 5.13a.) After an attempt in 2016, the climbers returned a year later to finish the 13-pitch route.** [Right] **Brittany Griffith leads the Lo-Brow crack (pitch nine, 5.11+).** *Eric Bissell*

their unfinished business with a new route on the striking and previously unclimbed east face. With promises of those cold beers, they convinced me to leave perfect climbing conditions in Siurana, Spain, to join them.

Located in the Samburu region of northern Kenya, Ololokwe has been climbed via multiple technical routes, mostly on the ledge-filled and lower-angle terrain on the west side of the mountain. In 2013, Alex Ficksman and Johannes Oos climbed the 1,400' south face at 5.10+ A2 (*see AAJ 2015*). Brittany, Kate, and JT first attempted the east face in 2016, picking a line on the left side of the steep wall that attempted to avoid some terrifying vulture nests and their accompanying 400' shit stains. The team's initial ground-up attempt faced major difficulties, as the wall had few continuous crack systems and steepened beyond anyone's expectations. After climbing two pitches and scouting some more, the team decided to leave their gear at Sabache Camp and return the next year.

On February 4 we all convened at a rooftop bar on a bustling bright night in Nairobi. A drought could be felt more and more intensely as we travelled to the rural north, herders walking livestock farther and farther for dwindling watering holes. We arrived at Sabache Camp to see workers attempting to repair a concrete water tank that had been destroyed the night before by a wild elephant. Luckily, the Tuskers were both delicious and hydrating.

We'd made the difficult decision to complete our route on Ololokwe on rappel. Bolting on lead appeared to be an impossible task, due to the nature of the rock and unfortunate likelihood of drilling holes into dead-end lines. A few crack pitches served as major landmarks, but significant traversing meandered between them. With limited time, we divided into teams and focused on sections, working out the exact path and where protection would be needed.

For roughly seven days we dangled around on the wall, usually hiding in a cave or under a boulder during the midday heat, when the sun would fire the rock like a kiln. JT and I focused on the lower half of the wall, while Brittany and Kate unlocked the upper half. The pitches turned out to be fantastic, varied, steep and technical. Pitch four (The Roof) launches 25' out into space, along a crack protected with a mix of gear and bolts (5.12d). The Red Dihedral of pitch five comprises the crux of the route and has incredible steep, dynamic crimping interspersed with a bizarre technical dihedral and slopers. Many pitches of 5.11 and 5.12 wait above.

100 Percent Not Losing (1,300', 5.13a) has 13 pitches in all and requires a standard rack to number 3, 15 quickdraws, and extra runners. Each pitch was redpointed, with each individual contributing a critical lead to the team ascent, but we were unable to complete a continuous free ascent. A single push from the ground will be a proud and enjoyable experience that all the members of the FA team look forward to hearing about someday. 📄 📷

– ERIC BISSELL, *USA*

Ines Papert high on A Private Universe (550m, 7b+), established in 2002 at Slanghoek Amphitheatre. The 2017 team repeated this route as a warmup for their new line Ruby Supernova (13 pitches, 5.12c). *Paul McSorley*

SLANGHOEK AMPHITHEATRE, RUBY SUPERNOVA

ON JUNE 15 and 16, Ines Papert (Germany), Joseph Pfnür (Germany), Luka Lindič (Slovenia), and Paul McSorley (Canada) established Ruby Supernova, the second route up the Slanghoek Amphitheatre in the Du Toits Kloof area. The 13-pitch route is 520m long and rated ED1 7b+ (VI 5.12c). The team used no bolts or fixed protection, finding mostly excellent quartzite that protected well with removable gear. A handful of stoppers and pitons were left behind at anchors for rappels.

The team began their trip to the region by making a two-day repeat of A Private Universe (550m, ED1 7a A1), established in 2002 by South Africans Hilton Davies, David Davies, and Mathew Sim, and later free climbed by Dave Birkett (U.K.) and Tinie Verseveld (South Africa) at 7b+. The 2002 team used 100 bolts for anchors and protection on the 19-pitch original route up this impressive wall.

Papert, Pfnür, Lindič, and McSorley then set

to work on a new line up an obvious corner system on the right side of the wall. In two separate teams, they pushed the route to within a hundred meters of the top, onsighting every pitch, before the storm of the century hit, smashing mature timber like toothpicks, depositing snow in the mountains, and causing widespread flooding throughout the Western Cape.

Over the next week, the team escaped to the inland areas of Rocklands and Montague while they waited for the line to dry. Returning with photographer Franz Walter, the foursome climbed nine pitches of familiar ground to a good bivy ledge and completed the climb the following day. They descended by rappelling roughly the same route.

Papert, Pfnür, Lindič, and McSorley are tremendously grateful to Hilton Davies, who provided them with logistical support, invaluable route beta, and gracious hospitality. After completing Ruby Supernova, they had the pleasure of climbing with Hilton and Tinie Verseveld on Table Mountain, enjoying the classic climbing with two pioneers of the zone. 📷 🔍

– PAUL MCSORLEY, *CANADA*

MADAGASCAR / TSARANORO MASSIF

TSARANORO BE, LALAN'I MPANJAKA

IN 2016, WHILE repeating Manara-Potsiny and Zaza Be on Tsaranoro Be, I observed that these routes crossed an overhanging zone at roughly the same height. These two routes had just 20m to 30m of overhanging rock, but farther right was a brown streak with a 150m overhanging headwall. Might this line be climbable? In September 2017, I returned with Chris-Jan Stiller to take a closer look. We both climb in the sandstone towers of the Elbsandstein in East Germany, so we're used to ground-up bolting. But we were not used to climbing with just one harness, one belay device, and an old 40m half-rope—when one of our haulbags did not arrive in Madagascar, we had to improvise.

Luckily, we had prepared for a luggage mishap by spreading our gear across four bags, so at least we could still rig a harness from slings. Our lead rope was missing, but we had a static rope and a 6mm tagline, which supposedly could hold two falls. To avoid testing this, I asked around in the village for another rope and found an old 8mm, albeit just 40m long. The first fall on that old rope was scary, as I dropped 10m due to unexpected stretch.

Despite the gear problems, we made quick progress on the first day, climbing 250m and placing 55 bolts for protection and anchors. We fixed our two ropes on the wall and hoped the missing bag would arrive soon. Thanks to Air France, the next day we were able to return to our original strategy. Armed with a portaledge and supplies for four or five days, we would not return to the ground until the route was completely bolted.

The more the headwall hung over us, the more we doubted that it could go free. The first overhanging meters had just enough holds to be climbable. At home on our sandstone towers we think carefully before placing a bolt, and here we had the same intention.

Before their missing bags arrived, the team had to improvise—here using a carabiner brake and an old rope for rappels. Tobias Wolf

Tsaranoro Atsimo (left) and Tsaranoro Be, showing approximate lines of 2017 routes: (1) Rivotra Mahery (700m, 8a+ A0). (2) Lalan'I Mpanjaka (600m, 8a+). Arrow marks potential finish by Vazaha M'Tapitapy. Many other routes are not shown. *Matteo de Zaiacomo*

We made sure to place bolts so you can clip them before the hard moves (which at times required placing them a meter lower than the skyhook from which we were hanging). We also eschewed the use of removable bolts—unfortunately, several existing routes in Madagascar have empty holes and don't mention removable bolts as essential gear.

We needed a full day to finish the headwall. There were three 5.13 pitches in a row, and one stretched to 60m to reach a no-hands belay stance. In several spots one missing hold would have made the line impossible. We spent five days bolting the route and two days redpointing all the pitches.

The route was stunning—we never imagined finding such a perfect line. Our opinion can't be objective, but we've made several hundred first ascents around the world and have not seen another line with such sustained and diverse climbing. Thus we named it Lalan'i Mpanjaka (600m, 11 pitches, 8a+, 7b obl), which means "king line" in the local language. [*Editor's note: This route starts left of Zaza Be (Gamio-Thomas, 2014) and crosses it on the second pitch. Although various published topos suggest otherwise, the German route stays left of Vazaha M'Tapitapy all the way to the top.*]

– TOBIAS WOLF, *GERMANY*

ZAZA BE, FIRST ASCENT AND FIRST FREE ASCENT: *Not previously reported in the AAJ, Zaza Be was established by Marc Gamio and Gérard Thomas (France) in June 2014 at 7c A0. The 500m, 14-pitch line stopped below the top of formation. Later in 2014, Mayan Gobat-Smith (New Zealand) and Ben Rueck (USA) freed the remaining aid on Zaza Be, graded the climb 8a (5.13b), and renamed it Solar Fusion. Tobias Wolf, who repeated Zaza Be in 2016, believes the route should be graded 7c+, with many pitches easier than earlier topos have shown.*

TSARANORO ATSIMO, RIVOTRA MAHERY

THE WALLS OF the Tsaranoro Valley are certainly not a new discovery, and Dimitri Anghileri, Marco Maggioni, and I (all members of the Gruppo Ragni di Lecco) were well aware of the dozens of routes already crossing the steep, smooth walls of dark granite. Our hope was to open a new route and leave our signature; however, on formations so famous we were prepared to give up this goal if forcing a new route would seem contrived.

On our third day in the country, we found ourselves on the Malagasy plateau, taking in the immensity of the walls we'd so often dreamed of. We spent an afternoon wandering the base of the cliffs, and Dimitri identified a possible line on a steep slice of wall on Tsaranoro Atsimo. We started to climb the next day. Route-finding proved to be difficult; sometimes we stalled for most of a day as we tried to find a logical line of holds, some so small we couldn't really see them until they were right in front of us. We alternated climbing and rest days, which gave us time to appreciate the valley and get to know the Malagasy people, who were always laughing and smiling.

There were many moments of discomfort in our effort, but morale remained high and we tackled the adversities together, reaching the top of Tsaranoro Atsimo after 12 days, having established 16 independent pitches, all on beautiful, compact rock. We took turns tackling the hardest free climbing sections and were able to solve the final 8a+ cruxes a few hours before the end of our trip. However, we did not have time to free the full route in a push. We named the route Rivotra Mahery (700m climbing distance, 16 pitches, 8a+ A0). The name is Malagasy for "strong wind," as the wind was our silent and faithful companion for the duration of our climb.

– MATTEO DE ZAIACOMO, *ITALY*

LA VÍA DE LAS RUBÍAS AND DREAMS OF YOUTH: *The new Italian route on Tsaranoro Atsimo rises between La Vía de las Rubías on the left and Dreams of Youth on the right. Neither route was reported previously in the AAJ. La Vía de las Rubías (450m, 9 pitches, 7b+) was established by Spanish climbers Ramón Pérez de Ayala, Jordi Barrachina, and Ernesto Navarro over six days in July 2016 and was redpointed by Barrachina and Navarro on July 18. Dreams of Youth (700m, 18 pitches, 7c A0) was climbed in August 2011 by Tobias Baur, Lukas Binder, Philipp Hofmann, and Martin Schindele from Germany. Most of the hard pitches were not redpointed—the climbers estimated 11 of the pitches would range from 7c+ to 8c if free climbed.*

MORA MORA, SECOND FREE ASCENT AND FIRST FEMALE FREE ASCENT: *Sasha DiGiulian (USA) and Edu Marin (Spain) free climbed Mora Mora (700m, 8c) on the east face of Tsaranoro Atsimo. The route was established in 1999 by Francisco Blanco and Toti Valés and freed by Adam Ondra in 2010. DiGiulian and Marin spent most of July in the area, working on the climb. They each freed the route, swinging leads on their final three-day push, except for the 8b+/8c crux pitch, which each climber led free.*

Matteo de Zaiacomo stretches for a hold on the sixth pitch (8a+) of Rivotra Mahery, a new route on Tsaranoro Atsimo. *Dimitri Anghileri*

GEORGIA

Climbing the final section of the south-southeast ridge (Gvalia Route) leading to the main summit of Shkhara. The 2018 climb began on previously unclimbed terrain off-picture to the right, crossed the ridge line to the sunlit glacial basin at left, then reascended to the ridge to reach the summit. The round trip from advanced base camp took 13 days. *Archil Badriashvili*

THIRTEEN DAYS ON SHKHARA
A NEW ROUTE AND FIRST WINTER ASCENT IN THE CAUCASUS

BY ARCHIL BADRIASHVILI

SHKHARA (5,203M) IS Georgia's highest mountain—about 500m higher than well-known Ushba—and according to experienced mountaineers from our country, "It is better to climb Ushba in the worst conditions than to go to Shkhara in winter." Despite this, several attempts had been made to reach the summit from the south in winter. [*Shkhara previously had been climbed from the north— the first winter ascent was in 1986—and via a ridge traverse, but the complex south face had never seen a winter ascent.*] In 2016, Baqar Gelashvili, Giorgi Tepnadze, and I tried the south face but turned back after five days, acknowledging that we needed a different strategy.

In January 2018, Giorgi and I acclimatized in the Kazbek region and then, on February 2, with the help of friends, walked to an advanced base camp below Shkhara at 2,670m. The snow was much deeper than during our previous attempt. On the next day our friends helped us carry loads partway up the Shkhara Glacier toward the central couloir on the southwest face of Shkhara Southeast (4,620m), a prominent summit on the south-southeast (frontier) ridge of Shkhara Main. We took food and equipment for around 10 days and started climbing that day.

Over two days we climbed 1,000m up the couloir. During the afternoon of the second day, the weather deteriorated and small avalanches came down the couloir. We moved left onto a ridge, alternating between dry tooling on compact rock and climbing 70° snow, until we were able to dig out a tent platform at about 4,000m.

A blizzard kept us confined to the tent throughout our third day. On day four we climbed snow-covered rock to reach the most continuous technical section of our route, a narrow gully with climbing up to WI5. Avalanches and spindrift filled our mouths and eyes and froze our equipment.

We built a bivy ledge just big enough for two, and next day traversed up and left across an icefield, bypassing Shkhara Southeast, to reach a col on the south-southeast ridge below a large gendarme. Despite having now ascended 2,000m from advanced base, there was still a long way to go.

To outflank the gendarme, we descended the far (northeast) side of the ridge to reach a high glacier basin where, in 2013, I had spent four days in a tent with Austrian colleagues due to bad weather. (We had climbed an established route to Shkhara, finishing up the eastern ridge, and got stuck while descending.) The next day, Giorgi and I climbed back to the crest of the ridge, well beyond the gendarme, and, according to a topo, to the right of the couloir climbed by the Gvalia Route (Cheishvili-Gvalia, 1933), which reaches the basin from the Nankvan Glacier. We camped on the crest at 4,620m.

Next day, our eighth of the climb, we cached the inner tent, took the fly, and started up the frontier ridge, following the Gvalia Route toward the main summit. We began by simul-climbing and then opened a new variant via a rocky pyramid with some fun mixed climbing. After this Giorgi led 10 pitches of ice to reach the summit ridge in a blizzard. The forecast had been for -38°C and 55km/h wind, but it felt worse—not least because by now it was dark. At 8:40 p.m. on February 10 we were standing on the summit: For the first time Georgians had climbed their highest peak in winter. We started to descend the same way, but at 5,000m decided to cover ourselves with the fly sheet and wait until dawn.

It took all of next day to get back to the tent. At one point, during a traverse, Giorgi took a 15m fall on blue ice and lost a crampon. That night the gas was almost gone, we had little food, and there was no chance to dry our clothes.

On our tenth day above advanced base we regained the glacier basin, where the snow was so deep we had to resort to an improvised crawling technique to cross it. It took half a day to reach the base of the couloir leading back up to the ridge. We camped again and spent the whole of the following day climbing just three pitches of 80° snow. At the crest we got a signal on our satellite phone and were able to call anxious friends. We rappelled the ice face on the far side, rejoined our ascent route, and next day were able to cross the rocky terrain and descend the central couloir. Our gas and food were now long gone, but by the end of the day we were safely at the bottom.

Unfortunately, we were faced with another

Archil Badriashvili and Giorgi Tepnadze enduring harsh conditions during the first winter ascent of the south face of Shkhara. *Archil Badriashvili*

surprise: An avalanche had stolen our poles and snowshoes. We decided to keep going and descended for another eight hours, through the night, to reach a hut in the valley, where we enjoyed a fire. Continuing down next day, we met with another surprise, this time most welcome: Our friends had organized a small helicopter to take us to the town of Mestia.

All of Giorgi and my previous expeditions, including the first ascent of Larkya Main in Nepal in 2017 (*see page 317*), had provided us with the experience and resilience to stay mobilized and enthusiastic for what is probably one of the longest routes in Georgia.

Summary: First winter ascent of Shkhara from the south. The route involved 2,500m of climbing (60-plus pitches) and was graded 6B (ED2) M5 WI5 75–80°. 📷 🔍

Robin Hill on Talgar. The peaks behind are on the west side of the Middle Talgar Valley. *Brody Leven*

TALGAR ON SKIS
WILD ADVENTURE JUST OUTSIDE THE BIG CITY

BY VITALY "RAGE" KOMAROV, *WITH ASSISTANCE FROM BRODY LEVEN*

THE ZAYLIYSKIY ALATAU, the most northerly mountain group of the Tien Shan, reaches its maximum elevation on Pik Talgar (4,973m). The region has a rich climbing history, beginning 100 years ago with the boom of mountaineering in the former Soviet Union. A large mountaineering camp was established in the Middle Talgar Valley, south of the town of Talgar, but this was destroyed by a mudslide in 1979. Today, despite rising only 30 kilometers from the metropolis of Almaty, these wild peaks are difficult to access and see only a few parties each year.

Pik Talgar was first climbed in 1938, and ascents of the normal route on the south side take five to seven days. But the most beautiful and complex lines lie on the kilometer-wide northwest face, clearly visible from Almaty. The idea of skiing from the summit had been rooted in many minds, but the insidious weather, avalanche-prone slopes, a multiday approach, and the steepness of the descent had deterred all.

In early summer of 2016, I joined Americans Robin Hill and Brody Leven for an attempt. On June 2, we hiked up the closed ski resort of Chimbulak, and, with the help of two friends acting as porters, traveled four days, via the snow-covered Talgarsky and Teu passes, to reach the upper section of the Middle Talgar Valley. We were lucky with the weather (it rained on only one day) and also lucky to see snow leopard tracks while crossing Teu Pass.

At 2:30 a.m. on day five we started up the South Talgar Glacier, then continued in a 35–40° névé couloir to reach a west-facing ridge on the face. In the icefall between the main and south summits, we had to bypass dangerous seracs and bridged crevasses. After ascending nearly 900m, we came to the crux, a steep 400m face. We opted for a gully left of the wide couloir between the south and main summits. This last part of the ascent followed previously unclimbed terrain: 60° ice and 75° mixed, with a few vertical mixed steps. At 11:30 a.m. we were on the summit. The weather was perfect, and I was convinced that, as legend says, you can see from this top to Khan Tengri and Pobeda—about 250km in a straight line.

After regaining our exit point onto the south ridge, we made one rappel down mixed ground (M2) and then slowly descended (Brody and me on skis, Robin on snowboard) a line close to but south of our ascent route. At times, a thin covering of snow lay over hard ice.

By making hop turns between rocky ridges and the icy face, we only had to make that one rappel. Once down the main face, we relaxed a little and allowed ourselves a more aggressive approach.

The difficulties didn't end there. During our access from Chimbulak, we had descended a glacier that we felt would be impossible to ascend safely. We therefore had to exit through Almatinsky Nature Reserve, making our way through real northern jungle, down the Middle Talgar Gorge and then, annoyingly, over a high pass. It was hard: We found ourselves covered with ticks, and a recent mudslide, which had demolished any flat ground or trail, left us traversing a steep hillside above the gorge for more than 20 hours and 30km. Through-out the expedition, we met not a single person. At the end we were exhausted: The mountain took everything from us, but in exchange gave back something more. ▤ 🖸

SUMMARY: Partial new route on the west face of Pik Talgar in the Zayliyskiy Alatau, followed by ski and snowboard descent, on June 6, 2016.

[Top] Brody Leven during the tick-ridden walk out the Middle Talgar Gorge. *Brody Leven Collection* [Bottom] Talgar (4,973m) from the south-southwest. The distant summit on the left is Pik Kopr (ca 4,750m). The 2016 first ski and snowboard descent is marked. A 2010 Vitaly Komarov–Denis Urubko route, reported in *AAJ 2011*, is farther left on the same face. *Brody Leven*

Pitch 15 (6c) of Alexandra Supernova, with wild rock formations above. *Benno Wagner*

PEAK 4,800M, NORTHWEST PILLAR, ALEXANDRA SUPERNOVA

FOR MANY YEARS I had dreamed of going to Kyrgyzstan to climb perfect granite walls above green meadows filled with wild horses. After much research I decided on the Ak-su branch of the Laylak valley, despite this area, unlike the neighboring Karavshin, not having a reputation as a free climbing Eldorado. [*Like the Karavshin, the Laylak area is divided into Kara-su and Ak-su branches; the main peak at the head of the Ak-su arm has two well-known tops named Snowy Ak-su and Rocky Ak-su.*]

Since the 1980s, Rocky Ak-su has been the mecca of former Soviet alpinists. In both summer and winter, hard-hitting alpinists with large haulbags, portaledges, pitons, and aid gear made their pilgrimage to the north-facing walls of Ak-su, Iskander, and Pik Alexander Blok. Spending five to ten days on an ascent and battling infernal storms at 5,000m were the rule. Free ascents of classic routes in this valley can probably be counted on one hand.

Nevertheless, a variety of 600–900m walls offer fantastic free climbing potential. Our plan was to free an existing aid route and/or open a new free route. Benno Wagner and I from Munich were joined by Paul Sass, a crack climbing specialist from the Elbsandsteingebirge, and by Henry Francis from Sheffield, England.

In August, with the help of horses and donkeys, we carried our hundreds of kilograms of gear and food 25 km from the mountain village of Uzgurush to the glacier moraine below the north face of Ak-su. The first week was very warm; it was well above 0°C at 4,000m, even at night. The surrounding walls rumbled often and violently with falling rock and ice. We looked for the safest good line and eventually decided on the compact northwest pillar of Pik 4,800m, a summit at the end of the west ridge of Pik Alexander Blok.

Working in teams of two, we took turns to establish the first pitches. The lower half of the wall was either very slabby or presented hard face climbing on compact granite, and we had to drill bolts regularly. In a week, we climbed, equipped, and cleaned the first 10 pitches. Two-thirds of the way up the 800m route, we reached considerably steeper ground, with crack systems that required far fewer bolts. The orange granite, illuminated in the afternoon sun, gave a Joshua Tree–like climbing experience, with hueco formations perfectly made for climbing.

Unfortunately, the initial warm weather did not last. In the afternoons, cold wind and shade made the use of a down jacket necessary, even while climbing. Snow fell at base camp. We completed all of the pitches through these harsh conditions, but the route still awaited a free ascent.

Sometimes you get lucky: In our final four days the sun came out, dried the wall amazingly fast, and we were able to free all the pitches, including two pitches of 7b.

We called our route Alexandra Supernova to give the nearby Alexander Blok, named for the Russian poet, some pleasant new company. We climbed 18 pitches, largely from 6a to 7b. After three weeks we returned to the valley through beautiful alpine meadows and green woods. In addition to the climbing experience and the scenery, the overwhelming friendliness of the Kyrgyzstan people remains a warm memory. 📷 🔍

– TONI LAMPRECHT, *GERMANY*

PIK ALEXANDER BLOK, WEST FACE, SUMMER BOUQUET

Martin Grajciar, Ondrej Huserka, Jozef Kristoffy, and I (Slovakia) spent seven weeks in Kyrgyzstan with the aim of making a new route on the west face of Pik Alexander Blok (5,239m). After travel by minivan from Osh to Uzgurush, we transported 500kg by horses and donkeys to the moraine of the Ak-su Glacier. Over the next few days of poor, windy weather, we carried gear up the Aktjubek Glacier to beneath the west face.

On August 6, having identified an unclimbed line on the right side of the face, we fixed rope

[Top Right] (A) West face of Pik Alexander Blok (5,239m), showing the line of Summer Bouquet (2017). Several earlier routes ascend this face farther to the left, as well as the southwest ridge (right skyline) and north face (left, in shadow); see photos online and in AAJ 2014. (B) Northwest pillar of Pik 4,800m with the line of Alexandra Supernova (2017). *Martin Grajciar–MANOfactory* [Bottom Right] Jozef Kristoffy leading the crux pitch (IX+) of Summer Bouquet on Pik Alexander Blok. *Vladimir Linek*

up four pitches of 60° ice. Two days later we added another 70° pitch to reach the base of the wall, where we climbed the first rock pitch at UIAA VIII. Bad weather continued over the next few days, but we continued up the overhanging wall, using a mixture of free and aid, to establish a portaledge camp at the top of pitch seven. Temperatures were consistently low—rarely above freezing during the day and -10°C at night.

On August 25, having established 16 pitches, we pushed for the top. After reascending the ropes to our high point, we completed one more pitch and then traversed 30m left to join the Gunko Route (2010). We followed this for 80m in a snow couloir (55°). Before reaching the summit ridge we were hit by a thunderstorm, forcing us to sit it out in the couloir for around half an hour. Finally, at 6 p.m., we were all on the summit.

Over the next three days we free climbed all the aid pitches. The hardest, pitch 13 (50m), was at around 5,000m and was led by Jozef at IX+ (5.13a/b). It features a bouldery start past four bolts, followed by hard slab climbing to an overhang. Jozef felt he was lucky to do this in a short window when the sun was shining for half an hour.

We spent August 6–28 establishing the route, during which we only had one complete day of fine weather. Summer Bouquet (900m, 22 pitches, IX+ 70°, 51 protection bolts, 36 on belays) is probably the hardest free line in the area. 📷 🔍

– VLADIMIR LINEK, *JAMES, SLOVAKIA*

KICHIK-ALAI, GEZART VALLEY, KORLY-TOO AND PIK KAMAR (A.K.A. DJUMAS)

IN AUGUST WE visited the Gezart Valley in the Kichik-Alai (Little Alai) mountains, establishing base camp at 3,550m, not far from the start of the Gezart Glacier. This was at least 10 hours of walking from the village of Ak Art, which can be reached by 4WD. The Kichik-Alai still has considerable scope for first ascents on 4,000m peaks, despite being relatively accessible from Osh.

David Brezovjak and I led a team of nine up Gezart (4,935m Russian map), climbing the ice and snow of the northeast ridge, approached via 4,481m Gezart Pass. This is considered the standard route, though Gezart is very rarely climbed.

Korly-too (4,913m) seen from Kamar to the west, and the route of ascent via the north ridge. The lower Gezart Glacier is visible at right. *Michal Kleslo Collection*

Josef Krena and Vaclav Stetina climbed what we believe to be a previously virgin peak, locally called Korly-too ("Snowy Peak" in Uzbek, 4,913m, 39°54'37.34"N, 72°26'8.48"E Google Earth). From base camp they walked east for around five hours, passing over large scree slopes and around hanging glaciers, to reach the 4,400m pass at the foot of the north ridge. They climbed a snow-ice arête (45°) up the ridge, with short pitches of rock (UIAA III), reaching the rocky summit in three hours from the pass. The grade was 3A.

Kamil Bartos and Martin

Krena climbed the southeast flank and upper east ridge of a rocky peak west of base camp, which they named Pik Kamar (4,324m Russian map, 39°54'35.56"N, 72°23'10.26"E Google Earth). [*Vladimir Komissarov, in his Mountaineering Regions of Kyrgyzstan, notes this peak as Djumas and the col immediately to its south as Djumas Pass.*] The grade was 1B.

— MICHAL KLESLO, *CZECH REPUBLIC*

PAMIR

MINDZHAR VALLEY, PEAK 5,860M, NORTHEAST RIDGE; PEAK 5,914M, ATTEMPT

In *AAJ 2017* I reported on first ascents near Mindzhar Pass, around 30km west of Pik Lenin. I returned in August 2017 to explore farther along the ridgeline, this time with Eduard Skukis.

Over three days, we traveled from Pik Lenin base camp to the Mindzhar Valley, climbed east to Mindzhar Pass (ca 5,050m), and continued south and then southwest over Pik 5,390m and Pik 5,414m to MAI 50th Anniversary Pass. To this point we were retracing our 2016 journey. We continued for one hour toward unclimbed Pik 5,860m before

Eduard Skukis on the summit of Pik 5,860m, with unclimbed Pik 5,914m behind and to the southeast. *Oleg Silin*

camping. Next day, over technically easy ground with many crevasses, we reached the top of 5,860m at 1 p.m. (39°21'5.20"N, 72°33'58.66"E).

We attempted to reach Pik 5,914m (39°19'57.69"N, 72°35'1.12"E), the next peak to the southeast, the following day. From our campsite, we headed directly for the summit across the upper icefall of the Kuzgun Glacier, but once through this obstacle Eduard became ill and we decided to retreat.

— OLEG SILIN, *LATVIA*

PIK LENIN, WEST-EAST TRAVERSE

In July, Markus Gschwendt (Austria) and Anton Sharobayko (Russia) made a lengthy and unusual traverse of Pik Lenin (7,134m), crossing over Pik Yukhin (5,112m), Pik 30th Anniversary of Uzbek Republic (5,700m), and Pik Razdelnaya (6,148m) en route to Lenin. They descended the northeast ridge, then slanted down the north face by an avalanche-prone couloir to the southwest of Lipkin Rocks. The round trip from Camp 1 on Lenin's normal route took nine days, and the total distance traveled was 51km. It is unlikely that these routes had previously been combined into such a grand traverse.

— LINDSAY GRIFFIN, *WITH INFORMATION FROM MARKUS GSCHWENDT, AUSTRIA*

SOKULUK VALLEY, CHON-TOR, NORTHWEST FACE, GLAZUNOV ROUTE

IN FEBRUARY 2016, just a few weeks after the presumed first ascent of Chon-tor (ca 4,180m) by Egor Suzdaltsov and Ivan Temerev from Russian Siberia (*AAJ 2017*), a new route was climbed on the northwest face of Chon-tor by the brothers Eugeny and Sergey Glazunov, also from Siberia. This 4,165m peak lies in the upper Sokuluk Valley (a.k.a. Belogorka), just 20km west of the Ala Archa.

On February 15 the two brothers left Bishkek and reached base camp at 4 p.m. Early the next morning, they started up the right-hand buttress on the northwest face. After a 30° approach couloir of deep, loose snow, there were around 20 pitches on the buttress, with largely enjoyable rock difficulties of V and VI, mixed climbing in crampons, and many sections of aid at A1/A2. They made one bivouac about nine pitches up and reached the summit around 3 p.m. on February 17. No bolts were placed. The overall difficulty of the 900m route was 6A.

The brothers noted other possibilities on Chon-tor and said they were surprised this area is so neglected. 📷

– LINDSAY GRIFFIN, *WITH INFORMATION FROM ELENA DMITRENKO, RISK.RU*

ALA ARCHA NATIONAL PARK, PIK SEMENOVA TIAN-SHANSKI, NORTHWEST FACE

ON SEPTEMBER 2, 2015, Mark Aitken (U.K.) and Aleksey Potockiy (Kyrgyzstan) climbed a direct new route up the northwest face of Pik Semenova Tian-Shanski (4,895m), the highest peak in Ala Archa. They ascended steepening ice slopes (up to 65–70°) to a pronounced snow shoulder at around two-thirds height. Above, 50° ice led to the final three, largely rocky pitches, at first in a gully then a steep ridge (V Diff to S). The full route was graded 4A (Alpine D). 📄 📷 ▶

– MARK AITKEN, *U.K.*

CENTRAL AND WESTERN AT BASHI, PIK RHIANYDD AND OTHER ASCENTS

THE OBJECTIVE OF our expedition, which was organized by the International School of Mountaineering (ISM) and led by Adrian Nelhams, was to explore unclimbed peaks in the At Bashi from the south. The southern approach was first made in 2010 by two ISM expeditions led by Pat Littlejohn and Nelhams (*AAJ 2011*); subsequent ISM teams in 2012 and 2014 made many more first ascents.

Our expedition entered the central At Bashi in August via the Kashkaratash Valley. Base camp

The Pik Rhianydd group and Kashkaratash Glacier in the Central At Bashi, as seen from the west ridge of Pik Arie Gabai. Pik Rhianydd, the high point, was climbed by the obvious snow and ice slope leading directly to the top. Mark Aitken

was established at 3,680m, and an advanced base later established at 4,012m, near the Kashkaratash Glacier. After eight days climbing in the central range, we relocated to the western part of the At Bashi, establishing a new base camp (3,762m) at 40°50'50.1"N, 75°36'01.8"E).

We were delighted to summit 11 peaks between 4,000m and 4,801m. Ten of these are believed to have been previously unclimbed. Our most captivating first known ascent was Pik Rhianydd (4,801m). This involved a long approach up the Kashkaratash Glacier, followed by a snow climb up the east face to about 4,600m. Our route then went up steep snow and ice (up to 60°) on the northeast ridge to gain the summit (AD). Prior to our ascent, the highest summit in the entire At Bashi Range had been thought to be a 4,788m peak at the southern end of a 2km ridge leading to Pik Rhianydd. Our ascent of Rhianydd confirmed that it is the highest known summit in the At Bashi.

The coordinates and climbers of each peak we ascended are detailed at the AAJ website.

— MARK AITKEN AND ADRIAN NELHAMS, *U.K.*

AT BASHI SKI MOUNTAINEERING

The At Bashi Range is particularly suitable for ski mountaineering and still has around 60 peaks above 4,000m that remain unclimbed. In 2016 our team explored the potential in the heart of the massif, which contains the highest peaks, and learned that it is too far to reach in one-day trips from a base at At Bashi town (*AAJ 2017*). For our next trip, therefore, we planned to operate from a yurt camp in one of the side valleys, and we chose the Tuyuk Bogoshti, which flows north down to the village of Birinchi May ("May 1").

We arrived in At Bashi on April 3 and the next day went to examine snow condi-

Approaching the head of the Kok-Moinok Glacier basin. Choku Bocia (4,135m) is the summit at far right. The obvious rock tower to the left is likely unclimbed. *Ruggero Vaia*

tions. They were bad: lots of wet snow with no crust, due to a few weeks of uninterrupted cloudy weather. On the 6th we visited our yurt camp and were disappointed to find it located at 2,400m, about 5km down valley from our proposed site. But it was comfortable, with beds, mattresses, blankets, and the yurts heated by coal stoves.

The weather improved and over the next four days we climbed and skied three peaks. On April 8 we moved south up the Tuyuk Bogoshti and then took an eastern tributary, eventually reaching the high glacial valley of Kok-Moinok, which allows access to a dozen summits over 4,000m. We opted for the closest top, which we reached via its west slopes and south ridge. We named it Choku Bocia (4,135m). We then made a fine ski descent of more than 1,700m, reaching the yurts at 5:30 p.m.

On the 9th we headed up a ridge on the western side of the Tuyuk Bogoshti and eventually reached a previously climbed top of 3,750m that the locals call Choku Kuumamy.

Next day we set off at 4 a.m. and again reached the Kok-Moinok Glacier and continued to its head. From there we climbed up to the watershed ridge and, moving west, reached a narrow summit of 4,256m, our highest during the expedition. We named it Choku Sonja, after our friend Sonja Brambati. It was a full 12km descent on skis to our camp.

— RUGGERO VAIA, *ITALY, SUPPLIED BY PAOLO VITALI*

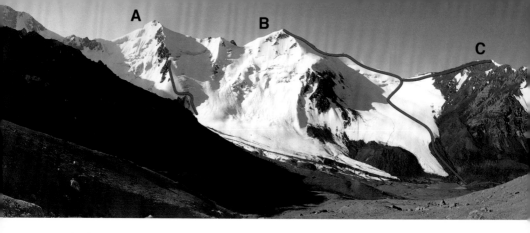

Looking from the north at (A) Pik 4,898.7m and attempt, (B) Pik 4,785.5m and ascent route via the west ridge, and (C) Pik 4,722.3m (4,727m GPS) and route of ascent via the southeast ridge. *Borkoldoy 2017 Expedition*

EASTERN BORKOLDOY, FIRST ASCENTS FROM KAINAR LAKE

THE BORKOLDOY RANGE lies due south of Lake Issyk Kul and north of the Western Kokshaal-too mountains and consists of two main valleys systems, one facing west and the other east. The western end of the Borkoldoy has seen many prior expeditions, but previous trips to the eastern valley were turned back by armed hunters. We were able to contact the local hunters in advance and agree a permit fee for access.

Unfortunately, when the vehicles dropped us off in our chosen valley, the packhorses we had prebooked were not there. After waiting a couple of hours, we decided to begin ferrying our 500kg of food and equipment to base camp ourselves. Consequently, our camp on the south shores of Kainar Lake (41°24'32.31"N, 77°52'53.09"E), although idyllic, was far lower than planned.

Nonetheless, between August 11 and 27, Stuart Gillan, Tom Harding, Matt Lewis, David Lyons-Ewing, Scott Martin, Hannah Meinertzhagen, and I (in various combinations) completed the likely first ascents of 14 peaks and made attempts on two others. We also documented the local distribution of observed wildlife and photographed 11 glaciers for Project Pressure, a charity that is documenting the world's glaciers. The eastern end of the Borkoldoy still offers potential for first ascents and new routes, though the rock quality is poor. We didn't make it to the head of the valley, so peaks there will be unclimbed from the east; most if not all have been climbed from the west. A full report is available at the AAJ website. 📄 📷 🔍

— NEIL COX *AND* BORKOLDOY 2017 EXPEDITION, *U.K.*

PIK CHAPAEV, SABER; PIK IRBIS, FIRST ASCENT, VIA NORTH FACE

THE KHAN TENGRI base camp on the South Inylchek Glacier is a crossroad of time and people. Here you can find real characters: from the mountaineering past and future; from Europeans to Africans; from alpine-style athletes to commerical guides. Everyone is flaunting ideas and it is easy to be charged with positive energy. The South Inylchek is still a great place for creativity.

Maria Cardell (Spain), Vera Rogovaya and Vladimir Ryazantsev (Russia), and I arrived here on August 8 after a three-day trek. A few days later we climbed Khan Tengri by the standard route from the South Inylchek. Cardell returned with numb toes but decided to accompany me on a new route up nearby Pik Chapaev (6,372m). Chapaev stands just west of Khan Tengri, and a shoulder of the peak forms part of the normal route up Khan Tengri from the north. On the 2,000m south face, it seemed a potential route on the left side was still unclimbed.

Maria and I left base camp (ca 4,000m) on the South Inylchek at 3 a.m. on August 25 and climbed through the icefall to a plateau at 4,700m. We stepped onto the west ridge at about 6,100m and followed it to the summit a little before 3 p.m. on the 27th, having climbed 35 pitches with technical difficulties of IV/4 M4 90°. We descended the same way. We took no tent, made three open bivouacs (in crevasses), and named our route Saber, rating the overall ascent 5A.

We then turned our attention to an unnamed peak of about 5,350m, a distinct high point midway along the long ridge that runs southwest from Pik Piramida (5,565m) toward the Zvez-dochka Glacier. Despite the close proximity to both Khan Tengri and Pobeda, there appeard to be no known previous ascent. Maria had to stay behind with her frostbitten feet, but Vera, Vladimir, and I left early in the morning of September 1, taking only chocolate and a few warm clothes. The north face looked to have maybe 12 to 14 pitches. We left our packs at the bottom. I'd drunk a cup of coffee before leaving and reasoned that I'd get another one back in the warmth and comfort of the tent that evening. This is climbing!

Twelve hours after leaving base camp, our group was not only far from any warmth and comfort, but also far from the summit. After 22 pitches we reached the summit ridge as the sun was setting. We climbed both the west and east tops, just to be sure we reached the highest point. We named the summit Pik Irbis ("snow leopard") and our route Twenty-two Ropes. We rappelled our line of ascent and returned to base camp 29 hours after leaving, greeted near camp by Maria with sweets and tea, our first liquid since setting out. This is training!

— DENIS URUBKO, *RUSSIA AND POLAND*

The new route on the south face of Pik Chapaev (6,372m). Other routes on this face not shown. *Denis Urubko*

TAJIKISTAN

GEN GLACIER BASIN: PIK 5,610M, NORTH FACE, PIK PATKHOR, NORTH FACE ATTEMPT

Seen from the northeast over the Gen Glacier basin: Pik Patkhor (left) and the 2017 attempt on the north face, and Pik 5,610m and the line of the 2017 ascent. *Spencer Gray*

PETE DRONKERS AND I (both USA) spent several weeks in August climbing in the central Rushan Range. We were drawn to the area by stable weather, unclimbed peaks, relatively simple access, and friends who had spent time recently in the range. We used donkeys from the village of Basid in the Bartang Valley to carry supplies as far up the west branch of the Devlokh River as possible. From there we double-carried for another two days to set up base camp on the moraine of the Gen Glacier below the north face of Pik Patkhor (6,083 m). After extensive research, we are unaware of other climbing parties having visited the Gen basin.

Patkhor is the highest peak in the Rushan Range, a somewhat overlooked subrange of the Pamirs with highly variable rock quality. [*This area lies just northwest of the Shadzud Valley; see AAJ 2017.*] Patkhor was first climbed in 1946 from the south by a 12-member Soviet party that included Evgeny Abalakov (brother of the inventor of the Abalakov anchor). Its north and east faces rise 1,600m above the bergschrunds. The outskirts of the Rushan Range boast some Sierra-quality granite, but most of what we found in the Gen basin was Pringles-like shale, the kind of rock that makes you an ice climber—or a beachgoer. However, the high-pressure system that dominates the Pamirs most of the summer was as good as one could hope. Temperatures at night above 5,000m were relatively warm, probably no cooler than -10°C to -12°C.

After acclimatizing we climbed a prominent unnamed summit (Pik 5,610m on the most recent Soviet map, but somewhat lower on our altimeter; 37°54'22.58"N, 72°10'24.01"E), the most appealing option in the Gen basin other than Patkhor. We reached the top via the north face (snow and ice up to 70°), climbing the route in a long day from an advanced base camp.

An attempt on the north face of Patkhor, starting up a couloir on the east-northeast face, ended after two days because of concerns about rock quality, some rockfall, and potentially dangerous rappels. It was a more ciruitous alternative to the most obvious line on the north face, which was continuous ice and snow except for 50m of overhanging crumbly rock.

We also climbed a 300m rock line, Apricot Heaven (5.10+), partway up a tower in the lower Devlokh Valley. Many thanks to Bo White and Odina Nurmamadov for their assistance. [*The online version of this report has many photos of this rarely seen area.*] 📚 📷

– SPENCER GRAY, *AAC*

View to the west-northwest from Brocca Peak. (A) Jinnah Peak (6,177m) and 2017 first ascent route. (B) Soot Gah (5,825m). (C) Iqbal Peak (5,820m). (D) Cima Alpinisti Vicentini (5,750m). *Francesco Rota Nodari*

HINDU RAJ

JINNAH PEAK, SOUTHEAST FACE AND EAST RIDGE

Since Franco Brunello's first expedition to the Chiantar Glacier area of the Hindu Raj in 1997, ten different Italian climbing and trekking parties have returned to these mountains, most recently in 2015. Only one 6,000m peak remained virgin: Peak 6,177m above the northwest corner of the Soot Gah (a.k.a. Suj Gah) Glacier on the watershed with the Chiantar. Anticipating climbing this mountain, we had already decided to name it Jinnah Peak after Mohammed Ali Jinnah, the first president of Pakistan.

Approaching via Ishkoman, we began our trek from the village of Ghotolti (2,530m). In 2009, the Montagne e Solidarietà Association, which is financed by Italian contributors, built an aqueduct and fountain here; in 2013 a new iron bridge (carried from Italy in pieces) was installed. A community climbing center is under construction—a refuge that can host tourists and mountaineers in this "forgotten" area, and which will give local people the opportunity for work.

Tarcisio Bellò planned to spend 30 days coordinating work on the refuge and then join Mara Babolin and me for an attempt on Peak 6,177m (Jinnah Peak). We established base camp at the Gashukis Lakes (3,894m) just below the Soot Gah Glacier. To acclimatize, we made an ascent of Brocca Peak (Broken Peak, 5,040m, 36°40'50.05"N, 73°46'21.02"E) via the west face and northwest ridge (220m, D+ 80° UIAA IV). Brocca Peak was climbed during a 2004 expedition, but it has been impossible to evaluate whether the climbers reached the true summit.

We then turned to Jinnah Peak (36°42'48.58"N, 73°42'28.67"E) and put a camp below the southeast face at 4,600m. Access to this face is barred by a jumbled icefall. To outflank this, we climbed a 400m, 45–50° couloir (dubbed Couloir Steck after the legendary Swiss who had recently died on Nuptse) between a rock buttress and the main face of the unnamed peak east of Jinnah (estimated to be 5,700m). This led to a notch at 5,050m, from which we descended for two rope lengths on the far side (toward Jinnah Peak) and then slanted left above the worst part of the icefall. At first there was icefall danger, but this lessened considerably as we gained height. Three pitches over rock (UIAA IV) brought us to the main slope leading to the east ridge. This went on forever: snow at 50° and four pitches of ice at 60–65°. We reached the east ridge at 5,800m, and from there the summit looked close. It wasn't, and there were icy sections guarding the top that needed screws.

From the summit we made seven rappels to regain the point at which we had reached the east ridge (snow stakes, Abalakovs, ice bollards) and another 25 rappels down to the top of the main ice fall. From there we climbed back up to the notch and made another seven rappels down the Couloir Steck.

We had begun the climb from our camp at 4:30 a.m. on June 30, reached the summit at 8 p.m., and regained our tent at 8 a.m. on July 1. Our timing had been perfect. By 11 a.m. it was snowing, and when we got back to base camp on the 2nd it rained for the next two days. We named the route Ghotolti Dreams (1,500m, TD 70° IV).

– FRANCESCO ROTA NODARI, *ITALY*

HIMALAYA

NANGA PARBAT, SECOND WINTER ASCENT, FIRST COMPLETE ASCENT OF NORTHWEST FACE, AND RESCUE

A LITTLE AFTER sunset on January 25, 2018, Tomasz Mackiewicz (Poland) and Elizabeth Revol (France) reached the top of Nanga Parbat (8,125m) to make the second winter ascent of the mountain. The pair had completed the first ascent of the northwest face to the summit, with Revol becoming only the second women in history to climb an 8,000m peak in winter (after the Swiss mountaineer Marianne Chapuisat, who climbed Cho Oyu on February 10, 1993). Their ascent was made in very lightweight style.

The northwest face had seen several previous attempts, including a 1991 Austrian team that reached 7,400m and a 2008 attempt that reached 7,760m, not far below the north summit. (*See AAJ 2017*.) Mackiewicz, a veteran of multiple winter attempts on the mountain, had attempted the northwest face with Revol in 2014-'15 and again the following winter. In 2018, they started along the same line but then angled right, eventually reaching the Kinshofer Route, which they followed to the summit.

After a first foray in early January, in which they reached Camp 2 at 6,600m, Mackiewicz and Revol began their summit attempt on January 20. On the 21st they made it back to Camp 2, where they discovered their tent still intact (the shovel they'd left there had blown away). It was very windy that night and the next day, making it inadvisable to move. On the 23rd, in early afternoon, they began to traverse right toward the Austrian-Canadian route on the northwest buttress (Göschl-Rousseau, *AAJ 2010*). Violent wind from the direction of Mazeno Pass forced them to stop for the night at a sheltered spot at 6,900m.

On the 24th the pair reached the buttress at 7,000m and then continued up and right, generally following the Austrian-Canadian route. However, at 7,200m Revol suggested that they try contouring right, as much as 200m below a similar traverse followed by Göschl and Rousseau, to hit the Kinshofer Route close to its standard Camp 4. At first the climbing was mixed, then two snowy couloirs were crossed before the two emerged onto the great snow slopes below the summit pyramid. They found a sheltered site for a tent in a crevasse at 7,300m and settled in for the night.

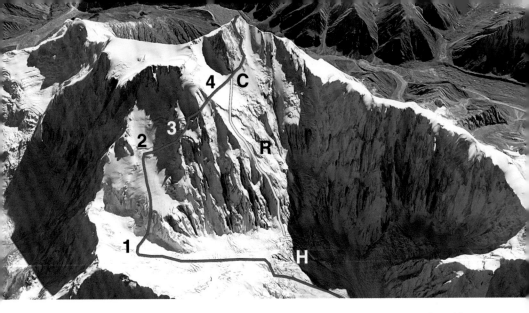

Nanga Parbat from the northwest. Red line shows the Mackiewicz-Revol route up the northwest face and traverse to the upper Kinshofer Route, with camps 1 to 4 marked. As far as Camp 2, Mackiewicz and Revol generally followed the line of past attempts on the northwest face; from there to Camp 4, they also were on or near ground that mostly been climbed before, but they were the first to link the northwest face to the main summit. (C) is the crevasse bivouac at 7,280m where Mackiewicz stayed after the descent from the summit. From there Revol continued down the Kinshofer Route (yellow line). (R) marks the approximate spot at 6,100m where Revol was found by Adam Bielecki and Denis Urubko. (H) marks the general area where the Polish were dropped off to begin the rescue. *Google Earth*

On the 25th they crossed the large plateau, quickly joining the normal line of the Kinshofer Route, and started the final ascent. At 5:15 p.m., with an extensive cloud sea below and the sun dipping down the Mazeno Ridge, Revol used her Garmin InReach to contact her husband and support team in France. She was at 8,035m. When Mackiewicz joined her, they discussed whether to continue, given the lateness of the hour, but both agreed to carry on. They reached the top between 6 and 6:15 p.m.

During the ascent they had been relatively sheltered from the wind, but now they received its full force, making it far too cold for Revol, who arrived first, to operate either her Garmin or GoPro. It was dark, and when Mackiewicz joined her he confessed he could not see Revol's headlamp, which she had switched on, and that she herself was a blur.

Alarm bells rang for Revol: The lack of vision might have originated with Mackiewicz neglecting to wear protection during the hazy summit day, but it also suggested the onset of cerebral edema. With Mackiewicz hanging onto her shoulder for guidance, Revol headed down immediately. The Pole was not able to move fast enough to keep warm. Partway down the main couloir he took four dexamethasone tablets, and this seemed to improve things for a while. The two continued down the snow slopes below the summit pyramid until about 7,280m. Here they would have needed to make a long traverse and a slight ascent to reach the tent, but Mackiewicz was by now completely exhausted, frostbitten, had signs of pulmonary edema, and was unable to see properly. Revol got them both inside a crevasse for the night, with no bivouac equipment.

Next morning it was obvious that Mackiewicz would not be able to move. By this time Revol had made several emergency calls. She was told that it should be possible to get a helicopter rescue to Mackiewicz, but that she must descend to a lower altitude herself, as it would be impossible to recover two people in a helicopter at this height. Reluctantly, next morning the Frenchwoman decided to descend the Kinshofer Route, on which altitude could be lost faster. Convinced at the time that a helicopter could rescue Mackiewicz, she anchored him inside the crevasse, then cut steps to the entrance so that he could climb out. That day she descended to 6,700m, where she spent the night in another crevasse.

Mackiewicz's wife in Poland, alerted to the situation by posts on Revol's social media, contacted a friend of Mackiewicz, who in turn contacted an official of the Polish winter K2 expedition. The offical called the Polish team at K2 base camp and asked if they wanted to help. Expedition leader Krzysztof Wielicki, with his team's blessing, reached out to Polish government officials, who began working with Pakistan's military to coordinate a rescue. Sheltering in her crevasse, Revol knew nothing of this. Exhausted and dehydrated, she began to suffer hallucinations. She perceived that someone was offering her hot tea but in return wanted one of her boots. Revol took off her left boot and only realized this serious mistake five hours later.

A little after noon the next day, the weather in Skardu cleared enough to allow two helicopters and four pilots, led by Lt. Col. Anjum Rafique, to set off for K2 base camp and pick up four climbers, Adam Bielecki, Jaroslaw Botor, Piotr Tomala, and Denis Urubko, to participate in the rescue. These four were flown to Skardu and then on to Nanga Parbat. En route, Rafique made the decision to continue past base camp and try to land at the base of the Diamir Face, as close to the standard Camp 1 (4,900m) as he could. After several attempts, all four climbers and equipment were dropped at around 4,800m.

Nanga Parbat from the west. Red line: the Mackiewicz-Revol ascent. The lower section of the route is hidden by Ganalo Peak. Yellow line: Kinshofer Route. The long arête right of the summit, curving toward the camera, is the Mazeno Ridge. *Guihem Vellut / Wikimedia*

At 5:30 p.m., Bielecki and Urubko, well acclimatized from K2, started immediately up the Kinshofer Route, carrying bivouac and medical equipment, hoping to reach Camp 2 before dawn. Botor and Tomala would set up a support camp at 4,900m. In the meantime, Revol, having giving up hope of being rescued from 6,700m, was descending toward Camp 2.

At 2 a.m. on the 28th, having put in a remarkable performance by ascending 1,100m in less than nine hours, aided by finding many useful fixed ropes, Bielecki and Urubko established voice contact with Revol at around 6,100m. They took her slowly down to Camp 2, where they sheltered for four hours in a bivouac tent, administering hot fluid and medicines. The temperature was -35°C and wind gusts estimated at 80km/hour. Although Bielecki and Urubko had originally discussed the possibility of continuing up, in the slim hope that they might be able to do something for Mackiewicz, it was now blatantly obvious that the conditions, a bad forecast for the following days, and a very weak Revol, frostbitten in the hands and left foot, made it imperative that they try to get the Frenchwoman off the mountain alive.

Bielecki and Urubko belayed Revol down the steep Kinshofer Wall and then the couloir below, until all three reached the bottom of the face. From there Revol was able to walk to Camp 1, where, at 1:30 p.m., she was evacuated by helicopter. 📄 📷

— LINDSAY GRIFFIN, *WITH INFORMATION FROM ELIZABETH REVOL, RODOLPHE POPIER (HIMALAYAN DATABASE), ERIC VOLA, KRZYSZTOF WIELICKI, PIOTR PACKOWSKI, AND MAJ. GEN. MUHAMMAD KHALIL DAR*

MAIDON SAR (A.K.A. DARMYANI PEAK), EAST RIDGE FROM THE SOUTH

RUSTY WILLIS AND I left the United States on July 14, 2016, aiming for Shispare Sar (7,611m). After a week of travel we set up base camp at around 3,960m, alongside the lateral moraine of the Pasu Glacier. During reconnaissance we placed a high camp at the top of a small snow bowl on the north side of the glacier, hoping to access the upper glacier and thus reach Shispare. Two weeks into the trip, Rusty received news that his mother had been hospitalized, and he returned home. Now down to a team of one, I decided to climb a

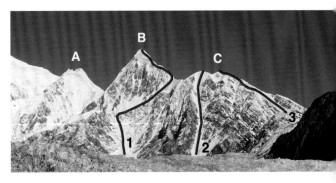

Looking northwest across the Pasu Glacier. (A) Noukarsich (6,498m). (B) Maidon Sar (6,085m). (C) Hiriz (5,550m). (1) 2016 route to Maidon Sar. (2) Southeast couloir of Hiriz (Peak 5,550m), climbed in 1992. (3) Spanish Route, continuing up the east ridge of Maidon Sar (1985). *Steve Su*

peak above our high camp that was designated 6,085m on our German map. Only later did I learn it had been climbed before.

On August 4, I spent the night at the high camp at a little over 5,000m. Snowstorms delayed my departure next day, but at 4 p.m., after the sun went behind the mountain, I set off up the glacier and climbed through a minor bergschrund and onto the main snow slope leading to the east ridge of Peak 6,085m. Once on the ridge, cornices forced me to climb on rock below, though the difficulties were no more than M4. Soon it was completely dark and my pace along the ridge slowed substantially. After some awkward climbing on steep, unconsolidated snow, I bellyflopped onto the summit ice cap and eventually found the top. It was a bit anticlimactic in the darkness, but after staring up at the starlit sky and seeing the occasional shooting star, I was rewarded. I would like to thank the Mugs Stump Award committee for supporting this trip.

Editor's note: Peak 6,085m, noted on the Polish map of the Batura Muztagh as Darmyani Peak ("Needle Peak," 6,085m), has had three known ascents, all by the east ridge, though each party reached that ridge by a substantially different route. The mountain was most likely first climbed in 1985 by Spanish climbers, who named it Maidon Sar. More information on all the ascents will be found at the AAJ website. 📄 📷

– STEVE SU, *AAC*

YAD SAR AND PEAK 5,855M

DUE TO WORK commitments, Steve Carratt, George Cave, Clay Conlon, and I could only afford three weeks away in August for our expedition to the Shimshal Valley. This was a risky plan, as the team would only spend a week at base camp and would be living above 4,400m after four

days. With the help of a fifth team member, local guide Karim Hayat, whom George had met in Yosemite on an AAC International Climbers' Meet, we found a number of unclimbed mountains between 5,800m and 6,000m, easily accessible from the Gunj-e Dur glacial system.

We took three days to walk from Shimshal to a base camp in the Gunj-e-Tang river valley, arriving on August 31. After three days of acclimatizing, advanced base camps were established below the First East and Second East Gunj-e Dur glaciers, from which two climbs were made.

From a 5,000m camp below the First East Gunj-e Dur Glacier, Karim, George, and I attempted the southeast face of Peak 6,200m (Polish Wala map) on September 5. Unfortunately, George had to descend from 5,500m due to altitude illness. Karim and I carried on to the summit ridge. This ridge is multi-topped, similar to the various summits along the crest of the Grandes Jorasses. We arrived at about the midpoint and climbed to the nearest summit, which we named Yad Sar (Remembrance Peak) and measured at 6,015m (36.60809°N, 75.58147°E). To the east, about 200m distant, the highest peak on the ridge appeared around 80m higher than us and was deemed unreachable given the current snowpack.

Our ascent route to Yad Sar, named Half Way House (900m, Scottish II/III), followed a wide, easy 300m gully in the center of the face to a more difficult hanging glacier about 500m high. We descended the same way, with eight rappels and some downclimbing.

[Top] Ross Davidson and Karim Hayat, dwarfed by a hanging glacier, at around mid-height on the southeast face of Yad Sar. *George Cave* [Bottom] Yad Sar above the First East Gunj-e Dur Glacier and the route Half Way House on the southeast face. The highest point along the ridge is to the right (east). *Ross Davidson*

Clay and Steve focused their attention on a peak of 5,855m (36.54698°N, 75.64537°E) above the Second East Gunj-e Dur Glacier, which they summited on September 4. The pair climbed the west ridge (1,000m above camp, PD) in seven hours. They crossed the summit and descended the northwest flank and glacier, regaining the tent shortly before nightfall. [*This seems to be the same as Peak 5,836m, attempted from the Shuijerab Glacier by Japanese climbers in 2002; they retreated 15m from the top, calling the peak Halshamas Sar.*]

We would like to thank the Austrian Alpine Club, British Mountaineering Council, Mount Everest Foundation, Alpine Club Fund, and Karabiner Club for financial support of this expedition. 📷

— ROSS DAVIDSON, *ALPINE CLUB, U.K.*

PEAKS AROUND BOESAM PASS

JAMES LAWSON, WILL Smith, and I initially planned to visit the Yashkuk-Yaz Glacier in northwest Gilgit-Baltistan, near the Afghan border. Unfortunately, our permit was denied at the last minute. Inspired by a report from Pete Thompson in *AAJ 2016*, we subsequently planned to visit the Virjerab Glacier and attempt unclimbed Khurdopin Sar (6,310m). However, on arrival in Shimshal we found that during the previous months the Khurdopin Glacier had advanced by a kilometer, preventing all access to the Virjerab.

Needing a new objective in the Shimshal Valley, we were informed of an area of unclimbed peaks a little under 6,000m, close to Boesam Pass (ca 5,000m), north of Shimshal village. We arranged porters from Shimshal and reached base camp, southwest of the pass, on our third day of trekking. Over the next three and a half weeks, we completed what we believe to be four first ascents.

Having set up a high camp on the pass, we climbed the northwest face of the snowy 5,700m peak at 36.53440°N, 75.36591°E in order to acclimatize (PD).

Several days later, we attempted Koh-e-Brobar (6,008m), which had been summited in 2001 by Samina Baig and her brother Mirza Ali, although we were not aware of this at the time. We headed up the long, sweeping ridge that runs northeast then north-northwest to the summit, a different route than Samina and Mirza's. We abandoned the climb at a shoulder due to poor snow conditions.

The northwest face of Peak 5,503m rising above Boesam Pass. In the background are peaks beyond Shimshal Pass. *Will Smith*

We next climbed the 5,503m peak immediately southeast of the pass, summiting via the 500m northwest face (AD). The snow was extremely poor in parts, with sections of chest-deep powder. We turned back about 3m below the true summit at an extremely unstable tower of choss.

After a frustrating period tent-bound in poor weather, we set a camp in a basin to the north, from which we climbed the 5,930m peak at 36.56241°N, 75.31744°E by its south ridge (AD). We named this Imtiaz Sar after our excellent guide.

We were then forced to remain in base camp for almost a week, as more heavy snow set in. When this eventually cleared, we established another camp in one of the valleys on the north side of the pass (west of Koh-e-Brobar). From here we climbed the 5,970m peak (36.572875°N, 75.319553°E) by its impressive east ridge, passing a number of rocky pinnacles (AD). The instability of the snowpack following recent snowfall was made very clear during our descent, with significant slab avalanches from the crest of the ridge. We named this peak Arman Sar, after our equally excellent cook.

The following day, Will and I attempted the ca 6,000m peak to the north of Arman Sar, but turned back on the east ridge at 5,700m due to poor snow conditions and warming temperatures. 📗 📷

— TIM SEERS, *U.K.*

Machu's southwest face with the west ridge on the left. The line atttempted in 2017 is off-picture to the left. *Peter Thompson*

MACHU, SOUTHWEST RIDGE, ATTEMPT

IN JUNE, AIDEN Laffey and I attempted Machu (6,630m, 36.234967°N, 75.051874°E) in the Hispar Valley. As far as I could ascertain from Internet research and from talking to the locals, it had not been climbed or attempted before.

We hired porters in Hispar village. In one day we crossed the Hispar River by a single-cable bridge and climbed steeply to the northeast for 1,400m to some shepherd huts at 4,442m in the Machu Valley. We then made two carries to set up an advance base camp on the Machu Glacier at 4,760m. Our aim was to climb the southwest ridge of Machu to a col and then continue up the west ridge to the summit. We climbed a 700m couloir to reach the southwest ridge at 5,530m, but heavy snowfall forced a retreat. We returned and climbed to 5,650m, where we found our way blocked by a rock peak with difficult ground to circumvent it. We again retreated. It appeared that another couloir farther up the Machu Glacier would lead to the southwest ridge beyond the rock peak. Unfortunately, this couloir did not look safe in the prevailing conditions.

— PETER THOMPSON, *ALPINE CLUB, U.K.*

EMILY PEAK, SOUTH FACE, LA VENGEANCE DE ROBÎNE

IN MAY AND June, a friend and I traveled to Pakistan to attempt virgin Pumari Chhish East (6,850m), above the Yutmaru Glacier. During acclimatization my friend fell sick, so I decided to attempt an easier peak alone. Leaving base camp on the north side of the Hispar Glacier on June 8, I climbed around 1,000m of easy terrain (mostly snow slopes up to 50°) and camped for the night at approximately 5,000m, below the main south face of a peak I thought at the time was unclimbed. [*See note below.*] The next day I climbed to the summit and back in 10 hours. The hardest part was the first 400m, a gully with sections of AI4 and M4. I self-belayed three pitches. Above, snow slopes up to 50° and moderate mixed climbing led to the top, where my altimeter read around 6,000m, and from there I descended easy snow slopes well to the left of my route. I named the route La Vengeance de Robîne (AI4 M4). 📷

— SYMON WELFRINGER, *FRANCE*

HISTORY AND ELEVATION OF EMILY PEAK: *This is the mountain soloed in 2008 by Rufus Duits and named Emily Peak (AAJ 2009). Duits soloed the southwest face (AD- 60°). The Jerzy Wala (Polish) map gives a summit elevation of 5,684m, and the Russian map shows 5,687m. Welfringer's altimeter watch suggested an elevation of 5,950–6,050m. An analysis of Duits' photos of nearby mountains from the summit, and of Emily Peak from an attempt on Hispar Sar, shows the peak is somewhat higher than the map elevations—perhaps around 5,850m, though not 6,000m.*

On a narrow, corniced section of the north ridge of Latok I during the 2017 Russian attempt. Each afternoon, the team spent three to four hours excavating a bivouac site. *Alexander Gukov*

NEAR MISS ON LATOK I
FIFTEEN DAYS ON THE NOTORIOUS NORTH RIDGE

BY ALEXANDER GUKOV

WE WOULD HAVE done it, I'm certain, but the weather was constantly against us. Our sirdar told us he couldn't remember such weather in August. It snowed all but the first two days of our 15-day attempt on the north ridge of Latok I (7,145m), which soars 2,400m above the Choktoi Glacier.

Anton Kashevnik, Valery Shamalo, and I arrived at base camp on August 6. During the approach an incident occurred that would play a significant part in the outcome of the expedition. While crossing a stream, Valery slipped and fell head-first into the water, eventually leading to a cough that would plague him during the climb. The rope came in handy, and Anton dragged him out a few meters downstream.

Over the next few days, we tried to acclimatize on an unnamed 6,000m peak, though we were all quite well acclimatized already—Valery from Elbrus, Anton from Trango, and myself from Denali. Snowfall kept us at base camp until the 17th, when things started to improve and a forecast predicted 10 days of fine weather.

We started up the couloir on the left side of the lower rock pillar of the north ridge, but on that day managed only 10 pitches. On the 18th we decided to cross onto the right side of the ridge. It looked like three or four easy pitches to reach the crest, but it turned out to be six, and two of these required aid. We bivouacked in a notch without erecting our tent. Next day we climbed the right flank of the ridge in worsening weather, aiming for a good campsite that Valery believed we would find atop a serac. *[Shamalo had attempted this route in 2012 with Slava Ivanov, Ruslan Kirichenko, and Oleg Koltunov, reaching about 6,400m.]* We climbed 10 pitches, realized we weren't going to make it, cut up to the crest, and spent many hours excavating a bivy site, eventually getting to sleep at 3 a.m.

On August 20 it snowed all day and we stayed put, enjoying the rest after the previous day's exertions. Next day we rappelled back to the right flank and started working up ice. Imagine our surprise on reaching the end of this section to find no serac. "It must have fallen off," Valery said. On the 22nd, Anton spent three hours working through the first 50m pitch with a shovel. A few pitches higher and it was time to look for another campsite, but it took three more hours until we reached a suitable spot.

Next morning brought serious work, overcoming a wall with horrendous, sometimes vertical ice. After five pitches we camped atop a slim serac, both sides of the tent hanging into the abyss. On the 24th we managed another six pitches until we reached a cave. Even though water dripped on us all night and our sleeping bags had long ago morphed into soggy lumps, there was a lot of space to stretch out. It snowed all the following morning, making us reluctant to leave. However, by lunchtime Anton and I decided to put up a few pitches, while Valery enlarged the cave for a second night. In the end we only managed two more leads.

On the 26th we climbed another four pitches on snow, ice, and verglassed slabs. While Anton was climbing the last pitch, I excavated a cave and we passed a relatively comfortable night. On the 27th it was still snowing and we only climbed four pitches. We couldn't see the top and were tired of guessing how far there was to go.

August 28 was our 12th day on the face. (We think the route could be climbed in 10 days, but no less. We had to spend three to four hours on most days chopping out tent platforms.) We had only a little porridge and the tail end of a gas cylinder remaining. Almost every day we got a forecast by phone that gave us hope it might become sunny and warm. But it continued to snow.

That day Anton climbed one and a half pitches up the vertical snow wall of a serac—how he climbed it I will never understand. After I jumared to him, I could see a large serac, above which, we knew, a terrace led to the west ridge. Relative to what we had done, it was not far— maybe three days to the summit in good weather. We were at around 6,700m. But we didn't want to die of hunger and fatigue. Also, Valery had developed a bad cough due to his immersion in the stream. Every day his health was getting worse—we had to go down.

On the morning of the 29th, we started the first of what we estimated would be around 40 rappels. Early that day I made a mistake. I was belaying Valery while he rappelled, and suddenly I heard a shout that I interpreted as him having reached an anchor. I clove-hitched the belay rope to my anchor and began to set up my own rappel. The belay rope suddenly went very tight. There was shouting and I realized that Valery had not made the anchor but was in fact dangling over an overhang. He couldn't get his weight off the rope; I couldn't release the clove hitch. In order to extricate himself from this situation, he cut the backup belay rope. The resulting jerk tore his pack from his shoulders, taking with it our tent and sleeping bags.

We made 14 rappels that day and spent the night with no bags, sheltering under a small hammock we had brought along to supplement our bivouacs. Unfortunately, we didn't take off our boots, nor change our wet socks, and this almost certainly led to the start of the frostbite suffered by Anton and Valery. All our gas was now gone.

On the 30th we continued our descent, and at 5 a.m. on the 31st we made it to the glacier:

I counted a total of 42 rappels, so I had nearly been right. We had planned to descend the south side of Latok if successful, and five days before we estimated we would be starting our descent, we had phoned our sirdar and asked him to call the porters, break camp, and head down to Askole with everything. Maybe I entered the wrong number, because he never got the message. We were overjoyed to see our camp still in place.

Getting to it was another matter. We were amazed by the amount of new snow on the glacier. In a normal state, we would have reached camp in a couple of hours. Instead it took eight hours, even after we abandoned all our gear. It was now clear Valery had serious frostbite to both fingers and toes, and Anton also had frostbitten feet. Valery also had a bad lung infection. But we felt we were heroes. We didn't need helicopters—we would walk out.

We all tried walking the next day, but Anton could not continue for long; from then on he was carried by a horse. Valery held out well at first, but on the second day he too found he couldn't walk; his pneumonia was progressing quickly. With some difficulty we found another horse, and with two dexamethasone pills he made it to civilization.

[Top] The magnificent and still unclimbed north ridge of Latok I (7,145 meters) from the Choktoi Glacier, showing the 2017 Russian attempt and high point, about 450 meters below the top. Only one team has gotten higher: the American expedition in 1978. [Bottom] Valery Shamalo on the north ridge. Shamalo had tried the same route in 2012, reaching 6,400 meters. This time he got 300 meters higher but paid a high price, losing all his toes and parts of some fingers to frostbite. *Alexander Gukov*

In the end, Anton lost a few toes. Valery eventually recovered from pneumonia but lost all his toes and parts of some of his fingers. Though we didn't summit, I'm confident I have a good chance next time, *inshallah*.

EDITOR'S NOTE: *There have been more than two dozen attempts on the north ridge of Latok I. The Russian attempt, which reached 6,700m, is believed to be the highest point attained since the first attempt, by four Americans, in 1978. They reached about 7,000m, approximately 150m below the summit, before storm and illness forced a retreat. This report was supplied by Elena Dmitrenko, Risk.ru, and translated by Emily Laskin.* 📷

The southwest side of Trango Tower (6,250m), seen from Uli Biaho Tower, showing Claire de Lune with the Russian direct start. (Other routes not shown.) The dashed line is the approach gully climbed during the first ascent of the tower in 1976. This gully was also used by the Swiss on Claire de Lune (1999). The section below the junction of the two lines is the new Russian start. The large peak on the left is Biale (6,772m), while the two pyramids, one behind the other on the right, are Muztagh Tower (7,284m) and K2 (8,611m). *Andrej Grmovsek*

TRANGO TOWER, SOUTHWEST FACE, CLAIRE DE LUNE WITH NEW START

ALEXEI KUROCHKIN, KONSTANTIN Markevitch, and Dmitry Skotnikov (all from Russia) established a direct start to the Swiss route Claire de Lune on the southwest face of Trango Tower (6,250m), adding around 600m of difficult climbing.

In 1999, Gabriel Besson, Claude-Alain Gaillan, David Maret, and Fréderic Roux (Switzerland) climbed their new route, Claire de Lune, on the southwest face: It follows the gully system taken by the tower's original ascensionists in 1976, then continues directly via the left side of a prominent gray rock scar. The 1,200m line, of which around 900m were new, was graded 6b A3.

The three Russians climbed the usual dangerous approach gully (ca 1,200m) for Trango Tower and established an advanced base below the wall. Taking a portaledge, they then climbed the front face of the tower from its base, to the right of the upper gully followed by earlier routes. There were several pitches of A3, many skyhook moves, and often-poor natural protection. This section of new ground involved around 600m of climbing (400–450m of vertical), and due to the weaving line it was often harder for the followers, with loads, than for the leader.

The Russians' original intention had been to force a new line via the right side of the huge gray scar above their start, but having reached Claire de Lune they realized that it would be far better to continue on the beautiful and logical existing line. The three spent a total of six and a half days reaching the summit and a further one and a half days in descent, using the original gully system. The overall grade was Russian 6A 6c A3+. 📷

— LINDSAY GRIFFIN, *WITH INFORMATION FROM ELENA DMITRENKO, RISK.RU*

ULI BIAHO GALLERY, MOUNTAIN MEDICINE AND SANDWASSER & KASNUDELN

IN THE SUMMER of 2016, Johannes Steidl and Vittorio Messini (Italy) climbed two new routes on Uli Biaho Gallery during an impressive trip in which they also climbed Great Trango and Trango Tower and attempted Uli Biaho, among other ascents. The new climbs on the southeast side of Uli Biaho Gallery are Mountain Medicine (400m, 6c C2) and Sandwasser & Kasnudeln (400m, 7a+). Details and photos are at the AAJ website. 📄 📷

— VITTORIO MESSINI, *ITALY*

GREAT TRANGO TOWER, NORTHWEST FACE AND SOUTHWEST RIDGE, INSHALLAH (NOT TO SUMMIT)

ANTON KASHEVNIK, YEGOR Suzdaltsev, and Ivan Temerev (all from Russia) climbed some new ground on the northwest face of Great Trango Tower in July. They started on the left-hand pillar and eventually slanted right, crossing several existing routes, to climb the wall parallel to and left of the upper part of Bushido (Raganowicz-Tomaszewski, 2013). They joined the latter at the point where it exits onto the southwest ridge, then continued up the 2004 Cordes-Wharton Route (Azeem Ridge). After a total of 11 days, they reached a point 200m from the south summit, where lack of time and food forced them to give up.

The team estimates the vertical interval of their line to be more than 1,500m, with a climbing distance of around 2,000m. They have given their partial new route the name of Inshallah (6b+ A4). A little later, Kashevnik joined Alexander Gukov and Valery Shamalo for an epic attempt on Latok I (*see earlier story in this section*). 📄 📷

— LINDSAY GRIFFIN, WITH INFORMATION FROM ELENA DMITRENKO, RISK.RU

KHALKHAL WEST, SOUTHWEST RIDGE; PRAQPA RI, SOUTHEAST TOP, EAST-SOUTHEAST RIDGE

ON JUNE 13, Andres Bosch, Armando Montero, and I arrived in Pakistan with the intention of exploring virgin peaks in the Khalkhal Valley, directly opposite Broad Peak. We knew Praqpa Ri was unclimbed, and there were three smaller peaks nearby.

From Broad Peak base camp, we reconnoitered the Khalkhal Valley to ascertain conditions on the glacier and find the best way to reach Khalkhal Pass (5,705m), at the foot of the southeast ridge of Praqpa Ri (7,156m), where we planned to establish a camp. We decided to attempt the higher of two summits southeast of the pass, which, according to Google Earth, was around 6,200m.

Returning to base, we planned for a four-day trip to the pass. During the two-day approach, we saw a nice snow and rock ridge leading directly to the summit of our peak from the southwest. We rested one day on the pass and then, at 3 a.m. on July 4, left our tent and descended back to the Khalkhal Glacier, from which we reached the start of the ridge at ca 5,300m. The first part of the route was mainly rock climbing up to UIAA IV. After 500m we put on crampons and climbed a snow ramp (45–60°) to a small col just 40m below the summit. A final pitch of 70° ice led to the snowy top, 12 hours after starting the ridge. Our GPS read 6,270m. Returning the way we'd come, we regained the glacier late at night and decided to keep going down to base camp, which we reached next morning. Our 1,000m route was graded D+ IV 45–70°.

Back home in Santiago, during discussions with Eberhard Jurgalski, we discovered this peak had been climbed on June 25, 1983, by Dutch climbers Ronald Naar and Gerard van Sprang. From a camp near the head of the Khalkhal Glacier, the two climbed the west flank of the northwest ridge to reach the crest and then followed it to the summit, with dangerous cornices near the top. They descended the southeast ridge (also corniced) and south face. They dubbed the summit Norit Peak, but this mountain and its lower eastern summit have long been labeled the Khalkhal Peaks, notably on Polish maps of the region. The most recent survey lists Khalkhal West at 6,250m and Khalkhal East (sometime referred to as Pastora Peak) at 6,206m.

After our climb of Khalkhal West, Armando returned to Chile, leaving Andres and I to attempt Praqpa Ri. With a good forecast, we headed back up to Camp 1 on the pass, arriving on

[Top] Khalkhal West (6,270m GPS) seen from Khalkhal Pass. The original Dutch route (1983) climbed onto the northwest ridge, facing the camera, from the right and followed the crest to the summit. The new Chilean route on the southwest ridge is marked. Khalkhal East is the lower summit immediately left, while the rocky summit to the right is Marble Peak. [Bottom] The Chilean route to the southeast top of Praqpa Ri (7,046m GPS), following the east-southeast ridge from Khalkhal Pass. The main summit is at far right. *Armando Montero*

July 12. At 4 a.m. on the 14th, we began climbing the east-southeast ridge, leading to Praqpa Ri's southeast top (7,026m on Polish maps; this is the same ridge attempted by Ralf Dujmovits and Nancy Hansen in 2016, *AAJ 2017*). After a short pitch of M3, we climbed 300m of snow (50–70°) with three 90° bergschrunds. Fortunately, we sometimes found ice under the snow, so it was possible to place screws. Above the snow, 300m of good ice at 60–70° led to a sharp, exposed ridge. Deep snow on this ridge made for slow progress. At 8 p.m. we camped in a nice spot beneath a large serac. That day we had belayed 10 pitches and simul-climbed the rest. The following day we rested and then set off for the summit at 11:30 p.m.

Before the expedition, our goal had been to traverse from the south summit to the main summit. However, after observing the upper ridge, the weather, and the long distance between the summits, we decided to focus on the southeast top. So, for our summit push, we left our tent and sleeping bags at Camp 2. The terrain above proved less technical, but the altitude and deep snow slowed progress. We first traversed left 50m and then climbed direct for 150m to a small plateau (possible campsite). After traversing left across this plateau, we climbed another ridge and then a long ramp of deep 50° snow to arrive on the southeast top at 10 a.m. on July 16. The GPS showed an altitude of 7,046m. The ridge leading toward the main peak was very sharp and corniced, and the higher peak was very far away; I think a more direct route will be the best way to reach the main summit.

In deteriorating weather we followed our footprints back to the tent. Bad visibility kept us in Camp 2 the whole next day, but the following morning a short window allowed us to escape, eventually reaching base camp on July 19. The 1,500m ascent to the previously unclimbed southeast top of Praqpa Ri was graded TD+ M3 50–90°. 📷

— ALEJANDRO MORA, *CHILE*

GASHERBRUM IV, EAST FACE ATTEMPT

THE EAST FACE of Gasherbrum IV (7,925m) appears to offer a relatively straight shot up snow gullies and occasional rock for 1,000m, and is known to have been tried in 1980 by Americans Craig McKibben and Steve Swenson, in 1993 by Yasushi Yamanoi (Japan), and in 1996 by a Korean team including Kim Chang-ho. Yamanoi did not get far above the floor of the 6,900m cwm separating Gasherbrum IV from III, while both the Americans and the Koreans were repelled low in the central gullies by "spindrift and compact rock." [*Kim Chang-ho and Lim Saeng-muk reported reaching about 7,400m before complete lack of protection forced them down; it seems likely their high point was 7,300m, the same as the 2017 expedition.*]

In early July, Marcos Costa (Brazil), Billy Pierson (USA), and I reached 7,300m on the face, finding 50° snow over slabs of unprotectable fractured marble. We turned around at a compact and obviously difficult marble slab that offered no protection or even any possibility of a belay. In a year with more winter snow, as seen in pictures we took in 2009, it might be possible to climb over some or all of the marble bands via unprotected snow.

A brief attempt on "Gasherbrum 4.5", a 6,950m peak along the ridge joining Gasherbrum IV to V, had to be stopped at 6,700m due to dangerous snow conditions. I would like to thank the Mount Everest Foundation, the British Mountaineering Council, and the Montane Alpine Club Climbing Fund for their generous support of the expedition. 🗄 📷

— **BRUCE NORMAND,** *SWITZERLAND*

KARAKORAM / MASHERBRUM RANGE

BEATRICE, SOUTHEAST FACE, THE EXCELLENT ADVENTURE, FREE ASCENT AND COMPLETION TO SUMMIT

RYO MASUMOTO AND Yusuke Sato traveled to the Charakusa Valley with the goal of free climbing a big wall in capsule style. Their attention was drawn to the sheer 750m southeast face of Beatrice (ca 5,800m) and to a single crack that rose from partway up the wall directly to the summit area. The pair started on August 1, with Sato aiding the first wet pitch before free climbing it. After another night at their advanced base on the glacier, the two jumared their fixed rope and climbed two more pitches, after which they discovered a bolt. This came as a bit of a shock, as they were unaware the line had been climbed.

In fact there were three existing routes on this wall, all thought to be unrepeated before 2017. In 1997 two British teams (Grant Farquar, Steve Meyers, and Mike "Twid" Turner, and Glenda Huxter, Kath Pyke, and Louise Thomas) climbed almost independent lines, sharing a common approach to the prominent snow patch 100m up. From there, the three women headed up left to create Hatija (VI E3 6a A3+), while the men continued directly up the continuous crack line to complete the Excellent Adventure (also VI E3 6a A3+). Both teams climbed to the top of the wall, but neither went to the summit. Two years later, Jimmy Chin, Evan Howe, and Doug Workman (USA) climbed a third route, farther to the right, which they named Wanderlust (VI 5.10+ A3). The Americans also skipped the summit, which was well guarded by snow-covered loose blocks. No team climbing the southeast face had reached the top of the peak.

[Top] **Yusuke Sato leading the overhanging crux pitch of the Excellent Adventure (20 pitches, 5.13a).** *Ryo Masumoto* [Bottom] **The southeast face of Beatrice (ca 5,800m). (1) Diaper Couloir (1988, first ascent of peak). (2) Hatija (1997). (3) The Excellent Adventure (1997, FFA 2017). (4) Wanderlust (1999).** *Marek Holecek*

On day four the two Japanese reached the large snow patch, where they established a portaledge camp. That day they climbed and cleaned two difficult pitches in the main crack system above, largely on aid. Over the next two days the pair climbed through very steep ground, part free, part aid, to reach somewhat easier terrain, where about half a dozen more reasonable jamming pitches led to the summit ridge. They followed this ridge over poor rock and loose snow to the top.

During the descent to the portaledge, they spent more time cleaning various sections of the route. Then, over days seven and eight, they freed the remaining pitches, despite some sections of persistent wetness. Sato led the crux 10th pitch at 5.13a. 📄 📷

– LINDSAY GRIFFIN, *WITH INFORMATION FROM YUSUKE SATO AND HIROSHI HAGIWARA (EDITOR, ROCK AND SNOW), JAPAN*

KARAKORAM / TAGAS MOUNTAINS

KONDUS VALLEY ATTEMPTS; DEOSAI MOUNTAINS, PEAK NIC, GOOD, NO GOOD

AFTER MONTHS OF waiting—and in the end only four weeks before we were due to leave Italy—Federica Mingolla, Simone Pedeferri, and I received a permit to climb in the Kondus Valley. [*Editor's note: The Kondus Glacier and Saltoro Mountains were put off-limits to non-military activities after 9/11. One year earlier, four Americans had climbed a prominent buttress (Tahir Tower) above Karmanding, a village at the entrance to the Kondus Valley. In 2016, a group of French climbers managed to obtain a permit to climb in the Kondus, but were stopped at Karmanding due to military exercises further up the valley; they turned their attention to the nearby Lachit Valley.*] We flew to Skardu, and after a long day's drive, negotiating many checkpoints, arrived at Khorkondus village, a little beyond Karmanding and one hour's walk below the start of the Sherpi Glacier. There we made a five-star base camp in a small building with adjacent hot springs.

A reconnaissance showed what appeared to be many exciting possibilities, and we chose a 1,200m rock wall close to base camp as a "warm-up route." However, contrary to appearance, the granite was sandy and the cracks choked with vegetation. After 400m we realized there was no chance of success and descended. We tried a shorter line elsewhere, but the result was the same. These walls lie between 4,000m and 5,000m, and we soon realized that every wall and spire in the area had the same rock, except perhaps two higher objectives, finishing at around 6,000m. [*The 2000 American team reported a mix of good and bad rock on Tahir Tower.*]

With only 10 days left, we decided to take the risk of moving to a new area. The Kiris Valley (on some maps the Shigarthang Lungma) is accessed from the Gilgit to Skardu road, a short distance from Skardu, and is on the eastern fringes of the Deosai Mountains. We may have been the first Westerners to venture into this valley, and certainly the first to climb there. We found a south-facing 800m wall at 35°19'27"N, 75°19'E; it begins at 4,100m and is composed of three tiers.

We established base camp at 3,700m, and over three days, July 14–16, climbed Good, No Good to the summit, using neither pegs nor bolts. A walk-off ledge above the first pillar allowed us to return to base camp each day. (The route name came from a repeated question by our cook about our activities.) In all, there were 16 pitches with difficulties to 7b (6b obl) A2. When we arrived at the 4,900m summit, we found it to be a large, grassy plateau, good enough for a picnic. Hence we called the mountain Peak Nic. We descended easily along the west ridge and down a couloir to base camp as our perfect three-day weather window came to an end. 📄 📷 🔍

– LUCA SCHIERA, *RAGNI DI LECCO, ITALY*

Looking over the K6 Glacier from the upper section of Ghiacciaio Marta to spectacular rock towers and the higher summits of (A) Hassin Peak (approximately 6,300m, climbed from the far side in 2011 by Kyle Dempster and Hayden Kennedy). (B) K7 (6,934m). (C) Link Sar West (6,938m, climbed in 2015 by Jon Griffith and Andy Houseman). (D) Unclimbed Link Sar (7,041m), with the southeast face pointing toward the camera. The northeast face, attempted in 2017, is out of view around to the right. *Marcello Sanguineti*

KONDUS GLACIER: LINK SAR, ATTEMPT, FIOST BRAKK, PUNTA CITTÀ DI BIELLA, AND OTHER ASCENTS

In 1979 a Japanese expedition made the first attempt on Link Sar (7,041m) from the Kondus Valley. After a long period of closure due to the Siachen Conflict, the Kondus Glacier area was re-opened in 2000, and the following year an American expedition (Swenson, et al) explored lines on the southeast, east, and north sides of Link Sar. After 9/11, the area was closed again and no one visited these sides of Link Sar for the next 16 years. [*Beginning in 2012 Jon Griffith (U.K.) made four attempts in successive years to climb the mountain from the Charakusa Valley to the west, eventually reaching the top of Link Sar West (6,938m) in 2015 with Andy Houseman.*]

Our primarily Italian team left Skardu on July 31 and drove to a provisional base camp at 3,400m on the east bank of the Kondus Glacier, just below the point where the Kaberi Glacier comes in from the left. Landslides on the road prevented us from driving further, and before this, several military checkposts had been difficult to negotiate.

From here Tom Ballard (U.K.), Michele Focchi, and Daniele Nardi began their acclimatization by spending two days completing a new rock route, Welcome to the Jungle (950m, UIAA VI+ A0), on a formation they named Scimitara Rossa (4,400m). Above their finish lay a really big wall, around 1,000m high, rising to a summit of around 5,600m that they dubbed Alison Peak.

In the meantime, Gian Luca Cavalli and I carried loads to a camp below the southeast face of Link Sar, the aspect attempted to around 6,000m by the Japanese. After looking at the face and talking with the Americans Steve Swenson, Chris Wright, and Graham Zimmerman, who had arrived a few weeks previously with the same objective, Gian Luca, Michele, and I decided we didn't have enough time to make a serious attempt on Link Sar; Tom and Daniele also decided against this aspect of Link Sar and focused on the northeast face instead. We moved base camp up to 3,600m, on the west side of the Kondus Glacier, directly below the east side of Link Sar.

Gian Luca, Michele, and I opted to explore an unnamed glacier (which we dubbed Ghiacciaio Marta) immediately south of the K6 Glacier, and in mid-August, with the help of porters, established a high camp at around 4,800m. We spent eight days there and climbed two new routes.

We first concentrated on a subsummit (Fiost Brakk, 5,850m, "Friendship Peak" in Balti) of a higher peak we named Black Rock Brakk (ca 6,150m). At 9 p.m. on August 17 we walked one

[Top] Panorama looking northeast to east over the Saltoro Range from Ghiacciaio Marta. (A) Baltoro Kangri (7,300m). (B) Sia Kangri (7,424m). (C) Mt. Hardinge (Sia Kangri South, 7,075m). (D) Silver Throne (6,630m). (E) Ghent (7,401m). (F) Sherpi Kangri (7,380m). *Gian Luca Cavalli* [Bottom] Gian Luca Cavalli on Via delle Poiane with Black Rock Brakk, Mattia Brakk, Elisa Brakk, and Fiost Brakk (the lower summit, climbed in 2017) behind. *Marcello Sanguineti*

hour from our camp to the bottom of a rock pillar, climbed several pitches up to UIAA VII+, then moved left onto a hanging glacier. Large seracs required strenuous climbing on thin icy ridges. Deep snow then slowed progress, and the final wall provided several technical pitches on poor ice that was difficult to protect. We reached the summit at 1 a.m. on the 19th after 27 hours of continuous climbing. After a bivouac with no overnight gear, we traversed sharp ridges, often à cheval, to another rock summit, from which we descended in 20 rappels. Sixteen hours after leaving the bivouac we were back in camp.

Our route was Amman in Kashmir (950m, 1,300m of climbing, ED+ 6b AI6 X; amman means "peace"). High above Fiost Brakk lie two unclimbed icy summits that we named Elisa Brakk and Mattia Brakk; they are estimated to be between 6,200m and 6,300m.

On the morning of the 21st we left early and climbed a rock spire on the north side of the glacier, below our camp. We named our route Via delle Poiane (450m, TD+ 6b+) and the summit Punta Città di Biella (approximately 5,505m). As the weather was deteriorating, we returned to base camp the following day. In the meantime, Daniele and Tom had attempted Link Sar, as reported below, and Kate Ballard (U.K.) and Cuan Coetzee (South Africa) explored the lower Kaberi Glacier and climbed the foresummit of an easy peak of around 5,500m they called Mt. Ulu (Owl). [*Many photos of this exceptional area will be found at the AAJ website.*]

— MARCELLO SANGUINETI, *CAAI, ITALY*

E   F

LINK SAR NORTHEAST FACE ATTEMPT: From our Camp 1 on the Kondus Glacier at 4,050m, directly opposite the mountain, Tom and I decided to attempt the northeast aspect of Link Sar via what we dubbed the Utopia Glacier. We climbed a wide glaciated couloir behind a prominent rock spire to reach Camp 2, at 5,200m on a snow spur. During the night, a large serac collapsed and swept the couloir.

The following morning we left for Camp 3. The sun was harsh, so we decided to leave late, hoping for some protection from clouds. The forecast was good for some days, but looking east toward the big peaks of Saltoro Kangri and Sherpi Kangri, I could see spiral-formation clouds building on their summits. In two hours it was snowing. We climbed around to the right of the first large rock tower on the spur above, where we found the best climbing of the day: 70° ice leading to fine mixed terrain. We reached Camp 3 (5,800m) at midnight. To this point we had climbed 1,700m of the 3,000m face. The section from Camp 1 to 2 averages 55°, with some vertical sections and objective danger from avalanches and serac fall; from Camp 2 to 3 there had been 14 pitches with difficulties up to WI5 M5.

We decided to rest one day at Camp 3 and soon realized the forecast had been very wrong: It snowed for three days, and on the morning of the fourth we started down. Before we reached Camp 2 a large avalanche came over the rock spur above. For a moment I thought it was all over, but after a little more than a minute the force died away, leaving me to clean up and get warm again. At Camp 2 we opted to wait for the coldest hours of the night before descending the couloir below.

This expedition was a crazy experience with exceptional companions. You can get the best out of yourself when you know you have your back covered by people on whom you can count.
– DANIELE NARDI, *ITALY*

LINK SAR, EAST FACE, ATTEMPT

STEVE SWENSON, CHRIS Wright, and I spent the summer close to the junction of the Kaberi and Kondus glaciers, near the border with India. While ultimately unsuccessful in our goal of climbing the east face of Link Sar (7,041m), due to bad weather, hard climbing, and complex route-finding on a dangerous face, the trip was amazing. The peaks near the Actual Ground Position Line between India and Pakistan (many of which remain closed) offer incredible potential. Huge thanks to the Mazamas, Mount Everest Foundation, Mugs Stump Award, and New Zealand Alpine Club for their support.

– GRAHAM ZIMMERMAN, *AAC, USA/NEW ZEALAND*

INDIA

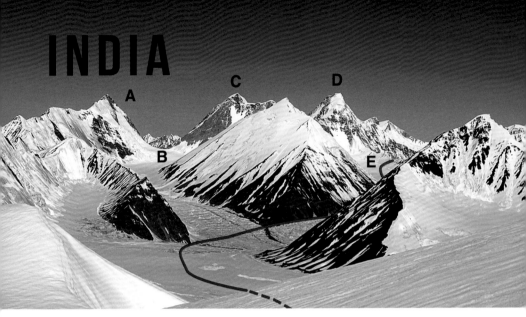

Looking northwest down the Sagtogpa Glacier to the junction between the East Phunangma Glacier (left) and South Argan Glacier. A portion of the route taken by the 2017 Indian expedition is shown. (A) Karpo Kangri (6,535m). (B) Konto La. (C) Argan Kangri II (6,640m). (D) Argan Kangri (6,789m). (E) Argan La, the crossing of which led to the North Argan Glacier. *Divyesh Muni*

A GRAND TRAVERSE
EXPLORATION AND A FIRST ASCENT IN THE EAST KARAKORAM

BY DIVYESH MUNI, *HIMALAYAN CLUB, INDIA*

WHEN OUR SIX-MEMBER team set out from Rongdo, a quaint village in Ladakh, we had little idea of our final destination. Our plan was to start trekking at the southernmost village in the Nubra Valley and work our way as far north as possible along the main axis of the mountains to the east of the valley. As the Dalai Lama was scheduled for a weeklong visit to the Nubra, it was impossible to hire any help, whether human or animal. However, the ever-efficient Rimo Expeditions solved the problem by arranging for a dozen horses to be transported by truck from Leh to Rongdo.

The group consisted of Sonali Bhatia, Huzefa Electricwalla, Rajesh Gadgil, Vineeta Muni, Ashish Prabhu, and myself, accompanied by Aditya Kulkarni, a cinematographer, with support from Pasang Bhote, Pemba Bhutia, Sanjay Thakur, and Sunil Thakur. We initially trekked up the Rongdo Lungpa, and after four days established base camp at 5,000m, past a lone shepherd's hut and up steep residual moraine of the Sagtogpa Glacier. From here we explored a route that would cross a high pass to the East Phunangma Glacier. An advanced base was established at 5,500m, and a second camp on the pass itself, which we named the Rongdo La, at 5,800m.

Unfortunately, while ascending to the pass, I slipped on loose rock and was knocked unconscious. Internal bleeding left a sizable bump, and as the blood settled toward my left eye, I began to look like a character out of a horror movie. The injury required that I travel back to Leh to consult with a doctor, who reluctantly let me return to the expedition. We all were back at base camp within a week

After regaining high camp on the Rongdo La, on August 1 we left at 6:30 a.m. and made our way to the base of a small peak to the northeast. A short, steep snow climb put us on the

southwest ridge, and the easy-angled crest led us to the summit. It was 10 a.m. and we named our first ascent Nga Kangri (Ladakhi for "Snow Peak Five," 6,165m). This peak lies on the watershed with the Central and Western Sagtogpa glaciers that flow east to the Ryong Kharu Valley, and is a little to the north of Sagtogpa Kangri (6,305m), climbed in 2015 (*AAJ 2016*).

We now set off to the north, and a gradual descent brought us to a camp at 5,628m. Next day we were at the junction of the East Phunangma and South Argan glaciers. After several hours of searching, we finally found a safe route to access the South Argan Glacier through a huge icefall. Above this the glacier flattened, and in five hours we were pitching tents at 5,777m, below the high pass that would allow us to cross the ridgeline east of Argan Kangri (6,789m). On August 6 we made the first crossing of the Argan La (5,950m) via a 200m climb, a traverse of a narrow ridge, and a 100m descent to reach the North Argan Glacier.

[Top] Looking southeast from the upper section of the South Argan Glacier. The 2017 Indian expedition ascended from the Sagtogpa Glacier in the distance, in front of the conspicuous snow pyramid, Sagtogpa Kangri (6,305m), climbed from the far side in 2015. [Bottom] A precarious trail on the descent of the Sakang Lungpa, badly affected by floods in 2016. *Divyesh Muni*

While this glacier began descending gently, it turned into a high, broken, dangerous icefall that posed a route-finding challenge. Once through this, we made our way to the base of the South Shukpa Kunchang Glacier and ascended this more easily for two days through amazing landscape, with the formidable Saser Kangri II dominating the horizon. We then made the first crossing of the Zamoriyon La (5,860m) to reach the Zamoriyon Glacier, which we followed down to the Sakang Valley. This was an exhausting day, which ended with a steep, difficult, and boulder-strewn slope and a final river crossing to grassy meadows below the snout of the Sakang Glacier, where we camped at 4,859m.

After a few days of badly needed rest, we trekked to the head of the Sakang Lungpa Glacier, where we decided to end the expedition at a high point on the glacier below Plateau Peak (7,300m). We turned around and descended the Sakang Valley, which proved to be the sting in the tail: Much of the route was washed out by the previous year's heavy rain, and we had to cross large sections of exposed mountainside on a nonexistent trail. We finally reached Tigur in the Nubra Valley on August 18.

We had completed more than 100km of traverse across pristine glaciers, crossed three high passes (two new), and made the first ascent of Nga Kangri. We were satisfied at having pushed our limits—both physical and mental.

A superb map of this traverse will be found at the AAJ website.

EAST KARAKORAM

SUMUR GLACIER, VARIOUS ASCENTS

UNTIL RECENTLY, THERE has been little exploration by foreign mountaineers of the more remote areas of the East Karakoram. In 2016 we managed to obtain permission to visit the lower Rassa Glacier (*see AAJ 2017*). But with so much more to be explored, we decided to return in 2017 in order to attempt some of the unclimbed mountains approachable from the more northerly Sumur Glacier. Our hope was that we could traverse from there to the upper Rassa Glacier via the East Rassa Col, a high pass crossed in 2014 from south to north by Divyesh Muni's expedition (*AAJ 2015*). Failing this, we would attempt virgin peaks bordering the Sumur Glacier.

Sumur Kangri (5,991m), as seen from the southern arm of the Sumur Glacier. The first ascent generally followed the snowy right skyline (west-northwest) ridge. The northwest face of unclimbed Nya Kangri is behind. *Derek Buckle*

Once again we received permission to visit this area with only just enough time for visa applications to be processed. Five Alpine Club members—Drew Cook, Jamie Goodhart (who unfortunately had to leave the expedition early), Rafal Malczyk, Howard Pollitt, and I as leader—planned a five-week trip lasting from August 31 to October 7. At the village of Sumur in the Nubra Valley, we arranged porters for the arduous two-day trek to base camp at 5,160m by the Sumur lakes.

Subsequent exploration led to two high camps on the southerly arm of the Sumur Glacier: Camp 3 at 5,500m and Camp 4 at 5,743m.

On September 16 we made an attempt on Peak 5,991m, aborted due to unstable snow conditions. On the 18th, after post-holing badly up the easy-angled glacier from the higher camp, four of us reached the convergence of three ridges at the head of the glacier (6,068m), which, since this turned out not to be a distinct mountain, we named Deception Point. Disappointingly, we could see no realistic way to reach the upper Rassa Glacier from this area.

There was little more we could do from this glacial arm, so we refocused on the arm immediately north, where, on the 21st, we established Camp 5 at 5,680m. On the 25th, all four of us made the first ascent of the twin-headed peak at the head of the glacier via its south face. We first climbed the rock-capped south summit (6,071m, PD), then traversed to the slightly higher and snow-capped north summit (6,078m, 34º41.068'N, 77º47.543'E). We chose to call this Tsagtuk Kangri (Ladakhi for "Twin Snow Peak"). From the northern peak, we returned directly to Camp 5.

Before returning to base camp, we made an exploratory foray to the foot of the East Rassa Col to establish the viability of using this north-facing slope as an access point to the upper Rassa Glacier. However, heavy bouts of snowfall had made all north-facing slopes extremely prone to avalanche. We therefore returned to Camp 3 for a second attempt on Peak 5,991m (34º38.184'N, 77º45.866'E).

On September 29, Cook, Malczyk, and I climbed this peak via the steep west-northwest ridge at AD. The corniced summit offered fantastic views of unclimbed Nya Kangri (6,480m) and beyond. On account of its dominant position, we chose to name this peak Sumur Kangri.

We are indebted to the Mount Everest Foundation, the Montane Alpine Club Climbing Fund, and the Austrian Alpine Club (U.K.) for financial support. We also thank Rimo Expeditions, as without them our task would have been immeasurably harder. 📄 📷 🔍

— **DEREK BUCKLE**, *ALPINE CLUB, U.K.*

LADAKH

KANG YATZE III, EAST FACE, DESESPERADOS

On October 21, Paulo Roxo and Daniela Teixeira (Portugal) made the second known ascent of Kang Yatze III (6,300m) via a somewhat convoluted route on the east face. They named the climb Desesperados (600m, AI2 M3). From the top, they descended the upper section of the northeast ridge, the route climbed in 2015 for the first ascent of the peak (*AAJ 2016*), then cut down to the east to regain the upper glacier. The pair made attempts on two other mountains but were thwarted by conditions or weather. A full account appears at the AAJ website. 📄 📷

— **LINDSAY GRIFFIN**, *WITH INFORMATION FROM DANIELA TEIXEIRA*

KARNAK VALLEY, HANUMAN WALL, MONKEY BUSINESS

On September 4 and 5, Cosmin Andron and Cristina Pogacean (Romania) completed the 14-pitch rock route Monkey Business (6a+) on a limestone wall in the Karnak Gorge, south of the Kang Yatze massif. (The wall is at 33.591351°N, 77.473961°E.) The route started at around 4,200m and finished a couple of meters below the crest of a ridge at around 4,700m. The first half of the climb was said to be good, then the rock got progressively looser, and the last four pitches were anything but enjoyable. A full report is available at the AAJ website. The rock and ambience of this gorge were thought reminiscent of Morocco's Taghia Gorge—a hidden limestone area in country full of granite. This valley is also home to the 2007 Swiss route Samsara is Nirvana (650m, 7b), a bolted climb of 16 pitches that was repeated for the first time (by Indian climbers) in September. 📄 📷 🔍

— **LINDSAY GRIFFIN**, *WITH INFORMATION FROM COSMIN ANDRON*

ZANSKAR

LALUNG VALLEY, MAHALAYA

On September 20, Korak Sanyal and Spandan Sanyal (India) climbed a northwest-facing rock buttress in the Lalung Valley, southwest of the Kargil-Padum road, to create Mahalaya (550m, UIAA VI+). The route was climbed with natural gear, and both climbers freed every pitch. The buttress tops out at 4,800m on the northwest ridge of unnamed Peak 5,200m, but the Indian pair did not continue to the summit. A full report is available at the AAJ website. 📄 📷

— **LINDSAY GRIFFIN**

RUCHO, EAST FACE AND SOUTH RIDGE

IN EARLY 2010 the government of India opened 104 peaks in the Zanskar region. One of these was unnamed "Peak 6,000m," located above the west bank of the north Hagshu Nala. It is a little north of Lagan (5,750m), which was climbed in 2014 by a Slovenian team, prior to their ascent of the north face of Hagshu (*AAJ 2015*). It is also the eastern summit of a higher unnamed peak (6,019m on Russian map).

With Takaaki Furuhata, we flew to Leh on July 19. Next day we began our road journey via Kargil, over the Pensi La, to the village of Akshow. On the 23rd we walked south up the northern Hagshu Nala (a.k.a. Akshow Valley) for around three hours, using Google Earth printouts for maps, until we spotted the peak on the right. We established base camp (4,150m) at the foot of a grassy slope, just above the lateral moraine on the west side of the Hagshu Glacier. The peak looked nothing like its image on Google Earth—it appeared much steeper and more jagged.

Google Earth suggested that the best approach would be from the southeast, where a spur of moraine led directly onto the glacier. Two days later, on July 26, we established an advanced base on the rocky moraine alongside the glacier, and the next day inspected the east face of the peak, the proposed line of ascent. The following day, Furuhata and Yamanoi climbed to 5,500m on the south ridge, depositing some food and gear for their planned descent route.

At 1:30 a.m. on August 1, the two Japanese left advanced camp, crossed the glacier in 45 minutes, and began climbing the east face. It was a clear, cold night and progress was swift, the terrain consisting of mostly hard snow with occasional ice patches (70° maximum). By the time it was getting light, at 5:30 a.m., the two were on the south ridge.

Rucho (5,970m) and the upper section of the Japanese route on the east face and south ridge, the first ascent of the peak. *Yasushi Yamanoi*

The climbers had pinned their hopes on reaching this point in one full day, but now found themselves there at dawn with a whole day in front of them. A traverse right on exposed 70° snow led to a bottleneck where the snow was thin and the rock loose. Above this obstacle, six pitches of snow climbing led to a final 20m of loose rock and the summit (5,970m GPS). It was 9:11 a.m., about 7.5 hours since they'd left advanced base. Their ascent was rated TD.

After retracing their route as far as the top of the east face, they continued down the south ridge. They debated stopping for the night—they were carrying a tent and food for three days—but time was on their side, so they continued down to advanced base, arriving at 4:30 p.m. Their decision had been sound: During dinner, clouds began to build, and it subsequently rained all night.

After much discussion the two have proposed naming the peak Rucho, which means "horns" in both local dialect and Ladakhi. Yamanoi was particularly happy with the success. In 2002 he lost many fingers to frostbite during a difficult climb and descent of Gyachung Kang (7,985m, Nepal). Since then he has put up new routes in China, Greenland, and Peru. But success in the Himalaya had eluded him until now. 📷 🔍

– YASUSHI YAMANOI, *JAPAN,* AND SARTAJ GHUMAN (LIAISON OFFICER), *INDIA*

RANGTIK TOKPO: CHAKDOR RI, JAMYANG RI, AND OTHER ASCENTS

Anastasija Davidova and I had visited the valley of Rangtik Tokpo in 2016, and I decided to return in 2017 with Matjaz Dusic and Tomaz Zerovnik. This valley and surrounding areas to the south of the Doda River are infrequently visited by mountaineers. The summits rise to around 6,400m, but the ridges and faces are roughly the same scale as those of the Alps, and there is great potential for first ascents at all grades. Approaches from villages along the Kargil-Padum road are not long; most mountains can be reached in one day. We established a base camp in the Rangtik Valley at 4,926m (33°28'30"N, 76°45'13"E). From here we made three first ascents.

Treasure of Zanskar on the southeast ridge of Chakdor Ri (6,193m), as seen from Remalaye. The 2017 route (750m, ED+) was the first ascent of the peak. *Anastasija Davidova*

In 2016 Anastasija and I made the first ascent of Remalaye West (6,266m, *see AAJ 2017*), but it was obvious the east summit (H5 on the 2012 Sakamoto map) was higher. Matjaz, Tomaz, and I decided to make this our acclimatization climb.

We left base camp on July 21 and followed our 2016 route to 5,900m, where we bivouacked. Next day we continued toward the west summit until we reached around 6,000m, where we headed right over good ledges to reach a prominent couloir on the southeast face leading directly toward the summit. We reached the east ridge just below the top via a section of M5+, which we realized later could have been avoided. The main summit was 6,278m and our route D+. We descended to our bivouac with a few rappels, spent a second night there, and went down to base camp on the 23rd.

According to locals, the handsome peak at the head of the valley is called Chakdor Ri (6,193m, H8 on the Sakamoto map). After spending a night at a camp on the upper glacier at 5,400m, the next morning, July 31, we started up a 55° snow/ice ramp that seemed to give logical access to the southeast ridge. After 100m we continued in rock shoes. We reached a bivouac at 5,850m, having spent an enjoyable time climbing warm granite to UIAA V+.

Next day we continued up the right side of the ridge on good granite with difficulties from V+ to VII-, using nuts, cams, and a few pitons. Later in the day, we moved to the sunny left side of the ridge, and finally reached the summit from the north. At that point a small electrical storm moved in, and within 10 minutes it was snowing. We didn't hang around, and after seven rappels were back at our bivouac. The following day, through a little rain and snow, we made it back to base camp. We named the route Treasure of Zanskar (750m, ED+ VII- 55°). The entire route was led free, and there was no jumaring, fixed ropes, or bolts, but we left five pitons in place. The summit ridge is horizontal and sharp but easy to climb. Given the weather conditions, we are not completely sure we stood on the highest point.

A rock spire visible from the Padum road guards the entrance to the upper Rangtik Tokpo. In 2016 locals told us it was called Phobrang. However, there is already a Phobrang

Jamyang Ri (5,800m) from the west. (1) Inshallah, Maybe, to the top of Torre Fanni (TF, ca 5,600m, Austrian). (2) Cunka (Slovenian). (3) Dust–From Dusk till Dawn (Austrian). *Matic Jost*

in the nearby Haptal Tokpo, so this year they suggested a new name, Jamyang Ri (5,800m).

On August 5 all three of us carried gear to the base of the west face, though only Matjaz and I would attempt the climb. We started up dusty cracks and chimneys with large jammed blocks to reach the start of a rightward traverse. This turned out to be two full 60m pitches, as we couldn't find any direct continuation. Higher, the rock became cleaner but sometimes far from perfect. We reached the southwest ridge and climbed delicate "boulder problems" on the exposed crest to gain the summit. The climbing had been consistently V to VII-, and we felt the 650m route warranted an overall grade of ED. We named it Cunka.

We rappelled a direct line down the west face to the start of the traverse, then continued down the lower section of our route, arriving in base camp at 10 p.m. We used only nuts and cams, and both of us climbed every pitch free.

— MATIC JOST, *SLOVENIA*

RANGTIK TOKPO AND SURU VALLEY, VARIOUS ASCENTS

At the start of August, Michael Groher, Thomas Holler, Timo Moser, Babsi Vigl, and I, all from the Alpinkader Naturfreunde Österreich (a three-year coaching scheme for alpine climbers), arrived in Leh. We traveled by road to Padum, where we had to scrap our original plans because of a lack of porters. Fortunately, we had seen alternatives during the drive. Not far west of Padum, above Sani village, is the valley of Rangtik Tokpo, in which we had seen a stunning monolith we dubbed Zanskar Cerro Torre. We didn't know that this peak had been climbed on August 5 by a Slovenian team who named it Jamyang Ri (5,800m, *see report above*). There was a small monastery, where we set up base camp.

On August 10, after acclimatization, Babsi and Thomas climbed an ice gully up the west face of a tower on the northwest face of Jamyang Ri, naming it Inshallah, Maybe (350m, M6 5c+ 60°), and the tower itself Torre Fanni (ca 5,600m). The same day, Michael, Timo, and I climbed a new route up the southeast face of Remalaye (H5 on the 2012 Sakamoto map, 6,278m), farther up the valley. The difficulties of our 1,000m climb were 4a 55°.

Our next goal was to reach the top of Jamyang Ri. We spied a line on the southwest face, which offered cracks, corners, and ramps of amazing, solid, Chamonix-type granite. We climbed to the headwall by sunset. Above, things looked difficult, so we rappelled to a ledge, bivouacked, and next day, August 16, found a way up hidden corner cracks until finally a slab led to the top. We named our route Dust–From Dusk till Dawn (500m, 6a A1).

With seven days left, we decided to move to the Suru Valley, home to the Shafat Fortress (ca 5,900m). Reaching it involved crossing a large river, over which we built a Tyrolean traverse.

For their final goal of the expedition, Thomas and Timo climbed the northwest face of the west summit (5,700m) of Shafat Fortress over August 21–22, later realizing this was more or less a repeat of the 2015 route Estética Goulotte (900m, V/5+ M5, Baró-Pellissa, *AAJ 2017*).

They made one bivouac during the ascent at 5,600m.

Babsi, Michael, and I added another route to the 4,700m slabby formation directly opposite camp, climbed in 2007 by a group of Italians via a 1,200m-long route, described as having great character and named the Chessboard (UIAA V+). This face sits below Peak Giorgio and the Golden Sentinel. On the 21st we climbed cracks and flakes to a point halfway up the face, then rappelled to the base and finished the climb next day, a little after sunset. Located well to the right of the Chessboard, the climb is named My Local River is a Nightmare (18 pitches, 6a+). We think that the face is 500m high. 📷 🔍

— LORIN ETZEL, *DALORIN@GMX.DE, GERMANY*

TETLEH KANGRI, FIRST ASCENT VIA NORTHWEST FACE

IN SEPTEMBER, JUAN Diego Amador and David Pérez (Spain) made the first ascent of Tetleh Kangri (6,025m altimeter reading; 33°12'45"N, 76°51'20"E) toward the head of the Tetleh Nala, one of the three main offshoots of the Raru Valley. The peak had been named, after consultation with locals, by the Slovenian team that visited the area in 2015 (*AAJ 2016*). It is the highest peak on the southern rim of the Tetleh Valley and was designated R10, 6,101m, on Kimikazu Sakamoto's sketch maps of the area (*AAJ 2013*).

The Spanish expedition left the road head at Raru on August 27 and two days later reached a base camp below the glacier at 4,800m. A reconnaissance showed the northeast face seemed exposed to stonefall, and while the north and northwest aspects were less exposed to sun, the north side featured large and ominous serac barriers. They established a high camp close to the face and returned to base.

After waiting through two weeks of poor weather they left high camp at 3 a.m. on September 16, crossed the glacier, and started up the northwest face, traveling light with no tent or stove. The first 450m was a snow/ice slope of 55–75°, then came a mixed section of 200m, followed by a final 200m section of snow and ice at 65–75° that led to the east ridge. The most difficult part was the steep mixed section.

At 8:30 p.m., having battled through a snowstorm and then darkness, the two men, realizing they were close to the top, found a small platform at 5,985m and decided to stop for the

Looking west toward the head of the Tetleh Glacier, with the north side of Tetleh Kangri (ca 6,025m) dominating the left skyline. The line of Don't Sleep (900m, MD, 2017), the first-ascent route, is shown. Arrow marks the descent route. *Anastasija Davidova*

night. They had little water or food and just the clothes they were wearing, it was blowing, and the temperature was -15°C, making it very much a night to remember. By 6 a.m. the warmth of the sun had begun to clear the clouds, and they quickly ascended the final ridge to the summit, though the visibility was still far from perfect. Now they had to get off.

They tried several directions, even the opposite side of the mountain, but new snow made all these alternatives dangerous. In the end they opted to descend the rocky northeast face. By noon it was snowing again. Using rock anchors until they reached ice, followed by Abalakov threads, the two rappelled the face. By 8:15 p.m. they were back at high camp on the glacier. Next day, insensitivity in various swollen fingers and toes made them give up any idea of further climbing, and they descended to base camp. They named their route Don't Sleep (900m, MD 75° M3/4), and because Amador comes from the Canary Islands, they dubbed the mountain Pico Islas Canarias. 📷 🔍

— LINDSAY GRIFFIN, *WITH INFORMATION FROM EXPEDITION REPORT AND MATIC JOST*

LENAK NALA, L8 (A.K.A. LAMA SOO), EAST FACE AND NORTH RIDGE

In August a team of Japanese college students (Gakushi Eguchi, Satoru Miyachi, Yuu Nishida, and Ryota Takanezawa) trekked into the Lenak Valley, planning to climb the east ridge of L8 (6,020m, 33°09'27"N, 77°02'08"E). L8 was first climbed in 2012 from the Raru Valley to the west by two Greek climbers (AD, *AAJ 2013*), who named the peak Lama Soo ("Monk's Tooth"); their altimeter registered 5,947m on top, and they descended the north ridge.

In a photo of L8, the east ridge had looked gentle and wide. But the Japanese found the crest to be full of loose rock and steep pinnacles. They decided to cross the ridge, descend north into another valley, and attempt to reach the north ridge, a gentle snow crest. On August 31, from Camp 2, at 5,400m, below the northeast face, all four set out at 7:30 a.m., climbed to the north ridge, and reached the summit at 12:25 p.m. 📷 🔍

— LINDSAY GRIFFIN, *WITH INFORMATION FROM KIMIKAZU SAKAMOTO AND THE ASIAN ALPINE NEWS*

KISHTWAR HIMALAYA

KIJAI NALA: PEAK 6,038M, NORTH RIDGE; ARJUNA, WEST FACE

Visiting the Kijai Nala had been on the bucket list for Hayden Kennedy, Marko Prezelj, and me since 2015, when we climbed together above the Chomochior Glacier in eastern Kishtwar (*AAJ 2016*). We had planned to head into this western Kishtwar valley at the end of that expedition, since there was so little information—who knows what interesting climbing objectives might lie in untraveled corners?

However, the climbing on Cerro Kishtwar kept us busy and we ended up postponing our planned visit to the Kijai Nala for the fall of 2016. Then, a week before our departure, we were shocked by the disappearance of our dear friend Kyle Dempster and his climbing partner, Scott Adamson, in the Karakoram. We canceled the climbing part of the expedition; instead, Marko and I traveled to India simply to check out potentially interesting objectives.

In the Kijai Nala we were most impressed by the magnificent west face of Arjuna (6,230m map height). This valley had been visited a few times in the late 1970s and early '80s, and then possibly not again until 2016, when Chris Gibisch and Jeff Shapiro climbed the south face of Bram-

Marko Prezelj starting the third pitch on the second day of All or Nothing, the first alpine-style ascent of Arjuna's main peak. Three challenging mixed pitches on this day took a total of eight hours to climb. *Urban Novak*

mah II (*AAJ 2017*). [*See this report at the AAJ website for a brief history of climbing in this valley.*]

Until this trip we had visited Kishtwar in the fall, but in 2017 we decided to go in spring, mainly because we expected to find much better conditions for mixed climbing. On May 29, Ales Cesen, Marko, and I established base camp on the west side of the glacier at 4,008m. Our first impression was that surrounding peaks were covered with much more snow than we'd seen the previous fall. For acclimatization, we decided to try Peak 6,013m, which Poles had climbed by the southeast ridge in September 1979 (*AAJ 1981*).

We climbed via the glacier to the west of our base camp, south of the mountain. We made our first bivouac at 5,000m and our second, at the top of the glacier, at 5,500m. From this point we ascended a dome-like side peak (5,700m), from which we got a good look at a possible route to the summit of Peak 6,013m.

On June 4 we climbed up to a plateau on the west side of 6,013m and traversed under its summit—below the northwest face—to reach the north ridge, which we followed to the top. Our GPS device measured the altitude as 6,038m (with +/- 4m accuracy). The overall grade was D. From the top, we had a clear view of Arjuna, and the line that really stood out was a gully to the right of the Polish central pillar. [*Poles Jerzy Barszczewski, Mirosław Dąsal, and Zbigniew Skierski climbed the central pillar of the west face to make the first ascent of Arjuna's main summit, fixing the lower 120m of the route (AAJ 1984).*] Highly motivated and full of expectation for the days to come, we descended to base camp that same day.

On the 10th, in variable weather, we carried part of our gear and food to the glacier under the west face of Arjuna. Storms prevented us from returning until the 15th, when we were able

The Arjuna group from the southwest. (1) 1983 Polish route (Barszczewski-Dąsal-Skierski) up the central pillar of the west face. (2) All or Nothing (Cesen-Novak-Prezelj, 2017). (3) West face of the south summit (Bender-Piasecki, 1983). (4) Gandiva (Graham-Hawthorn-Silvestre, 2017). (5) Descent used by the British climbers in 2017; apart from the top section, this line approximates the route followed in 1981 by the Poles (Bartos-Otreba-Puzyrewski) who first climbed Arjuna's south summit. They finished up the southeast ridge (approximately right skyline) to the summit. *Marko Prezelj*

to erect a tent and break trail to the base of the route. More snowfall postponed our departure until 8 a.m. the next day.

We found good snow and ice conditions in the lower section of the gully and climbed most of this unroped. We then climbed six pitches of mixed, where we had problems with occasional wet-snow avalanches. We bivouacked below what we expected to be the crux of the route.

Next day it took us eight hours to climb three hard mixed pitches. After this we climbed a steep ice pitch and then seven snow pitches, before bivouacking late at night about three rope lengths below the summit ridge.

We reached the main summit of Arjuna around noon next day. The GPS device read 6,250m. The same day we rappelled our ascent route and reached advanced base at midnight. We named the 1,400m route All or Nothing (ED+ M7+ WI5+ A0). It was the second ascent of the summit and the first in alpine style.

On the 19th we started down toward base camp. After half an hour it started to rain, and it didn't stop for the next three days. We left base camp with huge smiles on our faces: Rarely do you get to connect perfectly all the dots of conditions, weather, and personal feelings during an expedition. We very easily could have left the valley without an opportunity to attempt our main objective, but we left with heads held high. [*Read Cesen and Prezelj's reflections on this expedition at the AAJ website.*]

The Kijai Nala is an exceptional playground for modern-style climbing in all disciplines of rock, mixed, and snow/ice terrain. We believe it will get many visits in the future and is an "upgrade" of the popular Charakusa Valley in Pakistan. 📄 📷

— **URBAN NOVAK**, *SLOVENIA*

ARJUNA SOUTH, SOUTHWEST PILLAR, GANDIVA

Pete Graham and I have been climbing together in winter and on alpine terrain quite consistently for a few years. He was originally my mentor, but the relationship has grown into a healthy partnership. Each year we've managed to push ourselves a little further.

In January, on the suggestion of Mick Fowler, I contacted American climber Jeff Shapiro, who had climbed in Kishtwar in 2016, to ask about Arjuna. His photos showed a steep rock spur on Arjuna South (ca 6,100m), which could prove a fantastic end to a summer of rock climbing in the U.K. We enlisted Uisdean Hawthorn to join us in September.

Three days of walking through the Kijai Nala took us to base camp, and our first glimpse of Arjuna confirmed we had made a very good choice. The rock looked excellent, and the route itself seemed free from objective dangers. However, there appeared to be blank sections high on the spur, and choosing a descent presented an intimidating problem.

We acclimatized by moving gear to a high camp at the base of the route (4,700m) and walking to 5,300m on a ridge above base camp. We then waited out a spell of bad weather at base camp.

On October 2 we walked up to our advanced base and left at dawn the next day to climb a gully on the right flank of the pillar. After reaching a notch at the base of an imposing rock wall, we climbed three excellent steep pitches to the base of the arête. We had brought rock shoes for the leader and jumars for the seconds, and this proved the fastest and least stressful method of ascent. A further three pitches on lower-angled ground, which we could second in boots, brought us to a palatial bivouac.

Next morning I set off up the corner above, a fantastic technical exercise with a small roof at the top. I was surprised to find myself already at the section that had looked blank from below. The granite turned out to be covered with chicken heads providing face holds. Traversing around the arête, I found cracks leading to a small ledge below a menacing chimney. This was avoided by technical face climbing on lumps to access a steep hand crack, which led to another good stance near the arête. This last pitch was the rock climbing crux (5.11), though many of the pitches were only slightly easier. Above, high-quality climbing on Chamonix-style granite led to easier-angled though still complicated terrain, and at dusk we reached a small snow arête, where we spent a cold night.

Next morning, Pete took us to the top of the pillar via a couple of excellent pitches on huge chicken heads. We rappelled into the notch on the far side and discovered an anchor from the 1983 Polish team that had climbed the west face of Arjuna South, making its first ascent. We climbed directly up the headwall to the right of their line and made our third bivouac a little below the two "horns" that dominate the top of the mountain. After a good night's sleep we climbed the right-hand of two gullies via a hard mixed step to reach steep ice, the summit ridge, and finally the top.

Basking in the late morning sun, congratulating ourselves that we'd climbed every pitch free, we allowed ourselves to enjoy a short while on top. Before too long the prospect of descent became pressing, and we traversed to a point on the southeast face from which we could start rappelling. Pete led us bravely down the face in 12 long rappels, until we eventually reached a glacier south of the mountain, a short while after dark. We walked down this until a steepening required a further five rappels, and we stopped for the night in a notch atop the approach gully, 300m above our advanced base.

This proved a good decision, as we benefited from the cold of the next morning to descend steep, choss-covered slabs. A further four rappels brought us to the bottom, extremely satisfied to have climbed such a beautiful and imposing line on our first trip to Asia. We named the route Gandiva (1,400m, 5.11 M5). 📷

– **BEN SILVESTRE**, *ALPINE CLUB, U.K.*

Barnaj II (left) and Barnaj I (6,370m GPS) seen from the east-northeast in 2014, showing the 2017 route up Barnaj I, the first ascent of the peak. Barnaj II has seen repeated attempts from the south, but the highest point has not been reached. *Mick Fowler*

BARNAJ I, NORTHEAST BUTTRESS; THE CASTLE, SOUTHEAST FACE

Barnaj I (6,370m GPS) is a mountain that beckons to be climbed. After my 2014 attempt on the north buttress with Tim Dittmann and Jared Vilhauer, and knowing of at least one other attempt and several potential expeditions, I kept expecting to read that it had been done. [*Though the higher Barnaj II had repeated attempts from the south in the 1970s and early '80s, it is not clear whether Barnaj I received a serious attempt before 2014.*] However, by the end of 2016 this challenging mountain remained virgin, and Jared and I, together with Sam Hennessey, planned to return the following year. Unfortunately, Jared's Indian visa was delayed in Houston due to Hurricane Harvey. This, combined with untimely illness, saw him in India only a short time before he had to head home.

Sam and I left the village of Akshow with our LO and logistics crew, and established base camp at 4,350m above the west side of the Hagshu Glacier. After a few days of scouting and acclimatizing, we decided to attempt an unclimbed peak behind camp. The Castle, as we referred to it, is 5,760m and snow-free on its east and south aspects. On September 19 we climbed the southeast ridge and face. The route required a few hundred meters of scrambling and eight pitches of roped climbing on moderate to poor rock (IV 5.8+). We also made an attempt on Peak 6,200m, which sits above the huge, snowy basin west of base camp, but turned around at 5,850m due to unstable snow conditions.

On September 30, after a few days of unsettled weather, we moved to an advanced base near Barnaj I at 4,700m. Sam and I left this camp next morning and walked 30 minutes up the glacier before starting to climb snow aprons at the base of the impressive north face. We crossed the bergschrund at 4,920m and climbed nearly continuous ice all the way to the summit. The route had very little snow, mixed climbing, or calf-burning sheet ice—its caliber was reflected in pitch after pitch of quality ice climbing. Ever engaging, yet never desperate, the route was in good condition, with many pitches containing just enough ice for reasonable protection and swift passage.

On the first day we simul-climbed up the left side of the face until belaying a thin pitch of 80° ice. After 70m the angle eased, as did the spindrift, and we climbed several pitches of low-angle ice and occasional snow into a deep cleft defined by a massive granite spire on the right. Our route went up this only briefly before cutting straight up through a shallow, 300m gully system. The first 100m were steep, with sustained sections of vertical ice; combined with heavy packs, this provided the greatest pump on the route. The remaining 200m were no more than 10m wide, with sticky blue ice averaging 70°, ending at the start of a transverse snow band on the northeast aspect of the peak. A short step of M4 put us at the same point where we bivouacked in 2014, and we stopped for the night.

Knowing that our next protected bivouac site was only 250m higher, we had a late morning, resting and taking advantage of the sun to dry equipment. A few hours of traversing on snow, followed by a couple of ice pitches, then put us at our second bivouac site, which sits just left of the entrance to the upper ice chimney at ca 5,700m.

Seth Timpano leading an ice pitch low on the northeast buttress of Barnaj I. Continuous high-quality ice climbing characterized the line, which Timpano and two other climbers had attempted in 2014. *Sam Hennessey*

We had turned around at this point in 2014 due to rockfall, a result of thin rotten ice and warm temps. To mitigate this hazard, our strategy this time was to climb through the incredible ice-filled gash in the dark. We woke at 1 a.m. and worked our way through the chimney in four long pitches of fairly sustained ice. The climbing was brilliant and the sticks were solid, with the exception of one 20m section of steep rotten ice.

It had been difficult to assess the upper route beforehand, so we were pleasantly surprised to find the weakness continued upward. Although the route opened up a bit, and the angle eased slightly, the climbing was more delicate, and protection often scarce. After 10 more rope lengths of ice, averaging 75–80°, with a few vertical steps, Sam cut his way through the cornice and onto the summit ridge. A few minutes of easy snow climbing put us on the true summit, where our GPS devices read 6,370m.

We reversed the route with V-threads to our tent at 5,700m, where we brewed up and slept several hours before descending the lower half of the route the following day. Our 1,450m route had been WI5+ M4.

There is no doubt the true north face of Barnaj I is a more impressive problem, but navigating the ephemeral smears seems unlikely without much mixed and aid. While not as difficult, our route is the line—direct, sustained, and objectively safe. We feel fortunate, as it is rare to make an alpine-style ascent of such quality directly to the summit of an unclimbed mountain. We would like to thank the Mugs Stump Award for helping make this expedition possible. 📷

— SETH TIMPANO, *USA*

Stephan Siegrist leading a pitch on the steep pillar of Cerro Kishtwar. *Huber | Siegrist | Zanker Archive*

CERRO KISHTWAR, NORTHWEST FACE DIRECT, HAR-HAR MAHADEV

In 2011 Denis Burdet, Robert Frost, David Lama, and Stephan Siegrist climbed Yoniverse on the northwest face and upper south ridge of Cerro Kishtwar (6,155m GPS) to make the second ascent of the mountain. During his time on the climb, Siegrist's eyes were drawn toward the great rocky expanse of the direct northwest face to the left, an image he was not able to get out of his head.

On September 13, 2017, Siegrist was back at the base camp below Cerro Kishtwar, this time with Thomas Huber (Germany) and fellow Swiss Julian Zanker. Ideal weather allowed no opportunity for rest, and by the 18th they had established an advanced base at 5,050m. The plan was to climb up the front face of the large rounded pillar that characterizes the middle of the wall.

Their planned route lay to the right of an attempt in October 1991 by Brendan Murphy and Andy Perkins, who climbed the left side of this pillar to the top of the face but not the summit. After a total of 17 days and 28 pitches (A3 and Scottish 6), the British climbers slanted left to reach the north ridge, crossed to the northeast flank, and were 100m below the top when, exhausted and without food, they were forced to descend.

After fixing parts of the lower mixed section of the face and establishing a camp on a snow terrace at 5,450m, immediately below the granite pillar, the 2017 team set off with a portaledge on October 1 for what they hoped would be a five-day climb. In retrospect, they realized they had underestimated the difficulties; the route was sustained and very demanding due to the constant cold. After three days they had only reached the top of pitch seven, about one-third of the way up. Also, Siegrist was having problems with tendonitis in one hand. They chose to descend, resupply, and make a second attempt in a few days.

On October 8 they began again. The weather was typically clear and cold through the night and morning, with temperatures down to -20°C, then snowing in the afternoon. They made three portaledge camps on the wall, and it took seven days to reach the summit. Only on the last day did they climb in sunshine. All climbers came away with some degree of frostnip, especially Zanker. However, on the summit, they were treated to full sunshine and no wind. It was the fourth overall ascent of the mountain, and the second by Siegrist.

The route was named after an expression from Hindu mythology, Har-har Mahadev, which roughly translates as "raise moral values to overcome fear and dangerous situations"—as Huber put it, "Get a grip!" After the first 400m of ice/mixed (M6 80°), the 600m headwall involved 24 pitches up to A3+ and 6b; it only came close to the Murphy-Perkins line very high on the wall. Some bolts were placed on belays, while seven rivets and eight bathooks were drilled on lead. The team rappelled the route. [*This climb and an interview with Siegrist are featured in episode 3 of the AAJ's Cutting Edge Podcast.*]

Cerro Kishtwar (6,155m GPS) from the northwest. (1) The diagonal ice ramp followed by Mick Fowler and Steve Sustad on the peak's first ascent in 1993. (2) Brendan Murphy–Andy Perkins 1991 attempt to within 100 meters of the summit. (3) Har-har Mahadev (2017). (4) Yoniverse (west face and south ridge, Burdet-Frost-Lama-Siegrist, 2011). *Huber | Siegrist | Zanker Archive*

— **LINDSAY GRIFFIN**, *WITH INFORMATION FROM STEPHAN SIEGRIST, SWITZERLAND*

HIMACHAL PRADESH

MIYAR VALLEY, VARIOUS ROCK ROUTES

A NEW ZEALAND team comprising Nick Craddock (who has spent years working out of Manali), Llewellyn Murdoch, David Shotwell, and Alison Swintz reached base camp below the west face of Castle Peak in May. They climbed at least five possible new lines on the south face of Toro Peak (4,970m), from grades 17 to 22. They also did the probable second ascent of the original 1992 Italian route on the west face of Neverseen Tower (ca 5,750m) and established many single- to three-pitch rock climbs in the lower Takdung, a side valley off the Miyar.

Thibaut Tournier and his wife Muriel Zucchini (France), who climbed new routes in the Miyar during September 2015, returned in August 2017 with Thomas Auvaro, Florence Cotto, and Antoine Rolle. This group climbed two possible new routes (6a+ and 7a) on Goya Peak (5,163m) and two on the south face of Toro Peak, Waiting for Whisky (300m, 7a) and Positive Vibes (300m, 7a); the Toro routes are close to two of the New Zealand lines and may share some common ground.

Tournier and Zucchini climbed what is thought to have been a virgin pyramidal summit near the head of the Chhudong Glacier, which they named Chhudong Devlin. The 700m east face, on which they discovered a few old pitons until about half-height, gave a full day's climbing at 6b. The same pair, together with Cotto, climbed a route on the southwest ridge of Marakula Killa, but not to the main summit.

Full reports on these expeditions will be found at the AAJ website.

— **LINDSAY GRIFFIN**

LAHAUL, GHAR NALA, PEAK 6,113M, ATTEMPTS

A NINE-MEMBER EXPEDITION led by Rudra Prasad Halder made several attempts on an unnamed and unclimbed peak of 6,113m (dubbed Goutam Parbat, 32°34'43"N, 76°42'43"E) in the Ghar Nala, south of Thirot in the Chandrabhaga Valley. From a base camp at 4,400m, northeast of the mountain, the team tried climbing a long spur that descends east-northeast from the north ridge (eventually reaching Point 5,789m on the north ridge), as well as a spur to the south that falls more or less east from the summit. The team concluded that Peak 6,113m might be climbed more easily from the Chobia Valley to the west. 🗎 📷

– **LINDSAY GRIFFIN**, *WITH INFORMATION FROM RUDRA PRASAD HALDER, INDIA, AND NANDINI PURANDARE, EDITOR, HIMALAYAN JOURNAL, INDIA*

Peak 5,620m and the route of the Japanese first ascent. *Yukio Ueda*

KULLU VALLEY, PEAK 5,620M, EAST RIDGE

IN SEPTEMBER, MAKOTO Kuroda, Hiroyoshi Manome, and Yukio Ueda left Tos (Tosh) village in the Kullu Valley and walked up the Tos Nala to establish base camp on the west side of the Tos Glacier. Unaware of a Korean ascent earlier in the year (and indeed the first ascent in September 1985), they had come to attempt the west face of Dharamsura (6,420m). However, the weather was very poor, so they switched objectives to an unnamed rock tower at 32°11'23.52"N, 77°26'41.47"E (Google Earth), near the head of the glacier that rose west of base camp. The ridge that runs from this point to the west and then northwest to Indrasan (6,221m) carries what are known as the Malana Towers.

On October 2 the three ascended the glacier and camped at 5,090m at the base of the tower. Next day they left early, climbed 200m of mixed ground up to the east ridge of the tower, then along the crest on snow until reaching a prominent gendarme. A 30m rappel put them at the base of an ice face on the north flank, which they climbed for 200m to avoid the gendarme. At this point it was midday. They then climbed a steep rocky section and mixed ground to a short section of ice leading to the summit. Their altimeter recorded 5,620m. The three bivouacked once on the descent and reached base camp by evening the next day. The 530m (vertical interval) route was graded ED-.

The team had an average age of 47, and all three members are considered strong veteran alpine climbers in Japan. 📷 🔍

– **HIRO HAGIWARA**, *ROCK AND SNOW, JAPAN*

KULLU VALLEY: DHARAMSURA, NORTHWEST FACE, SECOND ASCENT; PAPSURA, SOUTH FACE DIRECT

AFTER LEADING THE first Korean Way project in 2016, climbing the south face of Ganga-purna (AAJ 2017), I led a second expedition with the concept of fostering a younger genera-tion of Korean climbers, developing their skills and experience. I was joined by my friend An Chi-young (40), and with us were the inexperienced Gu Gyo-jeong (25), Kim Ki-hyun

(31), and Lee Jae-hun (24). We left Seoul on April 26 and reached our base camp at Kuta Thach (4,260m) after a four-day hike from Tosh (Tos) Village in the Kullu Valley to the southwest.

Dharamsura (6,446m) was first ascended in 1941 by a British party led by J. O. M. Roberts via the south-south-east ridge. It is not often climbed, though other routes have been added, including the southwest ridge and various variations from the east. Our goal was the northwest face, of which we failed to find a picture on the Internet or in mountaineering publications from India.

[*At the time, the Koreans were unaware of the little documented but remarkable ascent of this face, via the exact same line followed by the Koreans, in September 1985. Alan Hinkes and Andy Lewis (U.K.) battled poor weather, shortage of food, and five bivouacs above 6,000m before emerging at the summit. On return to base camp three days later than expected, they found the other two members of their expedition, who had reached the summit via the southwest ridge, had presumed Hinkes and Lewis dead and departed the area, leaving neither message, food, nor money.*]

To look at the face more closely, we scrambled through the Sara Umga Pass (5,020m), west of Dharamsura and

[Top] The northwest face of Dharamsura and the line of the 1985 British ascent, repeated for the first time in 2017. [Bottom] The south face of Papsura. (1) Southwest ridge. (2) South face direct (Korean Way). (3) Original route (south couloir to east ridge). The west face, climbed and skied by an American trio in 2017 (first ski descent of the peak), is just around the rock buttress on the left. *Korean Way Expedition*

Papsura (6,451m), returning down the East Tos Glacier. The stunningly beautiful western aspect of Dharamsura resembled Jannu's north face.

Lee and I, and An and Gu, formed individual roped pairs, though we climbed together. Taking three ropes, two tents, small sleeping bags, short air mattresses, stoves, and climbing gear, we each began the ascent with 14kg packs. We moved up the East Tos Glacier to reach our first bivouac site at 5,395m. Next day we rapidly climbed 10 pitches of snow, ice, and mixed terrain to make a second bivouac at 6,100m. The following day it was snowing, so we took a rest.

The fourth day was the hardest as we negotiated a left-slanting ramp through the head-wall, formed by a diagonal crack below an overhang on the vertical rock wall. It snowed and visibility was poor. The 18th pitch was the most difficult: 20m long with a 20cm (8-inch) crack. After this section the weather turned better. We spent the night below a huge roof at 6,250m. Four more pitches next morning led us to the top, which we reached at 10 a.m. on May 24. We descended the southwest ridge and arrived at base camp that evening. Our five-day, alpine-style ascent had 25 pitches and an overall grade of ED+.

Kim Chang-ho leads pitch 18, the crux of the diagonal ramp on the headwall of Dharamsura's northwest face. *Korean Way Expedition*

Our next goal was Papsura. This was first ascended in 1967 by Bob Pettigrew's British expedition, following a couloir on the south face and the southeast ridge. Since then routes have been added up the southwest ridge, the west face, and the northwest ridge.

Kim, Gu, and I started in the middle of the south face, and over five days climbed more or less directly to the summit. The face is not steep up to 5,900m, but above this we encountered a complicated rocky section formed of downward-shelving rock. After this we bivouacked below a serac at 6,000m. The sky was clear next morning, June 3, when we reached the plateau-like top. After 15 rappels along the northwest ridge, we safely reached the glacier. [*The northwest ridge was first descended in 1977, but not ascended until July 2012, when it was climbed by a seven-member Indian team (including four Sherpas) led by Subrata Chakraborty.*]

– KIM CHANG-HO, *KOREA, TRANSLATED BY OH YOUNG-HOON*

Papsura Variation and First Ski Descent: In May, Americans Chris Figenshau, Jim Morrison, and Hilaree O'Neill climbed a variation start to the 1991 New Zealand route up the west face couloir and then skied back down it, completing the first ski descent of Papsura. They chose to approach the couloir from the right, as this presented far less objective hazard, then joined the New Zealand route at around one-third height and followed it to the top. A photograph of the west face appears with the online report.

WESTERN GARHWAL / GANGOTRI

SHIVLING, NORTHEAST AND NORTH FACES, PARTIAL NEW ROUTE

SINCE SHIVLING'S FIRST ascent in 1974, many different routes have been created on the "Matterhorn of the Himalaya." In 1980 a Japanese team sieged the north pillar from its base to the final headwall. There they made a long traverse to the right extremity of the wall to gain the summit slopes. In 1993, Christoph Hainz and Hans Kammerlander climbed the crest of a prominent pillar to the left (northeast) to gain the Japanese route at around 5,900m; they turned around in a snowstorm about 300m below the summit. It wasn't until 2000 that Thomas Huber and Iwan Wolf climbed the true finish to the north pillar, a direct line through the headwall (Shiva's Line, UIAA VII A4). This impressive line would be the goal for Simon Gietl and me.

Heavy snowfall just before our arrival in the Gangotri made access difficult and covered the ridges in white, unapproachable splendor. While hard rock climbing on Shivling's northeast pillar would now be problematic, an ephemeral ice line had appeared to the left. It looked steep and difficult to protect, certainly WI5.

On our first trip up the mountain, we climbed to about 5,900m, fixing 400m of rope. The ice line consisted of four long, steep pitches followed by super 70° styrofoam snow. We then descended to base camp at 4,300m for two days of rest.

On October 9 we jumared the fixed ropes, picked up our cached gear, and continued up less difficult but hard-to-protect terrain to reach the crest of the north pillar. One short pitch up the crest led to a bivouac site at 6,000m. Above lay the headwall and the prow of Shiva's Line. Wearing a thick down jacket and mittens inside good sleeping bags, we quickly decided it was far too cold for us to negotiate the A3/A4 climbing on the prow. Instead we would opt for the Japanese Route, which follows a right-slanting ramp below the headwall to reach the summit snowfields.

After a cold night with little sleep, we left most of our stuff in the tent and headed up right, taking a "shortcut" to reach the Japanese traverse. Passing old fixed rope, we reached a corner that led to the final snowfields and, at last, the warming rays of the sun. We reached the summit at midday and rappelled the route back to our tent, spending one more night before continuing down our route to the base.

We named our partial new route Shiva's Ice (ca 1,100m, WI5 M6). Apart from the altitude, it could be compared to the Colton-MacIntyre on the Grandes Jorasses, and in terms of the overall climbing, it is certainly one of the most uniform routes on the mountain. 📷

– VITTORIO MESSINI, *ITALY*

CENTRAL GARHWAL

NILKANTH, SOUTHWEST FACE, OBSCURED PERCEPTION

BETWEEN SEPTEMBER 29 and October 2, Anne Gilbert Chase, Jason Thompson, and I made the first ascent of the southwest face of Nilkanth (6,596m). Anne Gilbert, Jason, and Caro North had planned to attempt the southwest face in 2015, and they climbed most of the peak's west ridge, which would have formed their descent route. However, the weather did not allow them to set foot on the southwest face (*AAJ 2016*).

Two years later, Anne Gilbert and Jason were awarded an AAC Cutting Edge Grant for another attempt on the unclimbed southwest face. They invited me to join, and with assistance provided by Ibex Expeditions, we arrived in mid-September at a 4,115m base camp directly below the south face. The monsoon extended well into the month, bringing warm temperatures and heavy rain.

Access to the southwest face involved 1,000m of ascent over gravel-covered slabs, and featured brief periods of exposure to overhead objective hazard. Straightforward glacier travel then led to the foot of the wall. Our only opportunity to acclimatize through the unsettled weather was to ascend these approach slabs and establish an advanced base below the wall at 5,180m. At that time, the first third of the wall looked in poor condition, with high temperatures

Nilkanth (6,596m) from the west, showing the upper part of Obscured Perception, a 1,400-meter route climbed over five days. Bypassing the prominent rock buttress on the right, the Castle, on day three was the crux of the climb. The west ridge, first climbed in 2000 and descended by the 2017 team, faces the camera. *Tad McCrea*

melting the ice and exposing loose scrappy rock. Rain only began to turn to snow around 5,100m.

On September 27 a long weather window began, and although not well acclimatized, we decided this would be our opportunity. We left advanced base on the morning of the 28th, finding just enough ice on the lower face to afford reasonable passage. There were a few pitches of mixed climbing up to M5, simul-climbing on steep snow slopes, and a steep WI5 ice pitch. Our first bivouac was at 5,670m in a moat.

On day two we pitched most of the climbing, which consisted of technical mixed ground and some beautiful steep ice. We were unable to locate a tent platform that evening, so we chopped out a bench at 5,944m and succumbed to a sitting bivouac under the stars. On most days the mountain would see convective cloud buildup and light precipitation during the afternoon hours.

Day three was the crux. We needed to find a way to the top of what we'd dubbed the Castle, a steep granite formation. As we got nearer, we saw that our intended route would require big-wall tactics. Instead, we opted to navigate around the Castle's right side and found a delicate ice runnel leading into an overhanging cave. To exit, we tensioned over a slab and gained access to difficult mixed ground; this was followed by a steep ice pillar, eventually depositing us on top of the Castle at 6,248m. The bivouac here was the coolest ever, the exposure and views unforgettable.

Anticipating more straightforward climbing, we hoped day four would take us to the summit. However, the technical ground continued almost to the top. The rock quality deteriorated and route-finding became more difficult. By evening we had arrived at a false summit. The summit ridge looked steep, difficult, and exposed, so we opted to descend 30m to a flat bench and set up camp at 6,523m, the highest elevation any of us had slept.

After a cold and restless night, we awoke to another beautiful morning, sluggishly melted snow for water, and packed our bags to complete the summit ridge. This turned out to be straightforward, and a couple of hours later we were standing on the summit, psyched. Our route, Obscured Perception (1,400m, VI WI5 M6 A0 70° snow), had overall been of very high quality.

The west ridge was still fresh in the minds of Anne Gilbert and Jason, so we hoped for a fluid descent. We downclimbed névé ridges and made about 10 rappels, with Anne Gilbert doing a great job remembering the locations of the previously rigged anchors. Fifteen hours later, at around 2 a.m., we made it back to our advanced base, rested a while, and then continued our descent to base camp later in the morning. 📷

— CHANTEL ASTORGA, *AAC*

Chantel Astorga leading out on complex mixed terrain. Steep ice around the corner led to the top of the Castle and the team's third bivouac site, at nearly 6,250 meters. *Jason Thompson*

Franz Friebel on the northwest ridge of Pratibandhit Lek. The Kang La, below and behind, gives passage between Nepal (left) and Tibet (right). (A) Unnamed twin peaks at the head the Bholbihan Khola. (B) Asajya Tuppa (6,265m). (C) Absi (6,254m). (D) Kangla II (Ngomo Ding-Ding, 6,133m HGM Finn). (E) Lachama (a.k.a. Kubi Kangri, 6,721m). *Nils Beste*

NAMJA LAGUJA DANDA AND KANGLA HIMAL

FIRST ASCENTS OF SUNKALA TOPI, LEK FETT, AND PRATIBANDHIT LEK

SUPPORTED BY THE German Alpine Club, Nils Beste, Bernde Emmerich, Franz Friebel, Harry Kirschenhofer, and I flew to Jumla in western Nepal at the start of October. From there we drove 10 hours to reach Gamghadi, north of Jumla, and then trekked for five days, heading east up the Mugu Karnali Nadi and then turning north into the Mugu Khola.

Shortly before the Namja La on the border with Tibet, we turned northwest into the Takya Khola (Takya Valley), where we set up base camp at 4,666m (29°55.262'N, 82°20.214'E). We were now beneath the highest peak of the Namja Laguja Danda, a small range between the Kangla Himal in the west and Kanti Himal in the east. The Namja La appears to be an actively used pass for trade between Mugu and Tibet, judging by the Lhasa beer and Chinese Budweiser cans found along the way.

On October 12 we established a high camp at 5,148m, southwest of the highest summit, which we would subsequently name Sunkala Topi (5,865m). Harry felt unwell the next morning, but the rest of the team set out at 6 a.m. and climbed northeast up a ridge and through a maze of scree and boulders to a plateau. A rocky ridge then led us down onto the glacier that drapes the south flank of the mountain between the west and south summits.

We slanted up across this glacier to reach the crest of the south ridge of the main peak. After reaching a false summit at 5,856m (29°55'39.67"N, 82°31'12.25"E), we saw that the actual top, just to the north, would involve a difficult crossing. Nils was the only one to take up the challenge. Clouds and strong wind denied a decent panorama, but a glimpse to the west gave a brilliant view over the Kangla Group, where three pyramidal peaks above 6,000m caught our attention.

On the 14th we left the Takya Khola and crossed a pass into the western Chawarsing Khola (Chawarsing Valley). Shortly below the pass we camped at a lake (ca 4,800m), and from here Nils decided to try the border peak of Lek Fett (5,767m), the summit immediately north of the pass. His plan was to traverse rock and scree on the southwest face to a scree couloir that would lead to the northwest ridge. Once on the crest, he decided to avoid rock towers by descending to a relatively benign glacier basin on the far (northeast) side. This led to a 50° névé

slope, which he climbed for 150m to regain the ridge at around 5,550m. A wide snow crest led easily to the summit (5,767m, 29°56'55.11"N, 82°29'45.94"E). The crux had been crossing the open bergschrund between the glacier and the 50° slope.

That same day, we descended the Chawarsing Khola into the Take Khola and camped at the high meadow of Take Kharka (4,200m). On October 16, Nils, Franz, and I left this camp and entered the Kangla Khola. After 6km another valley branches northeast toward the Kang La on the Tibetan border. I felt weak thanks to a respiratory infection and stopped, but the other two continued another 3km to a campsite in a side valley at about 4,700m. Their goal was Pratibandhit Lek, the high peak immediately east of the Kang La. This pass is used for trade, and there is a good path on the southeast side of the valley, avoiding the glacier. In contrast to what is shown on old maps, there is no glacier to cross to reach the pass.

The two left camp at 4:45 a.m. and walked the 4km to the pass (5,400m). They then ascended scree, snow, and mixed terrain for 300m to reach the northwest ridge of Pratibandhit Lek at about 5,700m. This ascent was 55° and corniced, with steep drops on both sides ("more impressive than the Biancograt on Piz Bernina"). This ridge led southeast for 2km to the summit (6,130m, 30°00'13.63"N, 82°25'14.31"E). Observations from the top, and on Google Earth, indicate that Pratibandhit Lek is the highest peak of the Kangla Himal. However, since various peaks have similar elevations, further ascents are needed for confirmation.

[Top] Unclimbed Absi (Gorakh Kang), 6,254m, seen from Sunkala Topi to the southeast. [Bottom] Sunkala Topi (5,865m), seen from the Take Khola to the southwest, with the route of the first ascent marked. *Christof Nettekoven*

Another day of perfect weather gave a fantastic panorama over the Kangla Himal's unclimbed peaks. West of the Kang La is the unclimbed pyramid that we dubbed Kangla II (on the Japanese sketch map it is referred to as Ngomo Ding-Ding, 6,133m HGM-Finn) with a beautiful snow and ice northeast ridge. Behind lay unclimbed summits of the Gorakh Himal, including the impressive pyramid of Absi (a.k.a. Gorakh Kang, 6,254m). To the east the view stretched as far as Kanjiroba (6,883m), and to the southwest as far as Saipal (7,031m).

We completed the expedition by walking out to the west to Simikot. 📄 📷 🔍

– CHRISTOF NETTEKOVEN, *GERMAN ALPINE CLUB (DAV)*

NALAKANKAR HIMAL

TAKPHU NORTH, SOUTHWEST RIDGE FROM THE EAST

IN THE AUTUMN of 2016, a German Alpine Club (DAV) expedition under the leadership of Herbert Bader made the first ascent of Takphu North (6,142m, 30°18'8.03"N, 81°24'59.96"E), a peak on the border with Tibet, near the northwest tip of Nepal. It was brought onto the permitted list in 2014 and must have been one of the more remote unclimbed 6,000m summits in the country. The expedition's round trip from Simikot involved 240km on foot and about 11,000m of ascent.

Leaving base camp east of the mountain at 1 a.m. on October 12, Bader, Karl Joseph Hengge, Tassilo Hock, Josef Knitz, Annabelle Rochelt, Alois Sinz, and Bhai Krishna Khadka (Nepal) reached the summit at 10:30 a.m. The team appears to have climbed the southeast-facing glacier (about 35°) between Takphu North and Takphu Himal (6,395m) to the frontier ridge, and then followed this broad snow ridge northeast to the flat summit. The total distance from camp was estimated at 9 km. 🔍

– LINDSAY GRIFFIN, *FROM VARIOUS SOURCES INCLUDING THE HIMALAYAN DATABASE*

PALCHUNG HIMAL

DANPHE SHAIL, SOUTHWEST FACE

JUST OPEN a map of Dolpo and look at the far top, along the Nepal-Tibet border. There are very few peaks named, but one of them is Danphe Shail (6,103m, 29°40'18.38"N, 83° 0'29.10"E). When approaching Upper Dolpo, a pointed summit can be seen from afar, and many trekkers refer to it as the Dolpo Matterhorn. In 1909, Ekai Kawaguchi, a Japanese monk who traveled through Dolpo to Tibet, referred to it in his book, *Three Years in Tibet*, as "the mountain as a guide." (Lost in a storm, Kawaguchi was eventually able to find his way after glimpsing this mountain from a distance.)

However, what nearly everyone has seen is not just one summit but two—they are so close that it is easy to be confused. The sharp, Matterhorn-like pyramid lies entirely in Tibet and is 6,430m. It may be called Palchung Hamka. In front is a lower snow dome, which at first looks like a snowy shoulder of Peak 6,430m, but is in fact a separate summit, on the border, with easy glaciated slopes leading to its top. This, according to both altitude and the coordinates on the Ministry of Tourism list, is Danphe Shail.

The mountain was brought onto the permitted list in 2002, and the great Japanese explorer

Tamotsu Ohnishi planned to try the peak in the summer of 2011. However, during the long approach, insect bites infected his feet and he was unable to attempt Danphe Shail. In the spring of 2016, an expedition led by Ian Wall (U.K., resident in Kathmandu) reached the valley leading to the mountain and established advanced base at 5,519m, south-southwest of the peak. Storms and appalling snow conditions prevented much progress, however, and eventually they evacuated by helicopter.

The Dolpo Matterhorn, or Peak 6,430m, seen from the southwest. What appears as a snowy shoulder down to the right is in fact the separate summit of Danphe Shail (6,103m). *Etienne Principaud*

For us, the weather was perfect. No cloud and no wind—just pleasure. Despite the long march into the Upper Dolpo, it was a privilege to seek out the ancient Bon culture and visit the last village before the mountain, Ku. From there to our base camp at 5,040m, which we reached on October 3, it was a great wilderness experience.

We established advanced base at 5,750m on the 4th and then climbed to the summit and back to base the following day. Climbing in five separate pairs, and reaching the top, were Laurence De Fleurian and Dhan Magar, Bernard Vallet and Etienne De Fleurian, Jean-François Males and Etienne Principaud, Anil Rai and Deepen Bothe, and Sonia Baillif and Paulo Grobel. 📷

— PAULO GROBEL, *FRANCE*

DAMODAR HIMAL

PURKUNG, NORTH FACE; BELGIAN PEAK, WEST RIDGE; NEW TRAVERSE FROM THE TERI LA TO MUKTINATH

THE PRIMARY AIM of our trip was to climb summits of the Teri Himal, a small subrange northeast of the Teri La (itself northeast of the Thorong La) in the southern Damodar Range. I felt these 6,000m peaks would offer interesting climbing at a moderate grade, and in climbing them we would be promoting this "forgotten" region.

We first surveyed the trek up the Labse Khola above Naar. The nearby summits were ideal for our purpose, but unfortunately we didn't climb any. The weather was poor, and we had to leave enough time for the second part of the project: opening a trekking route from the Teri La, over the Yakawa Kang Pass, to the small village of Jhong, northeast of Muktinath Temple, all without crossing into upper Mustang.

This journey proved excellent, through pure wilderness, and the terrain made it somewhere between trekking and climbing. Along the way we climbed a couple of small, easy summits: Purkung (28°48'54.05"N, 83°59'25.20"E) and Belgian Peak (28°50'1.86"N, 83°57'35.58"E). The icing on the cake!

[Top] Looking northeast at unclimbed summits of the Teri Himal from the top of Purkung. [Bottom] Purkung and an unnamed 6,000m peak to its left (southeast). The 2017 route of ascent on Purkung more or less followed the right skyline. *Paulo Grobel*

On May 26 and 27, in two groups, we climbed Purkung (6,128m, a.k.a. Purkhang) from a camp at 5,795m, via the north-northwest snow slopes, at II/F+. The only previously known ascent of this peak took place in 2004, via the west ridge, by a large team of Japanese and Sherpas (*AAJ 2005*).

We climbed Belgian Peak (6,110m) on May 28 from a camp at 5,640m, via the west ridge and snow slopes, at II/F. This peak was probably first climbed from Muktinath to the west in May 2011 by the Belgian Jean-Francois Meyer. We returned via Jomoson and Pokhara.

The Teri Himal is a perfect location to conduct an adventurous trip. Apart from its unclimbed peaks, there is also potential for fine new lines farther south, including Purkung from the Mustang side or the northeast face of Yakawa Kang (6,482m). Just open a map, take the right permit, and go! More information is at www.paulogrobel.com. 📷

— PAULO GROBEL, *FRANCE*

CHULU WEST, WEST RIDGE, ATTEMPT

ON OCTOBER 19, Germans André Günzel, Manuel Möller, and Jürgen Schütz, along with Pasang Gomba and Dawa Gyalje, attempted the unclimbed west ridge of Chulu West (6,419m), generally thought to be one of the more difficult trekking peaks. Four of the climbers reached a junction with the southwest ridge, also thought to be unclimbed, at about 5,850m (900m above the glacier). The narrow, double-corniced ridge ahead would have taken too much time, so they retreated. On the 21st, the full team climbed the normal route (north ridge) to the top. 📖

— INFORMATION SUPPLIED BY RODOLPHE POPIER, HIMALAYAN DATABASE, AND STEFAN NESTLER, GERMANY

PERI HIMAL

HIMLUNG EAST, WEST RIDGE; TRAVERSE OF HIMLUNG HIMAL

I LIVE RIGHT below La Meije in the Ecrins Massif of France, and traversing a high summit like this is like opening the door to a new world. At the point where the trip is normally a success—the goal of the expedition—you are only partway through. Everything is different and interesting.

On the high summits of the Himalaya, only a few top climbers play this challenging game: The Mazeno Ridge on Nanga Parbat is one of the masterpieces of this decade—an inspiring success. I wondered what traverses might be possible for ordinary mountaineers in Nepal. After many expeditions to Himlung Himal by various itineraries, I felt confident to try a big journey at altitude, traversing this accessible 7,000er via a previously untrodden ridge, carrying more than four days of food.

Our plan was to climb the normal route up the northwest ridge of Himlung Himal (7,126m), without fixed ropes, put a high camp just below the summit, then climb over the top with all our gear and continue to unclimbed Himlung East (6,932m). The latter is a recently opened (2014) peak on the frontier with Tibet, on the ridge that leads north toward Ratna Chuli. We would then continue down this north ridge, over several tops, including Phu Kang (6,694m). [*Opened in 2003, this peak is still unclimbed. It is not to be confused with the 6,767m peak Phu Kang Go, which lies well to the southeast.*] We planned to carry on to the vicinity of Peak 6,566m, then descend the ridge west and eventually reach the valley north of Himlung Himal, so completing a "horseshoe" route.

It was a strange climb. We established five camps on the northwest ridge of Himlung Himal, the last on a flat shoulder at 7,050m, not far from the main top, higher than our eventual goal, Himlung East. We arrived at this camp at 11 a.m. on May 7. We had spent a lot of time acclimatizing so we could live safely at 7,000m, and now our schedule was tight. More importantly, the weather felt too unstable to commit to the full traverse. Reluctantly, we made the decision to make Himlung East our primary goal.

On May 8, Isabelle Guillaume, Jangbu Sherpa, Rajan Bothe, and I left camp and skirted the summit of Himlung Himal by the northern slopes to reach the east ridge, which we descended to a col. We then ascended the west ridge of Himlung East to its summit, completing the first ascent. On the return we climbed up the east ridge of Himlung Himal and over the summit, so making the first ascent of this ridge. By the time we had returned to camp the weather was poor again, but, fortunately, next morning the cloud level rose and we were able to make our descent safely. The ridge over Himlung East is fantastic and the continuation north is still there to be done (see www.paulogrobel.com).

– **PAULO GROBEL**, *FRANCE*

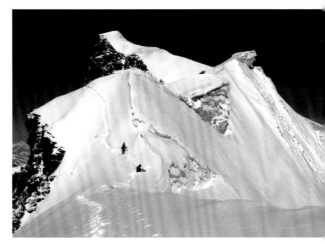

Isabelle Guillaume and Jangbu Sherpa descending the east ridge of Himlung Himal (summit visible behind) en route to the first ascent of Himlung East. *Paulo Grobel*

PANBARI, SOUTH RIDGE, ATTEMPT

PANBARI (6,905M) HAD been on my radar ever since the first ascent a decade earlier (*AAJ 2007*). A photo of the jutting south ridge was simply too much to resist. Leon Hiro Davis, Andres Marin, and I arrived in Nepal having learned just one day earlier that a French team (Thomas Arfi, Damien Tomasi, and Fanny Tomasi-Schmutz) had the same objective. We met up for dinner in Kathmandu, and it was quickly apparent that we would all get along well. It was a tough situation, since both teams wanted to be first, but we agreed to work together as long as we could.

Conditions in that part of the Himalaya were exceptionally dry in late 2017. Our photos had shown gullies choked with old snow low on the mountain, but we found these same gullies to be choked only with steep talus and shifting boulders. In mid-October, as we headed up a major gully toward the south ridge, the six of us were at about 5,100m when a volley of rocks came crashing down from an adjoining wall. Miraculously, no one was injured.

Both teams camped at around 5,400m, and the next morning the French decided (rightly) to descend. The rock ahead looked just as bad, and after witnessing a few rockfall incidents, we decided to go down too. There are many unclimbed routes that fill me with a desire to return. I am happy to let this one go. [*This expedition was backed by an AAC Cutting Edge Grant.*] 📄 📷

— CLINT HELANDER, AAC

ANNAPURNA HIMAL

GANGAPURNA WEST (A.K.A. ASAPURNA), NORTH FACE, ATTEMPT

SIMON MESSNER AND Phillip Pruenster (Italy) planned to attempt the north side of Gangapurna West (7,140m) from the Manang Valley in September. Deep snow plagued the expedition. On their first acclimatization trip up the route, the two plowed through knee- to hip-deep snow to an altitude of 6,000m. Before erecting their tent for the night, they were hit by an avalanche and swept some distance. Neither was hurt. They later made a second acclimatization ascent to 6,200m, where they left a tent. On September 22, after three days of snowfall, Messner headed back up alone. (Pruenster was ill.) When he got to the high camp, he found the tent had disappeared, probably swept away by an avalanche. The two abandoned the expedition. Gangapurna West was nearly summited from the south in 2016 by three Koreans climbers (*AAJ 2017*).

— *INFORMATION SUPPLIED BY* RODOLPHE POPIER, *HIMALAYAN DATABASE*

MANASLU HIMAL

LARKYA PEAK (LARKYA MAIN), FIRST ASCENT BY SOUTHEAST FACE

LARKYA PEAK (6,416M) lies on the ridge north of Manaslu North and is visible from the northeast along the classic Manaslu Circuit trek. From the south, many climbers ascending Manaslu's normal route have a clear view of Larkya Peak's impressive granite southeast face. However, the approach to the southeast face is long and difficult.

Thanks to the support from the Georgian Federation and the Ministry for Sport and Youth, we were privileged to climb outside the Caucasus. Georgians were pioneers of Soviet mountaineering but only within the Iron Curtain; until 2017 a Georgian team had not made a first ascent in the Himalaya. Larkya Peak—unclimbed, remote, difficult, and in an area of unstable weather—seemed the right challenge for us.

Bakar Gelashvili, Giorgi Tepnadze, Gia Tortladze, and I approached via Besisahar and the western part of the Manaslu Circuit. We crossed over Larkya La, continued east to Dharamsala, and from then headed southwest up the Syacha Glacier to a base camp at 4,550m, which we reached on September 16. Next day we established advanced base at 4,700m after a few hours of walking on difficult moraine. We then ascended post-glacial slopes to around 5,000m (satellite images show ice here only a few years ago), then 200m of ice. There was a certain amount of objective danger on this stretch, and Gia decided to head home. Our high camp below the wall was at 5,600m.

The southeast face of Larkya Peak (6,416m), showing the approximate lines of (1) Georgian Route, the first ascent of the peak, and (2) Directa Ecuatoriana. Both routes were climbed in autumn of 2017. *Roberto Morales*

The safest and most logical line on the face was directly up the center, left of a giant rock scar and close to what we had envisaged when studying photos at home. The wall was snow-free, despite storms, forcing us to carry an extra 10 liters of water to 6,000m.

We began climbing on September 22. The weather was bad, and by the time we had climbed three pitches over loose rock up to M4, we were soaked. We fixed three ropes and descended. Next day we hauled up all our gear, including the portaledge, and added one more, quality mixed pitch. On the 24th we climbed a further four pitches to 6,050m, hauled up all the gear, and spent the night.

The crux headwall rose from 6,070m to around 6,400m. On the 25th, Giorgi took the lead. Fortunately, it got warmer for a few hours as he aided through loose rock (up to A3+), climbed a 6a crack system in rock shoes, and then aided a 40m A4 pitch that took him a full five hours.

After a second night at the same portaledge camp, we took off for the summit with just a small bivouac tent. I led that day through three overhanging sections. We bivouacked at 6,200m, and the next day, the 27th, climbed very difficult terrain to reach the final snow slope. By headlamp we continued to the summit, on which we were all standing at 8 p.m., being loudly happy and toasting ourselves with a drop of whiskey. Our GPS recorded 6,425m.

We rappelled through the night to regain our portaledge at 6,050m, had a lazy day there, and then continued our descent through the next night to the foot of the wall. With 1,700m of ascent from advanced base, of which 700m were on the southeast face (17 pitches), our Georgian Route was rated ED1 6a M5 A4 80°. 📷

— ARCHIL BADRIASHVILI, *GEORGIA*

LARKYA PEAK (A.K.A. LARKYA MAIN), SOUTHEAST FACE, DIRECTA ECUATORIANA

WHILE REACHING THE summit of Manaslu, Esteban Mena caught a glimpse of Larkya Peak (6,416m) and later had no trouble convincing Roberto Morales and Nico Navarrete to join him for an attempt on the big rock wall of the southeast face. A few months later, they were eating their first chapatis in Kathmandu when they learned of the Georgian first ascent of the peak,

Setting out on pitch 10 of Directa Ecuatoriana on the southeast face of Larkya Peak, with Manaslu behind. *Roberto Morales*

just days earlier. However, they still wanted to establish their own route on this impressive wall.

Base camp was made in Dharamsala (4,500m) on the Manaslu Circuit trek, and the first step was a reconnaissance of the best approach. They first headed southwest up the never-ending Syacha Glacier, leading toward Manaslu North, then turned north and followed the upper glacier to the foot of the southeast face of Larkya Peak. They continued north, crossing a pass to the northeast of the peak that they named Ecuadorians' Col (ca 5,920m on the HGM-Finn map, between Larkya and Peak 6,039m), and descended the glacier on the far side. This led back to the Larkya Glacier and the Manaslu Circuit, but it turned out to be an extremely complicated and dangerous glacier. It was obvious there was only one way to Larkya Peak: the long way via the Syacha Glacier.

On October 14 they left Dharamsala and, in two days, with heavy loads, reached a camp at 5,600m below the southeast face. An unexpected snowstorm forced a welcome day's rest. On the 17th the three climbed the first three pitches of their proposed route (right of the Georgian line), fixed two ropes, and descended, inspired by the quality of the climb.

Next day they set off at 4 a.m. and enjoyed quality climbing until the 10th pitch, where unstable rock and technical difficulties began to slow them down. They soon realized that their anticipated one-day ascent was not going to happen, and at 6,200m prepared a bivouac.

After a night on a small snow patch, a cup of coffee and hydrated scrambled eggs put them in gear at 5 a.m. That day they lived through intense moments, with the final wall consisting of a series of vertical or even overhanging sections of rock that seemed to defy gravity. It was as if they were climbing the giant scales of a dragon, hoping not to wake it. Slowly they rose above the beast, and they were rewarded with a magnificent view from the top, having created the aesthetic Directa Ecuatoriana (700m, VI 5.11 R C2).

— ESTEBAN MENA, ROBERTO MORALES, *AND* NICO NAVARRETE, *ECUADOR*

PHUNGI HIMAL
FIRST ASCENT BY THE SOUTHEAST FACE

BY YURI KOSHELENKO, *RUSSIA*

SOME YEARS AGO, Anatoly Moshnikov commented, "I have already climbed that route in my mind, should we do it in reality?" I can't recall the mountain to which he was referring, but I remembered his words. They perfectly suited Phungi Himal (6,538m): I'd climbed it many times in my mind, but in 2017 I got the chance to compare dreams with reality.

In October 2010, Anatoly and I visited the Dana Khola, which rises below the southern flanks of Phungi Himal and Thulagi (7,059m), during a long exploratory trip to Nepal. From what we saw, we concluded that it would be best to first climb Phungi Himal, during which we could make a good inspection of Thulagi, with all its secrets and traps. Then, acclimatized, we could make a double: two unclimbed summits in the same area. But life turned out differently. In October of 2011, Anatoly died in the Altai mountains. Thulagi was finally climbed, after many attempts and two fatalities, in 2015 (*AAJ 2016*).

In 2017 I wanted to try a peak from my old secret stash. I discussed Phungi with Alexey Lonchinsky, whom I'd met at the Bezengi Camp in the Caucasus. On October 15, our small team of two climbers and Dandy the cook reached base camp at 3,655m in the Dana Khola. For two days the visibility was bad, but when we were finally able to see the mountain, we were surprised by how dry it was compared with seven years ago. We would have to find a different route from the one Anatoly and I had scoped.

Although not obvious from afar, a line on the southeast face now seemed the best option, starting with a couloir right of the summit fall line. We began early on the 26th, but rockfall was immediate, and we had to use the buttresses on each side for cover. We climbed mainly snow flutes, occasionally having to overcome the vertical back walls of crevasses. The couloir led to a groundhog-shaped rock below the narrows where we planned to bivouac. It was only 12:30 p.m. when we reached the groundhog, but rocks were flying down the narrows, so we chopped a sheltered site and pitched the tent.

Leaving at night, so as to reach a safe spot above the narrows before the rocks began flying again, we climbed ice and

[Top] **The southeast face of Phungi showing the route of ascent on the southeast face. The climbers descended the west ridge (left skyline) and southwest face. [Bottom] The west face of Thulagi (7,059m) seen from the first bivouac on the southeast face of Phungi.** *Yuri Koshelenko*

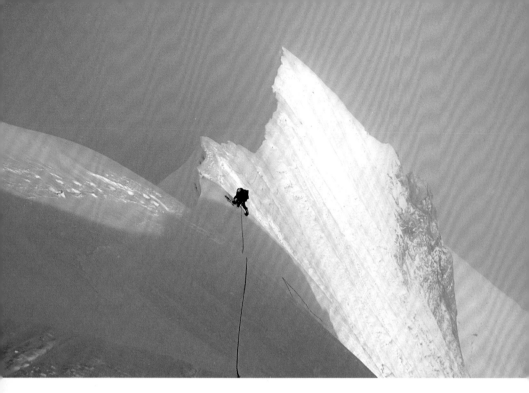

Alexey Lonchinsky on the east ridge of Phungi during the first ascent. *Yuri Koshelenko*

mixed for four pitches to the narrowest section, where a steep icefall led to the central ice flutes on the southeast face. Rockfall now was less of a problem. The face gradually got steeper as we approached the east ridge, and near the top we found a sheltered bivouac site below a serac, off the line of the route, at around 6,300m. We'd climbed almost 1,000m of ice that day (20 pitches from 60–80°), so were pleased with progress.

On the 28th the weather began to deteriorate. By 10 a.m. the temperature had dropped abruptly and it had started to snow. Nearing the east ridge, delicate icicles hung onto vertical blocks of snow. I'd faced this before while climbing Nuptse East in 2003: One wrong move and the structure breaks, leaving you feeling like a butterfly whose wings are frozen to the surface, holding the rest of your body above the void!

The last pitch to the ridge was intense. There was a strong wind, the cold was harsh, a cornice broke underneath me, and the metal gear I carried was making threatening sounds from static electricity. I retreated to a sort of crevasse and moved along it for a couple of pitches below the ridge.

Eventually things calmed down and we gained the crest in fresh snow. The angle was easy, so we trampled out a tent platform (ca 6,500m), left our gear, and went up to the summit, which we reached at 4:30 p.m. Next day we packed the tent, retraced our steps to the summit, and then went down the unknown west ridge. The weather deteriorated quickly, just like the previous day. With no visibility, our first three rappels were very much into the unknown. Then we circumvented a rock wall at around 6,100m, and even though we were eager to get down, our gut feelings told us to stop and wait for better conditions before continuing through the dangerous icefall.

Next morning we resumed the descent, and after three rappels found ourselves in a less steep part of the icefall. We moved together from then on, and although we couldn't make it all the way to base camp that night, it wasn't important. We'd managed to accomplish our goal. I dedicated the ascent to Anatoly. 🔲

GANESH HIMAL

PUNCHEN HIMAL NORTH, NORTHWEST FACE AND NORTHWEST RIDGE

PUNCHEN HIMAL (6,049M) lies on the Nepal-Tibet border, 30km north of Ganesh I (7,422m). In 2007, a Japanese party led by Tamotsu Ohnishi followed the northwest ridge from its base, with an excursion onto the face to the right, to reach Punchen Himal North (5,962m), but the climbers were unable to cross the connecting knife-edge ridge to the main summit (*AAJ 2008*). In 2009, a second Japanese expedition, led by Koichi Kato, attempted the south-southwest ridge direct to the main top, reaching 5,888m.

In mid-April we approached the peak via the Tsum Valley. After acclimatizing, we placed high camp at 5,161m, higher than, and farther east of, the 2007 Japanese high camp. On April 28 we summited Punchen Himal North with Dende Sherpa and Karma Sherpa. The snowy slopes of the northwest face presented a straightforward climb, apart from a 50m band of loose rock, and then we followed the northwest ridge over steep snow slopes to the top (PD+). [*The Japanese climbed the northwest ridge from its toe.*]

Looking along the summit ridge of Punchen Himal to the main top. The highest point may be the sharp rock pinnacle. *Mark Aitken*

We attempted to follow the connecting ridge toward the main summit. However, the avalanche risk was too high, with large and unconsolidated cornices on both sides of the ridge. With better consolidation, our proposed route would have been a viable option and likely AD+ or D. There is a possibility that the highest point is a steep rock pinnacle, which would be harder. We thank the BMC for providing a grant toward this expedition. [*Note: The online report includes interesting panoramic photos of this area.*] 📄 📷

— MARK AITKEN *AND* ANDY HEMINGWAY, *U.K.*

TABSAR SOUTHWEST TOP, NORTHEAST RIDGE

IFMGA GUIDE NARENDRA Shahi (Naren Thakuri), with Iman Gurung and Samir Gurung, all from Nepal, climbed one of several 6,000m-plus summits to the southwest of unclimbed Tabsar (6,065m), approaching via the Tsum Valley. The three ascended to the glacier southeast of Tabsar, followed this to an icefall, which gave some technical climbing with hidden crevasses, and made their high camp at a flat section above (ca 5,600m).

On October 1, the climbers continued southwest up the glacier, passing below the south ridge of Tabsar, to the northeast ridge of Peak 6,056m (HGM-Finn). They climbed this ridge (first rocky, then snowy) to the top. Their phone GPS recorded 6,110m. [*Peak 6,056m is one of three unnamed tops rising to the southwest between Tabsar and 6,425m Langu Himal. The other two are ca 6,100m and Peak 6,210m. The online version of this report also details the history of attempts on Tabsar.*] 📄 📷

— LINDSAY GRIFFIN, *WITH INFORMATION FROM NARENDRA SHAHI (NAREN THAKURI), NEPAL*

LAJO DADA (A.K.A. LANGU HIMAL), NORTHERN GLACIER AND WEST-NORTHWEST RIDGE

Norifumi Fukuda belays Kojuro Hagihara on his last steps to the summit of Lajo Dada, with the twin-summited Chamar (7,165m, north top) behind him to the west. *Yudai Suzuki*

ON OCTOBER 17 three young climbers from the Tomon Alpine Club—Norifumi Fukuda, a senior student at Waseda University, and two recent graduates, Kojuro Hagihara and me—made the first ascent of Lajo Dada (6,426m, 28°32'45.33"N, 85°3'12.18"E). This peak was opened by the Nepalese government in 2014 and lies west of the Tsum Valley, a little south of 6,065m Tabsar. Our only information about the peak was from Google Earth and a 1:50,000 map—this made the expedition quite adventurous, even for the approach.

We set up base camp at 4,650m, above Mu Gompa (monastery) in the main valley, and then Camp 1 at 5,200m on a glacier to the west of Mu Gompa, which we called Waseda Glacier. We then spent three days setting up Camp 2 at 5,730m, finding a way through the glacier maze.

We left for our summit attempt on October 15, spending a night each at Camps 1 and 2 before leaving the latter at 3:20 a.m. on the 17th. As I was climbing a 40° ice slope covered by 25cm of snow, I was avalanched for 15m. Fortunately, everything was under control, and after switching to an alternative line up ice, we reached a plateau at 5,850m.

We continued south up to a col on the Chhyosin Himal Ridge, which descends east-northeast toward the Tsum Valley, then followed the ridge southwest toward an unnamed, unclimbed peak of 6,200m. The ridge was mostly hard snow, with a steep drop to the south, but before reaching the summit there was a 3rd-class rock step that we simul-climbed.

We stood on top Peak 6,200m, at the western end of the Chhyosin Ridge, at 9 a.m., and then descended south to the plateau in front of Lajo Dada. This proved hard work, as we had to break trail through 40cm of snow. It took four hours to reach the base of the west-northwest ridge of Lajo Dada, at around 6,170m. This ridge was steeper than we had assumed. We did six pitches of 50° to 75° snow and ice, with the seconds jumaring. We reached the summit at 5:30 p.m., when it was beginning to get dark.

Without wasting time, we began rappelling the ridge, using snow anchors and V-threads. It was 9 p.m. when we reached the bottom of the ridge, and from there it took another eight hours to return to Camp 2, which we reached after a 26-hour day. Next day, with really sore bodies, we descended to base camp in 6.5 hours. 🗎 📷 ▶

— YUDAI SUZUKI, *JAPAN*

Langtang Lirung from the east. The original route, climbed in 1978 by a Japanese team, followed the right skyline (northeast) ridge after a difficult and dangerous glacier approach. Most subsequent ascents have followed the left skyline (southeast) ridge. (X) marks the spot of the climbers' proposed landing site above the icefall. From there, Dusserre and Girard hoped to climb snow slopes diagonally left before heading up to the northeast ridge. *Dusserre/Girard Collection*

LANGTANG LIRUNG AND SHALBACHUM: ATTEMPTS WITH PARAGLIDER

THERE ARE A number of attractive unclimbed faces in the Himalaya that have not even been attempted because the approach is considered too difficult or dangerous. On paper, our concept was simple: We would use paragliders to catch thermals and fly over the danger zone, landing at a safe site on the face. From there we would hope to climb in alpine style to the summit and back, and then descend by paraglider.

After extensive research on the mountains of Nepal, Julien Dusserre and I found that Langtang Lirung (7,227m) met all the criteria. Relatively few have reached the summit, and the peak is deemed highly dangerous due to constant avalanches. [*There are 14 known ascents, nearly all by the southeast or southwest ridges. However, unauthorized ascents are rumored.*] The east face remains virgin, and toward the right side there was a potential safe landing between 5,700m and 6,000m. Above lie snowfields that lead, seemingly easily, to the upper crest of the unrepeated northeast ridge, the route of the first known ascent (Japanese, 1978). Below the proposed landing site is a chaos of ice, where seracs fall almost constantly. And in this part of the world it is quite easy to find thermals up to 6,000m.

We trekked from Kathmandu through Helambu in poor weather. We each carried 37 kg (82-pound) packs, and we used no porters. When the weather improved and we had gained enough altitude and acclimatization, we packed everything, launched our paragliders, and flew to the Langtang Valley, eliminating three days of hiking with two hours of flight.

To finalize our acclimatization for Langtang Lirung, we decided to attempt a similar climb with two nights spent at altitude. Choosing a peak that had characteristics closest to our main objective, we settled for Shalbachum (6,707m), where there are several possible landing sites between 5,000m and 6,200m. The remaining ascent did not look too difficult. [*This peak was first climbed in 1959 by Japanese via the southwest face.*]

On April 30 we packed 18-kilogram (40-pound) rucksacks and flew from a height of 4,200m to a snow terrace on the southwest face of the mountain at 5,800m. Unfortunately, we were now in cloud. Moving through deep snow, we reached a higher terrace at 6,200m, where we decided to sleep. It was clear and cold that night, but the next morning large, dark clouds gathered in the west. It began to snow. In the middle of the afternoon we took advantage of a lull to downclimb, not without difficulty, to 5,800m, where we camped for our second night. Next day we descended another 250m, and after digging a takeoff runway and waiting for the wind to subside, we managed to fly down to the main valley.

After a couple of days of rest, we felt sufficiently acclimatized to take a shot at Langtang Lirung. Unfortunately, the weather remained unstable. From May 5 to 11, we made multiple attempts to fly up to Langtang Lirung carrying 12-kilogram packs, including food for three days. Sadly, the air currents formed a flying ceiling of little more than 4,600m. With no change in the forecast until June, we abandoned the expedition.

On the positive side, we now know that this system will work, and given the right weather conditions it is certain that paragliding will make it possible to discover new routes that were hitherto deemed inaccessible.

– ANTOINE GIRARD, *FRANCE*

KYUNGKA RI, SOUTHWEST FACE AND NORTHWEST RIDGE

DURING THE POST-MONSOON season there were a number of attempts on Kyungka Ri I (6,599m), an officially unclimbed peak close to the Tibetan border, northeast of Shalbachum, and at least one successful ascent.

First to arrive was a large expedition of six Koreans and four Sherpas led by Yuon Heon-mo. They established base camp on October 11 at 4,700m on the Shalbachum Glacier. Two camps were made on the southwest face, the highest at 5,700m. At 3 a.m. on the 15th, Oh Min-young, Han San-hum, Dawa Norbu Sherpa, and Pasang Norbu Sherpa left the high camp and climbed up to the northwest ridge, negotiating a wide crevasse. Between 10 and 10:30 a.m., all four claim to have reached the summit. However, while their summit photos are certainly from the upper northwest ridge, they obviously are taken on relatively wide and flat ground, whereas the summit is very sharp.

In November and December came a Japanese expedition led by Yoshichika Yamada, making his third attempt. (His first two were in 2010 and 2011.) Also attempting the southwest face to northwest ridge, Yamada, Yuki Shibata, and Yu Yamamoto found the route up to the ridge to be completely on ice, and having planned for snow and brought few screws, they were forced to retreat from 5,800m.

The true summit was definitely reached shortly after the Korean expedition, and via the same route, by a solitary climber who believes the Korean "summit" photos were most likely taken about 200m to 300m away and 40 to 50 vertical meters below the top. At this flat section of the ridge, the solo climber saw that an obvious line of blown-in footprints leading up the ridge appeared to stop, though at the time this was not thought significant, as the snow from there to the summit was firmer and more wind-scoured. The Korean team later said they took the photos a little lower than the summit because the latter was so sharp. 📄 📷

– LINDSAY GRIFFIN, *WITH HELP FROM OH YOUNG-HOON, KOREA, AND YU YAMAMOTO, JAPAN*

ROLWALING HIMAL

KORLANG PARI TIPPA SOUTH, WEST FACE AND SOUTH RIDGE

IN NOVEMBER, ROB Boulton, Joe O'Connor, Mark Rowland, Ian Stead, Dan Walker, and I, led by Dawa Rita Sherpa and Mindu Sherpa, made the first ascent of the remote Korlang Pari Tippa South (5,738m) on the Tibetan border. Our approach took us from Lamabagar (reached by 11 hours of very bumpy driving) to Lapche Monastery, and then up the right fork of the valley to base camp on a plateau at 4,800m.

From an advanced base at 5,300m, near the head of the valley, we climbed the west face and south ridge to the top on November 18. (The Sherpas had fixed 450m of rope the day before.) Although the height gain was only around 440m, scree and loose rock made for a tough ascent. At one point we reached a gendarme that we could neither go around nor over, so we took off our packs and squeezed directly through, making moves more akin to caving than climbing.

The summit was at 28°9'58.39"N, 86°11'32.46"E. (The erroneous coordinates given by the Ministry lie to the north and east, and entirely in Tibet.) About 1km to the north, at the northeast head of the valley, is another peak of similar, or perhaps slightly higher, altitude. We referred to this unclimbed summit as Korlang Pari Tippa North.

– BRIAN JACKSON, EXPEDITION WISE LTD., *U.K.*

CHEKIGO SANO, WEST FACE; BAMONGO, SOUTH FACE, TICK CHHA

FOUR MEMBERS OF the Spanish Alpine Team (Equipo Español de Alpinism)— Jesús Ibarz, Omar Juan, Pablo Ruíz, and Jorge Valle, accompanied by Sonia Casas, Jonatan Larrañaga, and expedition leader Mikel Zabalza—visited the Rolwaling in October and November. This was the culminating trip of a three-year mentoring program.

On arriving in early October at their base camp in Na (4,180m), the team discovered that south faces, normally the optimal aspect for post-monsoon climbing, were very dry. Instead, they first looked at west faces, hoping the the southern aspects eventually might come into better condition. To acclimatize, members of the

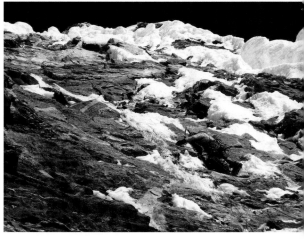

The final mixed section (M5) of Tick Chha on the south face of the Bamongo–Kang Nachugo ridge. *Pablo Ruíz*

group climbed Yalung Ri (5,650m) and Peak 5,794m. Ibarz, Juan, and Ruíz climbed the latter by a variant to the 2012 Rousseau-Villanueva route (*AAJ 2013*), following the north ridge in its entirety from the base and naming their line Moon (400m, UIAA V+ 65° M).

On the 28th, after a previous inspection of the line from a simple peak to the south, Larrañaga and Valle climbed the south ridge of Chugimago, only two days after the American first ascent reported below. They felt the 1,000m route was at least TD.

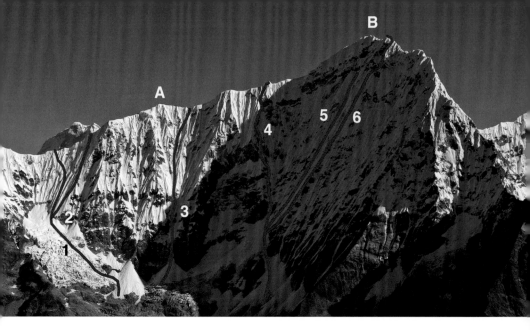

Kang Nachugo from the south. (A) Bamongo (6,400m). (B) Main summit (6,737m). (1) West Ridge (2008). (2) Che Guevara (Chinese-Nepalese, 2013, to Bamongo). (3) Tick Chha (Spanish, 2017). (4) Japanese Route (2016, continued to summit). (5) Gottlieb-Puryear 2008 attempt. (6) Monsoon (Kastelic-Padros, 2013) to southeast ridge but not to summit. *Joe Puryear*

Meanwhile, the rest of the group had set their sights on Chekigo Sano (6,121m, the west summit of Chekigo). On the 28th, Ibarz, Juan, and Ruíz climbed a direct line (probably the first) up the west face, which they named Danebat (900, TD+ WI5 M4/5). They started from a 5,000m camp close to the foot of the face at 2 a.m. and reached the summit at 4 p.m. The lower section gave ice at 70–80° and one mixed section (first crux), while the upper section, in a couloir between two flutes, featured ice to 80°. They rappelled the route, mainly from V-threads, reaching their tent at 10 p.m. It is not clear when the first ascent of Chekigo Sano took place, but it was certainly climbed from the northeast by Paulo Grobel's team in 2004.

On November 7, after a previous attempt four days earlier with Ibarz, Juan and Ruíz climbed a line up the south face of Kang Nachugo's west ridge, exiting onto the ridge just right (east) of the summit of Bamongo (6,400m). The 1,200m route was graded ED WI5 M6+ and named Tick Chha. They made more than 20 rappels down the route to regain their camp 25 hours after leaving.

That same day, Ibarz and Zabalza repeated an old French route on the southeast face of Chekigo Sano, climbing a couloir/depression between Sano and the main summit *(see AAJ 2015)*. Ibarz and Zabalza reached the base of the couloir via a rising rocky traverse from the right (steps of UIAA IV/V). The couloir itself had sections of M4, a rock step of V, and ice to 80°, steepest below the summit. The overall grade was considered TD (1,000m). 🗒 📷

— LINDSAY GRIFFIN, *FROM INFORMATION PROVIDED BY PABLO RUÍZ, SPAIN*

KANG NACHUGO, SOUTH FACE AND WEST RIDGE

I HAD INTENDED to try the unclimbed east face of Kang Nachugo (6,737m) in 2015, but the massive earthquake prevented access to this region. A year later, in the autumn of 2016, I hooked up with Hiroki Yamamoto to try again. We reconnoitered the east face, and although it looked good, each line had too many objective hazards. We turned our attention to the southwest face.

We found a thinly iced line, and on October 15, 2016, we ascended from Na to our 4,900m advanced base. As usual, the face was veiled in thick cloud during the afternoon, but when this cleared as the sun went down, we saw to our amazement that the thin ice on the steep section had vanished. Our only option now seemed to be a repeat of the route Monsoon (Kastelic-Padros, 2013), hopefully completing it to the main summit as they had been unable to do.

At 3 a.m. on the 16th, we reached the foot of the climb. But from here we could see another possible line, farther to the left, on the south face. It was unclear whether we could make it through the rock band below the summit ridge, but we decided to try.

After a pitch of classic WI4 with good ice, we mostly simul-climbed and quickly covered the first 500m in one lead block each. There were cruxy mixed sections and rotten ice, but generally the terrain was moderate. We reached our first bivouac spot, at 6,100m, just before dusk.

Next day we climbed a knife-edge leading to the final rock band. A slightly overhanging line of solid ice brought us to a flute of solid ice and deep snow. Just before noon we reached the summit ridge. With a bit of sketchy downclimbing, we arrived at a very flat spot where we could leave all our extra gear for a summit push. The Tibetan side of the ridge looked easy, but it was unclear if cornices might block the way to the summit. We chose to keep to the Nepalese side, which was more difficult and proved slow going, as we had only one snow stake. At around 3 p.m. on October 17 we stood on the summit, only the second known ascent of the peak, after David Gottlieb and Joe Puryear in 2008.

We discovered we could easily descend to the Tibetan side of the ridge, so we were able to follow moderate terrain back to our bivouac. On our third day we began rappelling the south face immediately below the bivouac. Eighteen rappels took us to the base; the first half of the descent was very exposed to avalanches and microwave-size blocks of rock and some ice falling past us. We celebrated our climb in Na with a stack of beers and Kukuri rum, which made us happy, even if it made my snow blindness worse. [*See a photo from this climb on page 1.*] 📄 📷

– **GENKI NARUMI**, *JAPAN*

CHUGIMAGO NORTH, NORTHWEST FACE; OMI TSO GO, NORTHEAST RIDGE; KHANG KHARPO, SOUTH-SOUTHEAST RIDGE

ON OCTOBER 23, Miha Zupin and I left Slovenia for the Rolwaling, and on the 28th reached the village of Na (4,150m), our base camp for the next three weeks. At the start of our stay there was afternoon snowfall, but other than that we had beautiful cold, clear weather the whole time.

On the 30th we walked to Tsho Rolpa Lake (4,580m), and the following day up to 5,200m at the base of the northwest face of Chugimago North (5,945m). On November 1 we climbed a similar line to the 2016 Mirhashemi-Pugliese route [*probably more to the right in the lower two-thirds*], reached the lower northeast

Khang Kharpo (a.k.a. Ripimo Shar) from the southwest, showing the line of Kranjski Greben (2017) on the south-southeast ridge. *Luka Plut*

Miha Zupin on the upper south-southeast ridge of Khang Kharpo with the peaks of the Mahalangur Himal (Khumbu and Barun) in the background. Large peaks visible on the distant horizon include (from left) Everest, Lhotse, Makalu, and Chamlang. *Luka Plut*

top (measured at 5,890m GPS), and descended northeast to the Tsho Rolpa. We don't recommend this descent, as it is very loose. Our 600m route had sections of snow and ice up to 80°.

On November 7 we climbed the northeast ridge of Omi Tso Go (6,332m), northeast of Kang Nachugo, on the border with Tibet. Although it is likely that Omi Tso Go had received one or more unauthorized ascents in the past, it was only brought onto the official permitted list in 2014. Early that same winter, American Scott Adamson reached 6,000m on the northeast ridge, climbing alone while his partner, Angela VanWiemeersch, remained in camp with altitude illness.

From a high camp at 5,600m, we climbed the ridge (up to 75°), measuring a summit altitude of 6,337m. Thinking it to be a first ascent, we were surprised to find fairly fresh footprints in the middle of the ridge. These disappeared 50m below the summit but could easily have been blown away by the wind. [*Climbers on nearby Bamongo—see report above—witnessed an unidentified solo climber descending from that peak one day earlier.*] We descended to our tent the same day.

The last mountain we climbed was Khang Kharpo (a.k.a. Ripimo Shar, 6,646m) at the head of the Rolwaling (Ripimo Shar) Glacier. On the 13th we reached the col (ca 6,000m) between Khang Kharpo and Dragnag Ri. The following day we made the first ascent of the south-southeast ridge of Khang Kharpo (6,641m GPS) and descended to the tent. We named our route Kranjski Greben (1,300m, UIAA IV 75°). This was the fifth known ascent of the mountain.

At the end of the expedition we were lucky to be invited to a traditional Sherpa wedding, where we consumed chang and dal bhat in great quantities. It was a perfect end to our first trip in Nepal. ⬛ 📷

– LUKA PLUT, *SLOVENIA*

LANGDUNG, SOUTHWEST FACE AND SOUTHEAST RIDGE

IN LATE 2017, Dawa Yangzum Sherpa, Nima Tenji Sherpa, Pasang Kidar Sherpa, and I obtained a permit for unclimbed Langdung (6,357m), spanning the border with Tibet at the head of the Rolwaling Glacier (a.k.a. Ripimo Shar Glacier). The peak had been attempted several times, notably in 2016 when a party reached a point close to the summit on the southeast ridge (*AAJ 2017*).

We headed for the mountain on December 12 and reached a base camp below it, at 5,097m, after a week of trekking. We only spent a day there before ascending the Langdung icefall to put a high camp (5,700m) on the upper glacier below the south face. We felt physically strong enough at that point to go for the top, but were concerned about the weather; cirrus clouds racing over the summit were a bad sign.

Next morning, December 20, we planned to leave for the summit very early, but it was so cold we didn't start until 6 a.m. In two and a half hours we climbed the 300m southwest face (45–60° ice) to reach the southeast ridge at around 6,000m. The crest above was longer and sharper than we had expected, mainly mixed with a few sections of loose rock that made it more challenging. We spent five and a half hours on the ridge before reaching the summit, where our satellite phone showed a reading of 6,350m.

After spending a short while soaking up the spectacular panorama, we made a quick descent down the southwest face in nine rappels [*more or less following the line of the 2016 attempt*]. Overall, we felt the 650m route was PD.

— DAWA GYALJE SHERPA, *NEPAL*

[Top] The broad Langdung Massif from the southwest. (1) Approximate line of 2016 American-Nepalese attempt, generally followed for rappel descent by the Nepalese in December 2017. (2) Nepalese route (2017). [Middle] Looking along the main axis of the Langdung Massif toward Langdung Central and West. Tibet is to the right. The large mountain in the distance is Gaurishankar, while the nearer face to its right is part of Menlungtse. [Bottom] Langdung summit selfie. *The Nepalese Langdung Winter Expedition*

Rolwaling Kang from the Drolambau Glacier to the south-southeast, seen over a foreground ridge. The summit is on the left and the south face, climbed in 2016, is hidden. *Yasuhiro Hanatani*

ROLWALING KANG, SOUTH FACE

IN OCTOBER–NOVEMBER 2015, we organized our first "Himalayan Camp," with the aim of helping Japanese newcomers to the Himalaya. Approaching through the Khumbu and then operating from a base camp in the Chhudunbo Valley, we climbed Langdak (6,220m) via the southeast ridge, a route more difficult than expected (Sho Kamasawa, Koji Shiogai, and me, November 8) and Raungsiyar (6,224m) by crossing the col to its south—between the peak and Pimu (Pamalka, 6,344m)—to reach the Drolambau Glacier, and from there traversing the mountain from south to north (Sho Kamasawa and me, November 14). *[These peaks likely have seen a number of climbs since their first ascents in 1952 and 1955, respectively, so it is not possible to say if any new ground was covered; see also AAJ 2016.]*

Our original plan had been to attempt Rolwaling Kang (6,664m, 27°53'51.44"N, 86°31'14.61"E), but the earthquake made the approach to the Rolwaling Valley impractical. So, in 2016, our second Japanese Himalayan Camp also targeted Rolwaling Kang.

We left Kathmandu on September 29. Because conditions on the approach were none too good so early in the season, we were forced to establish base camp at 4,700m, at the entrance to the Drolambau Glacier, lower than planned. After reconnaissance and acclimatization, we camped the night of October 18 at 6,100m, near the head of the glacial cwm south of Rolwaling Kang. That same day, Yuchiro Iida and I inspected a direct ascent to the south ridge but found it difficult to establish belays due to poor snow conditions. Instead, we climbed four pitches up the face to the left, cached some gear, and descended to our high camp.

We all left next morning at 5:30 a.m. It was sunny and windless. We split into two teams and climbed the broad south face, left of the south ridge, in parallel. There was more snow than expected, so finding good ice for anchors was difficult. We reached the edge of the summit plateau around noon and were pleased to find an easy walk northeast to the highest point, which we reached a little after 1 p.m. Summiters were Yuichiro Iida, Maho Ishio, Youhei Kayama, Keisuke Tsunoda, Takuya Yoshikawa, and me. This was the first known ascent of this mountain. 📷

– YASUHIRO HANATANI, *JAPAN*

CHUGIMAGO (A.K.A. CHUKYIMA GO), WEST-SOUTHWEST RIDGE

MIKE ARNOLD (USA), my client Tim Wheeler (U.K.), and I arrived at Lukla on October 5. We acclimatized in the Khumbu and then used the Tashi Laptsa pass to reach the Rolwaling, reaching the village of Na on the 18th.

Hoping to attempt Chugimago (6,258m), we moved up to the vicinity of Yalung Ri base camp on the 21st, and the same afternoon I made a solo ascent of the east ridge of Yalung Ri North (5,634m). It had difficulties up to 5.7 or 5.8 on several sections and plenty of loose scrambling. With some traffic, the route would offer a nice alternative to the more popular Yalung Ri. *[The first ascent of Yalung Ri North took place in 1952, though the exact line is uncertain.]*

On October 22, Mike and I carried a tent and equipment to the base of the west-southwest ridge of Chugimago, establishing a camp on the rocky ridge running south from Peak 5,794m. The following day, all three of us moved up to this camp. We spent the next two days climbing nearby lower summits, all of which had seen recent activity, and watching for an improvement in the winds, which had been quite strong.

On the morning of the 26th, Tim stayed in the tent while Mike and I went for a single-push attempt on Chugimago's west-southwest ridge. We had previously scouted a 250m ice gully on the northwest flank of the lower crest, which would allow us to bypass the very broken rock and a tower at the start of the ridge.

Leaving camp a little before 5 a.m., we started up the gully at 5,600m. By 7:45 a.m. we had reached the crest of the ridge, where we decided to cache one rope and some ice screws. The climbing above looked predominately moderate, with the difficult sections on broken rock.

For the next three hours we took turns leading in blocks, mostly staying on the crest. Low on the ridge, we came across a cache of six pitons, a few carabiners, and a Tibloc, all rusted; we estimate these dated from the early 2000s. By 11 a.m. we had reached about 6,000m and decided to stop and melt snow for water. At this point we left the stove for our return and also the rock rack, carrying only four ice screws and two snow pickets above. This ended up being a mistake: We had underestimated the difficulties of the upper mountain.

As we traversed the ridge, our height gain seemed minimal for the amount of climbing, much of which was on mixed terrain. Nearing the last few hundred vertical meters, the ridge steepened and various steep ice pitches appeared to require more screws than we carried. Instead, we traversed right onto rock that was horribly fractured and at times overhung. Near the top of the rock we gained solid ice, where a good screw gave us confidence to continue moving right on a series of ledges. Several more pitches of AI3 led to the summit ridge, where afternoon clouds began to obscure most of the views. It was 3 p.m. when we reached the top, where three ridges intersected and there was barely room for the two of us to stand. Two minutes later we began the descent, knowing that much of the terrain would need to be downclimbed.

Just as the last rays of sun were dropping into the horizon, we reached the cache where we had left the stove and rock gear. Both of us were hungry, thirsty, and ready to take a small break. The rest of the descent passed without much difficulty. We reached camp at 9 p.m., rating our ascent ED1/2 (5.7/8 AI3+).

Next day we packed camp and descended to base camp. On the 28th, while Mike moved some equipment down to Na, Tim and I climbed Yalung Ri. Both of us were pleasantly surprised by the quality of the climb. As we descended, snow started to fall, and it was clear we had squeezed in our last objective just before the weather turned.

– **KRISTOFFER ERICKSON**, *AAC*

High camp on the south ridge of Peak 5,794m with Chugimago behind. The gully approach to the west-southwest ridge is marked. Three known routes (2014–2016) ascend the left side of the northwest face, below the summit (see AAJ 2017). *Kristoffer Erickson*

TO THE TOP
SETTLING OLD BUSINESS ON PANGBUK NORTH

BY MAX BONNIOT, *GMHM, FRANCE*

AFTER SPENDING ALMOST 20 hours studying the pictures of the west face of Lunag Ri, I thought I'd finally found the line, which cleverly avoided objective hazards and verticality. It also seemed very blue, the sort of blue of which every mountaineer visiting Nepal dreams. Maybe I should have worried about the falling barometric pressure? Maybe I should have suspected something from the repeated rumbling above camp?

Max Bonniot leading out of the notch on the southeast ridge of Pangbuk North. The next 120m would comprise mostly unprotectable snow. *Pierre Sancier*

After sweating and stumbling, Pierre Sancier and I managed to establish a foothold on the Lunag Ri moraine, where we saw the evidence left by the anticyclone that had persisted across this part of Asia for a month. Instead of our long-anticipated ice flows on the west face, we saw flood waters similar to the Arve River through Chamonix in spring. After a few seconds of contemplation we switched to plan B—from a west face to a north face, from Lunag Ri to Pangbuk North (6,589m, although mistakenly 6,748m on the HGM-Finn). The unusual heat in the Lunag cirque appeared to have left Pangbuk North unscathed.

In 2009, a French-Nepalese-Swiss team tried to summit Pangbuk North via the northeast face and southeast ridge, but turned around at about 6,150m after exiting the face at a notch on the southeast ridge. [*The leader of this team claimed the first ascent of the mountain and attempted to name it after a corporate sponsor.*] In 2013 the peak was climbed via a direct route up the northeast face (*AAJ 2014*). We decided to try to finish the 2009 route, which would involve very steep snow on the ridge immediately above the notch and would give us a full 1,000m to express ourselves between the bergschrund and the summit we now coveted.

At 3 a.m. on October 18 we could still hear Lunag Ri's west face groaning, yet everything seemed quiet on Pangbuk North. We crossed the bergschrund at 5 a.m., the altimeter reading 5,450m. Shortly after, we reached the constriction at the bottom of the face, post-holing in soft snow. As the sun rose I had to take off my pack to climb the first block of vertical ice; I trailed a thin rope to haul the bag once I passed the crux. Spindrift was falling, making it seem as though I was breathing through a Ziploc bag. At the same time my fingers started to lose sensitivity, and when I reached the belay I was panting. By the time the steepness gave way to a long snow slope it was 7 a.m. The altimeter showed only 5,600m—a long way to go if we were to reach the summit that day.

Three hours later we reached the last section before the ridge, finding 200m of beautiful ice. It was 10 a.m. and falling rock was beginning to ricochet close by. We took the most sheltered path; the pitches were interesting and varied. On the last pitch of mixed climbing we found pieces of fixed rope from the 2009 team. At the snow-covered notch, I took a quick glance at the ridge above and was temporarily demoralized: 400m to go and

[Top] Pangbuk North from the east. (1) Tolérance Zéro (2017). (2) Purgation (2013). The peak behind on the left is Pangbuk Ri (6,716m). *Chris Wright* [Bottom] Pierre Sancier on the summit ridge. Behind him, the southeast ridge ends at Peak 5,777m. To the left the Lunag Glacier flows into the Nangpa Glacier; to the right is the Pangbuk Glacier. The Everest-Lhotse group and Makalu are on the far left. *Max Bonniot*

the next pitch looked really steep. Since Pierre was only interested in attempting this mountain as a second, I had agreed in advance to lead the entire route, and the idea of climbing the almost unprotectable snow pitch above the notch made me stop and think. When Pierre arrived at the ridge, we decided we'd stay the night there—after I'd led the 80° snow above and fixed our two ropes.

Somehow we managed to overcome the difficulties, return to our tent, rest well, and leave at dawn the following day. We ascended our ropes, after which the ground eased to 60°. At around 9 a.m., after traversing a gorgeous snow-covered ridge, we reached the summit and were treated to a breathtaking panorama over Tibet and four 8,000m peaks. The pleasure of witnessing such scenery left us blissfully happy. That night we rappelled 1,000m to reach the base of the mountain. To have been able to climb this elegant, logical, and technical route gave us tons of satisfaction.

SUMMARY: First complete ascent of the northeast face and southeast ridge of Pangbuk North in the Rolwaling Himal, by Max Bonniot and Pierre Sancier. The route was named Tolérance Zéro (1,100m, ED- WI5 80°). *This report was translated by Fanny Deplace.* 📷 🔍

The light from Jost Kobusch's headlamp is visible on the upper southwest face of Nangpai Gosum I during the night of October 2–3. He reached the south top and then continued across an upper plateau (hidden) to reach the main summit at left. *Raphael Schardt*

SOLO ON NANGPAI GOSUM

FIRST ASCENT OF ONE OF THE WORLD'S HIGHEST UNCLIMBED PEAKS

BY JOST KOBUSCH, *GERMANY*

At 10:24 a.m. on October 3, I reached the summit of Nangpai Gosum I (7,321m) all alone. This peak on the Nepal-Tibet border, southwest of Cho Oyu, had been considered by some to be the fourth-highest unclimbed mountain in the world. [*See editor's note below on nomenclature.*]

As far as is known, prior to 2017, it had had only two serious attempts. In 2006, Kazuyoshi Kondo's joint Japanese-Nepalese expedition fixed 2,600m of rope up the south ridge to reach what they referred to as the 7,240m south top. Despite the relatively early hour (11 a.m.), the team did not continue across a plateau to the main top, which looked quite far. A direct line up the south-southwest face, overlooking the Lumsumna Glacier, was attempted by four French guides in October 2016. After a bivouac at around 6,200m, they progressed to about 6,600m, where one of the team, Mathieu Maynadier, was hit on the arm by falling ice and injured (despite good conditions, every team member was hit by either ice or rock) and they retreated.

After acclimatizing in the region, I arrived in base camp on September 5, and over the next few weeks carried loads, including 500m of rope, to the base of the mountain. My idea was to fix these ropes on the very technical passages along the French line, so that they would only have to be soloed once; this also would allow a quick descent in case of bad weather or injuries.

One of the problems with this route is its south-facing orientation: Once the sun is up, the ice melts quickly, exposing granite. This not only makes the climbing difficult but also sends down a bombardment of rock. If it is snowing, avalanches regularly crash down the line.

On September 25, I made an attempt to reach the French high point and establish my Camp 2. During this attempt, I soloed an 80° ice wall at about 6,300m and then faced very dry conditions in the upper section, where there was a bottleneck (climbed by the French in 2016 and estimated to be M6/6+). There was no other option, but the ice was very thin, fragile, and ended on blank stone. To get an overview and hang my backpack, I built a temporary anchor from two ice axes and an ice screw. As I began to hammer in a piton, the entire belay ripped, leaving me hanging from the piton, which was only half in. The sun had been so intense it had quickly melted out the ice screw and axes. I decided to retreat. I'd felt safer when I climbed Annapurna, considered one of the world's most dangerous mountains.

Jost Kobusch on the summit of Nangpai Gosum I with the peaks of the Rolwaling behind. *Jost Kobusch*

I reached my Camp 1 at 6,100m in the middle of the night. Screws had melted out, ropes had been cut by rockfall, and I got hit several times and was lucky not to be seriously injured—what a day!

Back at base camp, the staff were preparing to leave. But I couldn't let go until I felt I had tried everything. I opted for another attempt, farther right, close to the Japanese line from 2006. I went light and fast, leaving most of my equipment, including any rope, at the base of the mountain. But I did take a harness in the unlikely case I needed helicopter rescue.

Starting from advanced base (5,600m) at 3 a.m. on October 1, I slanted up the southwest face of the south summit to a campsite at 6,400m (40–50° at the start, rising to 60–70° toward the end), and then the next day up to a second camp at 6,840m (50–55°). I left this camp at midnight and climbed through the night (generally 50° but with two short vertical sections). At the plateau beyond the south top, I struggled through almost waist-deep powder, but I reached the main summit in midmorning. Wind gusts up to 60 kmh (37 mph) made my stay short, but for a brief moment I stood still and felt like one of the adventurers I'd read about as a child. This wasn't following somebody's footsteps—it felt so much bigger than my previous climbs.

When I returned to base camp I found only my photographer, Raphael Schardt, waiting for me with a single tent.

SUMMARY: First ascent of Nangpai Gosum I in the Khumbu Section of the Mahalangur Himal. Jost Kobusch (Germany) soloed the southwest face to the south summit and traversed to the main summit, October 1–3, 2017. 📷

EDITOR'S NOTE: *The Nangpai Gosum peaks lie on a high ridge forming the Nepal-Tibet border, and confusion surrounds their nomenclature. Nangpai Gosum I (formerly referred to as Nangpai Gosum II or Cho Aui) is immediately east of Pasang Lhamu Chuli (7,350m), which used to be called Nangpai Gosum I or Jasamba but was renamed in 1993 after the first Nepalese female to summit Everest (she died on the descent). The nomenclature in this report is consistent with what we've used in the AAJ over the last 10 years.*

THARKE KANG, NORTHWEST RIDGE

THARKE KANG (6,710M) is a newly opened summit that sits on the northwest ridge of Hungchi (7,029m). This ridge rises from the Nup La (5,844m) and forms the frontier between Nepal and Tibet. A guided expedition led by Garrett Madison (USA) made the first known attempt on Tharke Kang in the autumn.

The team trekked to a base camp at around 5,200m by the Gokyo Fifth Lake, above the west bank of the Ngojumba Glacier. They then completely avoided the icefall by helicoptering over it and onto the glacier plateau near the Nup La, where an advanced base was established at 5,820m on November 1. Members of the team then climbed onto the crest of the northwest ridge and ascended about two-thirds of the way to the summit, fixing ropes on steeper sections.

On November 3, the team left advanced base at 2 a.m., crossed the glacier for 45 minutes, climbed about 150m up to the crest, and then continued up the northwest ridge to the summit, which the first group reached at 9:15 a.m. After descending to advanced base, the following day they experienced the culture shock of waking at 6 a.m., flying by helicopter to base camp, and then onwards to Kathmandu for a celebratory dinner. [*The online version of this report also describes the climbing history on neighboring Hungchi.*]

– **LINDSAY GRIFFIN**, *WITH INFORMATION SUPPLIED BY GARRETT MADISON*

BURKE KHANG, SOUTH FACE AND SOUTHEAST RIDGE

Looking north up the Gaunara Glacier to Burke Khang (6,942m) and the route up the south face and southeast ridge. The high peak to its left is Hungchi (7,029m), first climbed in 2003 by the southwest ridge. *Alex Buisse*

ON MAY 23, 2014, as I was hunkered down in my tent at high camp on the north side of Mt. Everest, the government of Nepal opened 104 new peaks for climbing. One of them was named after me. Thus began a three-year odyssey, which some have characterized as an obsession, to be the first person to climb my eponymous peak. [*Editor's note: Burke Khang was named by the government of Nepal upon the recommendation of the Nepal Mountaineering Association, in recognition of Burke's contributions to the promotion of mountain climbing, trekking, and tourism in the country.*]

Burke Khang (6,942m) lies on the frontier ridge east-northeast of Hungchi (7,029m). I made three unsuccessful attempts to climb it—in autumn 2015, autumn 2016, and winter 2017—failing each time because of conditions on the mountain or weather. I decided to make one last attempt in the autumn of 2017. I was joined for the climb by Noel Hanna from Ireland and Micah Kershner from New Jersey, supported by four Sherpas: Naga Dorjee Sherpa, Pemba Tshering Sherpa, Samden Bhote, and Tshering Tashi Sherpa.

On September 30 we arrived at base camp (5,300m) on the west side of the Gaunara Glacier. My planned itinerary called for rest days at each camp, and I informed the team that, at age 75, I would not deviate from that program. Noel and the Sherpas had arrived earlier and already had begun fixing lines up the mountain. Tshering Sherpa and I began our move up the east couloir of the south face on October 3. This was the toughest climbing of my life (much of it 75°+). It took 10 hours to reach Camp 1 (6,200m), where I pretty much collapsed in my tent.

On October 4, our weather forecast warned of heavy snow and high winds. Noel, Micah, and the Sherpa team planned to move to Camp 2. I felt strong and invigorated from my night of deep sleep, but I was not going to move up without a rest day. I told Noel unequivocally: If the team saw an opportunity to summit, they should not wait for me.

On the 5th, as Tshering and I began our move to Camp 2, I received a radio call advising me that Noel, Naga, Samden, and Pemba had left Camp 2 for the summit at 6 a.m. (Micah remained at Camp 2.) Their entire route was studded with deep crevasses, making navigation difficult. When they reached the nearly vertical headwall below the summit ridge, they moved east and attacked the headwall where it was shorter and less steep (70°). After crossing a false summit, at 12:05 p.m. the four of them reached the highest point, where Noel pulled out a bottle of champagne. It was a truly joyous moment for everyone on the Burke Khang team, though no one was more pleased than me. 🗎 📷 ▷

— BILL BURKE, *USA*

PEAK 6,010M, NORTH FACE AND EAST-SOUTHEAST RIDGE (ALMOST TO SUMMIT)

OUR ORIGINAL GOAL was to climb the north face of Lobuche West (6,145m). Joao Garcia and I approached up the Changri Nup Glacier from the village of Lobuche (ca 4,940m). Five hours of walking over difficult moraine took us to a base camp at 5,100m. On the afternoon of May 19, a large piece of Lobuche West fell off and swept the starting point of our proposed line. We changed our plan and instead went for Peak 6,010m on the ridge northwest of Lobuche West (between that peak and Nirekha).

The north side of Lobuche West and the line of the 2017 Spanish Route on Peak 6,010m to about 10m below the summit. A foresummit of Lobuche West is on the left. *Angel Salamanca*

We left the tent at 3 a.m. on May 20 and reached the snow cone at the foot of the 900m north face at 5 a.m. At first the snow was good (55–60°), but once the sun came up conditions worsened. The face steepened as we ascended and we reached a zone of flutes, similar to those found on Alpamayo in Peru. In this section we found very old, hard ice, at first 70° but occasionally up to 80°. We were carrying heavy packs, planning for a possible traverse along the ridge and bivouac, and in the last part this ice was such hard work that we had to reduce our pitch lengths to around 10m to 15m.

We eventually reached the summit ridge, and it began to snow heavily. Between rock outcrops the sharp ridge was split by crevasses covered with newly fallen snow, and I fell into one. Beyond the last rock the final section was a dangerous and thin cornice. In poor visibility, we stopped approximately 30m away and 10m below the top. Joao and I reversed the route, finally reaching our tent at 6 p.m. There appears to be no recorded ascent of this peak. [*The online report also describes the first known attempt on the north face of Lobuche West.*] 🗎 📷

— ANGEL SALAMANCA, *SPAIN*

Vlad Capusan on mixed ground at around 6,500m, below the third bivouac on the south face of Pumori. Difficult climbing and an afternoon snowstorm limited progress to 180 meters that day. *Zsolt Torok*

PUMORI, SOUTH FACE, ATTEMPT

OUR PROPOSED ROUTE on Pumori (7,148m) followed a direct line up the central section of the south face, well to the left of the 1986 Scottish Route. The project felt ambitious and would be totally reliant on the weather and mountain conditions, in an area known for heavy spring snowfall.

Zsolt Torok and I started acclimatizing on April 20, and for the next two weeks enjoyed almost perfect weather. On the 30th we climbed to 6,200m on Pumori's normal route, the southeast ridge, which we planned to use as our descent. In early May we received news of a short weather window, and our meteorologist said this might be the only chance we would have that season. We set off at 2 a.m. on May 6.

A giant crevasse and deep snow cost us many hours on the glacier, and it was only toward the end of the day that we reached the base of the wall and found what we hoped would be a protected bivouac site at 6,000m. However, there was frequent spindrift, and we had to clean the site every two hours. It was not the best night.

On the morning of the 7th we started up a chimney giving access to the main weakness left of the spur climbed by the Scots. We began by following a large dihedral. There was powder snow everywhere, and at each step we had to clean snow crust from the rock. We found no in situ gear or sign of previous passage in the short icy chimneys and passages of M5+. [*At this stage, the Romanians thought they might be following the initial pitches of a supposed Croatian route from 1986, which in some references is marked in this area of the face. However, these sources generally are based on an erroneous report in AAJ*

South face of Pumori (7,148m), showing (1) Southwest ridge, Japanese 1973; (2) Romanian attempt to 6,800m, 2017; (3) Scottish Route, 1986; (4) Czech Route, 1996; (5) French Route, 1972; (6) Jeff Lowe, solo, winter 1983; (7) British attempt, 1996; (8) Australian-American-Nepalese Route, 1984; and (9) Normal (original) route, German-Swiss, 1962. *Vlad Capusan*

1987 of a new Croatian route on the south face of Pumori. This was corrected to the south face of Ama Dablam in AAJ 1988.] We bivouacked that night under a large rock at 6,400m. It was quite cold, but our motivation was still high.

We woke at 3 a.m. on the 8th and continued climbing, encountering the hardest pitch so far. The weather was good, but by 2 p.m. a storm had arrived and we enjoyed it to the full for the rest of the day. We reached 6,580m, close to the start of what we dubbed the Ramp, before the weather finally stopped us. It snowed about 10cm and did not stabilize.

That night, after excavating a tent site, and just as we had managed to erect the flysheet, an avalanche buried me inside. The poles broke, but fortunately I was anchored and managed to extricate myself. We had to find another place to sleep—that night was the hardest of all.

On the 9th we woke at 2 a.m. with the aim of climbing the Ramp through the White Spider to a bivouac on the upper southwest ridge. However, at 5 a.m. black clouds swallowed the face, and soon it was snowing heavily. Despite this, we reached 6,800m, determined to push to the ridge. Unfortunately, at this point a large avalanche caught us in the middle of the Ramp. In the lead, I was swept off the wall and fell around 10m, but fortunately didn't suffer any real injuries, as my protection was good. However, I was coughing badly, our tent platform at 6,580m had been swept away, and the Ramp had been transformed into a huge avalanche funnel. We were sitting ducks.

We made the difficult decision to retreat and began 900m of rappels. It was night by the time we reached the foot of the face, and 3 a.m. on the 10th when we arrived at base camp (5,300m), completely exhausted. This expedition brought us to the limit of human condition, but we also laughed a lot and each morning woke up visualizing stepping onto the summit. The real summit is always back home; the rest is pure adventure. We will return. 📷

— **VLAD CAPUSAN**, *ROMANIA*

MAHALANGUR HIMAL / BARUN SECTION

LUNG-TA BUTTRESS

From the beginning, Jonathan Cooper, Japhy Dhungana, and I had the mindset of an exploratory expedition, seeking out unclimbed walls between the major Himalayan peaks. In November, we found many potential lines in the Barun Valley, which houses some of the best rock in the Nepal Himalaya.

We were armed for big wall, rock, and alpine climbing, in the hopes that the line would find us—and find us prepared. We were fortunate to find our line on only the fourth day of our approach trek, when a sweeping wall of granite was spied through a break in the rhododendron forest southwest of Yangle Kharka. The wall was situated above the south side of the Barun Valley, below an unnamed summit (ca 5,100m) on the long ridge extending southeast from Tutse (a.k.a. Peak 6, 6,758m).

We spent our first day carrying loads up 1,000m slopes to the base, scouting a line, and climbing and fixing the first few pitches. We returned in the evening of the second day and bivouacked at the base. Over the next two days, we climbed the left side of the buttress—our line mainly faces east—to the top of the wall, finding both pure rock pitches and mixed climbing. The Lung-Ta Buttress (500m of climbing, V 5.9 X A1 M5, steep snow) was predominantly free, with a pendulum on pitch six. There is potential for more lines on this peak and others nearby, where a high-quality band of granite forms several walls. 📄 📷

— **ZACH LOVELL**, *AAC*

Looking south from the col reached by Les Brasseurs Savoyacks at peaks in the little-known Chhochenphu Himal, rising to around 6,000m. *Grégoire Lestienne*

YANME KANG, SOUTH FACE

APPROACHING VIA YANGMA and the lakes of Nangamari Pokhari and Pabuk Pokhari, Grégoire Lestienne and Floriane Pugin (France) made the first ascent of Yanme Kang (6,206m, 27°56'59.64"N, 87°50'29.08"E), a peak opened in 2003 that lies on the border with Tibet to the northwest of Nangamari. On October 29, from a bivouac at 5,800m, they climbed the south face, comparing the route to ascending the Dome du Goûter in the Mont Blanc Range. A large crevasse that cut across the whole face at 6,000m was passable via a snow bridge. Their GPS measured 6,220m.

On the 30th they attempted the first ascent of Lang Chung Kang (6,475m), another border peak, between Yanme Kang and Nangamari. Access to the western flank of this fine pyramid is exposed to huge serac falls, as shown by a drone reconnaissance, so the two tried to climb the peak by crossing the border north of Nangamari and reaching the east face. They reached an altitude of 5,300m, where it began to snow and they retreated.

Moving south of Pabuk Pokhari, on November 2 they climbed a 400m northeast-facing ice/mixed couloir to a col at about 5,700m on the east-southeast ridge of Senup (6,265m). They named this ascent Les Brasseurs Savoyacks (M3 75°). [*The online report contains more photos of little-known peaks in this area.*] 📄 📷

– **LINDSAY GRIFFIN**, *FROM INFORMATION PROVIDED BY GRÉGOIRE LESTIENNE, FRANCE, AND RODOLPHE POPIER, HIMALAYAN DATABASE, FRANCE*

NANGAMARI II, NORTHEAST RIDGE FROM THE EAST

IN OCTOBER 2016, an expedition of the Kanzai section of the Japanese Alpine Club made the first ascent of Nangamari II (6,290m). [Nangamari I (6,547m) was climbed by an Australian team in 2010.] After establishing two camps, the higher at 5,600m, the Japanese climbed to the col between Nangamari I and II from the east, then continued up the northeast ridge of Nangamari II. The slopes were straightforward until a col between the north top and the main summit, after which a knife-edge snow arête had to be traversed. All nine team members reached the summit in early afternoon. A full account is at the AAJ website. 📄 📷

– INFORMATION FROM **TSUNEO SHIGEHIRO,** *JAC, TRANSLATED BY TAMOTSU NAKAMURA*

SHARPHU I, ATTEMPT; THA NAGPHU, NORTH RIDGE

SHARPHU IS A collection of peaks on a north-south ridge to the west of Kambachen, forming the watershed between the Ghunsa and Yangma valleys. There are six main summits in the group, and only the highest, Sharphu I (6,433m), is known to have been climbed: In 1963, Japanese climbers approached via the Sharphu Glacier to the southeast and climbed the south face and ridge.

In April, a Spanish-Argentine-Nepali group attempted Sharphu I via the Sharphu Glacier, reaching Camp 2 at 5,700m and finding the glacier to be much larger than depicted on their map. They also went up the Nupchu Khola (valley) to look at east faces of the Sharphu Group, and from here they climbed Tha Nagphu (5,980m) via the glacier to the northeast and eventually the north ridge (snow and rock to 80°). A report (in Spanish) with maps and photos of various faces in this area is available at the AAJ website. 📄 📷

– **LINDSAY GRIFFIN,** *WITH INFORMATION FROM MARÍA PILAR AGUDO, SPAIN, AND THE HIMALAYAN DATABASE*

JANAK HIMAL

LHONAK PEAK, SOUTH-SOUTHEAST RIDGE, ATTEMPT

TAKANORI MASHIMO'S SIX-MEMBER Japanese expedition, which made the first ascent of Dzanye II in October 2015 (*AAJ 2016*), also made an unsuccessful attempt on Lhonak Peak (a.k.a. Rifil Peak, 6,070m, 27.830876°N, 88.054761°E), a summit with no recorded ascent that was brought onto the permitted list in 2014. The expedition left the Lhonak Valley at around 4,600m and penetrated the gorge leading east to the Chhyatundinga Glacier (a.k.a. Broken Glacier). From an advanced camp below the entrance to the first glacier bay on the north side of the valley, they climbed onto the south-southeast ridge of Lhonak Peak, where they were stopped by loose terrain on the crest.

– **LINDSAY GRIFFIN,** *WITH INFORMATION FROM HIRO HAGIWARA, EDITOR, ROCK AND SNOW, JAPAN*

PANDRA, NORTHEAST FACE, PEINE PLANCHER

In October, Mathieu Détrie, Pierre Labbre, and Benjamin Védrines (France) made the second ascent of Pandra (6,850m map height, 27°51.897'N, 87°59.547'E) via a new route on the northeast face.

In November 2016, Kei Taniguchi and Junji Wada (Japan) attempted the right side of the northeast face, reaching the north ridge and continuing up this until 300–400m below the summit, where they retreated due to poor conditions, cold temperatures, and wind (*AAJ 2017*). Taniguchi died in a climbing accident in Japan just one month later.

Approaching from Ghunsa, the three French trekked for five days to a base camp at 5,140m, still some distance from the face. Next day, October 7, they established an advanced base at 5,500m, across the Chabuk Glacier from the northeast face, next to a small lake named Pokari. From here they could see that conditions on the face were much better than at the time of the Japanese attempt. Over the next two days they climbed a 6,200m peak just to the east of their camp to acclimatize.

[Top] The northeast face of Pandra. (1) Peine Plancher (2017). (2) Japanese attempt (2016). [Bottom] Mathieu Détrie on the crux ice pitch (WI6) on the second day of the northeast face of Pandra. *Pierre Labbre*

After four days' rest at base camp, they returned to advanced base, and on the 16th they set off at 6 a.m., crossed the Chabuk Glacier, and started climbing the face around 10:30 a.m., when the sun had moved off it. They took a line left of and entirely independent from the Japanese line, finding thin ice and a little mixed terrain, some of it very steep. They bivouacked at 6,000m. The next day began with a very hard pitch of thin ice. Above, steep ice climbing led to a pitch of M6, followed by steep snow to their second bivouac, a comfortable site at 6,400m.

Their third day involved ice and another section of hard mixed, followed by snow slopes to the top, which they reached at 2 p.m. They rappelled the route, arriving back on the glacier at 9 p.m., three hours after dark. The route was named Peine Plancher (1,200m, WI6 M6), and featured some sections of ungradable and impossible-to-protect snow, like that found in Alaska. The team said the northeast aspect protected them from the wind, so they never really got cold, and there were minimal objective dangers.

Although Pandra's official height on the HGM-Finn maps is 6,850m, on the first ascent of the mountain, in 2002 via the south face, three Danish climbers measured the altitude by GPS as 6,673m. The French carried no GPS device. 📷

— LINDSAY GRIFFIN, *WITH INFORMATION FROM RODOLPHE POPIER, HIMALAYAN DATABASE, FRANCE*

High camp at the base of Sauyr Zhotasy East. Although not technically difficult, the high point of this range, Sauyr Zhotasy (3,840m), has extreme topographic prominence for its size. *Mitch Murray*

SAUYR ZHOTASY EAST, FIRST KNOWN ASCENT

THE GOAL OF making the first documented ascent of Sauyr Zhotasy (a.k.a. Muztau), a remote 3,840m peak on the Xinjiang-Kazakhstan border, has been discussed for years. Although its technical difficulties and altitude are not great, its topographic prominence of 3,250m is perhaps the highest of any unclimbed peak. [*Previously, this accolade probably fell to Mt. Bois-ing, the highest peak of the Finisterre Range in Papua New Guinea. That mountain's first known ascent was in 2014.*] In addition, the small Sauyr Range and its glaciers hold the distinction of being the farthest from any ocean on earth. Hundreds of square kilometers of steppe and desert surround the range. Information on the peak was nearly impossible to find, and satellite images proved to have snow covering much of the terrain we wanted to see.

Months of attempted correspondence with Chinese authorities and expedition compa-nies resulted in disinterest and a certain paranoia due to the hazy security matters surround-ing Xinjiang's borders. The Xinjiang Mountaineering Association was not interested, as the summit lies below the height—4,000m—for which permits are required. Taking matters into our own hands, Eric Kowalski, Dr. Alex Mathews, Mitch Murray, and I decided to go ahead with a trusted friend, expedition collaborator, and logistics genius, Alex Tang from Chengdu.

From the razor-wire-girded Uighur restaurants and exotica of Urumqi, we crossed the Dzungar Basin to Hoboksar, a camel-trading outpost nearest the Kazakh frontier, deeply locked down with border paranoia, including Soviet-like security checks at every step. The Sauyr Range loomed beguilingly beyond the hotel windows, with only 25km of Gobi between us and it, but we took pains to conceal our interest, stating we were camel-watchers.

Prepared for anything, we crossed the expanse of endothermic Gobi to find intimidating patrol posts at the head of each valley, beyond which alpine walls, glaciers, huge buttresses, and snowy plateaus beckoned. Through binoculars we considered options ranging from the conservative to the cavalier, and then retreated to Hoboksar for permits, only to be blocked by military personnel wishing we would simply just go away.

We gambled on attempting Sauyr Zhotasy's glaciated main peak via a distant valley system, the only one in striking distance without a border post at the entrance. This would entail first summiting the most easterly main top of the range and then embarking on a 7km traverse of the exposed connecting ridge.

With supplies for a week, we walked 8km, with a height gain of 1,800m, to a launch camp below the snowline at around 3,500m. A second day of endless scree and boulder fields, merging into 50° snow, bought us to the base of the east peak's headwall, a crumbly mass of unstable rock and ice with no safe bivouac spots. However, there were great views back down the valley toward the Tarbagatai Desert and its strange ranges of eroded mountains.

Murray and I continued unroped along a rising traverse around the headwall, emerging onto the summit plateau, where I carried on for 1km through knee-deep snow to reach the east peak (ca 3,710m, 47.055189°N, 85.651908°E, Google Earth). Despite the summit's highest point showing no sign of previous visits, we saw blatant signs of human activity up to around 3,500m and a series of three possible ancient cairns on a feature at about 3,600m that may be visible from other vantages. Thus we claim the first *documented* ascent of Sauyr Zhotasy East.

It was clear the 7km ridge running westward to the main summit was punctuated by at least two technical ascents and descents, and a large section of the route was invisible to us. Although within our ability, the 14km round trip was deemed too risky at the time; any unplanned descent into the flanking valleys to the south would have resulted in detainment at their exit.

We had determined that the main peak would be possible to climb, once security and alpine problems are surmounted. Approaches from other valleys would be shorter and more dramatic, but would demand a plan for the ever-watchful border posts. Opportunities exist for pirate ascents, as per the tradition of Central Asian alpinism, but you didn't read that here. 📷 🔍

– ED HANNAM, *AUSTRALIA*

GANSU

ZHAWUDUO, WELCOME TO ZHAGANA AND GATE TO ASGARD

IN MAY, HE Chuan (China), China-based Ola Przybysz (Poland), who led the trip, and I visited the Tibetan village of Zhagana (2,800m) in southern Gansu to explore the Zhagana Stone Mountains. The area is becoming popular with Chinese tourists, but we learned of it from a photo on a climbers' chat group in summer 2016. Supposedly, an inexperienced Chinese climber had visited Zhagana, but locals said we were the first climbers to visit the area.

Our primary objective was the area's iconic limestone peak, towering above and to the east of the village. We learned on arrival it was named Zhawuduo (34.239956°N, 103.212854°E). Our first two days were spent reconnoitering the peak, finding the west and east faces very steep off the deck and with little obvious natural protection. However, a crack system on the south face, beginning higher up the hillside, appeared to offer more moderate climbing and better opportunities for gear placements.

We opted to make the 1.5- to 2-hour uphill approach each day, returning to the village to eat and sleep. Over five days (with one rainy rest day), we established Welcome to Zhagana

[Above] **Looking east to the village of Zhagana and the dramatic peak of Zhawuduo. The new routes climbed in 2017 are just beyond the right skyline.** [Right] Ola Przybysz leads pitch two (5.11a) of Gate to Asgard on the south face of Zhawuduo. *Garrett Bradley*

(300m, seven pitches, 5.10+ A1), leading to the higher, eastern summit at 3,800m. We placed a few bolts but still encountered some runouts. However, the rock on this face has generally decent friction and is quite featured.

On our way down we bolted the upper pitch of a new sport route, 40m to climber's right of Welcome to Zhagana, fixing ropes the rest of the way down. Chuan had to go back to Beijing for a few days, but in the meantime Ola and I bolted the remainder of the route. After Chuan returned, he and Ola climbed the nine-pitch Gate to Asgard (5.12a) all free, while I shot photos. With the exception of a hard sequence of moves on the first pitch, the route offered moderate, enjoyable sport climbing in the 5.10 to easy 5.11 range.

Zhagana is surrounded on three sides by towering limestone peaks, with a concentration of mountains to the north and northeast. Zhawuduo, the main peak, still has numerous unclimbed lines on the south face and steep sport climbing potential on the east and southwest faces. The area has much more to offer, and while the peaks up valley to the north will require a longer approach, they will likely provide bigger walls and longer routes. 📖 📷

— **GARRETT BRADLEY,** *USA*

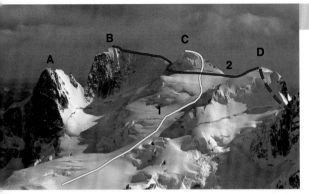

CHOLA I, SOUTH-SOUTHEAST SPUR AND WEST RIDGE

IN AUGUST, AN American-Chinese team likely became the first to stand atop the highest point of the Chola Shan. There has been much confusion in the past as to what has been climbed in this group.

Chola I (6,168m) has two tops, east and west. In 1988, a joint Chinese-Japanese expedition reported reaching the summit of Chola I, making its first ascent. (A second ascent was reported in 1997 by Charlie Fowler, climbing solo, but this turns out to be a different peak—see below.) In 2003, a Chinese team led by Jon Otto (USA) repeated the 1988 route. However, it was clear to Otto that both the 1988 and 2003 expedition had climbed to the west top, which Otto measured at 6,148m GPS. (This summit is now often reached by guided parties.) Around 450m to the east, along a difficult and narrow ridge, rose another summit: the east top. Was it higher? It looked roughly the same, but only by climbing both with a GPS would it be possible to clarify.

In August 2017, Gao Jun, Liu Junfu, and Otto set a base camp at 4,060m at the southern end of the large Xinlu-hai lake. The normal route up Chola I heads west up a glacier, around the north side of a rognon, and up the glaciated north face to the summit. The

[Top] Chola I seen from Chola II to the north-northwest. (A) Peak 5,898m, possibly unclimbed. (B) Chola I (east top, 6,168m). (C) Chola I (west top, ca 6,150m). (D) West shoulder, reached from the far side by 2017 expedition. (1) The normal route to Chola I west top. (2) Route from the west shoulder to the higher east top climbed in August 2017, starting on the far (south) side. [Bottom] Chola II seen from the northwest. (1) Costa-Dempster-Normand (2015). (2) Approximate line climbed by Charlie Fowler in 1997 during the first ascent of the mountain. This line was described incorrectly in *AAJ 2016*. *Bruce Normand*

American-Chinese team opted to start up the opposite side of the mountain. They moved south-southeast from the lake to reach a glacier on the south side of Chola I, where they established Camp 1 at 4,900m. Moving up the glacier, they made a second camp at 5,400m and a third at 5,820m, the latter below a south-southeast-facing spur that leads to the main ridge at a shoulder a little west of the west top. Climbing this short spur (50–70°), the three reached the shoulder, then traversed below the west top to reach the col beyond via a vertical step. From the col, they spent another two hours crossing the sharp ridge to reach the east summit on August 9.

Two GPS readings were taken on Chola I's east top: 6,163m and 6,157m. On the return, Gao and Otto descended directly to the north glacier from the col, but Liu continued to the west top, where he made two readings with the same GPS units: 6,146m and 6,139m. This implies the east top is higher by around 17m or 18m. (The most recently available Chinese map marks 6,168m squarely on top of the east summit.)

The 2017 climb thus appears to be the first known ascent of the highest point of Chola I. It now seems certain that Fowler was confused about what he climbed—the confusion no doubt aided by the poor mapping available at the time (and no Google Earth!). Fowler's described route and photo-diagram of Chola I (*AAJ 1999*) are actually on Chola II, a difficult rock and ice pyramid around 3km to the north-northwest of Chola I. He climbed a steep route on the northwest face to make the first ascent of the mountain. Another route, parallel and to the left, was climbed in February 2015 by Marcos Costa, Kyle Dempster, and Bruce Normand (*AAJ 2016*).

Fowler reported climbing another peak, which he called Chola II, making its first ascent, but this is actually a straightforward snow peak another 3km north-northwest again, with a height of 5,802m. This is sometimes referred to as Chola III (31°50'26.58"N, 99° 0'59.04"E).

— **LINDSAY GRIFFIN,** *WITH HELP FROM TOM NAKAMURA, AAC HONORARY MEMBER, BRUCE NORMAND,*
SWITZERLAND, AND XIA ZHONGMING, GERMANY

SICHUAN / SHALULI SHAN

KEMAILONG, NORTH FACE AND EAST RIDGE

In October, with the support of a Grit & Rock First Ascent Grant, Galina Chibitok (Russia) and Marina Kopteva (Ukraine) climbed the first route from the north on Kemailong (5,873m), making the second overall ascent of this elegant rock pyramid (see *AAJ 2013*).

The team, which also included Anastasia Petrova (Russia), spent four days finding an approach to base camp. (This northern side of the mountain reportedly had been visited previously only by monks.) Unfortunately, on arrival at base camp, Petrova was taken ill. Chibitok and Kopteva made the reluctant decision to attempt their planned route—the left side of the north face onto the east ridge—as a pair.

A first attempt was not successful and cost a rope and a lost day of good weather. On their second attempt, starting on October 5, they climbed the steep, short north face (250m, mainly A2) to the ridge, with two nights in their portaledge. Although they originally estimated they might continue up the east ridge to the summit in just two or three days, it soon became apparent that this route would not be

Kemailong from the south. (1) South ridge (ca 1,000m, 5.10 M5, Anderson-Yi, 2012). (2) East ridge (On the Way to Amsterdam, 970m, 6b A2, Chibitok-Kopteva, 2017). The east ridge team first climbed a 250m wall on the north (far) side. *Marina Kopteva*

overall Russian grade 5, as expected, but grade 6. After a final 16-hour push, they reached the east (main) top at 7 a.m. on October 12. The descent took a further 20 hours.

The full route took eight days to ascend and was named On the Way to Amsterdam (970m, 1,280m of climbing, 25 pitches followed by 140m of easy rock to the summit, 6A/ED 6b A2).

— **MARINA KIPTOVA AND MASHA GORDON,** *RUSSIA*

The west face of Mt. Edgar (E-Gongga, 6,618m). (1) The Moon's Power, solo new route by Tomas Franchini. (2) Colpo Finale (2017). (3) Start of the southwest ridge (right skyline). *François Cazzanelli*

MT. EDGAR, WEST FACE, JIAZI, SOUTHEAST RIDGE, AND OTHER ASCENTS

I BECAME AWARE of the Minya Konka massif while looking through Tom Nakamura's book *East of the Himalaya*. I was so attracted to the pictures of the east face of Mt. Edgar that I decided I needed to see these Chinese mountains myself. On September 25, Fabrizio Dellai, Matteo Faletti, and I, all from Trentino, and three friends from the Aosta Valley, François Cazzanelli, Emrik Favre, and Francesco Ratti, left Italy with the aim of reaching the wild valley of Nanmenganggou and attempting the northeast ridge of Edgar (E-Gongga, 6,618m).

After bureaucratic problems with both the Chinese embassy and our porters, we established base camp at 3,850m and started to acclimatize in the nearby mountains. On October 1, Fabrizio, Matteo, and I climbed a wonderful peak at the end of the eastern extension of the northeast ridge of Edgar, which we named Little Edgar (5,060m). We climbed a rock route on the north-northwest face that we named Buon Compleanno Toni (Happy Birthday Toni, 650m, UIAA VI), as October 1 is my dad's birthday.

Our friends from the Aosta Valley wanted to climb the southwest ridge of Edgar, and Fabrizio, Matteo and I wanted to explore descent options should we reach the summit via the northeast ridge. We therefore all established a route to the glacier plateau below the west face of Edgar, placing a high camp at 5,250m. From there the whole team reached the col at the start of the southwest ridge, from which Emrik, François, and I turned southwest and climbed a snow ridge up to virgin Peak 6,174m (Peak 6,130m, Chinese map), which we named Twenty Shan (29°43'35.94"N, 101°54'8.11"E).

During the descent I kept looking across at the west face of Edgar (this face was attempted in 2011 by Russians, who retreated after 400m, see *AAJ 2012*). I had a strange feeling, as if the mountain were calling me. I tried to dismiss it from my mind, as the team had already defined its plan. But the calling was strong. After dinner and heading to my sleeping bag, I instinctively decided

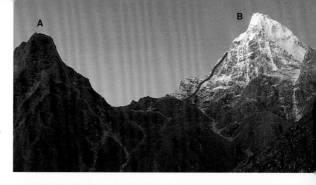

[Top] Seen from the upper Nanmenganggou, (A) Little Edgar with the route of first ascent, via the north-northwest face, and (B) attempt on the northeast ridge of Mt. Edgar to 5,840m. *Matteo Faletti* [Bottom] Tridente Trentino on the north side of the Nanmenganggou and the route of the first ascent. The pointed tower up to the right is Pilier Gerard Ottavio, also climbed in 2017. *Tomas Franchini*

to go for the unclimbed west face alone. Shortly after midnight, I headed out, illuminated by the full moon.

On the face, I climbed a series of difficult *goulottes* through steep terrain, with sections of thin and delicate ice. In the final part I had to overcome a section of mixed climbing to reach the ridge, which was laden with powder and snow mushrooms, like you see in Patagonia. Here, I had to use all my strength and concentration. A large snow structure broke away just in front of me and fell into the darkness. I had a bad fright! At 6.15 a.m., still in the dark, I reached the summit. I couldn't believe what I had just done: the first ascent of the face and the third overall of the summit. I tried to maintain full concentration during the descent of the southwest ridge (the 2001 Korean route of the first ascent of Edgar) until I reached base camp, where I celebrated with my friends. Climbed on October 7, the Moon's Power is 1,000m, WI4+ M4+, with thin ice.

Over the next few days we concentrated on smaller peaks that we could access from base camp. These included Pilier Gerard Ottavio (4,903m) by the route Meteopatia (seven pitches plus scrambling, VII, October 9); a traverse of the three summits of the Cresta delle tre Sorelle (Punta Barbara, 5,530m; Punta Elisabetta, 5,740m; Punta Patrizia, 5,852m; UIAA IV M4, October 12 and 14), and Vallee Shan (5,645m, four pitches up to VI+ on the initial rock pillar followed by classic mixed terrain at IV), all by Cazzanelli, Favre, and Ratti. In the meantime, Dellai, Faletti, and I had climbed Tridente Trentino (4,910m, by a steep 500m rock wall at VI+) on the 9th, and Peter Shan (5,645m) and Leonhard Shan (5,500m), both on the 11th. Most of these peaks lie on the north side of the valley, northeast to southeast of Jiazi. [*Coordinates are at the AAJ website.*]

Matteo and I then made the third ascent of Jiazi (6,540m) via a new route up the southeast ridge. We did this in one long day on October 15. The vertical interval of ascent was 1,600m, but the climbing distance around 3,000m. We named the route the White Line (sections up to 85°). Previous ascents had climbed the south ridge from the west (1982) and west face (2011).

As the weather was still good, we then tried our main objectives. Team Aosta Valley tried the unclimbed northwest ridge of Edgar but were stopped at 6,450m by technical difficulty and very dangerous, unstable snow. They descended with 25 rappels. Fabrizio, Matteo, and I tried the northeast ridge and spent two days getting to 5,840m, above which there appeared to be no safe lines. As the weather was very hot, we retreated on day three.

After these attempts, I needed to free my mind and again have contact with rock, so on the 20th I free soloed an unclimbed rock pillar of 4,850m via a 300m face of steep slabs, naming the route Animal (VII) and the summit Pilastro dei Pensieri.

In the final days of good weather we mixed the party: Emrik, Fabrizio, and Francesco reached the summit of Edgar via the Korean route up the southwest ridge, while François, Matteo, and I climbed the right side of the west face and continued to the summit via the Korean route to produce Colpo Finale (600m to the southwest ridge, WI5 90° M). The cherry on the cake was that we all arrived on the summit together, at 1 p.m. on the 25th. As we climbed the final crest to the top, I could still make out my descent tracks from nearly three weeks ago.

The trip was a great success for us all, but my greatest satisfaction was the solo climb of the west face of Edgar, a difficult psychological ascent where there was just me, the moon, and the mountain—nothing else.

– TOMAS FRANCHINI, *ITALY*

MT. GROSVENOR, ATTEMPTED NEW ROUTE ON WEST FACE

ONDRA MACEK AND I attempted a new route on the right side of the 1,300m west face of Grosvenor (a.k.a. Riwuqie Feng, 6,376m). We left our advanced base below the wall on September 27 and climbed eight pitches up to AI4/5 (80–90°), reaching an altitude of about 5,600m before retreating in a snowstorm.

– JAN KREISINGER, *CZECH REPUBLIC*

XIAO GONGGA, NORTHWEST RIDGE, LONG'S ROUTE (VARIATION)

ON NOVEMBER 28, four members of Summit Experience Mountain Co.—Sun Bin, Liu Hai Chuan, Zhang Bao Long, and I—made the sixth known ascent of Xiao Gongga (5,928m, a.k.a. Little Konka, Ruiche Gongga, or Tshiburongi). It was the first time most of us had gone together to the mountains, without clients, for the purposes of training.

We arrived at base camp (4,000m) on the 24th and the next day established Camp 1 below the north side of the mountain at 4,600m. On the 26th we walked for two hours to the bottom of the glacier, from which an icy line led in 600m to the crest of the northwest ridge. With Zhang Bao Long in the lead, this took around 10 hours to ascend, belaying 10 pitches up to AI3+. We reached the crest in the dark, in a temperature of -10°C and winds gusting 50km/h. We were forced to descend the ridge a short distance to find a comfortable campsite at around 5,350m.

On the 27th we fixed two pitches at the start of the upper ridge. We set off shortly after 6 a.m. on the 28th, and with Zhang still taking the lead, climbed for eight hours to reach the summit (around 14 pitches), encountering 60° snow. In cold, snowy weather, the descent was dangerous, as constructing reliable rappel anchors proved difficult. Thirteen hours after leaving, we returned to high camp, where we thawed out and ate the remaining food. The

Xiao Gongga from the north. (1) Northwest ridge, 2014 ascent. The Italian party gained the ridge just to the right of the rocks at far right. They saw evidence of a prior attempt or ascent on the route. (2) Variation start (Long's Route, 2017). *Vittorio Messini*

following day we descended the lower section of our route, trekked all the way out to the road, and drove back to Chengdu, where we arrived at 3 a.m. on the 30th to hot food and beds.

Editor's note: On October 18, 2014, Simon Gietl, Vittorio Messini, and Daniel Tavernini left a 4,600m high camp below the north flank of Xiao Gongga and climbed to the northwest ridge, at a point much further right (west) than that reached by the 2017 party. They followed steepening ground, eventually rising to 60°, to reach the summit at 1 p.m. Their 1,300m ascent was rated 60° M5 (AAJ 2015), and they saw evidence of a previous attempt or ascent.

– TOM CONNELLY, *SUPPLIED BY XIA ZHONGMING*

HENAN

LINZHOU, MERRY CHRISTMAS

OVER CHRISTMAS 2016, pictures of a large icefall strongly resembling a Christmas tree circulated on WeChat, a messaging and calling app widely used throughout China. It took He Chuan and Liu Yang five days to determine the location of this formation, and when they finally arrived on January 7, 2017, they discovered the icefall had collapsed.

The waterfall was some 700km from Beijing, southeast of the town of Linzhou in Henan Province. On January 26 a picture of the Christmas tree icefall appeared once again on WeChat, along with a message that two Chinese climbers were off to attempt it the next day. These climbers failed on the first pitch due to a huge flow of water between the ice and rock. He Chuan, Lie Feng, and Liu Yang were back in Linzhou the very next day, and He and Liu decided to make their attempt on the 31st, at the end of a four-day period of cold weather.

The start of the climb featured a pillar only 2m in diameter, but the most dangerous part was discovered 5m above the belay at the end of the first pitch: a large window in the ice revealing the waterfall underneath. He moved onto the "branches" of the tree to find better ice, and Liu then led the 50m third pitch, where a 10m section of overhanging thin ice below a large cauliflower formed the crux. The fourth pitch, also 50m, was a 3m-diameter pillar.

He Chuan has spent three recent winters ice climbing in Norway and Canada, and says that Merry Christmas (140m, WI6) is the most beautiful ice route he has ever seen, and also the most fun to climb. [*Editor's note: In early 2018, Canadians Will Gadd and Sarah Hueniken repeated this climb.*]

– LINDSAY GRIFFIN, *WITH INFO FROM XIA ZHONGMING, GERMANY*

He Chuan leading the fourth pitch of Merry Christmas (140m, WI6).
See another photo on page 6 of this edition. *Lie Feng*

NEW ZEALAND

Steven Fortune descending off the summit of Mt. McPherson after making the first ascent of Dark Waters, a new route on the southeast face. *Ben Dare*

SOUTHERN ALPS

NOTABLE CLIMBS OF 2017

A GENERAL TREND of unsettled and wet weather plagued the summer months in New Zealand and limited the amount of activity in the alpine. The most notable ascents were repeats: the second ascent of Maid Marian (1,000m, 22/5.11c A2, Dare-Joll, 2013) on the south face of Marian Peak in the Darran Mountains, by Daniel Joll and Gavin Lang; and the second ascent of Megawatt (600m, 17/5.9, McLeod, 1996) on the east face of Townsend Peak in the Hooker Range, by Steven Fortune and Conor Smith.

In early winter, a lack of precipitation led to thin conditions. Despite this, a number of new ice and mixed routes were established in the southern ranges. During the annual Darrans Winter Climbing Meet, in July, Steven Fortune and I climbed a six-pitch mixed route on the left-hand wall of the upper McPherson Cirque. Dark Waters (220m, III, 6) climbs the center of the southeast face of Mt. McPherson (1,931m), between the existing routes No Country For Old Men (Charles-Howells-Uren, 2000) and the Crossing (Harrison-Steward, 2012). I followed this up with two successful trips into the Earnslaw Burn, below the south face of Mt. Earnslaw (2,830m), where I established three new water-ice routes, two solo and one with Caleb Jennings.

The last act of winter occurred in heart of the Southern Alps, where Ben Ellis, Jack Grinsted, and Josh Mitchell made the first winter ascent of the pinnacled Maximilian Ridge on Mt. Elie De Beaumont (3,109m), more than 66 years after the first ascent in the summer of 1951 by Ed Cotter, Ed Hillary, George Lowe, and Earle Riddiford. Over six days, the trio made the long approach via the remote Whataroa Valley, on the west coast of the South Island, then completed the climb and descended the Tasman Glacier, on the opposite side of the range, to Mt. Cook Village. Ellis said the overall winter grade would be "in the ballpark of the summer grade" (4+ on the Mt. Cook scale), with a crux of about seven pitches leading to the summit ice cap.

Late spring brought a sustained period of calm, settled weather to the Southern Alps, and I was able to make two more first ascents. In late October I climbed the first route up the south face of Peak 2,472m, in the Huxley Range, at the head of the Ahuriri Valley. Phoenix (500m, IV, 5+ [M4, AI4]) follows a series of thin ice leads up a large corner system through the middle of the face.

In mid-November I ventured up the Hooker Valley to climb a probable new route on the south face of Aoraki/Mt. Cook (3,724m). From the upper Noeline Glacier, I linked ice flows and snowfields into a final mixed headwall below the upper south ridge to establish Remembrance (550m, V, 6 [WI4 M5]). [*This route is to the right of Sodom and Gomorrah (Alder-Vass, 1988) and completely independent of it. A route called Pounamu (Schmidt–Braun-Elwert) was climbed in the same general area in 2011. Elke Braun-Elwert remembers climbing mostly to the left of Dare's 2017 route, but the exact line of Pounamu has not been determined.*] Remembrance is named in tribute to Conor Smith, who, along with climbing partner Sarwan Chand, tragically lost his life in April. I had originally attempted the climb with Conor the previous year, and it was our last alpine climb together.

– BEN DARE, *NEW ZEALAND*

[Top] The south face of Peak 2,472m (left), showing the line of Phoenix (500m, IV, 5+). The west face of Mt. Huxley is on the right. [Bottom] Caleb Jennings on the second pitch of Dream Theatre in the Earnslaw Burn. *Ben Dare*

BOOK REVIEWS

EDITED BY **DAVID STEVENSON**

KARAKORAM: CLIMBING THROUGH THE KASHMIR CONFLICT

Steve Swenson. Mountaineers Books, 2017. Hardcover, 315 pages, $26.95.

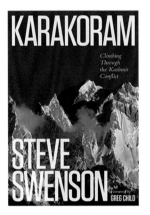

In *Karakoram*, Steve Swenson describes the climbs he attempted and accomplished in this great range from 1980 to 2015, during 15 discrete expeditions. Greg Child, who wrote the foreword, counted Swenson's days in the Karakoram at 1,200. An ascent of Everest, the only outlier, is included almost as a postscript to his K2 climb and is the only occasion he is attached (very loosely) to a larger expeditionary framework. The Karakoram climbs are done with small groups of friends, alpine style, and without oxygen.

The reference to the Kashmir conflict in the subtitle is not mere lip service. Every trip is contextualized within the ever-shifting violent political realities of the region. The only other mountaineering book I know that makes such an insistent and effective case for including such an extensive detailing of regional politics is Bernadette McDonald's *Freedom Climbers*, which connects the post–World War II economics and politics of Poland to the character of the superb alpine achievements of Polish climbers. Note that Swenson's works-cited page includes three titles on climbing and 16 on political conflict.

Swenson's first four trips to the region—two to Gasherbrum IV and two to K2—did not result in summits, but he would reach the summit of K2 via the north ridge with Greg Child and Greg Mortimer in 1990. This scenario gave me pause to wonder how many climbers failed to summit in their first four big trips, but went on to further success? The summit of G IV would elude him two more times before he turned his eyes to other goals. And yet there is not much wailing or gnashing of teeth over this. One of Swenson's many strengths is an ability to see the big picture, as if all these ventures were part of a larger whole, which includes his marriage, parenthood, a successful engineering career, and the lasting friendships with climbing partners old and new. His friendship with Ghulam Rasool, his Pakistani cook on an early K2 attempt, spans not only cultures and years but generations.

It's probably not fair to quote one of the few passages where Swenson uses an expletive (excluding when he's quoting Marko Prezelj!), but this seems essential: "It was the kind of fear that got my brain to say things like, 'Don't fuck up now, kick a step, make sure it's stable, stand up, shove your ice axe shaft into the snow, don't fuck up.' Over and over. Managing this state of heightened anxiety for hours on end was what I had been working on for years."

Swenson describes many moments that leave indelible impressions on the reader: his harrowing descent off Nanga Parbat with Doug Chabot after completing the first ascent of the Mazeno Ridge (to the Mazeno Gap: six miles!); Mark Richey's careful treading over loose snow on the north ridge of Latok I (Richey's photograph of the ensuing bivy is the stuff of nightmares); and his 2011 climb of Saser Kangri II with Richey and Freddie Wilkinson, a late high-light, though he barely mentions receiving a Piolet d'Or for it.

The maps are plentiful and first-rate, so that even as the locations change frequently the reader always knows exactly where the treks and climbs are located. Likewise, the index, so frequently omitted these days, is accurate and exhaustive. Any first-time Karakoram climber who chooses not to read this book is making the first of what will undoubtedly become many mistakes.

Swenson's Karakoram forms a triumvirate with Steve House's *Beyond the Mountain* and Barry Blanchard's *The Calling* (both writers share a rope with Swenson in these pages). While House may have charged harder and wore his obsession more visibly on his sleeve, and Blanchard is the more natural raconteur, Swenson emerges as the steadiest, who best shows us *how to be* in the mountains, and maybe, in the world.

– DAVID STEVENSON

THE PUSH: A CLIMBER'S JOURNEY OF ENDURANCE, RISK, AND GOING BEYOND LIMITS

TOMMY CALDWELL. *Viking, 2017. Hardcover, 352 pages, $27.*

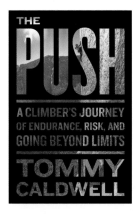

HOW TO EXPLAIN boundary-defining climbing to non-climbers? And how to encapsulate the motivation required by top athletes who push these boundaries to their extreme? Future biographers would do well to take note of the breadth of narrative in *The Push* by Tommy Caldwell, along with the techniques of co-writer Kelly Cordes (not credited on the cover but generously thanked inside).

The reach of the story is exemplified by the title. *The Push* most obviously refers to Caldwell's successful ascent of the Dawn Wall, an epoch-defining effort that received unprecedented media coverage. The last quarter of the book describes in satisfying detail the Dawn Wall push, the presumed culmination of his career. If this were the entirety of the book it would resemble other recent climbing autobiographies, focusing solely on the athletic achieve-ments of the climber. But Caldwell also infamously pushed his captor off a cliff in a youthful misadventure in Kyrgyzstan, an event the reader comes to view as pivotal in his emotional development. Just as Caldwell's first marriage, based primarily on climbing, was not successful, so too fail climbing narratives that are narrowly confined to recording ascents.

Halfway through the book we learn that Caldwell's future wife, Becca, "seemed more excited about cracking open my heart" than interested in him as a climber. The reader can be thankful that he was also open with Cordes, his longtime friend. As Cordes told me in an email, "Our relationship allowed Tommy to be fully vulnerable.... So often it seems high-end athletes don't reveal themselves. Maybe they can't, in a way, because it is too difficult, even too scary, to separate themselves from the shield of invincibility that many carry, which enables them to perform at such mind-blowing levels." Caldwell worded it differently to Becca during one of the six years of efforts on the Dawn Wall, eventually climbed with partner Kevin Jorgen-son: "With Kevin I have to show optimism and toughness. With you I can be vulnerable." Many climbing biographies are inferior stand-ins for YouTube compilations of the star in action. Film is incontestably a better medium for showing the sport of climbing, but as *The Push* demonstrates, a book is unrivaled in delving deeply into the psychological state that makes such feats possible.

There is enough detail about the Dawn Wall project to appeal to the climber who wants insight into tactics, training, and mental state. More noteworthy are the techniques used to appeal to the non-climber, so often left in the dark by the intricacies of our sport. Free climbing is simply "using one's body (primarily fingers and toes) for upward progress, truly climbing without relying on direct aid from the equipment to hoist oneself up." Why have so many commentators had so much trouble explaining the aid/free dichotomy when it can be done as succinctly as this? Descriptions of a hold is "similar in shape and color to Madonna's mole" or writing that one can count to ten before toothpaste spat from a portaledge hits the ground demonstrate the polished tool kit of an accomplished writer explaining our increasingly popular sport to the uninitiated in ways satisfying to longtime climbers.

In accepting a jury special mention at the Banff Mountain Book Festival, Caldwell revealed that on publication day he suddenly questioned what he had done in baring his soul to all who chose to read *The Push*. The answer, in part, is that providing such insight into his personality has gone a long way to demystifying the source of his greatness.

– IAN WELSTED

THE CLIMBERS

JIM HERRINGTON. *The Mountaineers, 2017. Slip-cased hardcover, 189 pages, $59.95.*

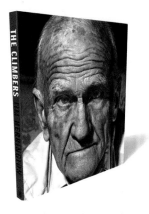

When you stand outside, looking to your climbing objective, you study the ridges, the lines defined by the terrain, and you analyze the peak you intend to climb with great patience and longing. I had a parallel experience when I first laid eyes on Jim Herrington's masterpiece of portrait photography, the grand prize and mountaineering history award winner at the 2017 Banff Mountain Book Awards.

The book comes encased in a black canvas cover with the spine of the book revealing its name, *The Climbers*, in bold red font. I traced my fingers over the outward-facing print, like fingers over a topographic map. The coffee-table book is heavy, and my arms tired while holding it. This is not a book that I wanted to read at a quick pace, like a sport climber racing for the chains. This was a book I wanted to savor and enjoy––I took my time unveiling its rich content, just as an alpinist may do while hiking toward his objective in the mountains. With each page, just like each bend and incline of the trail, I found new rewards and mystery in the folds that lay ahead.

The book's print content is well placed, up front, and is not messy with distractions–– simple, clean text, spaced in such a way that it allows the reader to breathe it all in for easy reading. The introductory pages serve as a guide to the importance of the portraits that await, beginning with a timely foreword from Alex Honnold, who is himself a climbing history buff. Herrington reveals the motivation behind his obsession with photographing his heroes, and then the meat of the text is a captivating and educational history penned by climbing luminary and entertaining writer Greg Child. His 42 succinct pages give a comprehensive overview of climbing in the 21st century, offering insight into the characters focused in front of

Herrington's soul-revealing lens. The subjects range from the familiar, such as Ament, Beckey, and Robbins, to the lesser known (to North American audiences) such as Euro luminaries Sonia Livanos or Robert Paragot.

As a photographer, I have a lot of respect for Herrington's choice to use the timeless medium of black and white, even though digital photography took hold during his creative odyssey. Herrington's book is a testament to an artist's belief in the power of a photograph as a statement—a picture *is,* or *can be,* worth a thousand words. To understand that comment you must look to Herrington's day job as a celebrity photographer, shooting portraits of greats such as the Rolling Stones and Cormac McCarthy. Instead of resting on those laurels, enjoying weekends in the mountains from his Sierra Nevada home—he is a longtime climber—he shouldered the load and spent his own hard-earned money and free time to research, find, and ultimately travel the world for more than 20 years, capturing real—and at times not the most flattering—photographs of his heroes. The completion of this book illustrates the same grit and tenacity that its featured subjects have embodied in the mountains.

– JAMES "Q" MARTIN

A MOUNTAINEER'S LIFE

ALLEN STECK. *Patagonia, 2017. 255 pages. Hardcover, 255 pages, $35.*

READERS OF THIS treasure of an American memoir, packed with fascinating color photographs, have to wait until page 58 to see a picture of the author himself (one with his face showing). And typically, that picture shows Allen Steck in a group of grinning climbing buddies, just back from a 1950 trip to Mt. Waddington in British Columbia, where they made various first ascents and had an all-around good time.

It's not that Steck was shy or without ego as a young climber. It's just that his natural habitat is with people. This book is full of accounts of friendships, his partners described astutely and with feeling. At the same time, Steck's character comes quietly through: steady temperament, always on for the hardest pitches, super-sharp mind. Like Fred Beckey, his great North American contemporary, Steck in his prime was masterful both as a rock climber and as an alpinist. The unassuming way he recounts his self-education as a climber, from first scramble up an ice chimney near Mt. Maclure in the Sierra to massive walls in the Austrian Alps and the Dolomites, then back to California for the iconic Steck-Salathé Route on Sentinel Rock, then to Waddington, then the Cordillera Blanca in Peru, then Makalu for the first American attempt on an 8,000er, makes it seem like just about anybody could do it.

That's not true. Steck is now officially old—91 as this book was being published—but his writer's voice is that of a man in his physical and mental best years. Partly that's because some of these chapters were written some time ago, as articles in the Sierra Club *Bulletin* or the *AAJ,* but the chapters written just last week have the same authoritative grip on reality, the same mortal seriousness leavened with absurd humor. A Steckian sentence has color, high focus, balance, and liveliness. It has a lot of the qualities you imagine he had as a climbing partner. An absurdly lethal, as yet unrepeated, ascent such as the 1965 climb of the Hummingbird Ridge on Mt. Logan was only possible because someone was keeping it all together, refusing to freak out as the team of six pals took 37 days inching farther and farther out on a thinly corniced knife-edge, way beyond the point of no return. Steck refuses to make himself the hero of this epochal story, and that's surely correct—there were six madmen-heroes. But again, I say, *someone* was refusing to freak out, the implacable calm was emanating from *somewhere*.

This is one of the most enjoyable, best-written, thrilling, and immediate works of climbing history I've read in the last decade.

– ROBERT ROPER

THE ART OF FREEDOM: THE LIFE AND CLIMBS OF VOYTEK KURTYKA

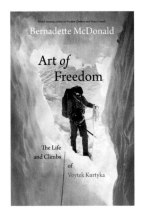

BERNADETTE MCDONALD. Rocky Mountain Books, 2017. Hardcover, 256 pages, $32 (CDN).

I CAN'T STAND it. Reviewing another dumb climber/hero worship story about rising above oneself in search of: meaning, a higher calling, aesthetics, purity of line, boldness, creativity, loss and redemption, blah, blah, blah. The human tale and so damn predictable. Please let this be different. I can't hate this book! It's Bernadette McDonald's work—Bernadette, the patron saint of Dead Poles—and this biography is about the most influential alpinist of the last 50 years: Voytek Kurtyka! The Mick Jagger-est cat who envisioned and executed the greatest alpine climb of all time (so far), the Shining Wall on Gasherbrum IV. I am in deep trouble. Trapped between a most certain social death if I say what I expect I will have to say and the self-loathing that awaits if I sell out.

Just put your head down, Charlie, and return to the predictable drivel. Bad rock: check. Winter conditions: check. Cheating to get what you want: check. Oppressive government: check. Parents don't get it: check. But…wait a minute. Slowly, the man emerges and somewhere in the middle of the book I forget my prejudices and am swept up in the story of Voytek. McDonald's skillful storytelling somehow sneakily transforms from her voice to Voytek's and it's very effective.

Perhaps it is natural that there is little reflection of Voytek's early life here because, like most of ours, it is unremarkable. But as soon as he tastes rock and begins to sense a greater world, he is driven to experience life through climbing exclusively on his own terms. Be they family, governments, peers, climbing clubs, religion, or relationships—Voytek rejects all authority. It's only later, as a mature person, that he derives meaning through human relationships. The tenderness and understanding he expresses for his climbing partners Erhard Loretan, Krzysztof Zurek, and Jerzy Kukuczka offer palpable insights into the man (and into his partners as well).

As a climber and student of the natural world, what sets Voytek apart is the consistent sound decisions he makes in the most dire situations. Whether the genesis of this judgment is a developed intuition or a keen intellect is impossible to say, but what is revealed in McDonald's work is that he is totally aware…all the time. One obvious consequence is that he and his partners manage to survive some very hard and deadly experiences. Reading between the lines of an epic on on Changabang, I can almost hear Voytek saying, "What did I just hear? What is this feeling? What is this doubt?" as Krzysztof Zurek, exhausted and spent, rationalizes setting a faulty belay with "I have a lot of pitons in. It's good." In response, Voytek refuses to move, and when Zurek climbs a few meters higher he falls, ripping the intended belay stance from the wall.

The Art of Freedom captures the full arc of a man's life, from early arrogance and bravado to the carefully scripted nuance of being a mature and hopelessly flawed human. In the end, Bernadette McDonald has treated us to the tale we all wanted to hear, ever since Kurtyka and Robert Schauer walked out from under the Shining Wall. This is story worth keeping close to your heart.

− CHARLIE SASSARA

WILD ADVENTURES WE HAVE KNOWN: MY LIFE WITH WILLI UNSOELD

Jolene Unsoeld, with lectures by Willi Unsoeld. Unsoeldstories.com, 2017. 407 pages, $30.

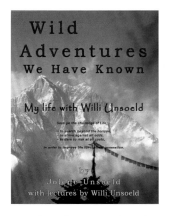

Wild Adventures We Have Known is a trip through the attic of a fascinating family, a trek to the top of the world, a descent into double tragedy, and a journey to one woman's recovery and activism. It focuses on her earlier life with mountaineer/philosopher Willi Unsoeld, legendary for his West Ridge ascent, traverse, and bivouac on Mt. Everest with Tom Hornbein in 1963. The book is beautifully illustrated, its images supporting the caption beneath a poster found in the Unsoeld home: "A ship in a harbor is safe. But that's not what ships are for."

Jolene Unsoeld is a night owl, conducive to quiet reflection on a life in which personal loss has been with her for 40 years, since the mountaineering deaths in 1976 and 1979 of her daughter and husband. She is a master storyteller on the early joys of that life, its tensions and triumphs.

The Unsoelds went to Nepal with Willi serving as deputy director of the Peace Corps in the country. And then came the 1963 Everest climb. The reader is left breathless by the book's intimacy. Jolene Unsoeld was resistant to her husband making the climb. He had already been on three Himalayan expeditions: Nilkanta (1949), Makalu (1954, and Masherbrum (1960). "Prior to my departure for Kathmandu, Jo and I separated three times, and we were set for divorce," Willi is quoted in the book. "I don't see how it could be otherwise, because to go to Everest you really have to lay it all on the line...your family, the future, the life that you've planned together."

Yet, weeks later, with Willi on the mountain, the couple exchanged letters of extraordinary warmth. Jolene Unsoeld shares those letters. "Let me be with you, Bill," she writes. "I need you so. Unless I am part of your happiness and sadness and searching, I am nothing."

Willi Unsoeld would lose nine of 10 toes to frostbite, the cost of a bivouac at 27,900 feet. The Unsoelds would settle into a new life, with Willi present at the creation of the Evergreen State College and Jolene embarking on a career of citizen activism.

Wild Adventures culminates with twin tragedies. Vibrant, athletic daughter Nanda Devi Unsoeld, at 23,000 feet on a climb of the Himalayan peak for which she was named, says "I'm going to die," lapses into unconsciousness and is gone within five minutes. The account by Willi, who was there, and the decision "to commit her body to the snows," is aching. The body is committed with a final yodel, so often the way Willi and Devi communicated.

"There was no time to process," Jolene Unsoeld writes. Willi had come back sick from

Nanda Devi. Jolene's mother had drowned in the Columbia River. Son Krag Unsoeld was injured in a bicycle accident. Three years later, leading Evergreen students on a climb of Mt. Rainier, Willi Unsoeld and student Janie Diepenbrock were killed in an avalanche.

The book ends with a lesson entitled, "How to Handle Grief." Writes Jolene: "It was several years before some sort of a transition took place where that vision of beauty no longer overwhelmed me with grief. And then, one day, I was driving down I-5 and received a blast of beauty from a sunset. And there was no more pain. I could feel Bill and Devi in the car with me. We were all together again."

She is now in her 80s and marks the Everest climb's anniversary each year by talking on the phone with Tom Hornbein. Still, in her words, Jolene Unsoeld is "ready to start again. I am ready for my next wild adventure."

– JOEL CONNELLY

THE OGRE: BIOGRAPHY OF A MOUNTAIN AND THE DRAMATIC STORY OF THE FIRST ASCENT

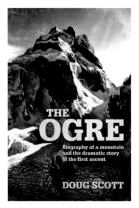

Doug Scott. Vertebrate Publishing, 2017. Hardcover, 192 pages, $26.72.

THE OGRE'S FIRST ascent by a six-member British expedition in 1977 might have been "just another" significant summit in the amazing climbing career of Doug Scott—that is, Sir Doug Scott, CBE. (Readers will find that his other "career" was rugby.) But fate, and perhaps hubris, had other plans. Just below the summit, at the end of a rappel that required much traversing, and in a moment of inattention, Scott's foot slipped. The ensuing pendulum into a wall shattered both of his tibiae. What followed is a lesson seemingly forgotten in our modern world: how to act when splattered with the foul aftermath of our mistakes, and with self-rescue as the only option.

What would each of us have done in such a situation? What would our partners have done? Sir Doug and his three partners seemingly followed their only option and continued their descent, setting up rappels or following their previously fixed ropes. Scott writes that traversing was much more painful than simply rappelling vertically, which seems immediately obvious and painful upon reflection. However, the most difficult and painful crawling was along the final five kilometers of glacial terrain to base camp, where a cadre of hired porters could assist. Here, the story could use more metaphor or simile, allowing readers to better imagine the pain of crawling so far, with or without bilateral tibial fractures!

Throughout the book, Scott takes readers to many places and to many ideas, among them an exploration of British schemes for empire. Sir Scott also refers to a "Pax Britannia" that arose from the Crown's imperial expansions into central Asia and justifies those expansions as countering Russian goals in the "Great Game" between the two powers. Perhaps we should expect such an attitude from a man who was "knighted" for his significant contributions to British alpinism. But of course, this review is intended for the alpine journal of a nation that is sometimes seen as expansionist, propagating a "Pax Americana."

In the chapter "Scottish Contribution to Empire," we find the following: "The British empire since the Battle of Waterloo (1815) and the American Civil War (1865) had expanded by 100,000 square miles every year." This is more than trivia: Scott's attention to Britain's Empire helps the reader understand the attention that alpine-oriented Brits gave to certain sweeps of geography, and the relative ease of obtaining official permission to explore.

The book has some sloppiness: misspellings, typos, and forced wording. But these are rare and some may be idiomatic. And certainly, an index would be useful to most readers. Surprisingly, the end pages list of "Further Reading" doesn't include Mo Antoine's account in the *Alpine Journal* (1978) or Chris Bonington's in the *AAJ* (1978). Both are engaging reads, and Antoine's, predictably, is humorous and nonchalant.

"The Climbers" (Chapter 6) is worth its weight in the coin of the realm, and the bond between the author and the other climbers is clear and poignant. A reader will feel the trust and respect that Scott has for all members of the loose team of acquaintances. They were not an expedition, but several small teams, each engaging a major alpine objective in its own way and perhaps by its own route, and still looking out for the others. Readers will be prompted to ponder times when they've been reduced to a speck in a vast alpine environment, and their mate or mates are their only solace if an accident occurs. When we've been reduced to a "crawl," or perhaps further, whom else do we have?

— CARL TOBIN

HONOURING HIGH PLACES: THE MOUNTAIN LIFE OF JUNKO TABEI

Junko Tabei and Helen Y. Rolffe, translated by Yumika Hiraki and Rieto Hotven. Rocky Mountain Books, 2017. Hardcover, 376 pages, $32 (CDN).

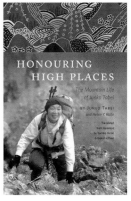

When Junko Tabei stepped on to the summit of Everest in 1975, there were 38 men who had done so before her. But Tabei was to make climbing history as the first woman on top of the highest mountain in the world.

Today, a woman climbing Everest while using supplemental oxygen and accompanied by a Sherpa guide doesn't qualify as a notable mountaineering feat. But at that time, Tabei and her contemporaries were up against considerable challenges to get to the mountain in the first place, not least a widely held opinion that the mothers on the expedition should be home caring for their children, and that women—in general—wouldn't be physically able to climb at altitude. "It was considered unrealistic, unproductive and most of all, detrimental to our families," she writes. (In this light, I especially appreciated Tabei later describing their female porters not only carrying small children on top of their 30-kilogram loads but also knitting while walking.) There was no roster of experienced high-altitude women climbers in Japan from which to choose expedition members. Recruiting team members took place by travelling around the country and visiting women's climbing and hiking clubs, as well as "chatting up" women climbers/hikers in Tokyo train stations as they headed out on their weekend trips.

Tabei makes it clear that they were well supported on the mountain and climbed with Sherpa men. Still, 1975 was long before one could book a commercially guided expedition on Everest and the sheer logistics of their Women on Everest expedition were impressive. In preparation for the climb, Tabei and her team made their own sleeping bags and sewed over-gloves and other gear from recycled car seats. They dehydrated food, assembled equipment, and packed and shipped thousands of pounds of supplies from Japan to Everest base camp.

About a third of book is taken up by Everest. The rest covers Tabei's numerous other climbs, including Annapurna II, Aconcagua, and Carstenz Pyramid, as well as her years in fundraising and activism: cleaning up trash on Everest, helping the survivors of the 2011 Tohoku earthquake, volunteering for various causes, all while engaged in a courageous battle with cancer in the later years of her life.

The translation is excellent, with a smooth-flowing narrative, though sometimes over-packed with details. The book provides a comprehensive reference to Tabei's climbing career, as well as numerous reflections and insights, and entertaining stories with enjoyable glimpses of Tabei's world through her unique lens: "Sato was popular among the Sherpas and porters because she was cute, and she was the only smoker among the women. When she ran out of her Japanese-made cigarettes, the Sherpas and porters were quick to offer their local stash. Her posture when she smoked—left hand casually placed in pants' pocket and a gentle lean forward while she inhaled—was the subject of much mimicking by our comedian, Mr. Gopal."

Most endearing, however, is Tabei's recurring acknowledgment and appreciation of those around her, including her husband whose unwavering support was remarkable for that time, as well as other women climbers: her insistence that Pan Duo, the Tibetan woman who climbed Everest 11 days after Tabei be included in a gathering in France organized by Maurice Herzog; Tabei's admiration of Alison Hargreaves and her grief at Hargreaves death, not so much as a climber, but as a mother; and the way Tabei seemed so taken with Lydia Bradey, the first female to climb Everest without supplemental oxygen. Tabei writes: "She was tall and blonde and full of humour; her mischievous nature made me feel like we had been friends for a long time." The book is peppered such examples, and it's in these gracious moments where the reader really falls for Tabei and sees her as the wonderful ambassador of adventure she became.

– SHANNON O'DONOGHUE CHILD

FOUND: A LIFE IN MOUNTAIN RESCUE

BREE LOEWEN. Mountaineers Books, 2017. Paperback, 224 pages, $17.95.

IN THIS AUTOBIOGRAPHICAL work, Bree Loewen describes the hardships, sacrifices, and intense satisfaction associated with back-country search and rescue. She is a longtime member of the Seattle Mountain Rescue team, an extremely busy organization with two to three missions per week. The often overstretched volunteer group operates out of two vehicles with no building to store gear or hold meetings.

Loewen is unique in that she is an almost full-time volunteer who finds the time, even with a young daughter, to attend numerous search and rescue missions, many of which run late at night, in inclement weather, and conflict directly with personal engagements, work, study and family events. But that is her life, and she would not have it any other way. In the book she describes her personal experience on many of these memorable missions.

As a technical member of the Alaska Mountain Rescue Group for 17 years, I strongly identified with many of her experiences. Loewen describes critical misinformation on many missions, the lack of the right equipment or people, the risks, and the strong friendships developed with members of the team through shared misery. She accurately describes the intense emotions of dealing with body recoveries from accidental falls or suicides, where no professional organization is able or mandated to do it, and it is left to volunteers to recover the body for family and friends. She observes that the consistent thankfulness of friends and relatives for a body recovery is often contrasted with the incongruous lack of appreciation for a life-saving rescue, when the subject is whisked off to definitive care, never to be heard from again.

The difficulty of access to the rescue subject is usually the focus of her narrative, with the actual medical treatment and technical extraction often glossed over. Those wishing to learn search management and technical rescue techniques will be disappointed. However, details such as the skill required to tactfully manage the critical working relationship with law enforcement agencies, the tying of shoes at successive stoplights on the way to the mission, the malfunctioning personal headlamp, the use of a cell phone light to pinpoint a subject on a cliff at night, the transformation of searches with the ubiquitous use of mobile phones, location tracking, and GPS coordinates are all accurately rendered and resonate with my own experience.

In between detailing various missions, Loewen thinks deeply about why she is so committed to search and rescue, and why she is able find a way to drop whatever she is doing and rush out, often far from home, for many hours or even days to help someone that she usually does not know. She skillfully articulates that her selfless priority in life is to help people in need, ahead of her family, work, vacations, and financial betterment. The title of the book is as much about her finding her place in the world as it is about finding people lost or hurt in the backcountry and bringing them home.

The search and rescue community will certainly enjoy reading this book, but it should also appeal to the broader climbing enthusiast looking to gain an appreciation for the motivation behind search and rescue volunteers.

— MATT GREEN

IN BRIEF: POETRY AND FICTION

THE SNYDER-WILCOX EXPEDITION on Denali in 1967 was not only North America's most tragic mountaineering incident—seven deaths—but also one of the most reported, most recently by Andy Hall in *Denali's Howl* (2014). Add Jessica Goodfellow's **Whiteout** (University of Alaska Press) to the bibliography. Goodfellow's uncle was one of the lost climbers, and these poems explore her family's loss and grief. ~ **Cinema Vertigo** (Imaginary Mountain Surveyors) is *Gripped* publisher David Smart's second historical novel set in the wartime Alps, following *Beyond the Reich*. Here, Smart fictionalizes the story of the filming of *First Man on the Rope*, Nazis included. Grand storytelling on the big stage. ~ Gisèle Villeneuve's **Rising Abruptly** (*University of Alberta Press*), a collection of seven short mountain fictions, won the Banff Mountain Book Award for fiction and poetry in 2017. Villeneuve writes, "Even the unassuming day trips deliver their moments." The stories, too, are unassuming. The mountains they portray are at once familiar and fresh: We know them but have never quite viewed them through this lens. And, "the moments"? The author delivers them: glinting shards of glass scattered throughout her fields.

— DAVID STEVENSON

IN MEMORIAM

These tributes cover the period from January 2017 to January 2018. Most articles have been edited for length; the full pieces may be found at publications.americanalpineclub.org. Here, readers also will find tributes to Norman Hardie and Tom Zajicek, as well as climbers who will be remembered in AAJ 2019, including Jim Bridwell, Tom Higgins, Ryan Johnson, and Marc-André Leclerc.

FRED BECKEY, 1923–2017

IN JULY 1938 the north face of the Eiger was finally climbed, after many attempts and multiple fatalities. It was Europe's greatest prize in climbing at the time and a widely celebrated ascent.

During the same period, a similar race was taking place in North America for the first ascent of Mt. Waddington in British Columbia's Coast Mountains. After 16 unsuccessful attempts and one fatality, German-born Fritz Wiessner finally succeeded, partnered with Bill House, in July 1936. The climb was of comparable difficulty to the Eiger's north face, but in very remote wilderness, not right above the hotels and telescopes of Kleine Scheidegg.

Just a few years after Wiessner's ascent, in 1942, the climb was repeated by two unknown teenagers from Seattle. Fred Beckey was 19 years old, and his brother Helmy turned 17 the day after the climb. It was shocking news to the climbing world. This was long before Facebook, but it was the sort of radical surprise that today would be talked about on every climbing website worldwide. The modern equivalent would be two high school students going to Pakistan over summer break and climbing a new route in alpine style on Gasherbrum IV.

Fred made his first first ascent, of Mt. Despair in Washington's North Cascades, in 1939. He continued making first ascents, both of mountains and routes, for seven decades. His legacy of climbs, considering the difficulty and volume, is absolutely unparalleled, not only in North America but in the entire world. He wasn't establishing just one-pitch rock climbs or new routes on faces where several already existed, but first ascents of huge mountains, often very remote, and nearly always by technical lines.

In the Cascades alone it would take over an hour to list all of Fred's first ascents, but some highlights are Forbidden Peak, Inspiration Peak, Crooked Thumb, Nooksack Tower, Liberty Bell, the South Peak of Hozomeen, Prusik Peak, the Northeast Buttress of Goode, the Price Glacier on Shuksan, Yocum Ridge on Mt. Hood, the Complete North Ridge of Mt. Stuart, and the Northeast Buttress of Slesse.

In need of both greater difficulty and new mountains to climb, Fred went often to Canada and Alaska. Again, his first ascents are too numerous to list, but some highlights are Kate's Needle, Devils Thumb, Mt. Asperity, the north face of Mt. Edith Cavell, the north face of Mt. Sir Donald, the west buttress of South Howser Spire, and the first winter ascents of Mt. Sir Donald and Mt. Robson.

Fred's 1954 trip to Alaska is the most successful Alaskan expedition of all time. In one season he made the first ascent of the Northwest Buttress of Denali, the first ascent of Mt. Deborah, and the first ascent of Mt. Hunter. Each of these climbs represented cutting-edge alpine climbing at the time. But Fred ticked them one after the other in the span of a couple of months.

I think that young climbers today can easily misjudge Fred for an "old-time mountaineer." He was in fact one of the best rock climbers in North America during the 1940s, '50s, and '60s. Yvon Chouinard said that when he teamed up with Fred, in the 1960s, he always had to ask to rope up before Fred felt the need. Fred established most of the early hard routes in Leavenworth and Index, and at one time nearly all the hard routes in Squamish were his. As usual there are too many to mention, but some that have become modern classics are Outer Space and Orbit on the Snow Creek Wall, and Squamish Buttress, Angel's Crest, and Tantalus Wall on the Stawamus Chief.

In July 2003 I was fresh out of high school and Fred was already in his early 80s as we stood together on the summit of Mt. Adamant in British Columbia's Selkirk Mountains. Although his age slowed him on the summit snow slopes, Fred was as graceful as ever on the steep, white granite buttress below. Watching his calloused hands work their magic, I wondered how many thousands upon thousands of feet of alpine rock those hands had touched.

Fred's legend goes far beyond climbing achievements. He more or less invented the lifestyle of the dirtbag climber. He chose to eschew climbing fame, financial security, marriage, and all other aspects of the American dream in pursuit of climbing, back when it was an unheard-of choice. Thousands of young climbers across North America are now copying Fred's ideal.

He wrote more than a dozen books, which are astoundingly well researched. The Cascade Alpine Guides are, I think, the only example in the world of such comprehensive, in-depth guidebooks to such a vast mountain range. Keeping track of climbing routes is one thing, but he was also a knowledgeable geologist and extremely accomplished historian. If you gave his *Range of Glaciers* to someone unfamiliar with Fred, they would deduce it was written by a decorated professor of history at a prestigious university, not a dirtbag climber who stole condiments packets from restaurants and slept half of his nights on the side of dirt roads. In fact, after publishing *Range of Glaciers*, Fred was offered a professorship at the University of Washington, but of course he declined.

During his climbing career he witnessed the development of crampons, nylon ropes, harnesses, helmets, nuts, rock shoes, and cams. He partnered with, and outlasted, multiple generations of celebrated climbers. Fred was without a doubt the most accomplished climber ever to come out of North America, and is among the all-time greats—right alongside figures such as Ricardo Cassin, Herman Buhl, Lionel Terray, Walter Bonatti, and Reinhold Messner.

– COLIN HALEY

EDITOR'S NOTE: *This article is drawn from a talk Colin Haley prepared for the Mountaineers' annual dinner in 2015. Alex Bertulis' remembrance of Fred Beckey can be found at the AAJ website.*

PAUL B. CREWS, 1917–2017

PAUL BEATTY CREWS, pioneer Alaskan climber and founder of the Mountaineering Club of Alaska (MCA), died in Anchorage on July 20. He was just 18 days shy of his 100th birthday. He had led an exciting and inquiring life, and as a natural leader he became a focal point for Anchorage climbers in an era when homegrown expeditions tackling unclimbed peaks in Alaska were still relatively uncommon.

Trained as an engineer, Paul served as an ordnance officer in the South Pacific in World War II. He moved with his family to Anchorage in 1952, founding a well-respected local engineering firm. Paul was the organizer and first president of MCA (1958-'59) and its first Honorary Lifetime Member. He made the first ascents of a number of peaks, primarily in Anchorage's backdrop Chugach Range and in the Tordrillo Range on Anchorage's western skyline. A sailor and private pilot, he was a co-author of the 1999 book *Tordrillo: Pioneer Climbs and Flights in the Tordrillo Mountains of Alaska, 1957–1997.*

Paul's leadership proved to be vital in the successful rescue of the "John Day Expedition" from Denali in May 1960. The Day party, which included Pete Schoening and Lou and Jim Whittaker, suffered a fall at 17,000 feet below Denali Pass. Day sustained a broken leg, and Schoening a likely concussion and later frostbite. In the first such use of a radio high on Denali, Paul coordinated the recovery of Day by helicopter from 17,000 feet (a Denali altitude record at the time).

Paul was a skilled woodworker, handcrafting musical instruments, and he enjoyed retracing legendary 19th-century Arctic explorations, making several trips aboard former Soviet icebreakers into the High Arctic. He was an avid cross-country and alpine skier to his 90th year.

– TOM MEACHAM

NORMAN GÜNTER DYHRENFURTH, 1918–2017

NORMAN DYHRENFURTH DIED September 24 in Salzburg, Austria, just short of a century old. He is best known as the creator and leader of the 1963 American Mount Everest Expedition (AMEE), which has been regarded by him and others as the *magnum opus* of his life as mountaineer and cinematographer. For those of us who were privileged to be actors in the 1963 AMEE drama and to contribute to its outcomes, what he pulled off was clearly the overriding yet underappreciated component of the expedition, setting the stage for its many accomplishments.

Norman was born on May 7, 1918, in Breslau, Germany (now Wroclaw, Poland), the youngest of three children of Himalayan explorers Günter Oskar and Hettie Dyhrenfurth. The family moved to Austria when he was five years old and then to Switzerland two years later. His father, a renowned German-Swiss geology/geography professor and mountaineer, led the 1930 International Himalayan Expedition to Kanchenjunga that succeeded in climbing nearby Jongsong Peak and a 1934 expedition to the Karakoram. His mother, a tennis champion who acquired a love of climbing by marriage, was the first woman to climb higher than 7,000 meters, summiting Kashmir's 7,442-meter Sia Kangri in 1934.

Having left Germany for Austria just after World War I, his family foresaw the storm clouds of another war emerging in the 1930s. His mother, who hailed from a family of prominent Jewish industrialists, emigrated to the U.S., followed by Norman in 1937; both became dual Swiss-American citizens. She urged her family to join her, but Günter wouldn't follow for lack of a professorship. Norman wound up spending three decades in the United States.

In his 20s, Norman found work as a ski instructor in Franconia, New Hampshire, and as a mountain guide in the Tetons. His Army service won him U.S. citizenship and some trusted government jobs; his climbing and cinematography took him from the Tetons to Alaska with Bradford Washburn. In his 30s, he served as head of the cinematography department at UCLA, where he became acquainted with some of Hollywood's leading lights. However, Norman's heart, like his father's, remained in the mountains.

In the fall of 1952, Norman was hired as cinematographer for the second Swiss attempt that year on Mt. Everest. Three years later, he was back in Nepal, leading an attempt on Lhotse, his first experience as expedition organizer. After serving as cinematographer for the successful Swiss expedition to Dhaulagiri in 1960, Norman applied for and was granted a permit to attempt Everest in 1963. Thus was AMEE born. Norman spent three years doggedly laying the groundwork to realize his dream. He solicited sponsors, set up science experiments, crafted military-scale logistics, and put together the climbing team.

Several ingredients were critical to AMEE's success. Most of all was Norman's determination, chutzpah, and organizational talents. To go beyond what had been done before, he envisioned ascents of Everest, Lhotse, and Nuptse, synchronized with scientific research that complemented, rather than competed with, the mountaineering objectives. His efforts to obtain support from the White House elicited a polite rejection letter from President John F. Kennedy. Norman, undeterred, used President Kennedy's best wishes for a successful effort as leverage to gain backing from the National Geographic Society and other supporters. His tenacity and style, aided by luck, won the day.

Norman's next *tour de force* was in choosing a team. While looking for strong, motivated climbers, he avoided prima donnas, those whose summit-at-all-costs ambitions ran counter to the essence of expedition-style mountaineering. Many came to the team as strangers, but they bonded well on the long walk in from Kathmandu. His success in this effort became even more apparent as the expedition unfolded, morphing into two teams, the South Col'ers and the West Ridgers, each competing for Sherpa carrying power, supplies, and priority. The situation was rife for problems, but the two teams managed to disagree in mature, agreeable ways, by no means a universal in Himalayan climbing history. Far more a facilitator than a military commander, Norman encouraged the team to resolve differences through open discussion and consensus.

On May 1, 1963, the day the expedition put the first American, Jim Whittaker, on Earth's highest point, Norman, at 44 the expedition elder, achieved an altitude well above 28,000 feet, returning to base camp near frazzled exhaustion.

The first of Norman's post-AMEE years were spent in the U.S., where he worked as a cinematographer, notably involved with Clint Eastwood's *Eiger Sanction* in 1975 and with Fred Zinnemann's *Five Days One Summer* in 1982, starring Sean Connery and also filmed in the Alps. However, Norman's hopes that the Everest expedition would open doors to major recognition and employment never came to pass. On the personal front, Norman's marriage ended in divorce in 1966. He returned to Europe and spent the final decades of his life in Salzburg with his partner Maria "Moidi" Sernetz, herself an accomplished golfer and skier. Both enjoyed good health into their 90s. Next to their apartment, Norman kept a small, tidy home office—

more of a tiny museum—where he showed visitors the news clippings, awards, and other memorabilia from his adventures.

Norman's dream, I suspect, proved a life-changing event for all of us on the AMEE team. In a way, it's as if, when we got back from Everest, the expedition was just beginning—traveling uncharted territory but propagating among the team continuing and at times deepening relationships as we confronted the various challenges of life. That is an unanticipated, inextricable piece of Norman Dyhrenfurth's dream. Thanks, Norman.

— TOM HORNBEIN, WITH SIGNIFICANT CONTRIBUTIONS FROM JOHN HEILPRIN

ELIZABETH HAWLEY, 1923–2018

The legendary Himalayan historian Elizabeth Hawley passed away on January 26, 2018, at the age of 94 in Kathmandu. Although her remarkable life encompassed several distinctive chapters, climbers knew her as the chronicler of mountaineering in Nepal.

I first met Elizabeth at her apartment in Kathmandu in 2004. I was hoping to write her biography, and I'd planned ten days of interviews with her. She was skeptical, and I was nervous. Almost everyone who knew her warned me that she had no patience for anyone who was unprepared, that she insisted on being called Miss Hawley, that she preferred men over women, and that she liked gifts. Although I couldn't do much about my gender, I *had* done my research, and I came laden with whisky and chocolate.

She was smaller than I expected, thin, and slightly stooped. Still, her eyes were dark and clear and her gaze didn't waver. I sensed in her an innate curiosity, a confident intelligence, a no-nonsense approach, and a sharp tongue.

There was much to admire in her. Born in Chicago in 1923, Elizabeth was a go-getter from an early age. When asked by a high school teacher what she might want to be upon graduating, she replied that she had no idea, but she was sure that she didn't want to be somebody's secretary. She graduated from the University of Michigan in 1946, and departed with a deep interest in American history and international affairs, social philosophy and the meaning of freedom.

She began working at Fortune magazine as a researcher and fact-checker, but her curiosity led her far beyond her New York apartment. By living frugally, she was able to launch a series of solo voyages that took her to the United Kingdom and to Central Europe, where she observed the ravages of the Second World War. She gambled in Monte Carlo and rode the Orient Express to Trieste, Italy. Gaining confidence, she ventured farther afield, meeting up with foreign correspondents in Yugoslavia, Finland, Georgia, Poland, Morocco, Sudan, Nepal, and Japan. She was clever. She was curious. And she was alone. As such, she stood out, meeting an endless number of interesting and sometimes powerful people.

She arrived in Kathmandu in 1959. In her words, "I didn't plan to stay. I just didn't leave." For Elizabeth, Nepal felt remote, exotic, less affected by the rest of the world. It was also on the cusp of its very first general election. In her words, it was "a place where you can see what the world is becoming." Elizabeth wanted to be part of that experience.

She worked at various jobs, reporting for Reuters and organizing trips for an emerging adventure travel company. She served as New Zealand's Honorary Consul in Nepal, and she played a key role in the New Zealand Himalayan Trust. Some of her first stories as a journalist were about climbing expeditions in Nepal, including the 1963 American Mt. Everest Expedition, winning a scoop on its success through some clever skulduggery. Although she socialized regularly with royalty and the most powerful politicians in Nepal, it was climbers who captured her imagination.

She became a fixture in Kathmandu as she motored around town in her baby blue Volkswagen Beetle, tracking down expedition leaders in order to learn of their plans and to document what they did or didn't climb. She became skilled at sleuthing fact from fiction, and she rarely erred. "I don't mean to frighten people," she said, but then she added that a little fear might help in ferreting out the facts. She wrangled the biggest egos in Himalayan climbing into submission, and many of them became her dearest friends. Sir Edmund Hillary once described her as "a bit of a terror." But he freely admitted that her friendship was gold standard—one that lasted a lifetime. Reinhold Messner called her a "first-class journalist." Kurt Diemberger described her as a "living archive." Together with Richard Salisbury, Elizabeth transformed her vast archive of climbing data into the Himalayan Database, which remains a priceless resource for climbing historians.

As the numbers of expeditions increased in Nepal, it eventually became clear that Elizabeth could no longer handle all of the work without help. Respected historians and climbers came to help her chronicle the climbs. One of those was Billi Bierling, from Germany. Over the years, their professional relationship grew into a deep friendship. In Billi's words, upon learning of her passing, "I cannot put it into words how much this amazing woman has meant to me, how much she has taught me, and how much I will miss her in my life."

My lingering memory of Elizabeth was of her standing at the top of her stairs with a slightly lopsided smile, waving good-bye, after our first intense ten days of getting to know each other. We had laughed and cried, debated dates of climbs and details of her love life, searched through dusty files, and drank a lot of tea.

Elizabeth Hawley: a pillar of society in Kathmandu, an icon in the mountaineering community, a fiercely independent woman, and a dear friend to many.

– BERNADETTE MCDONALD

FREDERICK O. JOHNSON, 1927–2017

FREDERICK O. JOHNSON died in his Berkeley, California, home of heart failure following dinner with his wife of 67 years. A fourth-generation Californian, Fred was born in Los Angeles and was a longtime resident of Berkeley. He entered Cornell University, served briefly in the Navy at the close of World War II, then received his Ph.D. from MIT. He worked as an executive chemist for 20 years at Chevron Chemical, then moved into commercial real estate.

Fred was a treasured, hard-working member of several clubs and the longest-serving volunteer for the *American Alpine Journal*. In 1956, he was recruited to compile the Club Activities section of the AAJ by then-editor Francis Farquhar, and he continued in this role for 60 years, only stopping when this section was dropped from the book in 2016. "It's been a rewarding, long run for me," he said at the time, "with the chance to do a small part for the Club, of which I've been a minor but enthusiastic member since 1950."

– THE EDITORS, *WITH INFORMATION FROM THE SAN FRANCISCO CHRONICLE*

HAYDEN KENNEDY, 1990–2017

ELEVEN YEARS AGO, on an ordinary cold spring morning in Castle Valley, Utah, I met a 16-year-old kid who unexpectedly would become my best friend. The memory is still vivid. After frantically trying to catch an inspiring father-son climbing team out in front of us on the Rectory all morning, I reached out my hand to introduce myself to a proud dad. Although I didn't recognize him until he said his name, he was my climbing hero Michael Kennedy, and his son was Hayden.

Over the next ten years, Hayden and I would return to the desert many, many times in search of adventure. Our friendship took us to some of the wildest places in North America and gave me some of the richest experiences of my life. As Hayden grew older, I realized that he quickly absorbed the knowledge of his mentors and used that understanding to express his talent toward his own vision for what adventure meant to him.

It was truly an honor to watch Hayden become one of the greatest climbers of our time. His unlimited talent, ability, and futuristic vision took him to summits most alpinists had only dreamt of—new routes on K7 and the Ogre in Pakistan, a new route on Cerro Kisht-war in India, the first "fair means" ascent of Cerro Torre's southeast ridge, and many, many more. Along with the enormous influence of his family, the mountains forged Hayden's depth and character. He approached his community, friends, family, and the mountains he passed through with profound humility, respect, and a deep gratitude.

With Hayden you always knew where he stood. While choosing his path in life, he wouldn't hesitate to admit his struggles in finding the right balance of life, love, and his passion for climbing. He shared his dreams with those close to him, whether it was climbing a virgin summit in unexplored India, starting a bakery and cafe in downtown Lander, or his vision for life with his sweet partner Inge Perkins.

In Hayden's own words, climbing was a very small part of his life, yet the lessons he learned from it affected all of life's aspects. Hayden learned to listen to his instincts, to question his own ego, and to pursue many things other than the mountains. He was a musician, a bread baker, a voracious reader, and a hopeless romantic. Hayden took the time to really listen in conversation and to connect with anyone he found himself sharing a room with. Despite being among the best in the world at his craft, he realized that learning was where the magic lay in life and that he always needed to learn from those around him.

The news of Hayden's death took me to the ground. The thought of him not in our lives is a reality that is still hard to accept for all of us. His friends miss the gum wrappers left in our cup holders, the unawareness of his open mouth chomping food, the morning egg tortilla dish he had mastered, and the continuous blatant and profound honesty he offered all of us. We all miss the countless rounds of "would you rather," the random postcards from his latest travels, and the daily photos of the bread loaves he had just proudly baked.

Almost exactly ten years after meeting him in Castle Valley, Hayden and I returned there together one last time. Atop of Castleton Tower, I tried to say good-bye to him as he sat in the form of white crystalline ash in my palm. Opening my hand to the wind and watching him return to the earth, I realized that saying good-bye to Hayden will be a lifetime process—one that I never will fully be able to complete. I try to think of Hayden as a gift, a gift that you can't keep but one that you can live. Hayden's example, and aspiring to be a bit more like Hayden, is his greatest gift to us, his community, and for that we are so grateful.

– JESSE HUEY

ROYAL ROBBINS, 1935–2017

THE MORNING OF March 14, 2017, Royal Robbins passed away, a man who stamped us with his elegance and class. The *American Alpine Journal* published an article of Royal's in 1963, when I was a high school kid. I was moved especially by one line:

What was the significance of our adventure? None. So we took it for what it was, a meaningful experience which awakened our minds to a lust for life and a keener awareness of beauty.

I still like that passage, the way it describes what it is to climb and the paradox that something can be of no significance yet be meaningful and mind-awakening. I was young, and his words made me think.

Every climber worth his salt has a sense of Royal's many accomplishments. A few stand out. Years ago, I listened intently when Royal told me of his repeat of Tom Higgins' Jonah (6 pitches, 5.10+ R) on Tahquitz Rock in 1964. He later would write to me about it, "It was very hard, and I was determined to get up it, because Higgins had done so. I got up it, but I remember it as the hardest climb I had done up to that point." Soon after, also in 1964, Royal led Athlete's Feat in Boulder Canyon: four pitches of 5.10, the first of which he managed without chalk, entirely unprotected, at the risk of a ground fall onto a blade of rock. This pitch would be identified a few years later as solid 5.11, among the first in the country and one of the boldest. The crux is now bolt-protected.

Of course there were Royal's great pioneering adventures in Yosemite, which included a fast, day-and-a-half second ascent of the North Wall of Sentinel (later called the Steck-Salathé) in 1953, with similarly young Jerry Gallwas and Don Wilson, all three in tennis shoes, and in 1956 the first ascent of the Northwest Face of Half Dome, with brave Gallwas and Mike Sherrick. Half Dome was the first wall in this country of such an order of magnitude. Royal's climb in 1960 of the Nose of El Capitan, the wall's second ascent, with Joe Fitschen, Tom Frost, and Chuck Pratt, was a visionary, committing achievement without fixed ropes. Above all, perhaps, was Royal's sojourn in 1961, with Pratt and Frost, up into the white granite of El Cap's Salathé Wall.

It is hard to imagine so great and strong a soul could be reduced by illness, along with older age, to near paralysis. He had reached a point where he no longer was able to say much. He could not see the chess board or play Sudoku. His PSP (progressive supra-nuclear palsy) had made things increasingly difficult for Liz, his wife, for quite a long time, even with helpers. She was his faithful companion to the end. I spoke for an hour with Royal's daughter Tamara the early evening after he passed away, and she shared with me things about their family, a few of which verged on guarded secrets. Every famous or even slightly famous person fears that the realities of his or her life will be exposed. I have never been intimidated or disappointed by the imperfections of my friends. It is my belief that we are here to learn, and there would be nothing to learn if we were perfect. Tamara said Royal's faith had more or less failed, by the end. I did not care about this, because given another few months or years he would have turned it around again. There was enough greatness, in any direction one wanted to look, to define him.

Robbins, our Royal, that mighty heart that traversed high, our captain, the bearded Duke of Exeter, with that professional grade of seriousness, was and would remain precious to us. His name is in all of Yosemite's declivities. When I met him, in 1963, he seemed so...evolved. I had no idea how people could come to the world so far "ahead" in many ways. People such as Royal and John Gill seemed to know about integrity before anyone could have taught them. For others of us, many of life's most important ascents have only in part to do with rock. Each of us, Royal included, is a potpourri of imperfections, and our life is, if not to fully overcome, to know and confront those imperfections.

In an email dated October 30, 2008, Royal reflected about an extremely well-attended show Layton Kor gave in Boulder: "The more I hang around, the more clear it becomes to me that I have many sorry qualities, and that wanting to be a 'hero' is one of them."

Royal was his own enigma, which reminds me of a line from a poem by Howard Nemerov, poet laureate of America:

...it is not knowing, it is not keeping,
But being the secret hidden from yourself.

I loved Royal when I first saw him in those early AAJ photos from the Salathé Wall. I loved him the evening at the Longs Peak shelter cabin in 1963 when we stepped surreptitiously into each other's lives, and I would love him at every point along the way after that. When he and I climbed, I tried to avoid any little *cri de coeurs* of distress or indignation, which were a bit more readily at the flow when I was roped to Layton Kor, that beautiful gatekeeper between happiness and fear. I think of a photo I took that was published in *Quest* magazine, in which Royal leads the steep Horn Pitch on Shiprock, in 1964, the caption, "Man Is His Own Star." Nothing was more true about a person than those words—to suggest a life, and *the* life, of Royal Robbins.

– PAT AMENT

ROBERT JOHN SECOR, 1956–2017

ROBERT JOHN SECOR, mountaineer, guidebook author, and adventurer, passed away on October 26 at the age of 61. R.J., as he was known to all, authored four well-known guidebooks: *Mexico's Volcanoes: A Climbing Guide; Aconcagua: A Climbing guide; Denali Climbing Guide,* and the tome most often referred to as "The Bible of the Sierra," *The High Sierra: Peaks, Passes, and Trails.*

R.J. was involved in the Angeles Chapter of the Sierra Club for more than 30 years, holding leadership roles with the Ski Mountaineers Section (1980–1985); the Trail Maintenance Committee (1987–1991); and the Sierra Peaks Section (1998). In 2013, R.J. received the prestigious Francis P. Farquhar Mountaineering Award for his contributions to both mountaineering and the Sierra Club's role in that field. He also was a founding member and president of the California Mountaineering Club (1989–1990).

R.J. was a consummate professional in collecting mountain information, while also being a prodigious mountaineer. He summited Denali (1995), Aconcagua (via the Polish Glacier in 1986), and Mexico's volcanoes, the latter numerous times. In the Himalaya he summited Mera and Imja Tse, he reached 24,000 feet on Broad Peak (1992), and he also attempted Cho Oyu, and Changtse. In his beloved High Sierra, R.J. was the second person to summit the 247 Sierra Club–listed peaks twice, and he was well on his way to completing a third lap on all of them. In total, RJ attained 737 "summits" in the Sierra Nevada. A noted ski mountaineer, R.J. also performed four trans-Sierra ski tours (1985, 1995, 2000, 2002), focusing on unrecorded routes.

R.J. was a kind, friendly, humorous, generous, and occasionally irascible, eccentric human being. In the high country, he was never without his *CFO* financial magazine. He had a minimalist approach to gear and attire, best described as "history is always in style."

In 2005, R.J. lost control of a glissade and fell 1,200 feet down a snow slope on Mt. Badly in Southern California, suffering skull fractures and other injuries. Over the next two years, he made an arduous and almost miraculous recovery, though his spark was diminished. In 2016, a fall in his backyard reactivated the effects of some of those same injuries, and he could not recover. He will forever be remembered as a pillar in the pantheon of Sierra Nevada explorer-writers. The number of people he introduced to the Range of Light is incalculable.

– STEVE PORCELLA

UELI STECK, 1976–2017

ON APRIL 30, the climbing world lost one of its all-time greats when Ueli Steck fell from approximately 7,100 meters on Nuptse in Nepal. He was 40 years old. In typical style, Ueli was climbing by himself, with nothing more than a day pack containing minimal supplies.

Ueli Steck grew up in Langnau in the Emmental Valley—rural Swiss cow country, far from the bright lights of Zermatt or Interlaken. He was the youngest of three boys and came from a family of athletes: His two older brothers played competitive hockey, but Ueli discovered climbing at the age of 12 and resolved to follow its pull instead. "I don't care what you do," Ueli's father, Max, told him, "just do it 100 percent." Ueli quickly excelled, climbing the Eiger's north face for the first time in 1995, when he was 18 years old.

Around that time, Ueli came under the wing of Kari Kolber, a veteran Himalayan guide who introduced him to the mountains of the Khumbu Valley, bringing him along as an assistant guide on a trip to Ama Dablam. While their clients rested, Ueli snuck out of base camp, summited the mountain, and returned that day—setting one of the first speed records of his career.

Ueli did his mandatory service in the Swiss Army, then trained as a carpenter, but mostly he climbed. In 2001 he ticked new routes on the Eiger and Pumori in Nepal; in 2002, he managed Blood from the Stone, a phenomenal mixed line up the east face of Mt. Dickey in Alaska. From the start of his career, friends noticed his drive. "He had a lot of talents," wrote Kobler, "but the most important thing is: I don't know any other mountaineer...this goal-oriented."

The Eiger kept calling. In 2004, Ueli soloed the north face for the first time. By 2007, he felt ready to attempt the speed record. It took several tries before he succeeded, cutting the previous mark by 46 minutes, to 3 hours 54 minutes. But Ueli wasn't done. In 2008, he fully invested himself in a training program designed with Simon Trachsel of the Swiss Olympic Training Center. In December of that year, he broke his own Eiger record by more than an hour.

It is somehow fitting that this signature achievement was more a statement of inner mastery than external achievement. It is also one of those perfect little ironies of life that such an intensely personal experience would rocket Ueli to new levels of professional stardom and public scrutiny. After the record-breaking ascent, Ueli and a close friend, photographer Robert Bösch, self-funded a shoot using a helicopter to capture Ueli re-soloing sections of the climb. The resulting footage of him literally racing up the Eiger's snowfields and insecure limestone appeared in the hit movie *The Swiss Machine,* stoking the imaginations of millions of people.

I met Ueli at the Banff Mountain Film Festival the following year. In front of a rapt audience, he told the story of his Eiger solo with pitch-perfect modesty and self-deprecating humour. The year after that, we climbed together in Nepal and I discovered how much the public persona I had seen on stage at Banff was simply a professional role for him to fullfil, rather than a personal calling. Ueli was a natural introvert who preferred exercise by himself and quiet conversations with one or two good friends. He would sometimes disparage the idle "blah-blah-blah," as he would put it, of many Westerners. As we trekked and climbed for a month in the Khumbu Valley, it was obvious he felt at home with the early-to-bed, early-to-rise pace of Sherpa life.

Ueli's last years followed a roller-coaster arc that don't seem befitting of the guy I knew. In 2013, he was caught up in a tussle on Everest when his partner misused a Nepali epithet, upsetting a group of Sherpas. As if determined to move beyond the ugly incident, Ueli soloed the majestic south face of Annapurna a year later, a feat that earned him a second Piolet d'Or and seemed to cement his legacy. Then questions began to arise from certain peers—Ueli had dropped his camera during the ascent and didn't have GPS tracking, and thus lacked empirical proof of the climb. Publicly, Ueli tried to shrug it off, but the fact that there would be a vague asterisk attached to the ascent must have eaten at him.

In between such intense efforts, Ueli found great joy in pleasure climbing with his wife, Nicole, visiting Patagonia, Nepal, Yosemite, and elsewhere with her on annual holidays. He learned to paraglide, wrote several books, and managed a brilliant enchainment close to home, climbing all the 4,000-meter peaks in the Alps one summer.

And yet death always seemed nearby. In 2014, two climbers he had teamed up with on Xixabangma died in an avalanche; in 2015, he lost a partner while completing the Alps project. As calculating a human as Ueli was, he would occasionally admit the odds were bound to catch up with him if he didn't quit high-stakes soloing. "I think he would love to not go solo anymore," said climbing partner David Göttler. "He liked the solo thing, because he could just concentrate on his own performance, but I had the impression that he really enjoyed being with a climbing partner. He just ended up being alone because no one could keep up with him."

It is fitting that his closest companion on his last Himalayan climbs was a young Nepali friend, Tenjing Sherpa. After climbing Everest without oxygen with Tenji in 2012, Ueli invited him to Switzerland and encouraged him to pursue a career in guiding.

Before he embarked on his last expedition to Everest, Ueli mused to journalist Devon O'Neil about his fascination with the region: "Maybe I'll just go back to the Khumbu my whole lifetime until I don't climb anymore, because I see so many mountains and routes I still want to climb."

After the fatal accident on Nuptse, Ueli Steck's body was cremated at the Tengboche Monastery, in the heart of the Khumbu Valley.

– FREDDIE WILKINSON

NIELS TIETZE, 1986–2017

SOMETIME ON NOVEMBER 13, Niels Tietze, 31, fell to his death in what appears to have been a rappelling accident on Fifi Buttress in Yosemite National Park. Niels and I met in early May 2011 when he rode into Camp 4 on a motorcycle adorned with a sheepskin pelt and a brimming haulbag for his first season with Yosemite Search and Rescue (YOSAR). His pilgrimage followed the death of his middle brother, Kyle, in 2010. He had dropped out of his university and come to Yosemite seeking salvation on what he called the "godly granite" of the Valley. His wry smile, penchant for philosophizing, and blatant grief instantly drew me to him.

Raised on the edge of Salt Lake City with Mt. Olympus as his backyard, Niels grew up the youngest of four—three boys and one girl. Part of a tight-knit clan of capable eccentrics, Niels easily outclimbed his older siblings. But as passionate as Niels was about the vertical realm, and as much as he relished his solitude, Niels felt compelled to contribute to the greater human experience. It was that duty that helped propel him, still grief-stricken, to YOSAR in 2011. Niels took his search for purpose a step further in 2012 when he spent three months cramped in a tiny room with the indefatigable Timmy O'Neill, training as ophthalmic assistants in Nepal. From then on Niels volunteered a few months each year with the Himalayan Cataract Project, helping to bring sight-restoring surgery to thousands across Nepal and Ethiopia.

As a man who was obsessed equally with beauty and the absurd, it would not be unusual for Niels to approach a climb in tattered denim and on horseback or with freshly picked flowers in his hair, a faded, superfluous scarf wrapped around his head, and Vivaldi's "Four Seasons" blasting from a duct-taped speaker. Joy often exploded from Niels as he indulged in adventurous exploits: gracefully climbing desert sandstone, playing a ceramic flute to drive his family's Dobermans into frenzied howls, or wrangling cattle on his friend's ranch in rural Utah. But such happiness contrasted with frequent torment. His parents wrote after his passing that Niels was "a man who in so many ways embodied the complexities of the Universe."

Capricious, well read, and strange, Niels was a modern-day Renaissance man. While his physical prowess was made evident by such varied climbing accomplishments as a free ascent of El Capitan's Salathé Wall and a rapid climb of the Himalayan peak Ama Dablam, Niels will be most missed for his frantic passion, his pure love of (dis)honest fun, and his bottomless affection for those nearest and dearest to his full, aching heart. He is at peace, at last.

— LIBBY SAUTER

EDITOR'S NOTE: *Libby Sauter and the editors condensed this tribute from a longer remembrance piece that she wrote for Alpinist.com.*

NECROLOGY

In addition to those covered above, AAC members who passed away in 2017 included:

SUE BENNETT	SCOT MACBETH	TONY WATKIN
WILLIAM EVERHEART	INGE PERKINS	JASON WOLFE
NEIL GEHRELS	ERNEST ROOTS	LOREN WOOD
HENRY GHOLZ	REBECCA RYAN	JOHN ZOBEL
JANUSZ KONIAK	DALE VRABEC	
CALEB LADUE	RITNER WALLING	

INDEX

COMPILED BY **EVE TALLMAN & RALPH FERRARA**

Mountains are listed by their official names. Ranges, geographic locations, and maps are also indexed. Unnamed peaks (eg. Peak 2,340m.) are listed under P. Abbreviations are used for the following: Cordillera: C.; Island: Is.; Mountains: Mts.; National Park: Nat'l. Park; Obituary: obit. Indexed photographs are listed in bold type.

the AMERICAN ALPINE club

AAJ

INTERNATIONAL GRADE COMPARISON CHART

SERIOUSNESS RATINGS

These often modify technical grades when protection is difficult

PG-13: Difficult or insecure protection or loose rock, with some injury potential

R: Poor protection with high potential for injury

X: A fall would likely result in serious injury or death

YDS=Yosemite Decimal System
UIAA=Union Internationale des Associations D'Alpinisme
FR=France/Sport
AUS=Australia
SAX=Saxony
CIS=Commonwealth of Independent States/Russia
SCA=Scandinavia
BRA=Brazil
UK=United Kingdom

Note: *All conversions are approximate. Search "International Grade Comparison Chart" at the AAJ website for further explanation of commitment grades and waterfall Ice/ mixed grades.*

YDS	UIAA	FR	AUS	SAX	CIS	SCA	BRA	UK	UK
5.2	II	1	10	II	III	3			D
5.3	III	2	11	III	III+	3+			D
5.4	IV− / IV	3	12		IV−	4			VD
5.5	IV+		13		IV	4+			VD
5.6	V−	4	14		IV+	5−		4a	S
5.7	V / V+		15	VIIa		5			HS
5.8	VI−	5a	16	VIIb	V−	5+	4 / 4+	4b	VS
5.9		5b	17	VIIc		6−	5 / 5+	4c / 5a	HVS
5.10a	VI	5c	18	VIIIa	V	6	6a	5b	E1
5.10b	VI+	6a							E1
5.10c	VII−	6a+	19	VIIIb		6+	6b		E2
5.10d	VII	6b	20	VIIIc	V+	7−	6c		E3
5.11a	VII+	6b+		IXa			7a		E3
5.11b		6c	21				7		E3
5.11c	VIII−	6c+	22	IXb	VI−	7+	7b		E4
5.11d	VIII	7a	23	IXc			7c	6a	E4
5.12a	VIII+	7a+	24	Xa		8−	8a		E5
5.12b		7b	25		VI	8	8b		E5
5.12c	IX−	7b+	26	Xb		8+	8c		E5
5.12d	IX	7c	27				9a	6b	E6
5.13a	IX+	7c+	28	Xc		9−	9b		E6
5.13b		8a	29				9c		E6
5.13c	X−	8a+	30	XIa		9	10a	6c	E7
5.13d	X	8b	31		VI+		10b		E7
5.14a	X+	8b+	32	XIb			10c	7a	E8
5.14b		8c	33				11a		E8
5.14c	XI−	8c+	34	XIc		9+	11b	7b	E9
5.14d	XI	9a	35				11c		E10
5.15a	XI+	9a+	36	XIIa		10	12a		E10
5.15b	XII−	9b	37		VII		12b		E11
5.15c	XII	9b+	38	XIIb			12c		E11